Writing in an Electronic Medium:

Research with Language Learners

edited by

Martha C. Pennington

ATHELSTAN

© 1999 Athelstan

ISBN: 0-940753-14-6

Athelstan
2476 Bolsover, Suite 464
Houston, TX 77005
USA

www.athel.com
info@athel.com

Martha C. Pennington
Powdrill Professor of English Language Acquisition
Spires Research Centre
2 Adelaide St.
University of Luton
Luton LU1 5 DU UK
e-mail martha.pennington@luton.ac.uk
fax 44 1582 743701

CONTENTS

Preview

Contributors

PREVIEW

This book is a collection of research studies on writing in an electronic medium carried out with mature (late adolescent or adult) language learners in second and foreign language instructional contexts. The computer medium of these studies embraces not only word processing but also e-mail and hypertext used to create web pages on the Internet. The research, which involves both English and French as target languages, has been carried out in a range of settings in different countries, including Canada, England, Hong Kong, Turkey, and the United States. As the first collection of original investigations involving writing by second or foreign language learners in electronic environments, the attempt has been made to present both a broad-ranging perspective of this research context and an in-depth discussion of findings. The presentation and discussion of findings in the research chapters is supplemented by editor notes and an introductory chapter that provides background and a theoretical framework interpreting the research on writing in an electronic medium.

The contributions represent a variety of approaches to assessing the implementation of writing with electronic media in the second or foreign language curriculum. The introductory chapter explores the nature of writing on computer by seeking to link the findings of different investigations within a model of the effects of word processing in relation to other computer media. Four of the chapters form a group of quasi-experimental studies involving the use of word processing in relation to process writing and revision. A fifth study investigates temporal aspects of text production based on quantitative keystroke data. The other four research studies, which include two centering on use of e-mail in the language curriculum and one investigating students' acquisition of computer skills through the development of web pages, are more qualitative in orientation.

In Chapter 1, "Word Processing and Beyond: Exploring the Effects of Writing in an Electronic Medium", Martha C. Pennington reviews the effects of electronic writing, including word processing, e-mail, and other computer-based utilities that allow production of text and alignment with various resources to produce a range of outcomes that may aid the writing of second and foreign language learners. Computer effects are described as facilitative, quantitative, and qualitative outcomes on writing, which are mediated by the characteristics of the user, the type of computer application, the setting of computer use, and the amount of time spent on computer. It is shown how the electronic medium creates unique modes of writing and communicative functions that exploit the special features of computer resources and settings of use.

The findings of the first of the quasi-experimental studies (Chapter 2) identify the specific effects of the computer within a process writing curriculum. The second of this group of investigations (Chapter 3) shows the advantage of peer feedback over computer-based feedback in the context of word processing. The third of the quasi-experimental studies (Chapter 4) investigates the value of peer feedback compared with self-assessment as a mode of feedback in a computer context. The last of this group of studies (Chapter 5) suggests the value of training revision strategies within a computer medium. Taken as a group, these four investigations indicate the positive potential of the electronic medium for developing and supporting the writing processes of language learners, while also helping to tease out the effects of word processing as against those of various instructional interventions. The final quantitatively orientated study (Chapter 6) is an exploration of the method of keystroke analysis and the types of writing process information that can be derived from it. In contrast to the types of "product" data which are the focus of Chapters 2-5, the data generated through keystroke analysis offers a view of the writer's operations during text production. These data are open to both a "surface" interpretation in terms of the fluency of the writing process and a higher level interpretation in terms of the writer's cognitive process.

Chapter 2, "Word Processing in the EFL Classroom: Effects on Writing Strategies, Attitudes, and Products", is the first of the four quasi-experimental studies included in the collection. In this chapter, Ayse Akyel and Sibel Kamıslı investigate the effects of word processing in a process writing curriculum in a Turkish university EFL setting. In a two-group comparative research design using quantitative and qualitative measures, the researchers examine the effects of word processing vs. pen-and-paper composing in a process approach. Although the word processing group, in contrast to the pen-and-paper composing group, wrote significantly more words in their posttest compositions than in their pretest compositions, the difference at posttest between the two groups was not significant. The findings of Akyel and Kamıslı's investigation also demonstrated no advantage for word processing on writing quality nor on use of general or deep-level writing strategies; both groups had a similar level of improvement in these features from pretest to posttest. However, members of the computer group revised more at posttest in the categories of organization, sentence structure, word form, and spelling than members of the pen-and-paper group. They also exhibited a writing process at the end of the investigation that showed less preplanning, and more pausing and rescanning, than in the writing process of the pen-and-paper group. Attitudes in both groups were positive, with the computer group's comments suggesting a favorable response to the computer and perceptions of its positive impact on their writing and educational experience more generally.

The second in the group of quasi-experimental studies is the investigation reported by Mark N. Brock and Martha C. Pennington in Chapter 3, "A Comparative Study of Text Analysis and Peer Tutoring as Input to Writing on Computer in an ESL Context". In a study carried out in a Hong Kong tertiary institution, Brock and Pennington compared computer-based text analysis and peer feedback as aids to generating and revising written work within the context of word processing. Repeated measures analysis of variance determined that both groups made equivalent composition gains as judged by holistic scoring. However, the peer feedback group made more revisions overall and more content-level revisions per assignment than the text analysis group. The peer feedback group also wrote significantly more words at posttest and significantly more words, sentences, and paragraphs per draft of five composition assignments completed during their course than the text analysis group. Thus, the students who combined word processing and peer tutoring for the generation and revision of their written assignments wrote more and revised their texts more substantially than those who worked with word processing supplemented by computer aids to generating and revising written text.

Chapter 4, "The Effect of Peer Feedback versus Self-Assessment on the Quality and Revision of Compositions Word-Processed by Advanced ESL Learners", is a comparative study of the value of self-assessment and peer feedback for helping Arab students enrolled in a UK secondary school to revise in a computer-mediated writing environment. This study stands out for the thoroughness with which the authors, Sultan Al-Hazmi and Phil Scholfield, analyze and interpret their findings to tease out the full implications of their investigation, using statistical techniques as well as comparison to other relevant studies in the word processing and general writing literature. The presentation and discussion of results suggest many directions for future comparative research on word processing under different conditions. A main implication of the findings is that peer feedback in the context of word processing can help relatively unskilled student writers to make between-draft improvements that help 'close the quality gap' between them and their more skilled peers, who made better use of self-assessment. The reader's careful attention to the detail of the findings as presented by Al-Hazmi and Scholfield should be amply rewarded by the insights the discussion affords into the relationships between revision, writing skill, writing quality, and forms of measurement in these three areas.

In Chapter 5, "Effects of the Teaching of Revision Strategies in a Computer-based Environment", Jocelyne Bisaillon reports on a study of word processing and revision in three groups of learners of French as a second language in Canada. The aim of the research was to assess the effectiveness of teaching revision strategies in the context of word processing, based on pretest and posttest measures of revision and composition quality. Significant improvements occurred from pretest to posttest in revisions of content and organization, as well as language, and in composition quality in these three areas as well. Bisaillon's findings demonstrate the positive effects of teaching revision strategies in a computer context, particularly, for improving sentence-level coherence and organization.

In Chapter 6, "Investigating Academic Writing On-Line: A Study of Temporal Aspects of Text Production", Kristyan Spelman Miller uses the technique of keystroke logging to investigate a group of first and second language university students' pattern of text production while writing a timed examination essay on computer. The device of keystroke logging allows the researcher to record all keyboard operations performed by subjects during the composing process, including keypresses, cursor movements, and pausing, and to save each record in a logfile. The logfile can then be analyzed to show the pattern of writing behavior of individual writers or groups of writers in terms of their fluency of generating text and the specific locations of pauses. Such data offer a window on the cognitive operations of writing such as planning points and the writer's degree of engagement. Spelman Miller's findings focusing on pausing behavior suggest a relatively fluent writing process for two different essay tasks at the level of individual clauses/sentences, with major pauses occurring at clause or sentence and paragraph junctures. This pattern can be taken as indicative of rereading and planning at these major grammatical and rhetorical boundaries. The keystroke log further demonstrates a more effortful writing process in the second language group, who were predominantly Greek, in that they paused more in frequency and duration than the first language English speakers. A further exploratory aspect of the study examined individual subjects' keystroke record in terms of their pausing behavior at different thematic points in the text.

The first of the qualitatively focused studies (Chapter 7) characterizes patterns of response to the electronic medium in a longitudinal view of the adoption of word processing by a group of mature ESL students. In comparison with the research presented in the first group of studies, this study makes clear the degree to which individual factors affect the results of computer implementations within educational contexts. The next two chapters investigate curricular initiatives to put students in touch with electronic mail partners. In the first of these (Chapter 8), students were given opportunities for realistic communication with on-campus partners via e-mail, while in the other study (Chapter 9), e-mail was used to connect students in two different countries for mutual support in learning each other's language. The first of these e-mail studies helps to characterize the unique properties of e-mail as an electronic medium quite different from non-networked word processing. The other e-mail study focuses on practical matters of implementing inter-institutional e-mail as part of a language learning curriculum. Consonant with this focus, the final study of the collection (Chapter 10) also has a practical curriculum orientation, but in this case one which goes beyond the development of word processing skills or use of e-mail. This final investigation offers a unique view of the electronic writing context in seeking to determine effective means of instructing computer-based composition that includes word processing, hypertext, and web page design for an audience of second language (French) learners who are also majoring in computer studies.

Ruru Rusmin, in the first of the more qualitatively oriented studies, "Patterns of Adaptation to a New Writing Environment: The Experience of Word Processing by Mature Second Language Writers", offers a detailed examination in Chapter 7 of adaptation patterns in the optional use of the computer in a university writing course geared for mature students. While the majority of the students were positive towards the computer, differences in reactions over four assignments allowed Rusmin to classify subjects into one of six adopter categories, from 'devotees' to 'skeptics'. In-depth discussion of the factors that may relate to the adoption profiles of the group adds a dimension to the literature on how different people respond to word processing and make use of the computer as a writing tool. The examination of the changing pattern of response over time also represents a valuable addition to the relatively small number of investigations that have studied adjustment to the computer from a developmental or longitudinal perspective.

In Chapter 8, "Student E-mail Letters: Negotiating Meaning, Gathering Information, Building Relationships", Leslie K. Nabors and Ethel C. Swartley present an investigation into the nature of the language use and content of e-mail exchanges carried out at a US university between ESL student writers from Africa, the Middle East, Asia, Europe, and Latin America, and their electronic penpals, both first language English speakers and advanced second language English speakers. In their analysis and discussion of the e-mail data, the authors make links to the research traditions of second language acquisition, sociolinguistics, and psychology. Their study, which illustrates the substantial differences between e-mail and other forms of written communication, is especially significant for its investigation into how language is used to build and maintain relationships in an electronic environment. Nabors and Swartley break new ground in identifying twelve different relationship-building strategies used by the ESL e-mail penpals, including such acts as giving personal information and sharing feelings. In developing categories of analysis on the basis of a large set of e-mail data from second language speakers, in linking their findings to those of other studies of negotiation and conversation, and in identifying many areas for needed research, the authors provide a valuable basis for future studies of e-mail discourse involving language learners and/or first language speakers.

Paul Slater and Catrine Carpenter in Chapter 9, "Introducing E-mail Use into a Course in French as a Second Language", report on an attempt to make use of e-mail as a medium for communicating across languages, countries, and cultures. For their e-mail project, they paired two small classes of learners studying French in a UK university with a class of learners studying English in a higher education institute in France. Members of each group were to send questions written in their target language (i.e., French for the group in the UK and English for the group in France) via e-mail to paired 'keypals', for whom this would be the first language. Answers were to be written in the same language as that in which the questions were asked. Learners in each group therefore had a chance to send and receive e-mail messages in both languages. Unlike the US e-mail project described by Nabors and Swartley, in the UK project, the researchers attempted to structure the e-mail exchange so that the information obtained by the UK students from their e-mail partners in France could be incorporated into a specific curricular goal of giving an oral report on a choice of topics. Although its design was based on a review of the literature on e-mail use with language learners, the project faltered when the students were unable to accomplish the assigned task. Much of Slater and Carpenter's discussion of the project focuses on reasons for its limited success and ways to avoid the problems encountered when setting up future e-mail initiatives.

In the final selection, "Composing with Computer Technology: A Case Study of a Group of Students in Computer Studies Learning French as a Second Language", Chapter 10, Isabelle Marcoul and Martha C. Pennington investigate the features of writing produced in different media by a group of computer-literate students using French as a second language, based on student diary records of their writing activity. The comparison was made on a sequence of written products generated by different means, including: (1) pen-and-paper, (2) word-processing, and (3) hypertext used by students to create their own web pages as part of a university on-line newspaper. It was found that the students produced more surface corrections in word-processing mode than either pen-and-paper or hypertext mode, while they produced more changes in content and paragraph structure in the hypertext environment. The latter mode seemed to draw students' attention away from the details of language and towards the visual presentation of the text, at the same time as it sparked students' creativity and individuality of expression. In designing their web pages, students developed unique voices and original ways of communicating with an audience through a combination of words, images, and sound. On the basis of the comparative findings and the students' observations at the end of the course, Marcoul and Pennington are able to offer recommendations for teaching the use of these computer tools.

Each of the chapters of this volume exemplifies a different type of instructional intervention and research design examining the use of electronic media for learning to write in a second or foreign language. As an in-depth discussion of an investigation in a particular research context, each of these reports might serve as a model and impetus for further research on the writing of second or foreign language learners in an electronic medium. In the variety of their applications, research approaches, and findings regarding use of electronic media in the writing curriculum, both the individual studies and the collection as a whole also offer direction for teachers and curriculum developers wishing to implement word processing, e-mail, or hypertext in applications such as on-line newspapers and web pages as part of a second or foreign language instructional program. As a collection of studies exclusively focused on second and foreign language contexts, the findings presented in this volume can be compared with those which have resulted from employing electronic media to teach writing in other types of settings, thus aiding in the process of testing and validating research models and outcomes. In all these respects, the chapters of this book make a contribution to furthering our understanding of the impact which the computer, in its various manifestations as electronic writing device, is having and will have on language learning and communication more generally.

CONTRIBUTORS

Ayse Akyel

Bogazici University
Istanbul, Turkey

Sultan Al-Hazmi

*Imam Muhamed Ibn Saud Islamic
University*   Saudi Arabia

Jocelyne Bisaillon

University of Laval
Quebec, Canada

Mark N. Brock

Carson-Newman University
Jefferson City, Tennessee, USA

Catrine Carpenter

University of Brighton
Brighton, UK

Sibel Kamıslı

Sabanci University
Istanbul, Turkey

Isabelle Marcoul

City University
London, UK

Leslie K. Nabors

Harvard University
Cambridge, Massachusetts, USA

Martha C. Pennington

University of Luton
Luton, UK

Ruru S. Rusmin

Bergen Community College
Paramus, New Jersey, USA

Phil Scholfield

University of Essex
Colchester, UK

Paul Slater

University of Brighton
Brighton, UK

Kristyan Spelman Miller

University of Reading
Reading, UK

Ethel C. Swartley

Drexel University
Philadelphia, Pennsylvania, USA

1. Word Processing and Beyond: Exploring the Effects of Writing in an Electronic Medium

Martha C. Pennington

ABSTRACT

In this chapter, the documented effects of writing on computer using word processing alone or aligned with other types of resources such as networking utilities or multimedia are described in terms of a chain of effects that involve an interaction of the computer's capabilities and the context of use. Word processor capabilities that facilitate the generation, revision, and dissemination of text create the conditions for quantitative and qualitative effects on language learners' writing process and products. When augmented by other computer resources, some of the functions and outcomes of word processing in the way of text generation, revision, and dissemination may be enhanced. However, these other resources also create their own unique effects and outcomes on users' writing which must ultimately respond to new standards of value. The different types of computer outcomes are mediated by the context factors of user, computer, setting, and time, which are mutually interactive. Thus, writing in an electronic medium is seen to be a complex interaction of writer and writing environment.

1.0. INTRODUCTION

We have reached a point in the history of writing where it is becoming almost impossible not to jump on the computer bandwagon. Most types of writing-based work—from publishing to office correspondence—are now performed predominantly or exclusively by electronic means, and there is a general expectation these days that office workers will have computer writing skills. Most writers will by now have tried writing on computer, and the majority of these will have been won over by the machine. A new generation of children writes on computer in preference to writing by hand, and there are fewer and fewer holdouts in the older generation who continue to work only with pen and/or typewriter.

Although there is some reactionary pressure to move back to a pen-and-paper ethic or aesthetic for writing, any such movement is bound to be marginal and short-lived. For the writing implements of the previous generation have become impractical for the writing tasks of the present age. Pen and typewriter have been surpassed as writing tools; even writing paper may not survive in an age of electronic transmission. The computer is thus the tool of choice for producing written text and is rapidly developing as an alternate means of sending (and receiving) written text over distances. It is not only a writing tool but also a writing environment, a place where text can be created, called up, transmitted, and received. From a device for creating, transmitting, and receiving text, it is a short step to the computer becoming a way to construct messages and disseminate information that bypasses hardtext, an environment for the sharing of ideas virtually mind to mind. In many senses the computer is therefore a superior writing medium, and for many forms of idea-sharing, a superior communications medium as well.

This chapter opens the discussion of writing in an electronic medium by reviewing the relevant computer capabilities and their potentials to influence the writing, both process and product, of language learners through word processing and other sorts of computer utilities offering additional resources and modes of communication. It is shown how a series of outcomes in writing process and products may result from different types of computer use and may ultimately change the quality of the user's writing experience and written text.

The discussion is divided into five parts. The first part focuses on word processing. Here the impact of the electronic medium on a computer user's writing is described as a linked series of outcomes in the way of facilitative, quantitative, and qualitative effects on the generation, revision, and dissemination of text. The second part extends the writing outcomes presented in the first part by describing the impacts on writing of additional computer resources such as networking and multimedia capabilities. These effects augment the outcomes of word processing but at the same time have their own impacts based on the unique attributes of the resources. The third part of the discussion describes a set of conditioning factors that affect and are in turn affected by the outcomes of computer use. These include the factors of user, computer, setting, and time. The fourth part draws implications from the discussion for the writing curriculum, and the fifth part looks at research needs in relation to writing in an electronic medium.

1.1.   WORD PROCESSING

As an automated writing device, the word processor has the potential to facilitate the writing process and ease the writer's mind, reducing any sense of 'rewriting anxiety'. Such physical and mental facilitation of wri-

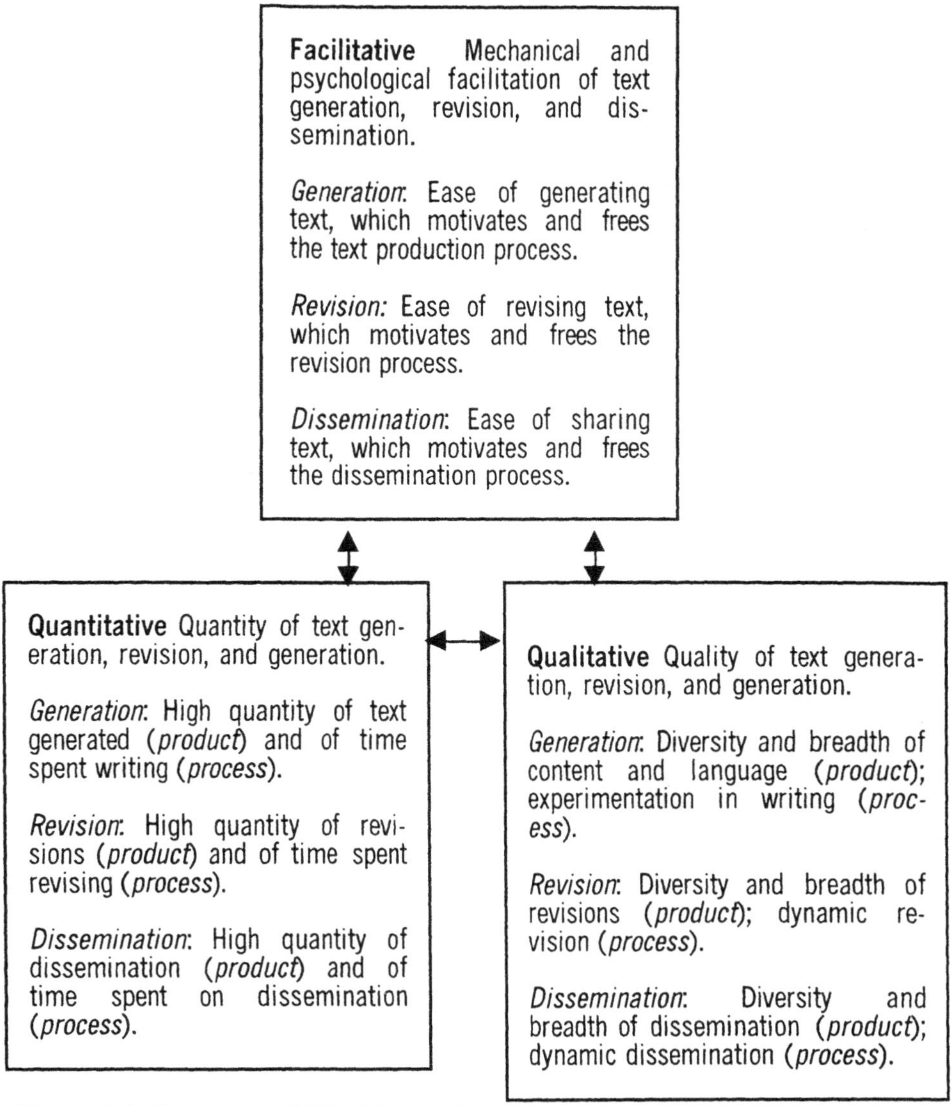

Facilitative Mechanical and psychological facilitation of text generation, revision, and dissemination.

Generation: Ease of generating text, which motivates and frees the text production process.

Revision: Ease of revising text, which motivates and frees the revision process.

Dissemination: Ease of sharing text, which motivates and frees the dissemination process.

Quantitative Quantity of text generation, revision, and generation.

Generation: High quantity of text generated (*product*) and of time spent writing (*process*).

Revision: High quantity of revisions (*product*) and of time spent revising (*process*).

Dissemination: High quantity of dissemination (*product*) and of time spent on dissemination (*process*).

Qualitative Quality of text generation, revision, and generation.

Generation: Diversity and breadth of content and language (*product*); experimentation in writing (*process*).

Revision: Diversity and breadth of revisions (*product*); dynamic revision (*process*).

Dissemination: Diversity and breadth of dissemination (*product*); dynamic dissemination (*process*).

Figure 1.1. Outcomes of Word Processing

ting is a key outcome of word processing that may lead to other types of outcomes on writing process and products (Pennington, 1993b; 1996b-d). Figure 1.1 offers a representation of three types of outcomes of computer use—*Facilitative, Quantitative,* and *Qualitative*—and their hypothesized interrelations, in relation to word processing. The placement of the Facilitative box at the top of the figure signifies that it is the primary outcome of word processing, i.e., the first type of effect to result from word processor use and the one upon which quantitative and qualitative outcomes are based. The two-way arrows between the outcomes boxes signifies that the three types of effects of word processing are interactive and mutually reinforcing.

1.1.1. Facilitative Outcomes

As Perkins (1985) observed: "Given word processors, people take advantage of their most immediate conveniences" (p. 14). These 'conveniences' include: a keyboard for typing, a video-based display for viewing, a printer for producing hard copy versions, a large capacity for storing, and text manipulation functions for altering and shifting pieces of written text. The most directly observable effect of the computer on writing is a facilitation of many of the physical acts involved in the writing process (Bruce & Rubin, 1993; Kozma, 1991; Roblyer, Castine, & King, 1988). Assistance in these physical acts of writing is what the word processor was designed to provide. In this sense, facilitative effects on writing are the most basic type of outcome of word processing and the starting point for any other types of effects on a computer user's writing process or written products.

A primary outcome, that of facilitation of writing, can thus be attributed to the computer's capabilities as a word processor that ease the generation and manipulation of text towards a finished product. It is therefore an expected and intended consequence of writing on computer that those who achieve a certain degree of mastery of the keyboard and word processing commands to add, delete, move, combine, format, save, and print text can more easily (i) produce text, (ii) modify that text, and (iii) share that text with others. Word processing therefore has the basic effects of facilitating the *generation, revision,* and *dissemination* of text. On the other hand, those who do not achieve a certain degree of mastery of keyboarding and word processing operations will not be able to take advantage of the word processor's potential to facilitate these writing operations (Dunn & Reay, 1989). The degree of mastery of word processing mechanics is therefore an essential conditioning factor in the chain of effects of computer use (Pennington, 1999).

The word processor's capabilities and attributes facilitate writing not only in the sense of easing the physical production and continuing alter-

4

ation of text towards a finished product. In addition to this *mechanical* type of facilitation of the writing process, the electronic writing device eases the psychological stress or burden of writing. This *psychological* type of facilitation results from an awareness of (i) the computer's attributes that aid writing and revising and (ii) the user's own ability to use the machine to produce and modify text at will. This awareness provides motivation to write and relieves the writer's apprehension about making errors and about having to revise or rewrite—an effect which may have particular value for language learners (Chadwick & Bruce, 1989; Neu & Scarcella, 1991; Phinney, 1991a; Pennington, 1999). It is often coupled with a general sense of empowerment or motivation (e.g., a 'novelty effect') associated with computer use (Daiute, 1985; Phinney, 1989). In addition, the visual attributes of computer text in terms of the brightness of the computer display, the size of visible text, the clarity of typed text appearing on the screen, the layout of text (and other elements on the screen), and the presence of a blinking cursor (Daiute, 1983) may help to capture and hold the computer writer's attention and to further motivate the computer user's writing process (Pennington, 1991; 1996b, ch. 1; 1996d).Freed from the anticipated labor of producing a readable and error-free text from a handwritten one, and given access to electronic tools that automate the production, the ongoing development, and the reproduction of text, the computer user is relieved of some of the usual mechanical and psychological constraints of pen-and-paper composing. As these constraints may be especially burdensome when writing in a second or foreign language (Jones & Tetroe, 1987; Phinney, 1989; Pennington, 1996b, ch. 3), the computer has special potential for the language learner. When some of the constraints of composing are reduced, the computer user writes in a freer and less encumbered manner than one writing with pen and paper. The mechanical and psychological facilitation resulting from the user's awareness of computer functions, coupled with the enhanced attention and motivation provided by the visually and psychologically captivating display of computer text, equates to a more engaged writing process. This greater freedom and engagement on the part of the computer writer applies as well to the process of revision. Generating and revising text unencumbered by the usual mechanical and psychological constraints of writing by hand, computer users may not only write and revise more than they would outside an electronic environment, they may also develop a writing process that is unique to the computer context (Pennington, 1996b-d). They may moreover disseminate their work more and in different ways.

1.1.2. Linking Facilitative and Quantitative Outcomes

The computer's facilitation of writing—the mechanical and psychological easing of the writing process in a word processing context—can be linked to effects on the quantity of writing produced by electronic means. Quantitative effects resulting from computer use, as described below, occur in the generation, the revision, and the dissemination of text in an electronic environment. These effects are interactive with the facilitative effects of computer use in that writing more increases the user's ability to make effective use of computer capabilities that ease the writing process.

It would seem a short logical step to assuming that if they can produce text more easily, computer users will produce text more efficiently than non-computer users in the sense of producing more text within a given period of time. Such a quantitative advantage for computer-aided writing has been documented in a wide range of studies where students produced compositions in computer or pen-and-paper mode under otherwise comparable conditions (e.g., Brady, 1990; Brock & Pennington, this volume; Etchison, 1989; Friedlander & Markel, 1990; Greenleaf, 1994; Williamson & Pence, 1989). The computer effect of writing longer texts has been confirmed by meta-analytical statistical procedures as the strongest and most consistent writing outcome attributable to word processing (Bangert-Drowns, 1993).

In addition, writers may write for longer periods of time on computer than off (e.g., Nichols, 1986; Womble, 1984). The quantitative *product* effect of a higher quantity of text generated is then complemented by a quantitative *process* effect of a longer time spent writing. This effect may be due to the ease of text production, so that computer writers become less fatigued by the writing process and stay with it longer. It may also be due to the greater attention and motivation, and hence the greater engagement, engendered by the computer writing context.

Thus, for those who develop at least a basic level of awareness and skill in the operations of word processing, there would seem to be a relatively direct causal link from facilitative to quantitative outcomes in the generation of text. In addition, once this link is established, it becomes two-way, in the sense that the more the computer user writes and makes use of computer capabilities to produce text, the easier it becomes to make use of them.

Beyond the effects on text production, computer writers, including second language (L2) writers, have often been found to revise more than those writing off the computer (e.g., Chadwick & Bruce, 1989; Cochran-Smith, 1991; Hawisher, 1989; Li & Cumming, 1996; Oliver & Kerr, 1993; Phinney & Khouri, 1993; Robinson-Staveley & Cooper, 1990). It can be assumed that this quantitative effect for revision is a relatively direct outcome of the use of computer capabilities that are designed to facilitate revision and the writing process more generally. In addition to the specific revision operations of adding, deleting, and moving text, the effect may be in part a result of the save and print functions which allow the writer to increase efficiency of revision by generating and revising text over more than one writing episode. Higher levels of revision may also be an effect of the visual properties of computer text which may focus attention and promote more reading of one's own text (Rodrigues, 1985).

Complementing the documented product effect for revision, a quantitative process effect for revision can be hypothesized which parallels that for text generation. Because of the ease of revision and the motivating context of the word processing medium, computer writers may engage in revision for longer periods of time than they would if working off the computer, and may "continue revising after planned changes [have] been made" (Phinney & Khouri, 1993, p. 271). In the view of Owston, Murphy, and Wideman (1992), "writing on computers seems to foster an ongoing and interactive process of revision of previously-written material" (p. 270). Moreover, as in the case of text generation, in the case of revision, there is a practice effect such that the more the computer user revises with the aid of the machine, the easier it becomes to make use of the computer's capabilities for revision. Therefore, as the computer user revises more, the revision process becomes more skilled and easier to execute.

In terms of dissemination, writing on a word processor makes possible the widespread dissemination of text, whether screen or hardcopy, at any stage in the writing process. The ease of making text available to others promotes more sharing of work in computer writing classes than in traditional writing classes (Greenleaf, 1994; Williamson & Pence, 1989). In a computer writing context, the easy accessibility of text can increase the quantity of dissemination in the sense that more writing products (e.g., individual drafts or sections of text) are made available to more audiences and in the sense that more time is spent in sharing one's writing with others.

1.1.3.   Linking Quantitative and Qualitative Outcomes

Many studies of word processing have found a computer advantage in both quantity and quality of writing (e.g., Robinson-Staveley & Cooper, 1990; Williamson & Pence, 1989), and a strong correlational link between document length and writing quality has been established in Bangert-Drowns' (1993) meta-analytical review of word processing studies. Such a link can perhaps be most transparently explained in terms of a text generation effect that impacts the quantity and quality of written content. In addition, some studies have noted a link between the high quantity of revision in a computer context and measured advantages for quality of writing (e.g., Oliver & Kerr, 1990; Robinson-Staveley & Cooper, 1990). As in the case of the causal link between facilitation of writing and quantity of writing (section 1.1.2), the quantitative-qualitative link is bi-directional.

In the usual case, the greater number of words produced in an electronic writing environment will represent an increase in the quantity of content or ideas as well. Content might also be increased by the ability to save text and then add material as newly generated or imported text from other files. This higher quantity of content does not in itself represent an increase in quality of writing, since the content produced may not be well-developed, representing more 'raw material' than finished product (Williams, 1992). However, this increased 'raw material' of both words and ideas that the writer has at hand during the writing process will usually mean an increased breadth or diversity of content and language which the writer can use in developing a topic. Moreover, writing for longer periods of time or over more than one session means staying with a topic longer and potentially establishing more connections among ideas (Pennington, 1996b-d).

A link from quantitative to qualitative outcomes can therefore be envisioned in terms of the word processor's impact on the development of the content of writing. Such *content* effects, which have been argued above on logical grounds, have a basis as well in some research findings on word processing. Friedlander and Markel (1990), for example, found that students in a university technical writing course produced essays on computer which were longer and contained "descriptions that were more complete and covered more of the necessary facts than...in papers written by hand" (p. 74). Similarly, an L2 writer studied by Li and Cumming (1996) obtained higher analytical ratings for content in compositions produced on computer than in pen-and-paper mode, as did a group of L2 writers studied by Lam and Pennington (1995).

A link from quantitative to qualitative effects in a word processing environment can be argued not only in the generation but also in the revision of text. The tentative nature of text created on a word processor can be seen in the tendency of students to make many more changes in their texts, particularly small or local ones, in a word processing mode than in a pen-and-paper mode (Cochran-Smith, 1991). Often this amounts to 'tinkering' with wording or grammatical structure that does not improve text and may even make it worse. This sort of tinkering, as observed in an example provided by Marcoul and Pennington (this volume) of a student's three drafts of a small piece of French text, does not survive into a hardcopy draft. Thus, as I have noted elsewhere (Pennington, 1993b; 1996, ch. 2), much of the process of developing a text in a word processing mode cannot be recovered on the basis of saved files or hardcopy drafts. Research such as that of Spelman Miller (this volume) using computer capabilities to gain a record of keystrokes and the rhythm of writing and pausing helps to bridge the gap between the students' writing process and the written products which ultimately result from that process.

The most common type of revision associated with word processing is surface-level editing such as for spelling and mechanics (Robinson-Staveley & Cooper, 1990). Some studies have also reported more attention to revision of larger syntactic or discourse units in a word processing medium, and indeed Robinson-Staveley and Cooper (1990) discovered that computer-users' compositions were not only more error-free than those of students not writing on computer but also contained longer and more complex sentences. In a comparative study of word processing and pen-and-paper composing by Turkish university students, Akyel and Kamıslı (this volume) found that the computer group revised more in the categories of organization, sentence structure, word form, and spelling. In a longitudinal study of one L2 writer, Li and Cumming (1996) report more syntactic and discourse-level revisions in computer than pen-and-paper mode. In addition, Kelly and Raleigh (1990) observe that those using word processing develop a wider repertoire of revising strategies, an effect noted as well by Chadwick and Bruce (1980), Cochran-Smith (1991), Oliver and Kerr (1993), and Phinney and Khouri (1993).

In sum, computer writers seem to revise more in general and also to make more revisions at the level of sentence and multi-sentence levels than those writing off the computer. Since they are more extensive and varied, and may affect larger units of text, the revisions of computer writers can be hypothesized to have a greater effect on the quality of their written compositions.

A link from quantitative to qualitative effects can also be hypothesized for dissemination, as an increase in the sharing of work implies a greater diversity and breadth of audiences, with concomitant increases in diversity and breadth of feedback from those audiences as input to the work. In the sense that it involves more readers, more acts of sharing, and more time spent in sharing along the way to producing a finished text, the writing process is qualitatively changed, becoming more interactive and collaborative. Ultimately, the expanded dissemination process has the potential of producing a more collaborative written product as well as a more collaborative, group mode of dissemination.

1.1.4. Linking Facilitative and Qualitative Outcomes

The computer's effects in the way of facilitating writing may result in qualitative improvements in writing. As the computer facilitates the writing process, the writer may become more engaged and involved in the writing process (e.g., Cochran-Smith, 1991; Greenleaf, 1994). Knowing that it is possible to both save and undo changes made, the computer writer may dare to be more experimental not only in writing process but also with language, structure, and content than when writing in a pen-and-paper environment (e.g., Cochran-Smith, Paris, & Kahn, 1991; Poulsen, 1991). Computer writers may also disseminate text more freely—i.e., more frequently, at an earlier stage, and to different audiences—than they would in a traditional writing context. In these senses, the computer's facilitation of text generation, revision, and dissemination promotes qualitative changes in the computer user's writing process that may be reflected as an effect of *creativity* or *diversity* in the types of text generated, the types of revision made, and the forms of dissemination or sharing of work with others. As in the case of computer effects on quantity of writing, there may be a 'washback' effect on facilitation of writing in the sense that writers working more experimentally or creatively will be motivated to explore and master computer capabilities to a higher degree, in order to facilitate an increasingly demanding writing process.

Being able to save text and modify it later not only helps to avoid fatigue and increase the efficiency of writing, it also encourages the computer user to work more on a particular written product to generate additional content or to (further) revise content already generated. Writing on computer thus facilitates the development of a multi-stage writing process in which material generated in one sitting is called up, reworked, and possibly combined with new text in another sitting.

Because of the tedium and drudgery of producing more than one draft, pen-and-paper composing is characterized by advance planning and structuring that seeks to avoid rewriting later on (Haas, 1989). Thus, the pen-and-paper writer devotes considerable cognitive effort to designing and pre-building as yet unwritten text, 'from the top down'. In this sense, traditional writing involves a great deal of preparation and projection of an imagined text. Because rewriting is a less burdensome activity and is generally performed in a recursive and cumulative manner at a local level, and because the text can be changed and printed as many times as needed, such preconceived texts are not necessary in an electronic medium. As Haas (1989) observed, word processing writers in comparison to pen-and-paper writers:

- plan less before beginning to write;
- do less higher level, conceptual planning;
- do more local, sequential planning.

In other words, computer-using writers do more in-process planning in relation to small sections of text as they are generated.

Similar effects on planning have been noted for L2 writers working in a computer writing environment. The L2 writer studied by Li and Cumming (1996) did more local planning and more intensive decision-making in computer than pen-and-paper mode, and the L2 computer writers investigated by Akyel and Kamıslı (this volume) did less preplanning and more rereading while they wrote than did pen and paper composers. Spelman Miller's (this volume) results suggest that L2 writers pause more frequently and to some extent at different points as compared to first language writers, suggesting a more effortful, less fluent computer writing process and some possible differences in planning behavior as well.

Another qualitative effect related to the computer's facilitation of writing is the apparently more dynamic and continuous process of revision (Owston, Murphy, & Wideman, 1992; Phinney & Khouri, 1993) and the more locally focused, micro-structural orientation of revision (Cochran-Smith, 1991) promoted by the computer's attributes and capabilities. On a computer, the whole recursive cycle of production and revision of text is more micro than in a pen-and-paper mode in the sense that smaller units of work are produced before revision begins. Indeed, generation and revision may be less separable in computer mode, where it is possible to write "close to the stream of consciousness" (Pennington, 1996, p. 113), than in pen-and-paper writing mode, which is often more labored and self-conscious. In this connection, Williamson and Pence (1989) describe a type of *recursive reviser* who revised continuously during text production and whose "locus of...revision... seemed to be tightly bound to the point at which text was being generated" (p. 116). These writers seemed to have adjusted their writing style to the electronic medium and to have made better use of the computer than some other university student writers in the Williamson and Pence (1989) study.

These qualitative differences in the revision process within a computer environment as contrasted with a traditional writing environment can be hypothesized to have an impact on the written text produced. There is in fact some evidence that the kind of focused, continuous micro-structural revision process promoted by the computer may lead to better writing. In a study comparing the computer-assisted and pen-and-paper writing of a group of eighth graders who were experienced computer users, Owston, Murphy, and Wideman (1992) discovered that the students' continuous process of micro-structural revision during text production on computer produced higher rated compositions than those generated by hand. In the words of these authors: "It may be that small, seemingly surface-level-only revisions have a differential impact on computer-produced writing because of their frequent occurrence, giving rise to a cumulative alteration of textual cohesion and coherence" (Owston, Murphy, & Wideman, 1992, p. 272). Thus, the text-generation and text-revision capabilities of the computer would seem to be effectively used for a tightly focused, micro-cycle of production and reprocessing of ideas that refines meaning and language simultaneously. The

11

computer may therefore help writers to realize the writing process as a "two-way street" (Taylor, 1981) in which content and form are continuously co-referenced and co-developed.

Research by Steelman (1994) with sixth grade students indicates that revision skills can be trained and that writing on computer helps learners to expand and deepen their focus in revision. Two experimental groups that received a systematic program of instruction geared to increasing their use of different types of revision strategies made more use of higher level strategies focused on language and organization than a control group taught by the same teacher. The control group made comparatively more use of lower level 'manuscript' strategies (those focused on production and formatting of text) and 'mechanical' strategies (those focused on punctuation, capitalization, surface grammar, and the like). Of the two experimental groups, the one that used the computer for their writing made the most use of the higher level strategies and the least use of the lower level strategies. In particular, the computer-using group focused most in their revision on organization strategies, using this type of strategy about three times as often as both of the other two groups.

Bisaillon's (this volume) findings for teaching revision strategies in a computer medium to students of French as L2 further demonstrate the positive effects of teaching revision strategies in conjunction with word processing, particularly, for increasing sentence-level coherence and organization. Moreover, the investigations of Brock and Pennington (this volume) and Al-Hazmi and Scholfield (this volume) both demonstrate the value of peer feedback for encouraging L2 students to make significant changes from one draft to the next when writing with a word processor. In this way, the dissemination process becomes intimately linked to that of the text generation-revision cycle.

1.1.5. Summary of Effects

To review, for those who achieve a basic mastery of word processing commands and keyboarding, computer capabilities which reduce the labor and hence the anxiety of generating, revising, and disseminating text have a facilitating effect on the writing process. A result is longer episodes spent writing with greater engagement and often to more audiences, as the writer continues to develop computer skills. The computer's facilitating effect leads to freer written products in the sense of producing more words and more experimental text with more audience interaction. It also leads to more tinkering and on-the-spot revision as pieces of text are being generated. The computer writer thus tends to generate a greater quantity of content with less pre-structuring and organization as 'raw material' in the continuing development of text towards a finished product. In place of the 'top-down' and global structuring of the pre-organized essay, where principles of cohesion and coherence re-lations must be worked out in advance of generating text, in a computer context cohesion develops 'bottom-up' and locally, through the writer's tinkering and discovery of natural relations of coherence existing in the content of the text. With increasing computer experience, the processes of text generation, revision, and dissemination are altered, and the boundaries between them become less clear, as text generation comes to incorporate aspects of revision (editing) and dissemination (audience) as well.

In general, it can be said that the writing process has been re-skilled in a way that matches the computer's capabilities, which are simply to produce strings of characters, manipulate them in some way, store the product, recall what has been stored for further manipulation, and repro-duce the result for dissemination. This *reskilling* effect can be viewed as the ultimate qualitative outcome of computer use. In the progression of computer effects from facilitation of writing to qualitative change in writing process and product, the writer can then be seen to move from computer-assisted writing, in which the computer assists the human writing process, to a computer-based writing process, in which the hu-man implements a computer writing process—what is perhaps most ac-curately termed *electronic writing*.

1.2.   BEYOND SIMPLE WORD PROCESSING

The functions of word processing and the facilitative, quantitative, and qualitative outcomes of computer use can be enhanced by the capabilities of other computer media. At the same time, linking the text generation-revision-dissemination utility of word processing with additional com-puter applications which afford access to different resources and modes of communication does not merely augment the effects of word process-ing; it engenders new types of effects related to the unique characteristics of the additional utilities.

The facilitative effects of the computer on writing are enhanced by access to the resources of databases, hypermedia, and local area and wide-area networks allowing connection to informational sources and other users through such capabilities as electronic mail and the Internet. In addition to facilitating the user's access to information and people, these capabilities also greatly expand the quantity of accessible informa-tion and the number of people with whom a computer writer may estab-lish contact—to a virtually unlimited degree. In this sense, these com-puter capabilities offer new resources for the development and dissemi-nation of information. In so doing, they offer additional opportunities and expanded potential to realize facilitative and quantitative outcomes of increased productivity or output per unit of effort, and qualitative changes in the processes and products of computer use.

1.2.1. Networking

The computer environment can be extended by linking individual users in a local area network (LAN) or wide area network (WAN). In the words of Hoffman (1996): "Networks connect language learners and language teachers and empower them by expanding and deepening their opportunities for communication in a range of contexts which support the learning and use of language, and which make possible the exchange of ideas on a scale far beyond that imaginable in the traditional classroom" (p. 77). Networked computers offer student writers a means of peer-oriented sharing and collaborative writing as well as access to their teachers as wanted (Bruce & Peyton, 1990; Bruce, Peyton, & Batson, 1993; Mabrito, 1991; Palmquist, 1993; Sayers, 1989). With e-mail and/or Internet access, the opportunities for interaction with others in the writing process becomes essentially limitless.

Networking expands the computer user's access to human resources as audiences and helpmates in the writing process. To an even greater extent than in a computer lab, on a network, the computer user can be writing to more people more easily, thus gaining more audience(s) and more input and feedback on ideas. Since there is a chance of receiving similar feedback from different people, and since the feedback is in a concrete (i.e., written) form that can be studied and fully digested, the salience and hence the usefulness of feedback for revision may be enhanced. There may also be more authors of a given work, as a user makes contact with a number of people to brainstorm and share ideas on a topic. In communicating with others on a network, the user is exposed to a greater number and a wider range of models for representing information. As an important part of this effect, the user working in an enhanced electronic environment gains access to more language and more types of language.

According to Hoffman (1996), communicating with e-mail over an institutional or larger computer network "provides an additional communication channel which prompts students to use the target language more, use it more communicatively, and helps them establish ownership of the language they are learning" (p. 67). In the view of Barker and Kemp (1990, p. 1), electronic networks can heighten the immediacy of the present moment, resulting in attempts to respond to it in novel ways. As I have noted elsewhere: "When writing over a network...the anonymity and ease of communication seem to encourage a spontaneous and playful form of 'speak-writing' that results in more creative and natural language than in some other environments" (Pennington, 1996a, p. 8). In addition:

> When married to a network, the computer...allows or encourages different voices and personas of students...and teachers... to emerge. The greater variety of voices and roles may eventually lead to better—clearer, more logical, more fluent, and more productive—voices and roles. (Pennington, 1996a, p. 2)

Baron (1998) likens the type of communication students engage in with e-mail to a creole that has properties of both speech and written language. Thus, networking offers the user new and different kinds of experiences for text generation-revision-dissemination that may result in not only a facilitative effect of easing access to ideas and a quantitative effect of offering access to more ideas, but also qualitative effects having to do with a different, more collaborative and unconventional writing process and product created in the computer environment.

1.2.2. Hypermedia

Hypertext is a computer resource for producing 'layered text' as a series of 'links' accessed by clicking on specially designated text or icons: "Like Chinese boxes, text can be nested within text, and huge texts can reside within tiny fragments" (Bernhardt, 1993, p. 164). Hypertext links provide a way for computer users to bring together ideas and other forms of expression in a network of connections that can be navigated by different audiences in different ways. It is also possible to combine hypertext with other media in hypermedia:

> *Hypermedia* is a database that consists of digitized visual, audio and textual information, and the connections among these pieces of information, delivered to a computer screen. The information is linked in multiple ways,...[and] [t]he end user of the system can navigate through the information as he/she chooses, thereby connecting information in potentially novel ways. (Acker, 1992, p. 210, emphasis as in original)

Using hypertext or hypermedia, the computer user is able to construct a 'hyperdocument' as a linked series of files containing text, digitized sound, or images of various kinds that can be accessed by a mouse.

In giving users immediate broad access to textual and non-textual media, and in offering a type of program in which these media can be mixed and manipulated as the user elects, hypermedia can enhance facilitative and quantitative as well as qualitative outcomes of writing on computer, offering ready access to more sources of information and a different type of access that may encourage more creative and engaged writing. Phinney (1996, p. 146) describes the positive experience and creativity of L2 writers using hypermedia systems to create electronic books and expository presentations built by a combination of text, pictures, and video. In a similar vein, Marcoul and Pennington (this volume) note the originality of the web pages produced by L2 students with hypermedia.

At the same time, the use of these media and the new options they provide for development and dissemination of information promote their own context effects on writing processes and products. As described by Ashworth (1996): "Hypermedia represents both a new medium for developing instructional programs, providing immediate access to multimedia resources, and a new communications medium in its own right" (p. 95). The availability of different multimedia tools for the content of hyperlinks offers different options for the representation and presentation of a writer's ideas, and the connections users elect to make are often fanciful and unpredictable. The result is a highly individual mode of expression which makes possible a highly individual experience on the part of the audience as well.

1.2.3.　Combined Media

With the added resources of the Internet, computer-driven video, music files, picture files, and other sound and visual resources, the creativity of an individual's writing style becomes virtually open-ended. Marcoul and Pennington's (this volume) study provides evidence of this enhanced creative potential in an Internet multimedia hypertext context, where hypertext users created web pages in which they presented themselves as different types of imaginary heroes or cartoon characters. These were in essence 'cyberspace characters' that projected the writer, both as person and as author, into the context of multimedia. As both a kind of play and a kind of creative dissociation from the writer's concrete, here-and-now context and from traditional writing norms, such a projection of self into an imaginary, virtual reality guise has the likely effect of enhancing the creativity and therefore affecting the quality of the texts produced. There is also evidence in Marcoul and Pennington's study that in the multimedia context of designing a web page, L2 writers may be pushed to improve their texts for a more concise and informative expression of ideas to fit into a smaller space, in order to leave room for non-verbal modes of expression on the same page.

With the extra resources available on computer, it becomes easier to do more as well as and more creative things as a writer. The greater access to physical and human resources of information and meaning-making may mean a greater interweaving and integration of sources and perspectives in written products that results in a more thorough and balanced coverage of a topic. Hence, the additional electronic resources may enhance the effects of writing on computer that ultimately result in qualitative improvements in written products. The greater variety of resources and the different types of access to and development of information that they make possible also create a different kind of writing experience—indeed, more different kinds of writing experiences, resulting in more different types of computer writing style:

> Thus, the forms of writing which emerge in a natural word-processing environment may be entirely new. Indeed, many new forms of writing may emerge in the different types of environments created by different software and hardware, including those created by networking and hypertext/hypermedia. (Pennington, 1996b, p. 117)

Ultimately, the definition of writing quality must respond to the differences in writing on computer vs. by traditional means, as a new aesthetic is required to embrace the new written products of the electronic age (Tuman, 1992). For an aesthetic of pen-produced works is not wholly relevant to the disk products and hardcopies of word processed text—much less can it be applied to web pages, electronic books, interactive stories, multiply authored 'brainbursts' created over networks, and the ephemeral, fluid, and interactive speak-write texts of e-mail. Interestingly, web pages have a permanence that e-mail and its 'cousin' spoken language do not, but unlike written products of an earlier age, the text of web pages is intended as only part of a larger presentation of images (Pennington, forthcoming).

1.3.   CONDITIONING FACTORS

The facilitative effects of word processing may not be as direct as at first appears. For the computer's capacity to facilitate a range of component actions that constitute the general act of writing is dependent on the user's awareness of and attitudes towards the relevant computer capabilities. In other words, any positive behavioral outcomes of the electronic medium in the writing activity of the computer user are dependent on a prior—as well as an ongoing—positive cognitive-affective response to the medium (Pennington, 1999). In addition, the characteristics of the user, the type of computer utility, and other aspects of the setting of computer use have a strong impact on computer outcomes. Most importantly, the amount of time spent on computer, and hence the skill and fluency of computer use, is a key factor affecting computer outcomes. The contexts of human-computer interactions can therefore be seen as made up of a particular constellation of *user, computer, setting,* and *time* factors, which continually affect and are affected by those interactions. In this way, the contexts, the interactions of human beings and machines, and the boundaries between them are in a constant state of flux, redefinition, and reconstrual.

1.3.1. User

Previous research has described individual differences in computer outcomes depending on users' inherent characteristics such as gender and age; prior knowledge and skills such as academic ability and experience with the computer; and attitudes and motivation with regard to the computer, English language, writing, and school in general (Bernhardt, Edwards, & Wojahn, 1989; Cross, 1990; Kozma, 1991; Pennington, 1993b; 1996b, ch. 2; Phinney, 1996; Phinney & Khouri, 1993; Phinney & Mathis, 1990; Piper, 1987). As observed by Piolat (1991), "the writing skill level of the student determines the type of assistance the computer can administer" (p. 261). In particular, more confident, academically stronger students may be able to master computer mechanics more easily than less confident, academically weaker or less motivated students and so benefit more from its potential to facilitate the writing process (Daiute, 1986). While some writers may find the computer exciting and liberating, others may find it intimidating or difficult to use (Phinney & Khouri, 1993; Williams, 1992).

Inherent characteristics

Knowledge and skills

Attitudes and motivation

Table 1.1. User Factors

Rusmin (this volume) provides ample evidence of individual differences in affective, cognitive, and behavioral responses to the computer on the part of L2 writers. She also shows how individuals' response to the computer might be relatively stable from first experience or might change over time to become more or less positive. The research of Nabors and Swartley (this volume) gives examples of a range of different ways in which individual users make use of the medium in communicating with others over e-mail and that of Slater and Carpenter (this volume) suggests the importance of language learners' pre-existing char-

18

acteristics, attitudes, and goals in determining the outcomes of computer use. In their study, e-mail 'keypals' on both sides of the English Channel (learners of French in the UK and learners of English in France) were not well-matched and had few common interests. In addition, the French partners seemed not to be motivated to assist the UK partners with a course assignment tied to the e-mail work nor in general to be as motivated as the English students, whose teacher initiated the e-mail project. The greater motivation of the e-mail contact on the part of the UK students learning French was the source of an imbalance in the effort expended in the project that caused it to be less successful than it might have been otherwise.

1.3.2. Computer

It is obvious that the type of computer application is a crucial factor in determining the outcomes of computer use, in particular, its effects on writing. The debate about the value of different computer enhancements for writing that has surrounded text analysis, which some have argued works against effective writing processes and products for L2 writers (see, e.g., Brock & Pennington, this volume; Pennington, 1992; 1993a; Pennington & Brock, 1992), may now be extended to networking and hypermedia. Like text analysis, these computer utilities exert a pressure, whether strong or subtle, towards different types of psychological, process, and product effects on writing. Marcoul and Pennington's (this volume) study provides evidence of different writing outcomes for word processing in comparison to hypermedia in an L2 context, and others (e.g., Bruce & Rubin, 1993; Hartman et al., 1991; Mabrito, 1991) have noted the different types of writing processes and products that results from writing in networked contexts. Some might argue that the differential effects promoted by different computer media may not necessarily be positive with respect to the ultimate goal of producing written texts of high quality. It may also be that the increasing availability of a diversity of resources, while a stimulus to good writing for some users, may be diverting or even overwhelming to others.

Whether using a simple word processor or a complex program linked to other users and resources such as networked hypermedia, there may be an interaction of the type of computer resources available to a user and the particular user's characteristics. Additionally, over time the computer-induced changes in user outcomes will be reflected in the computer characteristics of the hardware and the software, as administrators, programmers, and technicians seek to find the best fit between computer tools and the user's evolving state of computer writing expertise. The characteristics of user and computer can thus be seen to be linked in a cycle of mutual effects.

1.3.3. Setting

Crookall, Coleman, and Oxford (1992) describe the setting for computer-mediated learning "as a network of interactions, only part of which is that between the learner and the computer" (p. 100). At the broadest level, the setting includes the sociocultural context of computer use, which may evolve in different ways within different learning-teaching cultures and social groups. In addition, the emotional climate or psychological setting of computer use makes a difference in the effects which the electronic medium will have on individual users' work, as will the physical and instructional setting.

Sociocultural setting (culture, social grouping)

Psychological setting (pleasantness, emotional climate)

Physical setting (access, placement, comfort)

Instructional setting (curriculum, amount and mode of instruction)

Table 1.2. Setting Factors

The physical setting—e.g., the number and arrangement of computers—is an important determinant of both how and how much the computer is used. Gerrard (1989) maintains that "[t]he public nature of writing in a lab or classroom outfitted with computers may not suit all students..." (p. 105). However, Williamson and Pence (1989) have observed a positive "laboratory or workshop effect" of students working in a more engaged fashion and with greater interaction with others in a computer lab or classroom. In a study with Turkish students writing in English as L2, Kamıslı (1992) reports that the use of word processing in a writing lab setting fostered experimentation and the development of new, more collaborative approaches to composing in English that were potentially more effective for the students involved. Hoffman (1994) reports on the "warm" and friendly context for communication by ESL students that is created in a computer network environment. Thus, computer-induced changes in the physical setting of the classroom are related to both the sociocultural and the psychological setting.

A further setting factor linked to these others is that of instruction, including the curriculum design for students' use of computer tools and the manner and amount of instruction given in relation to computer use. As an example of this linkage, Pennington and Brock (1992) note a tendency for ESL students to become increasingly isolated from their peers under some conditions of writing on computer, such as when using a combination of word processing and text analysis. This is in sharp contrast to the interaction observed in computer labs or classrooms where peer interaction is encouraged. Mirroring the results of the earlier study, the Brock and Pennington (this volume) investigation of Hong Kong students' English writing demonstrates the differential effects of word processing when tied to peer work in a process writing curriculum rather than to computerized text analysis.

As another type of comparison, the instructional setting of the Slater and Carpenter (this volume) study for L2 students' e-mail interaction, which did not on the whole produce the desired positive effects, can be compared to a similar study reported by Woodin (1997). In Woodin's study, English-speaking learners of Spanish established e-mail contact with partners in Spain who were learning English. Woodin draws parallels between language exchange via e-mail contact and language exchange in a face-to-face context, where "[l]earners take responsibility for their own learning and also ensure that their partner also [*sic*] receives what he/she needs" (footnote, p. 22). Woodin also points out that in providing an opportunity for real communication one-on-one with speakers of the target language, e-mail is "acting as a bridge between the language classroom and the natural setting. There is the opportunity for contact with a variety of native speakers, but from within the safety of one's own environment" (p. 31).

In addition to the higher motivation of the Spanish e-mail partners in the Woodin e-mail project as compared to the French e-mail partners in the Slater and Carpenter study, another possible reason for the more favorable results in the Spanish e-mail project is the fact that the setting was viewed by students in more informal, communicative terms. This view of the context of computer use may have encouraged higher personal engagement and involvement in e-mail activity. The greater commitment and involvement on the part of the Spanish e-mail partners was no doubt due at least in part to the fact that in the Woodin study the students were free to communicate on any topic of interest whereas in the Slater and Carpenter study, the topics were preselected for them.

That this aspect, 'freedom of topic', of the instructional setting for e-mail use may be a key factor in students' level—and type—of participation by means of the medium is further suggested by the results of the Nabors and Swartley (this volume) research with e-mail partners for ESL students within an American university. As in the Woodin study, students in the Nabors and Swartley study were free to communicate on topics of their choice, with the result that the setting for use of e-mail promoted students' creative communication with their partners. Nabors and Swartley underscore the importance of students' being able to select their own topics for e-mail communication, as topic is a key factor in a speaker's attempts to promote the construction of an activity as an occasion for talk and conversational interaction. People display their interest in engaging in talk and interaction with specific partners by nominating topics which they think their interlocutors will find engaging. Topic selection, as Nabors and Swartley note, is also an indication of the proposer's view of areas (i) of shared knowledge or (ii) for the development of such knowledge.

Another factor in the disappointing results in the Slater and Carpenter study may be the fact that students were assigned to work in pairs on both sides of the e-mail exchange. This paired-sender condition for use of the electronic medium changes a characteristic setting feature of e-mail, that is, the sense of self-containment and privacy of use of the machine in communication. In short, the structure provided in the Slater and Carpenter implementation of an e-mail exchange for foreign language support may have countered some natural or common features of communication over a network.

Clearly, the setting not only affects but is affected by computer use and by the changing pattern of outcomes, as well as by the nature of the users, which changes interactively with the setting and with computer use. Thus, teachers' attitudes and behavior change in response to changes in the students' attitudes and behavior, and as student groups evolve a computer learning culture. Over the longer term, even more 'permanent' setting features such as physical facilities and curriculum will ultimately be changed by the users' evolving state of development.

1.3.4. Time

Time is an important variable in determining computer outcomes: "Except for some attitudinal benefits of writing on computer, most of the benefits in writing process or product of this electronic aid are not apparent in the short term" (Pennington, 1996b, p. 55). It takes time for users to master computer mechanics and so to realize the facilitative potentials of the medium. It also takes time for quantitative effects on computer users' writing to emerge, and additional time for qualitative effects to evolve in a computer writing context. As observed by Williamson and Pence (1989): "Word processing appears to change certain student writers' approach to text production, pointing the way to greater experimentation with their texts (however, more than 15 weeks of instruction ma be required for a significant number of students to realize the advantages)" (p. 120).

As an interactive effect, time spent on the computer can be seen to expand as facilitative and quantitative effects of computer use expand. This means that L2 writers can be expected to spend more time writing and to write more as both cause and effect of their increasing ability to exploit the computer's capabilities. In addition, the manner and quality of time spent on computer can be seen to change as the user's manner and quality of use change, and as the setting for computer use is impacted by the other conditioning factors.

1.4.   IMPLICATIONS FOR TEACHING

As observed by Baron (1998): "Human communication always involves choices—when to say what to whom and, at least since the development of writing, through what medium" (p. 158). Instead of a choice about *whether* to make use of the computer in the second or foreign language writing curriculum, choices exist in the *type* of electronic medium and the *manner* in which it will be used. Since different electronic resources, and combinations of these, promote different kinds of effects under different conditions of use, the choice should ultimately be governed by the learning goal, with attention as well to the characteristics of the learners and the other features of the learning context. Choices should also be made with an awareness of potential negative impacts of each medium (Pennington, 1991; 1996b; 1999).

Word processing responds to goals such as increasing text production, experimentation, revision, and dissemination to others. However, the quantity of text generated in a computer context generally requires extra time and effort for development and revision in order to become fully polished and coherent prose. In addition, inexperienced and L2 writers using word processing may benefit more from writing on computer if both writing process and revision strategies are explicitly trained. They may also benefit from instructional approaches that give a prominent role to peer feedback rather than relying solely on the computer to provide input for writing.

Computer labs and local area networks can help to develop peer interaction and collaboration in writing. However, writing activities such as freewriting or other kinds of independent work are more effectively performed in a quiet and private workspace. Moreover, some writers find it difficult to work in a relatively busy and noisy environment such as might be the case in a computer lab. Wide area networks such as e-mail and the Internet provide further access to sources of feedback and fresh ideas for writing in L2 contexts. At the same time, they may hold their own attractions which end up drawing attention away from writing. In addition, as noted by Woodin (1997):

23

> The skills needed for a successful e-mail partnership must not
> be underestimated. Participants need to form a relationship
> with a native speaker they have never met and cannot see, ne-
> gotiate a series of exchanges and obtain information of interest
> to them, write in the foreign language without the support of
> non-verbal clues and maintain the relationship once the initial
> excitement has disappeared. They need to be more explicit than
> in face-to-face conversations and yet be tactful so as not to of-
> fend. All of this must take place using the language which
> they are learning! [And] [w]e are, after all, still learning the
> language of e-mail and conventions are not yet clearly laid
> down. (p. 29)

Access to other writers or computer information sources such as
electronic databases can help L2 writers gain access to information. At
the same time, access to these resources may encourage these writers to
insert large amounts or a diversity of types of undigested information
into their texts. They may also promote quantity or diversity of information at the expense of quality of information or originality of writing.
Hypermedia makes available non-text resources to supplement and
combine with text. While responding to goals of originality, hypermedia
use tends to reduce the amount of text produced. It may also shift the
genre of texts produced away from academic writing style and towards
popular culture and its associated topics and language, thereby working
against some goals of the L2 writing curriculum.

On the other hand, as Murray (1995) remarks:

> [T]hose in positions of authority have been raised in the print
> culture, while those whom we teach, employ, or govern, are
> being exposed to a variety of media. These young people may
> not develop skills specialized primarily for reading; they will
> have a more diverse range of skills and media on which to
> draw. Indeed, they need this more diverse range of skills. (p.
> 113)

Writing teachers need to be open to the new values that inform writing in
computer contexts and the new genres which are inevitably developing in
these contexts. This is as true in L2 as in other educational contexts.

1.5.   RESEARCH NEEDS

The research on writing with electronic media has always been, and still
is, dominated by studies carried out in educational contexts in the United
States, with university-level freshman composition being the most com-

mon context of investigation. An encouraging exception is the recent emphasis on literacy in the global context of the World-Wide Web (see, e.g., papers in Snyder, 1998). More studies of all kinds with second and foreign language students, including those of pre-university age and especially for languages other than English, would provide much-needed breadth and balance, while also helping to clarify the effects of the electronic medium for different populations and teaching-learning circumstances.

More investigations of computer effects under different conditions of usage are needed to determine the computer's contribution to learning, as an independent or an interactive factor, within a specific instructional orientation or approach to the teaching of writing. As I have observed elsewhere:

> Given the increasing irrelevance of pen-and-paper composing, comparative studies of the differential effects of word processing and pen-and-paper composing should give way to comparative studies of word processing—and indeed other modes of electronic writing involving networking and hypermedia—under different conditions of instruction. In this way the differential effects of the computer and the context of instruction can be teased apart. Progress can also be made by designing investigations to test specific theories or models of computer-assisted writing.... (Pennington, 1999, p. 288)

More microscopically focused, longitudinal studies of computer users would help to trace the pattern of development of computer skills over time. There is a crying need for theoretically underpinned developmental studies of the acquisition of skills in electronic writing environments. A general research program can be proposed (see Pennington, 1996b, ch. 5, pp. 164 ff) to examine the evolution of learners' conceptions of the computer writing medium over time. Such a program requires a longitudinal focus to determine the learner's developing view and skills in terms of (1) computer, (2) writing, (3) language, and (4) interactions among these. It might also incorporate the developing views and skills of not only the learners but also their teachers and others in the educational establishment such as heads of schools or educational authorities. As I have described elsewhere:

> The goal of the research program is to characterize the users' initial models, or subjective theories, in each of these four areas and then to chart the ways in which, and the degree to which, each of those initial views evolves through exposure to writing on computer. This research agenda is sufficiently broad to allow for all kinds of computer writing treatments, while also providing a focus for comparison and contrast of different

learner populations, teacher characteristics, software and hardware, settings of use, instructional approaches, time periods of
the implementation, and measures of effects and effectiveness.
(Pennington, 1996b, p. 165).

There is a need as well for more meta-analytical studies, specifically,
of L2 writers. It is also perhaps time to train a critical eye on the field of
computer writing research and to examine the transformations which it
has undergone over the last quarter century, during which time the computer has evolved from fearsome machine to personal workstation and
connection-point to the world (Pennington, 1996a).

1.6.   CONCLUSION

This chapter has reviewed the capabilities and impacts of the computer in
its many guises as writing tool and environment. When complemented
by additional types of electronic resources, the text generation-revision-
dissemination functions that are basic to word processing may be enhanced, as the user's ability to produce, manipulate, and/or access information is expanded. At the same time, in emphasizing different aspects of writing and communication more generally, other computer resources also promote different kinds of effects, some of which may de-
tract from or work against the effects of word processing. The mutually
interactive context factors of user, computer, setting, and time impact
computer outcomes and are in turn impacted by those outcomes. Thus,
writing on computer forms a complex cause-effect cycle in which the
writer is changed by the writing medium and its context, as the medium
and the context of writing are also changed in the process.

2. Word Processing in the EFL Classroom: Effects on Writing Strategies, Attitudes, and Products

Ayse Akyel and Sibel Kamıslı

ABSTRACT

This chapter investigates the effects of word processing on writing and revision strategies, composition quality, quantity of writing, and attitudes of EFL students in an educational setting where computer use is not as yet widespread. Sixteen first-year university students were divided into equal groups: a pen-and-paper group and a computer group. Both groups were exposed to a 19-week process writing curriculum with a special emphasis on academic expository prose. The computer group spent half of the class time in a computer lab. The pen-and-paper group was taught in a traditional classroom. Data were collected through think-aloud protocols, semi-structured interviews, self-evaluation forms, and compositions. Findings revealed improvements in both groups but no significant group differences in terms of writing quality or quantity. However, the writing instruction seemed to influence the writing strategies of the students and their overall attitudes toward writing in a positive direction.

2.0.   INTRODUCTION

Despite the growing number of computers in schools and the consensus about their significant role in education, their place in the curriculum is still a subject of debate. However, one application of the computer, word processing, is recognized as a promising tool for improving composing skills, especially those of ESL/EFL writers. Moreover, research is widening its scope as to how this writing tool changes the way writers approach the composing process (Phinney, 1996).

Some studies examining the probable effects of computers on ESL/EFL writers' composing processes have focused on revision (Green, 1991; Johnson, 1986; Lam, 1991; Van Waes, 1994). Others have investigated the impact of word processing on the quality (Collins, 1991;

Kitchin, 1991; Lam & Pennington, 1995; Schcolnik, 1990; Silver, 1990) or the quantity of written work (Green, 1991; Johnson, 1986; Pennington & Brock, 1992). In addition, some studies have examined the influence of the computer on the social contexts or dynamics of classrooms (Hyland, 1993; Johnson, 1986; Kamıslı, 1992; Poulsen, 1991), while others have focused on the attitudinal effects of word processing (Benesch, 1987; Neu & Scarcella, 1991; Phinney, 1991a,b; Phinney & Mathis, 1990; Piper, 1987).

Researchers looking at the effects of computers on the revision behavior of ESL student writers have found that they revise extensively in a computer environment (Chadwick & Bruce, 1989; Green, 1991; Johnson, 1986; Lam, 1991; Phinney & Mathis, 1988). Moreover, two of these studies (Chadwick & Bruce, 1989; Phinney & Mathis, 1988) comparing the effects of word processing and pen-and-paper on ESL/EFL writers' writing processes report that these ESL/EFL writers use the computer to make changes both at the macro- and micro-structural levels of the text, i.e., exploiting the potential of the computer as a tool for revising and editing. However, the findings of one study conducted in the EFL context (Van Waes, 1994) suggest that word processing may not necessarily promote better revision strategies, as it encourages the writer to focus on only that portion of the text that appears on the screen. On the other hand, it has also been argued that the small portion of the text displayed on screen encourages intensive and repeated local processing (Pennington, 1991; 1993b). As Pennington (this volume) points out, this "locally focused micro-structural orientation of revision" (p. 17) renders the revision process more continuous and meaning-oriented.

In relation to the effects of computers on the planning behavior of ESL writers, the results of two comparative studies, one on ESL student writers (Chadwick & Bruce, 1989) and one on experienced EFL writers (Van Waes, 1994) show pen-and-paper writers spending more time thinking and planning before writing than computer users, who often start writing without preplanning. Moreover, other research findings indicate that the nature of the writing task may affect ESL/EFL writers' planning behavior in terms of quantity (Jones & Tetroe, 1987) and/or quality (Akyel, 1994; Friedlander, 1990). Pennington (1993b; 1996b,d; this volume) points out that word processing as a medium of writing may change the way that writers begin their writing task, encouraging a type of process in which initial planning is minimized.

Some studies looking at the attitudinal effects of word processing indicate that ESL writers using computers develop positive attitudes toward writing. Several studies, for example, show that student writers believe their writing benefits from using computers (Berens, 1986; Green, 1991; (Kamıslı, 1992; Neu & Scarcella, 1991; Pennington & Brock, 1992; Phinney, 1991a; Phinney & Mathis, 1990; Piper, 1987; Van Waes, 1994). However, a study by Chadwick and Bruce (1989) did not find any major changes in ESL writers' attitudes in terms of enjoyment of writing.

In general, researchers exploring the attitudinal effect of word processing in ESL/EFL contexts have found that the experience of writing on the computer may not be a reflection of writing with traditional methods, due to the computer's attributes and capabilities. One of the differences is that the impermanence of the electronic page may be able to ease some of the anxiety of writing. As the computer lessens the physical and psychological constraints of writing, this makes the process of writing easier and more pleasurable. Hence, the attributes of the computer can alleviate negative attitudes to writing (Pennington, 1991; 1996b; this volume).

The interactive nature of the computer is another important factor making the writing experience different than when writing with traditional implements. The blinking cursor constantly reminds the writer that s/he is engaged in a conversation, hence creating a sense of audience (Andrews, 1985; Daiute, 1985; Neu & Scarcella, 1991). This feature of the computer might be especially helpful to those writers who experience difficulties in transforming prose for an audience other than themselves, as the writer is encouraged to create "reader-based" rather than "writer-based" texts (Flower, 1979). This sense of writing for a specific audience may encourage the writer to spend more time trying out ideas and experimenting with language while searching for an appropriate expression to appeal to a particular audience. According to Faigley and Witte (1984), distancing oneself from the text, i.e., looking at the text with different eyes, can help unskilled writers to perform the kinds of revisions that are associated with skilled writing performance.

The effects of the computer environment on teaching-learning roles has also been observed by various studies in ESL settings, and it has been found that the computer reinforces the interactional dimension of the process approach to writing instruction. The findings of some studies suggest that the computer promotes productive teaching-learning roles and encourages collaboration among ESL writers (Hyland, 1993; Johnson, 1986; Kamıslı, 1992; Poulsen, 1991).

Studies on the impact of word processing on ESL/EFL writers are few in number in comparison to those on first language (L1) writers (for reviews, see Cochran-Smith, 1991; Hawisher, 1989; Pennington, 1993b, 1996b). To the knowledge of the authors, despite the increasing number of publications focusing on the impact of computers on English L1 and ESL writers, there have few studies, such as that of Van Waes (1994), on the effects of computer use specifically in EFL settings. Moreover, the participants in Van Waes' study were experienced writers who already had positive feelings toward computers and technology. Therefore, further empirical research is needed to explore whether or not and/or how computer use affects EFL students' writing processes and their attitudes toward writing and word processing. Moreover, it would be especially valuable to carry out research in an EFL setting where student writers are not as familiar with computers and technology as in some other ESL/EFL settings.

2.1.   METHOD

2.1.1.   Purpose

The present study investigates the impact of word processing on the writing processes and attitudes of EFL student writers in a setting where computer use has not yet been a widespread practice. The study also aims to test the findings of previous studies conducted in other ESL/EFL settings. Specifically, the study is designed to answer the following research questions:

> 1. Does word processing as a writing tool affect general writing processes and the deep- and surface-level revision strategies of EFL writers?

> 2. Does word processing as a writing tool affect the length and the quality of compositions?

> 3. Do student writers' attitudes toward writing change as a result of the use of word processing as a writing tool?

2.1.2.   Students

Sixteen first-year university students, all females between the ages of 18-20, who were enrolled in the English freshman composition course of an English-medium Turkish university participated in this study. When the study was conducted, there were three sections of the freshman composition course, one of which was the pilot computer writing course. Eight of the participants were from the computer writing section and the other eight students were enrolled in one of the ordinary pen-and-paper freshman composition sections. All of the student writers, as L1 speakers of Turkish, had passed a centralized, two-tier university examination and had gained a minimum score of 550 on the TOEFL (Test of English as a Foreign Language) together with a score of 4-4.5 on the writing component of the TOEFL or a corresponding score on the university's English proficiency exam, which is said to be equivalent to the Michigan Test of English (Hughes, 1988). The students were studying in the freshman year of a four-year teacher preparation program in Teaching English as a Foreign Language (TEFL) in Turkey.

2.1.3. Instruction

Both the computer and the pen-and-paper groups were exposed to process writing instruction with a special emphasis on academic expository prose. They were engaged in tasks to develop their knowledge of various genres and of coherence and formality at the discourse level, as well as in activities pertaining to various aspects of process writing (e.g., brainstorming, list making, looping, and cubing[1]).

Both groups were given writing instruction for three hours a week over 19 weeks by two experienced writing instructors who were the researchers' colleagues in the Department of Education. These instructors used the same textbooks (Neuflet, Gaudiot, Wiley, & Rigley, 1986; Raimes, 1986). The pen-and-paper group was taught in a traditional manner, i.e., they went through the writing process using pen-and-paper in a typical classroom setting. The computer group spent half of the instructional time in the classroom, where they were engaged in various writing activities as already described. The rest of the time they were in a computer lab working on their texts, which they had discussed with their peers or teachers previously. The student writers in this group were intensively exposed to computers and word processing features (e.g., copying, saving, and spellchecking) in the first weeks of writing instruction. They were encouraged to use the computer lab and were given tasks to accomplish outside class time in the lab, where they were helped by lab assistants as needed.

2.1.4. Tasks and Data Collection[2]

---

[1] These are techniques that help to discover and generate ideas. Brainstorming is an activity that lets one idea lead to another through free association and quick follow-up of related words, thoughts, and opinions. List-making is an activity that helps to recall ideas from memory. Looping means writing nonstop without self-censorship about anything that comes to mind. Cubing engages the students in considering a subject from six points of view—describe, compare, associate, apply, and argue for/against.

[2] The authors thank Dr. Emine Erktin for her suggestions on the statistical procedures to be used for this research. The authors also thank Yakut Gazi and Gülcan Erçetin for the statistical processing of the data. Many thanks go to Zeynep Koçoglu for her continuous help in data collection and in tabulation of the results. The authors also gratefully acknowledge Prof. Pennington for her incisive and substantive suggestions on an earlier draft of this paper. Finally, the authors thank Bogaziçi University Research Fund, without whose assistance in the way of a grant this project could not have been carried out.

Following the tradition of many studies on ESL/EFL writing (Akyel & Kamıslı, 1996; Kamıslı, 1992; Lay, 1982; Raimes, 1985, 1987), the student writers in both groups were asked to compose aloud in front of a tape recorder at the beginning and end of a 19-week writing course. Choosing between two topics assigned for each of the tasks, they composed in the descriptive mode—a rhetorical pattern that is frequently practiced in Turkish and English composition classes—in a natural setting without any time constraint (see Appendix 2.1 for prompts given for Tasks I and II as assigned at the beginning and end of the instructional period). As can be seen in Appendix 2.1, the prompts given to the student required them to use the same rhetorical pattern and to write on roughly similar topics in the compositions written at the beginning and end of instruction. This was done to avoid possible confounding factors related to topic or rhetoric.

Since think-aloud writing was a new task for the student writers, two consecutive orientation sessions on this data collection procedure were provided at the beginning of the writing course. First, the researchers demonstrated composing aloud in English. Then the student writers went through the same procedure, i.e., they reported what they were thinking while they wrote. Most of the students understood what they were to do and accomplished the task with little difficulty. Very few needed prompting before performing the task spontaneously. The orientation session ended when the researchers were assured that the subjects were able to write and compose aloud at the same time.

During the composing aloud process, the researchers observed and wrote down the students' observable behaviors. In cases when the student writers stopped reporting what they were doing, the researchers asked what the reason was and audiotaped the student writer's response. The mode of writing was pen-and-paper for both the groups at the beginning of instruction. At the end of the course, however, the computer group composed on computer while the other group wrote their compositions using pen and paper.

After each composing task, both groups responded to a self-evaluation form—a semi-structured questionnaire—and were interviewed to learn more about the student writers' composing strategies, past/current writing experiences in English, and their perceptions of and attitudes to writing in English. The self-evaluation form given to both groups at the end of instruction included items exploring whether they felt that the instruction affected their writing and if so, how. The computer group also responded to a question related to their feelings about the effects of computer use on their writing and their attitudes towards the use of computers (Appendix 2.2).

2.1.5. Variables and Measurement

In this study, general writing strategies (assessment and commenting, pre-planning, planning, rescanning, rehearsing, pausing, and reading the whole text), surface-level revision strategies (addition, substitution, punctuation, spelling, sentence structure, verb form, and word form), deep-level revision strategies (addition, deletion, substitution, reorganization, and combination), composition quality, and essay length, were treated as dependent variables. Two trained scorers who work in the School of Foreign Languages of the same university evaluated the student writers' compositions for quality using a holistic grading system, paying attention to content, organization, and language use. Based on the Pearson Product-Moment Correlation Coefficient, interrater reliability for the two raters was 0.91. The number of words in the compositions were counted by the researchers.

The composing-aloud tapes were transcribed and analyzed by the researchers independently using the coding schemes developed by Raimes (1987) and Pennington and Brock (1992). Accordingly, frequency counts of the specific composing strategies classified under three major categories were made as follows: general writing strategies, deep-level revision strategies, and surface-level revision strategies (Appendix 2.3). When differences in the frequency counts occurred, the researchers resolved the discrepancies through discussion.

The interviews were transcribed and the responses were grouped under three subcategories: the student writers' composing strategies, their past/current writing experiences in English, and their perceptions/attitudes to writing in English. In addition, subcategories for feelings and/or perceptions toward the initial encounter with the computer and writing with a computer in a writing class were added for the experimental group. Under these subcategories, the researchers looked for emerging patterns. These patterns were cross-validated with short "thick" descriptions which the researchers formulated for each student writer following Geertz's (1973) procedures.

The *Statistical Package for Social Sciences (SPSS)* was used for the statistical analysis of the data related to the writing and revision strategies utilized by both groups, the holistic scoring of quality, and the length of the compositions which students wrote at the beginning and end of the instruction. In accordance with the objectives of the study, two statistical measures, both non-parametric tests, were computed to check for differences between groups. These were: (a) the Mann-Whitney U Test to check for significant differences for the computer and the pen-and-paper group at the beginning and end of instruction, and (b) the Wilcoxon Matched-Pairs Signed-Rank Test to check for significant differences before and after instruction in each group. The level of significance was set at alpha = 0.05.[3]

2.2.   FINDINGS

2.2.1.   Between-Group Comparison

2.2.2.1.   Pre-Instruction

Mann-Whitney U tests were applied to see whether the computer and the pen-and-paper group differed from each other at the start of 19-week instructional program in terms of: general writing strategies, surface-level revision strategies, deep-level revision strategies, global quality of compositions, and length of compositions. Tables 2.1a, 2.2a, 2.3a, 2.4a, and 2.5a (Appendix 2.4, "pre-pre" section) present a comparison of the two groups before the instruction in terms of these variables. The results indicate that the two groups did not differ from each other at project start-up in terms of any of these variables.

2.2.2.2.   Post-Instruction Writing Strategies

To examine whether the computer and the pen-and-paper groups differed from each other after the 19-week instructional period in terms of the variables mentioned above, the same statistical procedure was followed. As indicated in Table 2.5a (Appendix 2.4, "post-post" section), a comparison of the computer and the pen-and-paper groups in terms of the frequencies with which they utilized all strategies classified under the three major categories of general writing strategies, surface-level revision strategies, and deep-level revision strategies indicated that the computer group had higher mean scores than the pen-and-paper group in all three categories: general writing strategies (computer group mean 37.25 vs. pen group mean 28.38), surface-level revision strategies (computer 7.75 vs. pen 4.50), deep-level revision strategies (computer 9.38 vs. pen 6.38). However, none of these differences were statistically significant.

General Writing Strategies. The pen-and-paper and the computer groups were also compared in terms of their use of each individual

---

[3] Some inferential power regarding the results of this study is lost by the decision to analyze within-groups and between-groups differences separately by means of non-parametric statistical tests. Compare the procedures employed by Brock and Pennington (this volume) and Al-Hazmi and Scholfield (this volume). (Editor's note)

34

writing strategy classified under the three major categories of revision. As can be noted in Table 2.1a (Appendix 2.4, "post-post" section), at the end of the instructional period the pen-and paper-group did significantly more preplanning than the computer group (pen 1.50 vs. computer 0.25, $Z = 2.60**$), the computer group had a significantly higher number of instances of rescanning (pen 2.00 vs. computer 5.00, $Z = 1.91*$) and pause (pen 3.00 vs. computer 4.20, $Z = 1.86*$) than the pen-and-paper group. These results are entirely consistent with other studies suggesting more in-process planning and a more recursive writing process for computer writers than for non-computer writers. Moreover, during their writing, the computer group planned and rehearsed more frequently than did the pen-and-paper group, with means of 8.25 (computer) vs. 6.13 (pen) for planning and 7.13 (computer) vs. 4.88 (pen) for rehearsing, though these differences were not statistically significant. Finally, the two groups did not differ from each other in terms of the categories of either assessing and commenting or reading the whole text.

Surface-Level Revision Strategies. As indicated in Table 2.2a (Appendix 2.4, "post-post" section), at the end of the instructional period, the computer group focused significantly more on spelling (pen 0.00 vs. computer 2.38, $Z = 2.21*$) and sentence structure (pen 0.13 vs. computer 1.38, $Z = 3.34***$) than did the pen-and-paper group, suggesting that some forms of micro-level revision may be facilitated by the computer. On the other hand, the pen-and-paper group focused more on word form than the computer group did (pen 0.50 vs. computer 0.00, $Z = 2.24*$). The two groups did not differ from each other in terms of the other categories of surface-level revision.

Deep-Level Revision Strategies. As indicated in Table 2.3a (Appendix 2.4), at post-test, the computer group had significantly more instances of reorganization than the pen-and-paper group (pen 0.88 vs. computer 1.75, $Z = 1.98*$).[4] Moreover, the computer group utilized the substitution and combination operations more frequently than the pen-and-paper group, with means for pen 1.38 vs. computer 2.38, and pen 0.88 vs. computer 1.50, respectively, for these two operations. However, these differences were not statistically significant.

Discussion. The results for writing strategies demonstrate that the computer writers spent markedly less time in initial planning and paused more frequently in the course of writing. Thus, it seems that instead of organizing their writing process from an initial, detailed text plan, they based their planning more on distributed periods of pausing, followed by rehearsing and writing at the level of sentences and paragraphs. The

---

[4] This finding is consistent with that of Bisaillon (this volume). (Editor's note)

findings also show that the computer writers from the very beginning of the writing process repeatedly alternated acts of formulating and revising the text, which means that their degree of recursivity was higher than that of pen-and-paper writers. In addition, the ease of writing with computers in general encouraged them to focus more than the pen-and-paper group on formal (surface-level) revision as well as content (deep-level) revision. These differences were statistically significant in terms of some of the surface and deep-level revision strategies (e.g., spelling and sentence structure as types of formal revision and reorganization as a type of content revision).

2.2.2.3. Post-Instruction Global Quality Scoring and Composition Length

Table 2.4a (Appendix 2.4, "post-post" section) presents the results of the comparison of the pen-and-paper and the computer groups in terms of global quality (holistic) scoring and length of compositions written at the end of the 19-week instructional period. As can be seen in Table 2.4a, the computer group scored higher than the pen-and-paper group in terms of global quality scoring (group means for computer 75.00 vs. pen 72.50) and length of compositions (group means for computer 430 vs. pen 411 words). These differences were not, however, statistically significant, suggesting that although computer writers may show differences in writing strategies related to use of the electronic composing tool, they may not necessarily outperform pen-and-paper writers in terms of quality and quantity measures when both groups are given process writing instruction over a period of time.

2.2.3. Within-Group Comparison

The two groups were also compared in terms of: (i) the writing strategies they utilized and (ii) the quality and the length of the compositions they wrote before and after the instructional period. For this purpose, Wilcoxon tests were applied. Tables 2.1b, 2.2b, 2.3b, 2.4b, and 2.5b in Appendix 2.5 present the statistical results for the two groups.

2.2.3.1. Pre- to Post-Instruction Writing Strategies

As can be seen in Table 2.5b (Appendix 2.5), there was a significant difference in the frequencies with which both groups utilized general writing strategies (pen group pre 18.00 vs. post 28.38, $Z = 2.52$*; computer group pre 18.13 vs. post 37.25, $Z = 2.52$*), and deep-level revision strategies (pen pre 4.13 vs. post 6.38, $Z = 2.19$*; computer pre 3.63 vs.

post 9.38, Z = 2.36*) before and after the period of instruction. These results suggest the impact of process writing on writing instruction and practice more generally in both groups. Moreover, both groups utilized comparatively fewer surface-level revision strategies during the post-instruction writing process than in the pre-instruction condition, with averages of pre 8.50 vs. post 4.50 for the pen-and-paper group, pre 9.25 vs. post 7.75 for the computer group. However, these differences were not significant.

General Writing Strategies. As indicated in Table 2.1b (Appendix 2.5), at the end of the course, the pen-and-paper writers utilized assessing and commenting (pre 5.25 vs. post 10.50, Z = 2.17*) in addition to planning (pre 3.13 vs. post 6.19, Z = 1.87*) and rehearsing (pre 3.38 vs. post 4.88, Z = 1.85*) strategies significantly more frequently than they did before the instruction. In addition, they had a significantly higher number of instances of pause (pre 1.75 vs. post 3.00, Z = 2.20*) during their assessed post-instruction writing process than during their pre-instruction writing process. Moreover, these writers had more instances of pre-planning (pre 1.13 vs. post 1.50) and they rescanned less frequently (pre 3.13 vs. post 2.00) after the instructional period, although these differences were not statistically significant. The reading-the-whole-text strategy (pre 0.25 vs. post 0.38) was observed to be used little in either the pre-test or post-test writing process of the pen-and-paper group.

Table 2.1b (Appendix 2.5) demonstrates that at the end of the course, the computer writers, like the pen-and-paper group, had a significantly greater number of instances of assessing and commenting (pre 5.50 vs. post 11.63, Z = 2.52*), planning (pre 3.13 vs. 8.25 post, Z = 2.52*), and rehearsing (pre 3.00 vs. post 7.13, Z = 2.52*). In addition, like the pen-and-paper writers, they paused more frequently (pre 2.00 vs. post 4.75, Z = 2.52*) during their post-instruction writing process than in their pre-instruction writing process. Moreover, as in the case of pen-and-paper writers, there was minimal use of the reading-the-text strategy (pre 0.50 vs. post 0.25) before and after instruction. Thus, both groups seemed to show similar effects of the treatment in these assessed areas. However, unlike in the case of the pen-and-paper writers, there was a significant decrease in the computer group's use of the initial planning strategy (pre 1.00 vs. post 0.25, Z = 1.82*) after instruction, consistent with other researchers' findings. In addition, again unlike the pen-and-paper writers, the computer writers rescanned what they wrote more after the course (pre 3.00 vs. post 5.00), but this difference was not statistically significant.

Surface-Level Revision. As indicated in Table 2.2b (Appendix 2.5), after the instructional exposure, the pen-and-paper writers carried out fewer surface-level revision operations in all categories except for punctuation (pre 0.13 vs. post 0.38), but the differences other than for sentence structure (pre 0.75 vs. post 0.13, $Z = 1.82*$) were not statistically significant. Further shown in Table 2.2b (Appendix 2.5), after the instructional period, the computer writers performed significantly fewer surface-level deletion operations (pre 1.13 vs. post 0.38, $Z = 1.67*$) and significantly more spelling operations (pre 0.25 vs. post 2.38, $Z = 1.75*$). Moreover, they utilized more sentence structure (pre 1.13 vs. post 1.38) and punctuation (pre 0.13 vs. post 1.00) operations, but the latter differences were not statistically significant. Thus, computer use does not necessarily mean less of a focus on surface-level revision.

Deep-Level Revision. As Table 2.3b (Appendix 2.5) shows, after the instructional treatment, the pen-and-paper group utilized significantly more deep-level addition operations (pre 0.38 vs. post 2.38, $Z = 2.36*$). Moreover, whereas they utilized substitution (pre 1.13 vs. post 1.38), combination (pre 0.75 vs. post 0.88), and reorganization operations (pre 0.50 vs. post 0.88) more frequently after instruction, there was a decrease during the instructional period in the use of deletion operations (pre 1.38 vs. post 0.88). However, none of these latter results were statistically significant.

As indicated in Table 2.3b (Appendix 2.5), the computer writers utilized significantly more addition (pre 0.50 vs. post 3.00, $Z = 2.17*$), substitution (pre 0.38 vs. post 2.38, $Z = 1.82*$), reorganization (pre 0.50 vs. post 1.75, $Z = 2.52*$), and combination (pre 0.50 vs. post 1.50, $Z = 2.36*$) operations at the end of the course. Moreover, they had significantly fewer instances of deletion operations (pre 1.75 vs. post 0.75, $Z = 2.02*$).

As mentioned in the previous section in relation to Appendix 2.4, both groups, after the writing instruction to which they had been exposed, utilized more deep level addition, substitution, reorganization, and combination strategies. However, as seen in Appendix 2.5, Table 2.3b, these differences were statistically significant for the four strategies only in the case of the computer writers. In the case of pen-and-paper writers, a statistically significant increase was observed only for addition operations (pre 0.38 vs. post 2.38, $Z = 2.36*$). Furthermore, although there was a decrease in the frequencies with which both groups used the deletion operation (pen 1.38 vs. 0.88, computer 1.75 vs. 0.75). Thus, the computer writers made more deep-level changes, and of more types, than the pen-and-paper writers. This decrease was statistically significant only in the case of the computer writers.

Discussion. Taking into consideration the findings that for both groups, there was a decrease in the use of some of the surface-level revision operations and an increase in deep-level revision operations, except for the deletion operation, it can be stated that both groups tended to put more of a focus on content revision than they did before the instruction, a result that may be attributed to the process approach or to exposure to writing instruction and practice more generally in both groups. However, as the comparison of the post-instruction writing strategies of the two groups presented in the previous section shows, this tendency was stronger in the case of the computer writers, reinforcing the view that use of word processing may enhance the content focus of a process approach. The findings also demonstrate that at the end of instruction the computer writers seemed to focus more on surface-level revision than the pen-and-paper writers, thus suggesting that computer writers make more changes of all kinds as compared to pen-and-paper writers. This may perhaps be attributed to the ease of writing with computers. Furthermore, there was a greater increase from beginning to end of the course in the frequency with which the computer writers rescanned and paused, suggesting a more intensive writing process than for the pen-and-paper writers. Finally, at the end of the course, the computer writers did markedly less initial planning than the pen-and-paper writers, confirming the findings of other studies.

2.2.3.2. Pre- to Post-Instruction Global Quality Scoring and Composition Length

Table 2.4b (Appendix 2.5) presents a comparison of the compositions written by both groups before and after instruction in terms of global quality (holistic) scoring. As indicated in Table 2.4b, both the pen-and-paper and computer groups had significantly higher mean scores for the compositions they wrote at the end of instruction than those written at the start of the instruction (pen, 64.38 vs. 72.50, $Z = 2.52*$; computer 64.38 vs. 75.00, $Z = 2.52*$). As also shown in Table 2.4b, the compositions written by the pen-and-paper writers before and after the period of instruction did not differ significantly from each other in terms of length (pre 379 words vs. post 411 words). However, the computer writers wrote significantly longer compositions at the end of instruction than at the start (pre 385 words vs. post 430 words, $Z = 2.52*$).

As these results demonstrate, both groups wrote significantly better compositions at the end of the writing instruction they were exposed to. However, as discussed earlier, when the two groups were compared in terms of their post-instruction composition scores, although the computer writers had slightly higher mean global quality ratings for their compositions than the pen-and-paper writers, the difference across the two groups was not statistically significant. The computer writers also wrote significantly longer compositions at the end of the period of instruction but again without any statistically significant difference in comparison to the post-tests of the pen-and-paper group.[5] Hence, although the computer writers tended to focus more on content revision, and their writing processes seemed to be more recursive than the pen-and-paper writers at the end of instruction, these differences did not show up as a significant difference in the quality of the compositions they wrote. This may be due to the fact that the period of instruction was not long enough (Pennington, 1993b; 1996b).

2.2.4. Attitudes to Writing with Computers

An analysis of the self-evaluation forms and the interview transcripts shows that the student writers in the computer group went through a phase in which they had difficulty adapting to the machine.[6] Although they probably encounter computers in their everyday life (e.g., in banks and offices), having to work in front of a terminal in a classroom was their first experience with the computer in an educational setting. Thus, as Student Writer 2 related:

> I was anxious. Can I do it? On computer, hmmm, it is different. The first time I used it I had anxiety. I questioned myself whether I can do it. How is it going to turn out to be?

Another difficulty resulted from not knowing the keyboard and so not having keyboarding skills. As Student Writer 3 commented:

> It was difficult to write on the computer at the beginning because I wasn't used to it. While writing, I would make grammar or spelling mistakes. While I was correcting that mistake, I would push the wrong key and the sentence would go down couple of spaces. Then I would try to get rid of the space totally forgetting to correct the grammar or the spelling mistake.

Not knowing the keyboard well made writing cumbersome and resulted in wasting a lot of time. According to Student Writer 6:

---

[5] The co-occurrence in the computer group but not in the pen-and-paper group of significant pre/post increases in both quality and quantity is consistent with the findings of a meta-analytical review of computer writing studies by Bangert-Drowns (1993). (Editor's note)
[6] Compare the findings of Rusmin (this volume) for computer users labeled converts and rededicateds. (Editor's note)

> At the beginning, I did not know the keyboard. I did
> not know the place of the keys. This would cause a
> lot of waste of time. I had to do a four page
> assignment for the freshman composition class. I
> spent a lot of time.

As can be seen from their own words, these student writers had difficulty and qualms about using the computer as a writing tool since the use of computers is not a widespread practice in Turkish education. As can also be noted from their comments, many of their difficulties were on a strictly mechanical level and similar to problems faced in a first encounter with a typewriter.

In spite of some of these problems, the findings of the self-evaluation questionnaire and the interviews show that both the pen-and-paper and the computer group reacted positively to the writing instruction to which they were exposed. As Student Writer 3 in the pen-and-paper group remarked:

> Now I can write on different topics. This course encouraged me and motivated me to write more. Maybe
> I don't write that well, but I think I will write well
> and I started thinking that I can write on my own. I
> can be autonomous. Writing in English does not
> seem to be difficult now.

Student Writer 2 in the computer group expressed the same feeling:

> We wrote on various topics in the class. Practicing
> helped a lot. Previously I had no desire to write.
> This is not the case now. Maybe I still do not write
> well, but it certainly became easier.

These comments indicate that as a result of the instruction, both groups started to enjoy the writing process more and felt more self-confident about writing. This may be one piece of evidence as to why the comments and assessments made by both groups on their writing increased in quantity and became more positive at the end of the instruction.

The questionnaire findings also demonstrate that the attitudes toward computer writing on the part of the student writers in the computer group changed over time. For example, in addition to having a positive attitude to the writing instruction offered, the student writers in the computer group developed an overall positive attitude to using the computer as a writing medium. Learning how to use the computer as a tool to express their ideas and feelings improved their attitudes to writing and built up their confidence about their ability to write in English, thus encouraging them to write more. As Student Writer 5 in the computer group expressed it:

> Writing with the computer by myself without the assistance of the instructor helped my confidence and I began to believe that I could actually write in English.

For these students, learning how to use the computer started a process of self-empowerment and confidence-building. Even those subjects who did not like writing started to have different feelings about writing. Thus Student Writer 1 commented:

> Although I do not like writing a composition, it is much better writing on the computer. Writing on the computer is more fun than writing by hand.

The aesthetic appearance or format of one's writing is another factor that the Turkish student writers pointed out as helping to build their confidence in themselves as writers. In other words, like the Chinese writers in Chadwick and Bruce's (1989) study, not having a messy paper or scribbled marks on the paper motivated these Turkish writers to write more. As Student Writer 1 in the computer group relates:

> When you write on the computer since what you write looks good, has a good format, you feel that what you have written is good. But when you write with pen-and-paper, there are scribbles on the paper that makes the paper look messy and untidy, therefore you get a feeling that what you have written is not really good.

The computer group students also commented that they were able to pay more attention to various aspects of their writing such as grammar and spelling. Student Writer 8 in the computer group stated:

> On the computer, I correct my grammar mistakes easily. I can do all kinds of editing. With pen-and-paper, there are a lot of scribbles. It is messy. There is no scribbles with the computer. You edit and then check the spelling.

Formatting features also encouraged the subjects to become more engaged in writing and to believe themselves to be better writers. Being able to change the font type or size helped them to feel in control of their written product. According to Student Writer 3 in the computer group:

> When writing on the computer, you do not experience or face the difficulties or inhibitions that you have with pen-and-paper. You can change anything you want, the font size, the font type etc.

Using computers especially satisfied those subjects who complained about their penmanship. In the words of Student Writer 7 of the computer group:

> The computer is an advantage to me because my handwriting is not good. With the computer, my compositions are legible.

The findings of the self-evaluation questionnaire and the interview helped to explain the statistical results in relation to the student writers' composing strategies, the global quality scores, and the length of the compositions they wrote. According to the findings, the computer writers felt that the computer facilitated many changes in the text during the process of writing. As Student Writer 8 of the computer group maintained:

> With the computer, it is very easy. I can edit, I can change, I can revise. The computer makes my life easier.

The ease of writing with the computer can perhaps explain to a certain extent why the computer group wrote longer texts than the pen-and-paper group at the end of instruction, although these differences were not statistically significant. This finding seems to support Pennington's (1996b,d; this volume) views that word processing stimulates quantitative effects in writing that result in longer texts:

> [W]ord processing stimulates quantitative effects in process and product in the sense of more time and energy spent on writing and a greater quantity of written output....The greater quantity of written output may be in terms of longer as well as a larger number of individual writing episodes and products. (Pennington, 1996d, p. 130)

In addition, the student writers' claim that they spent more time on certain aspects of writing, especially surface- and deep-level revision, strongly supports the statistical findings that the computer group focused more on content as well as surface-level revision than the pen-and-paper group.

Some of the student writers thought that the computer changed their writing processes. They reported that unlike writing with pen and paper, they started experimenting with their thoughts right away with the computer. The pen-and-paper writers claimed to devote more time to initial planning. This self-report supports the statistical finding that the computer group did significantly less initial planning than the pen-and-paper writers. Student Writer 1 (computer group) compared her writing process before and after the writing course as follows:

> With pen-and-paper, before starting to write, I devoted time to thinking. I did not do this with the computer. While by hand, I would look around, I would look at the people. However, on the computer, I just write. It goes flawlessly and fluently. It is different with the computer. You feel or think that whatever you are doing is good.

Thus, the students felt that the computer was compatible with the flow of their thoughts. In other words, for these writers, as in the case of the participants in a previous study carried out by one of the authors, "thinking and writing became simultaneous processes" (Kamıslı, 1992, p. 198). This finding reflects Pennington's (1996d) model of the development of "a natural" writing process on computer.

Using computers helped the student writers in this study to pay more attention to and focus more on what they were composing. They were more careful about and more engaged in what they were writing. This result is reinforced by the finding that the instances of general writing strategies of the computer group were significantly higher at the end of the period of writing instruction than at the beginning. As Student Writer 4 (computer group) remarked:

> While writing on the computer, one concentrates more on what one is doing, one becomes more productive, more careful. When writing on the computer, I can focus or zero in on what I am writing and I write faster. The computer increases the significance of what I am composing and I can think more broadly.

This comment seems to be related to the finding that the computer writers in this study did significantly more scanning than the pen-and-paper group.

Another reported advantage of the computer as a writing tool over pen-and-paper was that the speed of writing on the computer seemed to keep pace with the writer's development of ideas. This reported advantage can perhaps explain why the use of the computer led the student writers to concentrate more on surface- as well as deep-level revision strategies, as they could accomplish more in one writing episode. Moreover, analysis of the interviews and questionnaires indicates that the computer writers found it easier to plan during the process of writing than to organize their ideas based on an initial text plan. Hence, as Pennington (1996b) puts it: "In this way of approaching the writing task, a 'natural plan' is substituted for a 'tutored plan' developed prior to writing on the analogy of past read text" (p. 117).

In contrast, the pen-and-paper writers realized that planning before writing is important because during their manual writing process, it was difficult to formulate, rehearse, and make changes in the text. They felt that changes at the meaning level were more important than changes at the surface level and that making changes in a text was difficult at any rate because of the burden of rewriting. These findings seem to support the statistical result that after the instruction they received, the pen-and-paper writers did more initial planning and did less surface-level revision than did the computer users (although these differences were not statistically significant). These findings seem to support Pennington's (this volume) arguments that "on a computer, the whole recursive cycle of production and revision of text is more micro than in a pen and paper mode in the sense that smaller units of work are produced before revision begins" (p. 17).

According to the findings of the present study, although at the end of instruction, the computer writers tended to focus more on content revision, and their writing process seemed to be more recursive than that of the pen-and-paper writers, these differences did not seem to transfer to a significant degree to the quality of the compositions they wrote. The lack of transfer may be due to the fact that they did not have enough time for writing practice with the computer even though the period of instruction was longer than a semester.

Finally, in relation to the attitudes of the computer writers toward writing in the electronic medium, they felt that using computers would increase their chances of academic success. In other words, they felt that it was necessary to be computer literate in order to survive in an academic setting. In the view of Student Writer 5, one of the writers in the computer group:

> We need to learn using computers because it will help us a lot. We need it for writing assignments, papers, theses.

According to Student Writer 4, another writer from the computer group:

> We can ask somebody to type these for us, but it is
> not the same thing. Composing on the computer and
> writing directly on the computer is different. If one
> writes on the computer and then makes revisions, I
> think it would be better.

The computer group felt that all students should have a computer of their own and added that since the computer provides many advantages to students, there should be more time devoted to writing on computers and more access to the computer lab. Along these lines, Student Writer 7 commented:

> People should have their own computers. You need
> to practice a lot in order to use the computer effec-
> tively. Also, devoting an hour and a half on the
> computer is not enough. More time should be spared
> for writing on the computer during the writing class.

Although the computer writers liked using the computer, they wanted more exposure to it and more practice with it as a writing tool.

These student comments help to explain the findings of the study that although the computer writers made more deep-level revisions and had higher mean scores for composition quality and length, these results were not significantly different from those of the pen-and-paper writers (other than for the deep-level revision strategy of reorganization). As mentioned earlier, if the students had more time for writing with the computer, perhaps more significant or different results would have been obtained, specifically in the area of holistic improvements in writing products.

2.3.   SUMMARY AND DISCUSSION

This study compared the effects of a process-oriented EFL writing course offered over 19 weeks to Turkish university students in two different modes: pen-and-paper and word processing computer mode. The study examined the effects of these two modes of writing on the writing strategies and attitudes towards writing of this group of EFL learners, and on the global quality and the length of the compositions they wrote. The results indicate that both groups planned and rescanned more frequently and made more assessments and comments at the end of the period of instruction than they had at the beginning. In addition, they had more frequent instances of pausing during the process of writing at the end of the instructional period than at the beginning. These results which the two groups had in common are suggestive of the effects of the process writing instruction supplied to both groups.

In terms of contrasts between the two groups, at post-test the computer group did strikingly less initial planning and more rescanning than the pen-and-paper group. In addition, during their writing process at post-test they paused more than the pen-and-paper group. These results confirm the findings of previous studies, and support the views that computer writers do less initial and more in-process planning than do pen-and-paper writers. Moreover, according to the findings of the present study, the computer writers' composing processes reflected a more discernible pattern of recursivity, with alternating operations of formulating, rehearsing, and writing, than did the composing processes of the pen-and-paper writers. This finding concurs with the results of previous studies conducted in ESL/EFL contexts (e.g., Chadwick & Bruce, 1989; Van Waes, 1994), thus supporting Pennington's (1993b, 1996b,d; this volume) claim that word processing changes the way that writers begin their writing and minimizes initial planning.

In relation to the effects of computer use on the revising of the student writers, the finding that these EFL computer writers performed more deep-level revision operations than the pen-and-paper writers, especially in terms of reorganization of ideas, confirms the results of previous studies conducted in ESL/EFL contexts (e.g., Chadwick & Bruce, 1989; Phinney, 1989).[7] Another finding of the present study, i.e., that the computer writers carried out more surface-level revision operations, especially in terms of sentence structure and word form, than the pen-and-paper writers, supports the findings of a previous study conducted in an EFL setting, that of Van Waes (1994).

The findings of the present study that there were no significant differences between the two groups in terms of global quality and length of compositions are not consistent with the results of some other studies of the writing of students for whom English is not the mother tongue (e.g., Green, 1991; Johnson, 1986; Pennington & Brock, 1992; Silver, 1990).[8] This may be due to the fact that the instructional period was less than a full academic year and computer access was not extensive. Another reason may be that the instruction in both groups was of high quality, as both received process writing instruction from a committed and experienced teacher, so that the affect of the medium was probably over-ridden to some extent by instruction and instructor effects.

In relation to the attitudes of both groups toward the writing instruction they received, the findings indicate that both the pen-and-paper and

---

[7] See also Bisaillon (this volume). (Editor's note)
[8] See also Brock and Pennington (this volume). (Editor's note)

the computer writers felt they benefited from the writing instruction. Moreover, both groups gained positive affect towards writing and towards themselves as writers. In addition, for these EFL computer writers, like those in Piper's (1987) study, composing in a foreign language became an interesting and pleasurable process. These findings seem to support the argument that the computer changes the way that writers approach the writing process (Carrell, 1987; Phinney, 1996; Underwood, 1984).

However, in this study, the Turkish EFL students, similar to Berens' (1986) and (Kamışlı's (1992) subjects, stated that they experienced some difficulty related to the development of computer skills. These difficulties were the result of not having keyboarding skills and of coming from an educational system where computers are not yet part of language classrooms. Unlike Neu and Scarcella's (1991) subjects, they were not "computer savvy," and none of them had personal computers; but like those subjects, the Turkish students believed that the computer would increase the possibility of success in an academic setting and that this device is essential for survival in such settings.

2.4.   CONCLUSION

Computer use in the Turkish university setting has not yet become a widespread practice, but EFL teachers in Turkey are scrambling to implement computers in their curriculum. They have also developed an intuitive feeling, based on their experiences as writers and writing teachers, about the possible advantages of the computer as a tool for writing. Yet, as many have noted, the degree of success of computer use in ESL/EFL settings may depend on the nature of particular instructional contexts and the sociocultural settings in which they are embedded. An implication of this study is that curriculum designers should be cautious about the ways they incorporate the computer into their writing programs, taking into consideration the published results of research studies. With the insights gained, different types of experimental programs can be designed to incorporate clearly defined situational as well as methodological variables related to particular student writers at different levels of education. As Pennington (1993b; 1996b; this volume) stresses, the needs of students from different cultural and educational backgrounds, the approach of the writing instruction, the orientation to the computer, and the duration of the actual composing on the computer should be taken into consideration during the curriculum planning process.

The results of this study should be interpreted in the light of its small number of participants and the limited amount of time devoted to developing keyboarding skills and to composing on the computer. Further research with a greater number and variety of EFL student writers given more intensive exposure to the computer may yield valuable information and insights about the ways in which the computer affects writing processes and outcomes, and the kind of curriculum that can be designed for the integration of word processing into EFL instructional programs. Nevertheless, the present study stands as one of a growing number which indicate the potential of the computer to change writing processes and attitudes in potentially positive ways.

APPENDIX 2.1.

Tasks

Task I (pre-test).

Instructions: Write on <u>one</u> of the following:

> A) A friend of yours is going to come from the USA or England and stay with you for a year. You want to acquaint him/her with the place you live. Write a letter to him/her describing your neighborhood to give him a general idea about this place he/she is going to live for a year.

> B) Describe a person or a place that influenced your life.

Task II (post-test).

Instructions: Write on <u>one</u> of the following:

> A) Describe life in winter time in Istanbul

> B) Describe the lifestyle of a typical Turkish university student.

APPENDIX 2.2.

Self-Evaluation Form[i]

1. Have you ever written a composition similar to the one you just wrote? If so, when? What did you feel then? Do you see any differences between the two?

2. If you were to evaluate your composition, how would you rate it? Why?

     a) very good   b) good   c) fair   d) weak

3. Did you do anything before you started writing? If so, what?

4. Describe what you did during the process of writing your composition.

5. Was there anything that you paid particular attention during the process of writing?

6. What did you do just before you finished your composition?

7. Do you see any differences and/or similarities between the compositions you wrote at the beginning and end of the semester? If so, explain why?[ii]

8. Are there any differences between the way you wrote at the beginning and the end of the semester? If so, explain why and give specific details.

9. What do you think about the use of the computer in writing? Is there any difference between the way you write with the computer and with pen and paper?[iii]

---

[i] This self-evaluation form was given in Turkish to the student writers.
[ii] Both the pen-and-paper and the computer group responded to questions 7 and 8 at the end of the semester.
[iii] Only the computer group responded to this question.

APPENDIX 2.3.

Strategies Coding System

General Writing Strategies[iv]

A C	assessing and commenting
Pr	pre-planning
Pl	planning
R	rescanning
Rh	rehearsing
P	pause
RW	reading the whole text

Surface-Level Revision Strategies

a	addition
del	deletion
sub	substitution
sp	spelling
wf	word form
p	punctuation
v	verb form or tense
ss	sentence structure

Deep-Level Revision Strategies[v]

a	addition
del	deletion
sub	substitution
r	reorganization
c	combination

[iv] adapted from Raimes (1987)
[v] adopted from Pennington and Brock (1992)

APPENDIX 2.4.

Between-Group Comparisons

Table 2.1.a		GENERAL WRITING STRATEGIES								
		PRE-PRE					POST-POST			
		n	MR	M	s d	Z	n	MR	M	s d	Z
assess./	pp	8	8.13	5.25	5.55	0.32	8	8.19	10.50	4.38	0.26
comment.	c	8	8.88	5.50	4.84		8	8.81	11.63	6.00	
preplanning	pp	8	8.88.	1.13	0.84	0.34	8	11.38	1.50	1.20	2.60***
	c	8	8.13	1.00	0.76		8	5.63	0.25	0.46	
planning	pp	8	7.94	3.13	3.31	0.48	8	6.69	6.19	5.77	1.54
	c	8	9.06	3.13	2.10		8	10.31	8.25	2.05	
rescanning	pp	8	9.00	3.13	4.42	0.43	8	6.25	2.00	2.62	1.91*
	c	8	8.00	3.00	4.50		8	10.75	5.00	3.46	
rehearsing	pp	8	8.75	3.38	3.25	0.21	8	6.56	4.88	3.48	1.64
	c	8	8.25	3.00	3.12		8	10.44	7.13	3.00	
pause	pp	8	8.25	1.75	1.28	0.22	8	6.31	3.00	2.00	1.86*
	c	8	8.75	2.00	1.60		8	10.69	4.71	1.75	
reading the	pp	8	7.50	0.25	0.46	1.00	8	9.00	0.38	0.52	0.52
whole text	c	8	9.50	0.50	0.53		8	8.00	0.25	0.46	

PP = pen and paper
C = computer
MR = mean rank
M = mean

$^*p < 0.05$
$^{**}p < 0.01$
$^{***}p < 0.001$

Table 2.2.a			SURFACE-LEVEL REVISION							
			PRE-PRE				POST-POST			
		n	MR	M	sd	Z	n	MR	M	sd	Z
addition	pp	8	7.38	1.50	1.20	1.00	8	8.00	1.00	0.93	0.45
	c	8	9.63	1.88	0.83		8	9.00	1.25	1.17	
deletion	pp	8	7.50	0.88	1.13	0.89	8	9.50	0.75	0.89	0.97
	c	8	9.50	1.13	0.64		8	7.50	0.38	0.74	
substitution	pp	8	9.50	2.38	1.51	0.86	8	9.69	1.50	1.60	1.05
	c	8	7.50	1.75	1.39		8	7.31	1.13	2.10	
punctuation	pp	8	8.50	0.13	0.35	0.00	8	7.81	0.38	0.74	0.70
	c	8	8.50	0.13	0.35		8	9.19	1.00	1.60	
spelling	pp	8	9.13	0.50	0.76	0.65	8	6.50	0.00	0.00	2.21*
	c	8	7.88	0.25	0.46		8	10.50	2.38	3.46	
sentence structure	pp	8	7.31	0.75	0.71	1.11	8	4.81	0.13	0.35	3.34***
	c	8	9.69	1.13	0.64		8	12.19	1.38	0.52	
verb tense	pp	8	7.75	0.75	1.17	0.68	8	8.50	0.25	0.71	0.00
	c	8	9.25	1.00	1.07		8	8.50	0.25	0.71	
word form	pp	8	8.69	1.63	2.56	0.17	8	10.50	0.50	0.53	2.24*
	c	8	8.31	2.00	2.98		8	6.50	0.00	0.00	

PP = pen and paper
C = computer
MR = mean rank
M = mean

$^*p < 0.05$
$^{**}p < 0.01$
$^{***}p < 0.001$

Table 2.3.a		DEEP-LEVEL REVISION								
		PRE-PRE					POST-POST			
		n	MR	M	s d	Z	n	MR	M	s d	Z
addition	pp	8	8.31	0.38	0.52	0.18	8	7.94	2.38	1.51	0.48
	c	8	8.69	0.50	0.76		8	9.06	3.00	2.27	
deletion	pp	8	7.81	1.38	1.30	0.60	8	8.31	0.88	1.25	0.17
	c	8	9.19	1.75	0.71		8	8.69	0.75	0.71	
substitution	pp	8	9.88	1.13	1.36	1.27	8	8.25	1.38	1.19	0.22
	c	8	7.13	0.38	0.52		8	8.75	2.38	3.34	
reorganization	pp	8	8.25	0.50	0.76	0.24	8	6.38	0.88	0.64	1.98*
	c	8	8.75	0.50	0.53		8	10.63	1.75	0.89	
combination	pp	8	9.25	0.75	0.71	0.71	8	6.88	0.88	0.64	1.48
	c	8	7.75	0.50	0.53		8	10.13	1.50	0.93	

PP = pen and paper
C = computer
MR = mean rank
M = mean

$^*p < 0.05$
$^{**}p < 0.01$
$^{***}p < 0.001$

Table 2.4.a		GLOBAL QUALITY SCORE AND LENGTH									
		PRE-PRE					POST-POST				
		n	MR	M	s d	Z	n	MR	M	s d	Z
scores	pp	8	8.56	64.38	6.23	0.05	8	8.00	72.50	7.56	0.43
	c	8	8.44	64.38	6.78		8	9.00	75.00	8.45	
length	pp	8	7.50	379	191.78	0.84	8	7.25	411	160.12	1.05
	c	8	9.50	385	77.58		8	9.75	430	88.20	
Table 2.5.a		MAJOR CATEGORIES									
general writing	pp	8	8.25	18.00	11.71	0.21	8	6.94	28.38	16.19	1.32
	c	8	8.75	18.13	8.64		8	10.06	37.25	13.25	
deep-level	pp	8	8.81	4.13	2.36	0.27	8	7.88	6.38	4.10	0.54
	c	8	8.19	3.63	1.06		8	9.13	9.38	6.21	
surface-level	pp	8	7.69	8.50	5.83	0.69	8	7.44	4.50	2.93	0.90
	c	8	9.31	9.25	4.27		8	9.56	7.75	5.75	

PP = pen and paper
C = computer
MR = mean rank
M = mean

APPENDIX 2.5.

Within-Group Comparisons

Table 2.1.b			GENERAL WRITING STRATEGIES							
			PEN & PAPER				COMPUTER			
		n	M	s d	Z		n	M	s d	Z
assess./	pre	8	5.25	5.03	2.17*		8	5.50	4.84	2.52*
comment.	post	8	10.50	4.38			8	11.63	6.00	
preplanning	pre	8	1.13	0.83	0.94		8	1.00	0.75	1.82*
	post	8	1.50	1.20			8	0.25	0.46	
planning	pre	8	3.13	3.31	1.82*		8	3.13	2.10	2.52*
	post	8	6.19	4.32			8	8.25	2.05	
rescanning	pre	8	3.13	4.42	1.60		8	3.00	4.50	1.12
	post	8	2.00	2.62			8	5.00	3.46	
rehearsing	pre	8	3.38	3.25	1.85*		8	3.00	3.12	2.52*
	post	8	4.88	3.48			8	7.13	3.00	
pause	pre	8	1.75	1.28	2.20*		8	2.00	1.60	2.52*
	post	8	3.00	2.00			8	4.75	1.75	
reading the	pre	8	0.25	0.46	0.53		8	0.50	0.53	0.91
whole text	post	8	0.38	0.52			8	0.25	0.46	

M = mean   *$p < 0.05$

Table 2.2.b		SURFACE-LEVEL REVISION							
		PEN & PAPER				COMPUTER			
		n	M	sd	Z	n	M	sd	Z
addition	pre	8	1.50	1.20	1.04	8	1.88	0.83	1.27
	post	8	1.00	0.93		8	1.25	1.17	
deletion	pre	8	0.88	1.13	0.14	8	1.13	0.64	1.67*
	post	8	0.75	0.89		8	0.38	0.74	
substitution	pre	8	2.38	1.50	1.18	8	1.75	1.39	0.94
	post	8	1.50	1.60		8	1.13	2.10	
punctuation	pre	8	0.13	0.35	1.34	8	0.13	0.35	1.60
	post	8	0.38	0.74		8	1.00	1.60	
spelling	pre	8	0.50	0.76	1.60	8	0.25	0.46	1.75*
	post	8	0.00	0.00		8	2.38	3.46	
sentence structure	pre	8	0.75	0.71	1.82*	8	1.13	0.64	0.73
	post	8	0.13	0.35		8	1.38	0.52	
verb tense	pre	8	0.75	1.17	1.60	8	1.00	1.07	1.25
	post	8	0.25	0.71		8	0.25	0.71	
word form	pre	8	1.63	2.56	0.73	8	2.00	2.98	1.60
	post	8	0.50	0.53		8	0.00	0.00	
Table 2.3.b		**DEEP-LEVEL REVISION**							
addition	pre	8	0.38	0.52	2.36*	8	0.50	0.76	2.17*
	post	8	2.38	1.51		8	3.00	2.26	
deletion	pre	8	1.38	1.30	0.73	8	1.75	0.71	2.02*
	post	8	0.88	1.25		8	0.75	0.71	
substitution	pre	8	1.13	1.36	0.28	8	0.38	0.52	1.82*
	post	8	1.38	1.19		8	2.38	3.34	
reorganization	pre	8	0.50	0.76	1.60	8	0.50	0.53	2.52*
	post	8	0.88	0.64		8	1.75	0.89	
combination	pre	8	0.75	0.71	1.00	8	0.50	0.53	2.36*
	post	8	0.88	0.64		8	1.50	0.93	

M = mean $^*p < 0.05$

Table 2.4.b		GLOBAL QUALITY SCORE AND LENGTH									
		PEN & PAPER					COMPUTER				
		n	MR	M	*sd*	Z	n	MR	M	*sd*	Z
scores	pre	8	0.00	64.38	6.23	2.52*	8	0.00	64.38	6.78	2.52*
	post	8	4.50	72.50	7.56		8	4.50	75.00	8.45	
length	pre	8	4.33	379	191.78	0.70	8	0.00	3.85	77.58	2.52*
	post	8	4.60	411	160.12		8	4.50	430	88.20	
Table 2.5.b		MAJOR CATEGORIES									
general writing	pre	8	0.00	18.00	11.71	2.52*	8	0.00	18.13	8.64	2.52*
	post	8	4.50	28.38	16.19		8	4.50	37.25	13.25	
deep-level	pre	8	1.00	4.13	2.36	2.19*	8	0.00	3.63	1.06	2.36*
	post	8	4.50	6.38	4.10		8	4.00	9.38	6.21	
surface-level	pre	8	4.92	8.50	5.83	1.61	8	5.63	9.25	4.27	0.63
	post	8	3.25	4.50	2.93		8	3.38	7.75	5.75	

MR = mean rank
M = mean

*p < 0.05

3. A Comparative Study of Text Analysis and Peer Feedback as Input to Writing on Computer in an ESL Context

Mark N. Brock and Martha C. Pennington

ABSTRACT

This chapter describes a comparative study with two groups of Hong Kong ESL students on the effects of computerized text analysis and peer feedback as aids to revision. Students in both groups wrote three drafts of five course assignments as well as pretest and posttest essays on computer. The computer group did not outperform the text analysis group according to holistic scoring of the posttest, though they did write significantly longer compositions. Peer feedback was superior to computerized text analysis in promoting increases across drafts in the number of words, sentences, and paragraphs; in number and variety of revisions; and in revision of content.

3.0. INTRODUCTION

Computerized text analysis, those computer-based programs which analyze written text and provide feedback for improvement, is one of the most popular yet least studied computer writing aids available to student writers. Indeed, "while the number and popularity of text analysis programs have increased dramatically in the past five years, the amount of research examining this controversial writing aid has remained comparatively small" (Brock, 1995, p. 227). The extant research (e.g., Brock, 1991, 1993; Collins, 1989; Pennington, 1992, 1993a; Rabinovitz, 1991) suggests several problems with these computer aids, such as inaccurate analysis of text, limited scope of feedback, and a narrowing effect on student revising behavior resulting in a surface-level, editing focus. At the same time, many scholars see considerable promise in computerized text analysis. Gerrard (1989), for example, has claimed that computerized text analysis teaches a recursive writing process and then helps students control that process "by dividing it into stages" (p. 5). Lewis and Lewis (1987) believe that text analysis can help improve basic writing skills, while Frase (1983) has claimed that text analysis is "especially useful to authors whose native language is other than English" (p. 1889). As Pennington (1992, 1993a) has noted, the competing claims about the usefulness of computerized text analysis have largely been made without a basis of careful research.

This chapter adds to the research base examining computerized text analysis by presenting the results of a study examining differences in texts written by two groups of ESL student writers, one using computerized text analysis as a revising tool and the other revising their drafts after receiving peer feedback. Specifically, the study sought to compare the effects of text analysis and peer tutoring on the following measures:

- comparative gains in writing performance from pretest to posttest as reflected in the holistic ratings of two independent judges;
- the mean number of words, sentences, and paragraphs written from pretest to posttest;
- the mean number of words, sentences, and paragraphs written across three drafts of five assignments; and
- the number and types of revisions made on second and third drafts of five assignments.

3.1. METHOD

3.1.1. Students

Forty-eight students, all enrolled in the second year of a three-year Bachelor of Science degree program at City University of Hong Kong, participated in the study. The students were in their late teens or early twenties and spoke Cantonese as their first language. They were all Form 7 (equivalent to grade 13) graduates of a science-stream pre-university course. During the period in which the research was carried out, these students were taking a technical writing class, the third English class required by their degree program. Two groups of twenty-four students made up two sections of the class, which met three hours per week during a ten-week term.

3.1.2. Materials

Materials for the research included two text analysis programs, *Writer's Helper* (Conduit) and *Grammatik* (Wang), which were used by the text analysis group for receiving feedback on the first and second drafts of the five compositions they wrote during the study; revising protocols used by the peer tutoring group in responding to first and second drafts of the five compositions; two pre- and posttests; and *WordPerfect*, the word processing program used by all of the students participating in the study. Computer access was provided in the computer center within the Department of English at the City University of Hong Kong;

3.1.2.1. Text Analyzers

The two text analysis programs used in the study represent well the five categories of programs suggested by Smith (1989) and the three categories suggested by Wresch (1989) as desirable for computer aids to writing. The text analysis program used by students in the text analysis group for receiving feedback on the first drafts of their writing assignments was *Writer's Helper*. *Writer's Helper* manipulates surface features of a text in a way which reportedly focuses the writer's attention on content, organization, and purpose of the text. According to the developer of the program, *Writer's Helper* is designed to help students "think about their writing in an organized way" (Wresch, 1989, p. 67).

Writer's Helper is a set of about 30 programs, each with a unique purpose. The programs used for this study, designed specifically to prompt student revision of text, included: *Outline Document*, which prints first and last sentences of all paragraphs composing a text in isolation so that writers may view how logically they have developed their ideas; *Paragraph Coherence*, which prints the first and last sentence of individual paragraphs as a way of highlighting paragraph organizational coherence or lack of coherence; *Paragraph Development*, which prints a graph depicting the length of each paragraph along with the number of words and sentences in individual paragraphs as a way of highlighting paragraphs which may not be fully developed; *Readability*, which computes a readability index using the Fogg Index so that writers may consider how well they have met the expectations of their intended audience; *Transitions*, which reports the total number of transition words in a document, along with a list of common transitions and how many times each was used, as a way to help writers consider how well they have provided meaningful cues which help readers understand the writer's message; *References*, which reports the ratio of semantic references in a document to the total number of words to help writers consider how vaguely or specifically they have communicated their purposes; and *Sweet or Stuffy*, which compares words in a text to a dictionary of words (based on Gibson, 1966) representing a variety of styles, as a way to help writers consider factors contributing to the effect the text may have on readers.

Grammatik, the text analysis program which students in the text analysis group used for gaining feedback on second drafts of writing assignments, has the capability of parsing sentences and offering writers advice for improvement based on that parse. *Grammatik* analyzes text for three categories of error: **mechanical errors**, such as errors in punctuation and capitalization; **style errors**, such as use of overworked or trite phrases; and **grammatical errors**, such as errors in subject-verb agreement and number agreement. The program also provides statistical analyses of text, including readability scores calculated using the Flesch-Kincaid scale. *Grammatik* highlights 'style' errors by matching phrases in a text against a dictionary programmed to highlight certain words and phrases. The program detects errors in grammar and punctuation by parsing the text into parts of speech and analyzing the parse according to programmed decoding rules.

Grammatik was chosen for this study for two reasons. First, it has the ability to parse sentences and to flag errors in subject-verb agreement and number agreement with a fairly high degree of accuracy (see discussion in Brock, 1990a). These errors commonly persist in many final drafts of compositions written by students enrolled in course of study of the subjects in the present investigation. Second, *Grammatik* can be customized to better address the kinds of surface errors common to specific populations of student writers.

Before the study began, *Grammatik*, which students in the text analysis class used in revising second drafts of the five writing assignments, was customized using data gathered from assignments written by students enrolled in the first author's sections of the same class in the previous academic year. More than 300 compositions written for the same assignments as students participating in the present study were analyzed for surface-level errors. Ten percent of these compositions were analyzed by two other experienced writing teachers for comparison, achieving 77.5% agreement in the error analysis (Brock, 1993). Following the procedures discussed in Brock (1990b), *Grammatik* was customized to highlight as many of the types of errors identified in the error analysis as possible. In addition to the errors drawn from the error analysis, data from pretests and from error analyses of texts written by previous classes of technical degree students at the same university were incorporated into the customized version of *Grammatik*.

The error analysis showed that the most common types of grammatical errors made by students previously enrolled in the class included the following:

* errors in using prepositions
* agreement errors
* misuse of the perfect tenses
* errors in verb usage
* sentence fragments

While *Grammatik* was capable of highlighting some of these errors—in particular, many errors in agreement and verb usage—other errors were outside the scope of the analysis which the basic program provides. Thus, an attempt was made to customize *Grammatik* to highlight as many of the errors uncovered in the error analysis as possible. A total of 596 rules were added to the version of *Grammatik* customized for students in the text analysis group.

3.1.2.2. Revising Protocols

Students in the peer tutoring group used revising protocols in responding to their partner's drafts. For the first draft of each composition, students received a list of questions and issues that were to be considered in responding to their partner's composition. Similar to the reported purpose of *Writer's Helper*, the questions and issues were formulated to focus the peer tutor's attention on content, organization, and purpose of the text. In responding to second drafts of compositions, students received a revising protocol that was designed to focus their attention on some of the common surface-level problems that were previously identified (Brock, 1991, 1993) in final drafts of students who had previously completed the same course.

3.1.2.3. Pre- and Posttests

Students were randomly assigned to complete one of two tests as a pretest at the beginning of the study (week one) and the other as a posttest at the end of the study (week ten). Both tests required students to write an incident report, with context and some content provided in the test questions, in the computer center using *WordPerfect*. They were allotted two hours to complete the tests.

3.1.3. Instruction

Each of the two classes met three hours each week for ten weeks. Students completed five writing assignments during the term. The first two assignments were memo-style reports; the third and fourth assignments were business letters; and the final assignment was a formal investigative report. Two simulations supplied the context and some of the content for writing the report and letter-writing assignments of the course. Students spent two hours in the computer center revising each of the first four assignments and three hours in the center revising the fifth assignment. Treatments for the two groups differed in that one group received feedback solely from two text analysis programs, while the other group engaged in peer tutoring as feedback for revision. The first author, who was also the instructor for both classes, served as facilitator for both groups.

In week two of the course, the instructor led two-hour workshops for both classes that familiarized students with the revising techniques they would use during the course and gave them opportunities to practice these techniques. Using a sample composition, students in the text analysis group were instructed in using *Writer's Helper* and *Grammatik* for receiving feedback and making content-and surface-level revisions in the sample text. They were then given a second sample text with which to practice receiving feedback and making revisions using the two text analysis programs. Using the same sample compositions, students in the peer tutoring group were instructed in using revising protocols for giving and receiving feedback and making content- and surface-level revisions.

During the study, the instructor served as a technical facilitator for both groups. In the text analysis group, the instructor assisted students in operating the two text analysis programs and understanding the feedback they received. In the first hour in which students revised their assignments, they used *Writer's Helper*; in the second hour, they used *Grammatik*. During revising sessions, the instructor did not offer interpretative advice or suggestions for how the students should use the feedback offered by the text analysis programs. Those decisions were made by the students. In the peer tutoring group, the instructor facilitated tutoring by preparing revision protocols that focused student attention during the tutoring sessions. The protocols employed during the first hour were designed to focus student attention on content, purpose, and organization. In the second session, the focus was on language use.

A similar instructional process was followed for each of the five written assignments. Students participated in the simulation providing a context for the written assignment. After the assignment was given, students used *WordPerfect* to write their first drafts either at home or in the computer center. In the next class period, students brought a word-processed disk copy and two hard copies of their first draft to the computer center. They submitted one hard copy to the instructor and kept the other for reference while revising. Students in the text analysis group then downloaded their first drafts to the server, analyzed the draft with *Writer's Helper*, and revised the draft using either the text editor in *Writer's Helper* or by accessing the network version of *WordPerfect*. At the end of the first hour, students saved their drafts on disk and printed two copies—one for the instructor and one for their own reference when revising the second draft. In the next hour, students in the text analysis group downloaded their second drafts in order to analyze and revise them with the customized, network version of *Grammatik*. At the end of the period, students submitted both a printed copy and a disk copy of the final draft.

Students in the peer tutoring group followed the same procedure but did not have access to the text analysis programs. These students worked in self-selected pairs to read and respond to their partner's drafts using the revision protocols provided. As with the text analysis group, they brought a disk copy and two hard copies of their first drafts to the computer center, submitting one hard copy to the instructor and exchanging the other with their peer tutor. Using the protocols, they read and responded to their partner's first draft. Students then revised the draft using *WordPerfect*. At the end of the first hour, they submitted a hard copy of the revised draft to the instructor and kept one for themselves and their partner. During the next hour, the process was repeated, with the peer tutors focusing on surface-level concerns. At the end of the second hour, students submitted a hard copy and a disk copy of the completed final drafts to the instructor. Table 3.1 summarizes the different treatments the two groups received.

Text Analysis	**Peer Feedback**
	<u>Draft 1</u>: Written at home or in student computer center; based on information given during simulation; students bring disk and hard copy to next class.
<u>Draft 2</u> (*Writer's Helper*): Students revise with program that focuses attention on content, organization, and purpose; then students revise (one hour).	<u>Draft 2</u>: Students respond to partner's essay using protocols that focus attention on content, organization, and purpose; then students revise (one hour).
<u>Draft 3</u> (*Grammatik*): Students revise with program that focuses attention on surface-level concerns (one hour).	<u>Draft 3</u>: Students respond to partner's essay using protocols that focus attention on surface-level concerns; then students revise (one hour).

Table 3.1. Treatment Received by the Two Groups

3.1.4. Data Analysis

Data statistically compared for the study included the following:

- mean holistic scores of pre- and posttest essays;
- mean number of words, sentences, and paragraphs written on pre- and posttests;
- mean number of words, sentences, and paragraphs written on three drafts of five assignments;
- mean number and types of revisions made from first to second and second to third drafts of five assignments.

All statistical analyses were completed using the *Statistical Package for the Social Sciences (SPSS)*, Version 4.1.

The pre- and posttest essays were holistically scored on a nine-point scale by two experienced raters using a scoring rubric the raters had previously used in rating placement essays. The interrater reliability obtained was 0.789 on the prettest and 0.799 on the posttest. As a matched test design was employed to avoid a practice effect on posttest scores, pretest scores along with the number of words, sentences, and paragraphs written by members of the two groups on the two forms of the test were compared using paired t-tests to determine if there was any significant difference in the two forms of the test. Pre- and posttest essay mean scores of the two groups were then compared using multivariate analysis of variance (MANOVA). In addition, the mean number of words, sentences, and paragraphs written on pre- and posttest essays were compared for statistical significance using MANOVA.

Each draft of the five compositions written by students in the two groups was analyzed as well to determine the number and types of revisions made. The revisions completed between drafts one and two and drafts two and three were coded using coding categories adapted from Raimes (1985) and developed by Pennington and Brock (1992). Content-level revisions were designated as those that affected the informational content of a text, while surface-level revisions were considered to be those that did not change the informational content.

To determine the reliability of coding, ten percent of the essays, randomly selected, were coded by a second coder instructed in the use of the coding categories. A match of 74.1%, which was considered adequate, was found between the two codings. The categories used in coding and explanatory parameters for each category are listed in Table 3.2. After the revisions were coded according to the categories given in the table, multivariate analysis of variance was conducted to compare the performance of two groups for the total number and categories of surface- and content-level revisions completed across drafts and assignments.

Surface-Level Editing Changes		Content Changes Affecting Meaning	
a	addition[i]	a	addition
del	deletion[ii]	del	deletion
sub	substitution[iii]	sub	substitution
sp	spelling	r	reorganization[v]
wf	word form	c	combination[vi]
p	punctuation		
v	verb form or tense		
ss	sentence structure[iv]		

Adapted from Raimes (1985)

Table 3.2. Coding Categories Used to Determine Number and Type of Revisions

3.2.   FINDINGS

3.2.1.   Pretest and Posttest Essays

The two groups were determined to be comparable at the beginning of the investigation, as the paired t-tests revealed no significant differences (with the level of significance set at $p = 0.05$) for the two groups in either the holistic scores or the mean number of words, sentences, or paragraphs on the two forms of the pretest. To investigate the differential

---

[i] Refers to addition of a word [a(w)], phrase [a(phr)], or sentence [a(s)]. These coding symbols are used for instances of surface editing and for instances of revision affecting meaning. A special category is addition of a transition word (e.g., moreover, in conclusion, in addition, etc.), designated [a(tw)]. These words are classed under surface editing changes, though a case can be made for their affect on meaning. They are, at least, an 'in-between' class.

[ii] Refers to deletion of a word [del(w)], phrase [del(phr)], or sentence [del(s)]. These coding symbols are used for cases of surface editing and for cases of revision affecting meaning.

[iii] Refers to substituting a word [sub(w)], phrase [sub(phr)], or sentence [sub(s)] for a previously used word, phrase, or sentence. These coding symbols are used for cases of surface editing and for cases of revision affecting meaning.

[iv] Refers to a change in sentence structure which does not affect meaning.

[v] Refers to a major reorganization within a paragraph or across paragraphs which alters meaning.

[vi] Refers to the combination of two sentences or paragraphs.

69

effects of the two instructional treatments, multivariate analysis of variance was used in answering the following questions:

Are there differential gains in writing performance between the two groups from pretest-to-posttest as reflected in the holistic scoring of two independent raters?

Are there significant differences between the two groups in the mean number of words, sentences, and paragraphs written on pre- and posttest essays?

3.2.1.1. Holistic Scores

The descriptive statistics for pretest and posttest holistic ratings of essays are presented in Table 3.3. A two by two (two groups by two administrations of the test) repeated measures analysis of variance was conducted to compare the change in holistic scores from pretest to posttest between the two groups, yielding no significant difference, $F(1, 46) = 0.25$, $p = 0.619$. However, the pretest to posttest improvement as measured by holistic scoring was statistically significant for all students, $F(1, 46) = 72.25$, $p = 0.000$, with those in the peer feedback group increasing by an average of 3.0 points from pretest to posttest and the text analysis group increasing by an average of 2.6 points.

Group	N	Pre	Post
Text Analysis	24	9.42 (1.53)	12.08 (1.93)
Peer Feedback	24	9.58 (1.91)	12.58 (1.81)

Table 3.3. Holistic Scores, Pretest to Posttest—Means (Standard Deviations)

3.2.1.2. Number of Words

Table 3.4 shows pretest-posttest differences in number of words written in each group. Statistical analysis revealed a significant difference from pretest to posttest between groups for the total number of words written, $F(1, 46) = 4.55$, $p = 0.038$. The mean number of words written from pretest to posttest by members of the peer feedback group increased by slightly more than 107, while the mean increase from pretest to posttest for the total number of words written by members of the text analysis group was 47. Thus, students in the peer feedback group wrote a mean of over 60 words more on posttests than on pretests compared to the text analysis students. The pretest to posttest increase in total number of words was also statistically significant across all subjects, $F(1, 46) = 30.07$, $p = 0.000$, with the combined subjects on average writing 77 more words on the posttest than on the pretest.

Group	N	Pre	Post
Text Analysis	24	474.75 (75.37)	522.04 (71.16)
Peer Feedback	24	469.13 (96.08)	576.63 (80.58)
Total Sample	48	471.94 (85.48)	549.33 (80.10)

Table 3.4. Number of Words, Pretest to Posttest—Means (Standard Deviations)

Group	N	Pre	Post
Text Analysis	24	28.21 (4.15)	29.13 (3.60)
Peer Feedback	24	29.00 (4.32)	32.04 (4.39)
Total Sample	48	28.60 (4.21)	30.58 (4.24)

Table 3.5. Number of Sentences, Pretest to Posttest—Means (Standard Deviations)

3.2.1.3.   Number of Sentences

Table 3.5 presents the means and standard deviations for the number of sentences. There was no significant difference from pretest to posttest between groups for the number of sentences written, $F(1, 46) = 1.82$, $p = 0.184$. However, the pretest to posttest increase in total sentences was statistically significant across all subjects, $F(1, 46) = 6.30$, $p = 0.016$, with subjects on average writing two more sentences on the posttest than on the pretest.

3.2.1.4.   Number of Paragraphs

Table 3.6 gives descriptive statistics for number of paragraphs in pretests and posttests. Statistical analysis uncovered no significant difference from pretest to posttest between groups for the number of paragraphs written, $F(1, 46) = 0.40$, $p = 0.528$. However, the pretest to posttest increase in total paragraphs was statistically significant across all subjects, $F(1, 46) = 24.58$, $p = 0.000$, with an average of 1.6 more paragraphs on the posttest than on the pretest.

Group	N	Pre	Post
Text Analysis	24	6.75 (1.54)	8.17 (1.74)
Peer Feedback	24	8.08 (1.67)	9.92 (1.74)
Total Sample	48	7.42 (1.72)	9.04 (1.94)

Table 3.6. Number of Paragraphs, Pretest to Posttest—Means (Standard Deviations)

3.2.1.5. Summary of Pretest-Posttest Findings

The holistic ratings received by members of the peer feedback group increased by an average of 3.0 points from pretest to posttest, while scores of the text analysis group increased by 2.6 points. This difference was not statistically significant, though the combined group of all students showed a statistically significant growth in writing performance from pretest to posttest as reflected in the holistic ratings of two independent judges.

Those exposed to peer feedback as a writing aid wrote significantly more words, an average of 60 more, from pretest to posttest than did those exposed to text analysis. This was the only significant pretest to posttest difference between the two groups. In terms of number of sentences and paragraphs produced, the combined group demonstrated a significant increase in these measures.

3.2.2. Drafts of the Five Assignments

3.2.2.1. Word, Sentence, and Paragraph Statistics

For the three drafts written for each of the five assignments completed during the study, multivariate analysis of variance was used in answering the following question:

> Are there significant differences in the mean number of words, sentences, and paragraphs written by members of the peer tutoring and text analysis groups on three drafts of five assignments completed during the study?

Number of Words. Table 3.7 presents the descriptive statistics for the number of words written on each draft of the five assignments. A two by five by three (two groups by five assignments by three drafts of each assignment) repeated measures analysis of variance was conducted to compare the total number of words written across drafts between the two groups. The two groups varied significantly in number of words per draft. Members of the peer feedback group wrote significantly more words across drafts than members of the text analysis group, producing a mean of 19 more words from first to third drafts across the five assignments than members of the other group. A significant difference was also found between the two groups in the total number of words written across drafts of different assignments, $F(8, 368) = 2.62$, $p = 0.009$. On assignment one, the mean number of words written by the text analysis group decreased by one word from draft one to draft three, while the peer feedback group increased the number of words written across the three drafts by a mean of 15 words. On assignment two, the text analysis group increased the number of words written across drafts by 5, while the number of words written by members of the peer feedback group increased by 23. On assignment three, the text analysis group increased the number of words by 1; the number of words written by members of the peer feedback group increased by 6. On assignment four, the text analysis group increased the total number of words by one, while the peer feedback group wrote 11 more words on draft three than on draft one. On assignment five, the number of words written by members of the text analysis group increased by two, while the peer feedback group increased the number of words written across drafts by 51.

In addition, the changes in total number of words across drafts were significantly different across all subjects, $F(2, 368) = 24.47$, $p = 0.000$, with a mean total of 254, 264 and 266 words written on drafts 1, 2 and 3, respectively. There was also a significant difference for all subjects in the total number of words per draft in different assignments, $F(8, 368) = 3.12$, $p = 0.002$, and across drafts regardless of assignment, $F(2, 368) = 16.85$, $p = 0.000$.

Group	N	Assignment	Draft 1	Draft 2	Draft 3
Text Analysis	24	1	207 (65)	207 (65)	206 (65)
		2	302 (74)	308 (70)	307 (74)
		3	205 (59)	207 (58)	206 (57)
		4	228 (64)	231 (64)	229 (63)
		5	291 (65)	293 (67)	293 (67)
Total Text Analysis			246 (47)	249 (48)	248 (48)
Peer Feedback	24	1	236 (58)	249 (58)	251 (56)
		2	336 (68)	355 (72)	359 (73)
		3	206 (48)	210 (44)	212 (43)
		4	228 (55)	237 (50)	239 (52)
		5	302 (80)	342 (73)	353 (71)
Total Peer Feedback			262 (55)	279 (66)	283 (68)
Total Sample	48		254 (49)	264 (56)	266 (59)

Table 3.7. Number of Words Written Across Three Drafts of Five Assignments—Means (Standard Deviations)

Number of Sentences. The means and standard deviations for the total number of sentences written on each draft of the five assignments are given in Table 3.8. The two groups differed significantly in the total number of sentences written across drafts, regardless of assignment, $F(2, 368) = 4.24$, $p = 0.017$. The peer feedback group wrote significantly more sentences than the text analysis group, producing a mean of 0.40 more sentences from first to third drafts across the five assignments than members of the text analysis group. The change in number of sentences across drafts, regardless of assignment, was also significantly different across all subjects, $F(2, 368) = 26.65$, $p = 0.000$. No significant difference was found in number of sentences written across drafts in different assignments for the two groups, $F(8, 368) = 0.31$, $p = 0.963$, nor for the sample as a whole, $F(8, 368) = 1.01$, $p = 0.431$.

Group	N	Assignment	Draft 1	Draft 2	Draft 3
Text Analysis	24	1	10.8 (3.6)	11.0 (3.6)	11.0 (3.5)
		2	17.9 (4.5)	18.3 (4.4)	18.6 (4.3)
		3	14.7 (5.4)	14.8 (5.3)	14.7 (5.3)
		4	14.1 (4.1)	14.5 (4.2)	14.4 (4.1)
		5	16.5 (4.7)	16.8 (5.2)	16.9 (5.2)
Total Text Analysis			14.8 (2.7)	15.1 (2.8)	15.1 (2.9)
Peer Feedback	24	1	12.5 (3.0)	13.1 (3.0)	13.4 (2.9)
		2	20.6 (4.7)	21.5 (4.9)	21.7 (4.9)
		3	14.8 (5.0)	15.2 (4.8)	15.3 (4.8)
		4	14.2 (4.8)	14.5 (4.7)	14.6 (4.4)
		5	17.9 (5.7)	18.8 (5.3)	18.7 (5.2)
Total Peer Feedback			16.0 (3.2)	16.6 (3.4)	16.7 (3.4)
Total Sample	48		15.4 (2.9)	15.9 (3.1)	15.9 (3.1)

Table 3.8. Number of Sentences Written Across Three Drafts of Five Assignments—Means (Standard Deviations)

Number of Paragraphs. Table 3.9 gives the means and standard deviations for the number of paragraphs written on each draft of the five assignments. Members of the peer feedback group wrote significantly more paragraphs than members of the text analysis group, $F(2, 368) = 9.64$, $p = 0.000$, producing a mean of 0.30 more paragraphs from first to third drafts across the five assignments, while the number of paragraphs written by members of the text analysis group remained unchanged across drafts. In addition, the change in total number of paragraphs from one draft to the next were significantly different across all subjects, $F(2, 368) = 10.28$, $p = 0.000$. Statistical analysis revealed no significant difference between the two groups in the total number of paragraphs written across drafts for different assignments, $F(8, 368) = 0.92$, $p = 0.503$, nor in the sample as a whole, $F(8, 368) = 1.07$, $p = 0.385$.

Group	N	Assignment	Draft 1	Draft 2	Draft 3
Text Analysis	24	1	4.0 (1.2)	4.1 (1.2)	4.0 (1.1)
		2	5.1 (1.4)	5.1 (1.3)	5.1 (1.3)
		3	4.2 (1.0)	4.2 (1.0)	4.1 (1.1)
		4	4.3 (0.9)	4.4 (0.9)	4.4 (1.0)
		5	4.8 (1.3)	4.8 (1.2)	4.7 (1.0)
Total Text Analysis			4.5 (0.5)	4.5 (0.4)	4.5 (0.5)
Peer Feedback	24	1	4.2 (0.2)	4.5 (0.9)	4.7 (0.9)
		2	5.1 (1.3)	5.5 (1.5)	5.5 (1.5)
		3	4.2 (0.9)	4.3 (1.0)	4.3 (1.1)
		4	4.5 (1.1)	4.7 (1.0)	4.7 (1.0)
		5	5.1 (1.2)	5.4 (1.4)	5.3 (1.4)
Total Peer Feedback			4.5 (0.5)	4.9 (0.5)	4.9 (0.5)
Total Sample	48		4.6 (0.4)	4.7 (0.5)	4.7 (0.5)

Table 3.9. Number of Paragraphs Written Across Three Drafts of Five Assignments—Means (Standard Deviations)

3.2.2.2.   Surface- and Content-level Revisions

In examining the revisions made by students on second and third drafts of the five assignments, multivariate analysis of variance was used in answering the following questions:

> Are there significant differences between the two groups in the mean number of surface- and content-level revisions made across drafts on the five assignments?

> Are there significant differences in the frequency of certain categories of surface- and content-level revisions made by members of the two groups?

76

A two by five by two by two (two groups by five assignments by two drafts by two types of revisions [surface and content]) repeated measures analysis of variance was conducted to compare the number of surface- and content-level revisions between the two groups.

Group	N	Assignment	Draft 2 Surface	Content	Draft 3 Surface	Content
Text Analysis	24	1	2.0 (2.8)	1.0 (2.6)	1.8 (3.0)	0.1 (0.6)
		2	0.9 (1.6)	1.7 (3.1)	5.3 (4.3)	1.0 (2.1)
		3	0.9 (1.5)	0.5 (1.4)	2.6 (2.6)	1.1 (1.7)
		4	1.3 (1.5)	0.9 (1.1)	2.8 (2.0)	1.0 (1.5)
		5	1.8 (2.3)	1.8 (3.8)	4.3 (3.4)	1.4 (1.9)
Total Text Analysis			1.4 (2.0)	1.2 (2.6)	3.3 (3.3)	1.0 (2.0)
Peer Feedback	24	1	3.8 (3.2)	5.7 (5.2)	2.0 (2.9)	0.3 (1.0)
		2	4.7 (5.7)	4.6 (4.7)	3.7 (4.2)	0.9 (1.5)
		3	2.3 (2.4)	2.4 (2.8)	2.5 (2.9)	1.1 (1.9)
		4	2.2 (2.1)	2.8 (2.3)	2.6 (2.7)	1.5 (2.1)
		5	4.7 (4.1)	4.4 (5.3)	3.8 (3.3)	1.1 (1.7)
Total Peer Feedback			3.5 (3.9)	4.0 (4.3)	2.8 (3.2)	1.0 (1.7)
Total Sample	48		2.4 (3.3)	2.6 (3.8)	3.1 (3.3)	1.0 (1.9)

Table 3.10. Surface-and Content-Level Revisions on Drafts 2 and 3 of Five Assignments—Means (Standard Deviations)

Table 3.10 gives the descriptive statistics for the total number of surface- and content-level revisions made on second and third drafts of the five assignments. The groups were found to be significantly different in the number of revisions of each type, regardless of assignment or draft, $F(1, 184) = 2.89$, $p = 0.036$. Members of the peer feedback group made on average 6.3 surface-level revisions per assignment, and 5.0 content-level revisions, while members of the text analysis group made a mean total of 4.7 surface-level and 2.2 content-level revisions per assignment. The peer feedback group thus made a mean total of 1.6 surface- and 2.8 content-level revisions more per assignment than the text analysis group. In addition, the changes in revision type across drafts two and three were significantly different for all subjects, $F(1, 184) = 32.67$, $p = 0.000$, with the combined group making significantly more content-level revisions made on second than on third drafts and significantly more surface-level revisions made on third than on second drafts. Additional statistical analysis uncovered no significant differences between groups across drafts, $F(1, 184) = 0.03$, $p = 0.276$; across assignments $F(1, 184) = 0.51$, $p = 0.102$; nor across drafts of different assignments, $F(1, 184) = 1.84$, $p = 0.122$.

3.2.2.3.   Categories of Surface-level Revisions

Changes for surface-level revisions in each of five categories are presented in Tables 3.11-15. As there was no variance for ten percent of the variables compared for different types of verb form changes, this category was collapsed into the category of surface-level word form changes in the analysis of variance. In addition, the category of surface-level sentence structure changes was eliminated from the analysis, as there was no variance for forty percent of the individual variables compared in this category. A two by five by two (two groups by five assignments by two drafts) repeated measures analysis of variance was conducted to compare the number of surface-level revisions for each of the five categories between the two groups.

Surface-Level Additions. The means and standard deviations for surface-level additions in the second and third drafts of the five assignments are given in Table 3.11. When changes in the total number of surface-level additions across drafts were examined between groups, regardless of assignment, the difference was found to be significant, $F(1, 184) = 9.93$, $p = 0.003$. The peer feedback group made 0.30 more surface-level additions than the text analysis group on second drafts, while on third drafts the mean number of surface-level additions made by both groups was 0.18. As to the main effect for draft, the changes in the total number of surface-level additions from second to third drafts were significantly different for the two groups combined, $F(1, 184) = 4.56$, $p = 0.038$. On second drafts subjects in the two groups combined made a mean total of 0.28 additions, while on third drafts the mean number of surface-level additions fell to 0.18. No statistically significant difference was found for surface-level additions across drafts in different assignments between the two groups, $F(4, 184) = 1.72$, $p = 0.146$, nor for the two groups combined, $F(4, 184) = 1.42$, $p = 0.230$.

Group	N	Assignment	Draft 2	Draft 3
Text Analysis	24	1	0.04 (0.20)	0.04 (0.20)
		2	0.17 (0.48)	0.33 (0.70)
		3	0.08 (0.28)	0.13 (0.34)
		4	0.04 (0.20)	0.04 (0.20)
		5	0.29 (0.75)	0.33 (0.64)
Total Text Analysis			0.13 (0.44)	0.18 (0.48)
Peer Feedback	24	1	0.71 (0.99)	0.04 (0.20)
		2	0.67 (1.57)	0.21 (0.42)
		3	0.17 (0.57)	0.21 (0.51)
		4	0.17 (0.38)	0.17 (0.64)
		5	0.46 (0.83)	0.25 (0.53)
Total Peer Feedback			0.43 (0.98)	0.18 (0.48)
Total Sample	48		0.28 (0.77)	0.18 (0.48)

Table 3.11. Surface-Level Additions on Drafts 2 and 3 of Five Assignments—Means (Standard Deviations)

Surface-level Deletions. The surface-level deletions on drafts two and three of the five assignments can be compared in Table 3.12. The difference between groups for changes in the total number of surface-level deletions across drafts, regardless of assignment, was significant, $F(1, 184) = 11.81$, $p = 0.001$. On second drafts, members of the peer feedback group made more surface-level deletions than members of the text analysis group, producing a mean of 0.47 more surface-level deletions on second drafts, while on third drafts, members of the text analysis group made 0.15 more surface-level deletions than members of the peer feedback group. In addition, though the two groups did not differ in the number of surface-level deletions across different drafts and assignments, $F(4, 184) = 1.91$, $p = 0.110$, the combined groups made significantly more changes in the total number of surface-level deletions across drafts in some assignments than in others, $F(4, 184) = 2.91$, $p = 0.023$. As to the main effect for draft, the changes in the total number of surface-level deletions from second to third drafts were not significantly different across the two groups, $F(1, 184) = 0.35$, $p = 0.554$.

Group	N	Assignment	Draft 2	Draft 3
Text Analysis	24	1	0.50 (1.06)	0.17 (0.48)
		2	0.08 (0.28)	1.08 (1.21)
		3	0.04 (0.20)	0.21 (0.42)
		4	0.21 (0.51)	0.63 (0.92)
		5	0.21 (0.51)	0.79 (0.93)
Total Text Analysis			0.21 (0.61)	0.58 (0.90)
Peer Feedback	24	1	0.75 (1.07)	0.29 (0.55)
		2	0.79 (1.72)	0.54 (1.18)
		3	0.50 (0.66)	0.33 (0.57)
		4	0.46 (0.93)	0.42 (0.65)
		5	0.92 (1.35)	0.54 (0.93)
Total Peer Feedback			0.68 (1.20)	0.43 (0.81)
Total Sample	48		0.45 (0.98)	0.50 (0.86)

Table 3.12. Surface-Level Deletions on Drafts 2 and 3 of Five Assignments—Means (Standard Deviations)

Surface-Level Substitutions. Table 3.13 presents the means and standard deviations for surface-level substitutions across drafts. When changes in the total number of surface-level substitutions across drafts between groups were examined, regardless of assignment, the difference was statistically significant, $F(1, 184) = 20.43$, $p = 0.000$. The peer feedback group made a mean total of 0.81 surface-level substitutions on second drafts and 0.44 on third drafts. The text analysis group made a mean total of 0.42 surface-level substitutions on second drafts and 0.91 on third drafts. The combined groups made no significant changes across drafts, $F(1, 184) = 0.48$, $p = 0.490$. Other statistical results showed no significant differences for different assignments between groups, $F(4, 184) = 0.63$, $p = 0.639$, or in the combined groups, $F(1, 184) = 2.24$, $p = 0.066$.

Group	N	Assignment	Draft 2	Draft 3
Text Analysis	24	1	0.63 (1.02)	0.50 (1.02)
		2	0.17 (0.48)	1.25 (1.78)
		3	0.21 (0.51)	0.83 (0.96)
		4	0.38 (0.77)	0.79 (1.06)
		5	0.71 (1.20)	1.21 (1.47)
Total Text Analysis			0.42 (0.86)	0.91 (1.31)
Peer Feedback	24	1	0.92 (1.02)	0.13 (0.34)
		2	0.96 (1.46)	0.63 (0.97)
		3	0.50 (0.72)	0.33 (0.92)
		4	0.50 (0.78)	0.38 (0.71)
		5	1.17 (1.37)	0.75 (1.45)
Total Peer Feedback			0.81 (1.12)	0.44 (0.96)
Total Sample	48		0.61 (1.02)	0.68 (1.17)

Table 3.13. Surface-Level Substitutions on Drafts 2 and 3 of Five Assignments—
Means (Standard Deviations)

Surface-level Changes in Word Form. Table 3.14 presents the means and standard deviations for surface-level changes in word form across drafts. The between-groups difference in number of surface-level changes in word form across drafts, regardless of assignment, was statistically significant, $F(1, 184) = 21.95$, $p = 0.000$. The peer feedback group made a mean total of 0.72 more surface-level changes in word form on second drafts than the text analysis group, while on third drafts the text analysis group made a mean total of 0.09 more surface-level changes in word form than the peer feedback group. The difference in the total number of surface-level changes in word form from second to third drafts were significantly different as well across all subjects, $F(1, 184) = 45.66$, $p = 0.000$. On second drafts the two groups combined made a mean total of 0.73 surface-level changes in word form, while on third drafts the number of surface-level changes in word form fell to 0.18. Further statistical results showed no significant differences either

81

between groups, $F(4, 184) = 1.33$, $p = 0.261$, or in the combined group, $F(4, 184) = 0.14$, $p = 0.967$, for differences in assignments.

Group	N	Assignment	Draft 2	Draft 3
Text Analysis	24	1	0.54 (1.06)	0.21 (0.59)
		2	0.38 (0.83)	0.50 (1.10)
		3	0.33 (0.92)	0.13 (0.34)
		4	0.47 (0.72)	0.04 (0.20)
		5	0.15 (1.75)	0.21 (0.42)
Total Text Analysis			0.37 (0.93)	0.22 (0.41)
Peer Feedback	24	1	1.04 (1.40)	0.13 (0.34)
		2	1.42 (1.86)	0.13 (0.34)
		3	0.71 (1.49)	0.04 (0.20)
		4	0.79 (0.93)	0.08 (0.28)
		5	1.50 (1.75)	0.29 (0.75)
Total Peer Feedback			1.09 (1.42)	0.13 (0.34)
Total Sample	48		0.73 (1.50)	0.18 (0.47)

Table 3.14. Surface-Level Changes in Word Form on Drafts 2 and 3 of Five Assignments—Means (Standard Deviations)

Surface-level Changes in Punctuation. Table 3.15 presents the means and standard deviations for surface-level changes in punctuation across drafts. When changes in the total number of surface-level changes in punctuation across drafts were examined between groups, regardless of assignment, the difference was not statistically significant, $F(1, 184) = 3.28$, $p = 0.077$. The peer feedback group made a mean total of 0.22 surface-level changes in punctuation on second drafts and 0.13 on third drafts. The text analysis group made a mean total of 0.17 surface-level changes in punctuation on second drafts and 0.22 on third drafts. As to the main effect for draft, the changes in the total number of surface-level changes in punctuation from second to third drafts were not significantly different across the two groups, $F(1, 184) = 0.28$, $p =$

0.597. On second drafts, members of the two groups combined made a mean total of 0.19 surface-level changes in punctuation, while on third drafts the number of surface-level changes in punctuation was 0.17. In this category of analysis, there were also no significant differences across drafts for different assignments, either between groups, $F(4, 184) = 2.28$, $p = 0.063$, or for all subjects combined, $F(4, 184) = 0.32$, $p = 0.868$.

Group	N	Assignment	Draft 2	Draft 3
Text Analysis	24	1	0.25 (0.74)	0.21 (0.59)
		2	0.08 (0.28)	0.50 (1.10)
		3	0.08 (0.28)	0.13 (0.34)
		4	0.17 (0.38)	0.04 (0.20)
		5	0.25 (0.68)	0.21 (0.42)
Total Text Analysis			0.17 (0.51)	0.22 (0.62)
Peer Feedback	24	1	0.21 (0.51)	0.13 (0.34)
		2	0.38 (0.65)	0.13 (0.34)
		3	0.13 (0.45)	0.13 (0.34)
		4	0.04 (0.20)	0.08 (0.28)
		5	0.33 (0.70)	0.29 (0.75)
Total Peer Feedback			0.22 (0.54)	0.13 (0.42)
Total Sample	48		0.19 (0.52)	0.17 (0.53)

Table 3.15. Surface-Level Changes in Punctuation on Drafts 2 and 3 of Five Assignments—Means (Standard Deviations)

3.2.2.4. Categories of Content-level Revisions

The across-draft differences for content-level revisions in each of three categories are presented in Tables 3.16-18. As there was no variance for forty percent of the variables compared for reorganization and for ninety percent of the variables compared for combination, these categories were eliminated from the analysis of variance. A two by five by two (two groups by five assignments by two drafts) repeated measures analysis of variance was conducted to compare the number of content-level revisions for each of the three categories between the two groups.

Group	N	Assignment	Draft 2	Draft 3
Text Analysis	24	1	0.38 (1.25)	0.04 (0.20)
		2	1.33 (2.82)	0.88 (1.87)
		3	0.25 (0.85)	0.71 (1.62)
		4	0.42 (0.78)	0.33 (0.57)
		5	0.88 (1.75)	0.33 (0.82)
Total Text Analysis			0.65 (1.69)	0.46 (1.22)
Peer Feedback	24	1	3.42 (3.21)	0.21 (0.83)
		2	3.21 (3.59)	0.46 (0.93)
		3	1.25 (1.45)	0.79 (1.62)
		4	0.38 (1.53)	0.71 (1.04)
		5	2.75 (3.63)	0.46 (0.93)
Total Peer Feedback			2.40 (2.95)	0.53 (1.11)
Total Sample	48		1.53 (2.56)	0.49 (1.16)

Table 3.16. Content-Level Additions on Drafts 2 and 3 of Five Assignments— Means (Standard Deviations)

Content-level Additions. Table 3.16 summarizes the changes in content-level additions across drafts. Changes in the total number of content-level additions across drafts, regardless of assignment, were significant between groups, $F(1, 184) = 30.87$, $p = 0.000$, with the peer feedback group producing a mean of 1.75 more content-level additions on second drafts than the text analysis group. On third drafts, the peer feedback group made 0.07 more content-level additions than members of the text analysis group. In addition, the changes in the total number of content-level additions from second to third drafts were significantly different for the two groups combined, $F(1, 184) = 46.54$, $p = 0.000$, as on second drafts the subjects made a mean total of 1.53 content-level additions, while on third drafts the number of content-level additions fell to 0.49. Although content-level additions across drafts for different groups and assignments revealed no statistically significant difference, $F(4, 184) = 1.67$, $p = 0.158$, there was a significant difference in the total number of content-level additions across drafts for different assignments for all subjects, $F(4, 184) = 4.69$, $p = 0.001$.

Group	N	Assignment	Draft 2	Draft 3
Text Analysis	24	1	0.25 (0.53)	0.04 (0.20)
		2	0.13 (0.34)	0.13 (0.45)
		3	0.04 (0.20)	0.29 (0.99)
		4	0.08 (0.28)	0.25 (0.74)
		5	0.25 (0.53)	0.13 (0.34)
Total Text Analysis			0.15 (0.40)	0.13 (0.47)
Peer Feedback	24	1	0.63 (0.88)	0.04 (0.20)
		2	0.54 (0.66)	0.08 (0.28)
		3	0.50 (1.06)	0.08 (0.28)
		4	0.29 (0.62)	0.58 (1.02)
		5	0.13 (0.34)	0.33 (0.76)
Total Peer Feedback			0.42 (0.76)	0.13 (0.45)
Total Sample	48		0.28 (0.62)	0.13 (0.46)

Table 3.17. Content-Level Deletions on Drafts 2 and 3 of Five Assignments— Means (Standard Deviations)

Content-level Deletions. The descriptive statistics for content-level deletions across drafts are shown in Table 3.17. When changes in the total number of content-level deletions across drafts were examined between groups, regardless of assignment, the difference was significant, $F(1, 184) = 6.56$, $p = 0.014$. The peer feedback group made a mean of 0.27 more deletions on second drafts than members of the text analysis group, while members of both groups made 0.13 content-level deletions on third drafts. An examination of content-level deletions across drafts for different groups and assignments revealed a statistically significant difference as well, $F(4, 184) = 3.08$ $p = 0.018$. As to the main effect for draft, the changes in the total number of content-level deletions from second to third drafts were significantly different across the two groups, $F(1, 184) = 8.30$, $p = 0.006$. On second drafts members of the two groups combined made a mean total of 0.28 content-level deletions, while on third drafts the number of content-level deletions fell to 0.13. When changes in the total number of content-level deletions across drafts were examined for differences in assignment, regardless of group, these changes were also statistically significant, $F(4, 184) = 3.29$, $p = 0.012$.

Group	N	Assignment	Draft 2	Draft 3
Text Analysis	24	1	0.25 (0.90)	0.08 (0.41)
		2	0.17 (0.38)	0.29 (0.69)
		3	0.83 (0.28)	0.29 (0.99)
		4	0.38 (0.58)	0.50 (0.72)
		5	0.58 (1.86)	0.79 (1.35)
Total Text Analysis			0.29 (0.98)	0.39 (0.91)
Peer Feedback	24	1	1.33 (1.88)	0.04 (0.29)
		2	0.50 (0.72)	0.25 (0.53)
		3	0.50 (0.78)	0.17 (0.38)
		4	0.96 (1.57)	0.58 (1.02)
		5	1.17 (2.35)	0.25 (0.68)
Total Peer Feedback			0.89 (1.60)	0.25 (0.64)
Total Sample	48		0.59 (1.36)	0.32 (0.79)

Table 3.18. Content-Level Substitutions on Drafts 2 and 3 of Five Assignments—Means (Standard Deviations)

Content-level Substitutions. Table 3.18 presents the means and standard deviations for content-level substitutions across drafts. Analysis of the changes in number of content-level substitutions across drafts, regardless of assignment, uncovered a significant between-groups difference, $F(1, 184) = 25.65$, $p = 0.000$. On second drafts, the peer feedback group made a mean total of 0.60 more content-level substitutions

86

than the text analysis group, while on third drafts the text analysis group produced a mean of 0.14 more substitutions than the peer feedback group. As to the main effect for draft, the changes in the total number of content-level substitutions from second to third drafts were significantly different across the two groups combined, $F(1, 184) = 13.68$, $p = 0.001$. On second drafts members of the two groups combined made a mean total of 0.59 content-level substitutions, while on third drafts the number of content-level substitutions fell to 0.32. The results of the statistical analysis were non-significant for differences in assignments, both between groups, $F(4, 184) = 0.88$, $p = 0.475$, and for all subjects, $F(4, 184) = 2.17$, $p = 0.074$.

3.2.2.5. Summary of Findings for Drafts of the Five Assignments

Members of the peer feedback group wrote significantly more words, sentences, and paragraphs across drafts than members of the text analysis group, both overall and in individual assignments. Those in the peer feedback group made more content-level revisions than those in the text analysis group, producing a mean of more than twice as many content-level revisions per assignment; the number of surface-level revisions completed by the two groups was not significantly different.

In their second drafts of assignments, members of the peer feedback group made more revisions in each surface- and content-level category, while in their third drafts, members of the text analysis group made more surface-level deletions, substitutions, and changes in word form and punctuation. They also made more content-level substitutions in third drafts, whereas members of the peer feedback group made more content-level additions and deletions in second drafts.

3.3. DISCUSSION

3.3.1. Quality and Quantity Measures

As in many comparative studies of writing by pen-and-paper vs. computer means (Pennington, 1993b, 1996b, chs. 1-3), in the present study of word processing effects under different input conditions, quantitative difference or change was not associated with qualitative change as measured by holistic scoring. Both groups increased the total number of words written on posttests compared to pretests; but the fact that members of the peer tutoring group increased the total number of words written on posttests by more than 60 words compared to members of the text analysis group is noteworthy. There are at least three possible explanations for this significant difference.

One explanation for the significant difference in total number of words written from pretest to posttest is that members of the peer feedback group may have spent more time revising their compositions with word processing during the study and this more extensive experience using the word processing program resulted in the significant difference in total words written on posttests. Both groups used word processing in writing first drafts of each assignment. However, on subsequent assignments, the peer tutoring group engaged in peer feedback and used the word processing program to make subsequent revisions in their compositions, while members of the text analysis group used two text analysis programs along with the word processing program for revising their texts. It is possible that members of the text analysis group actually spent less time using the word processing program in revising their drafts and that this difference resulted in the differential effect for the total number of words written by the two groups on posttests. The power of this explanation is, however, weakened by two factors. First, all students participating in the study were experienced users of the word processing program employed for writing and revising assignments. Second, the actual time spent reviewing and revising texts with the word processing program, though not formally measured during the study, may not have been significantly different for members of the two groups, as every student used the word processing program to complete at least some revision of second and third drafts.

A second explanation for the significant difference in the total number of words written on posttests is that the differential effect is directly related to the use of computerized text analysis as a revision aid. That is, the use of text analysis, as Sirc (1989) has suggested, may have limited the parameters within which members of the text analysis group revised drafts of their assignments; and those limitations may actually have affected the total number of words written by those students even when, as on the posttests, they were not using text analysis as a revision aid. Rather than freeing the text analysis students for the task of meaning-making through writing, resulting in an increase in the number of words written on subsequent drafts, it is possible that text analysis so focused the attention of these students on surface-level concerns that more global concerns such as organization, content, and information flow were given less attention, resulting in shorter second and third drafts of assignments and shorter posttests.

The third explanation for the difference between the two groups in the total number of words written from pretest to posttest is twofold and relates directly to the possible positive effect of peer tutoring on the writing performance of members of the peer tutoring group. These students' participation in peer tutoring may have had an effect on their writing performance that resulted in their writing significantly more words on posttests compared to students in the text analysis group. Furthermore, the interaction of peer tutoring and word processing may have resulted in the difference between the two groups in the total number of words in posttests. Human interaction (peer tutoring) in combination with word processing, as opposed to human-computer interaction (the use of text analysis) in combination with word processing, may have contributed to the differential performance of the two groups on the total number of words written on posttests.

While the slightly higher scores received by members of the peer feedback group may indicate a trend towards greater gains in overall writing performance as compared to gains made by members of the text analysis group, this difference was not statistically significant. It is possible that the difference in writing performance as measured by holistic scoring may have been greater had the time in which the study was conducted been extended. Ten weeks may be too brief a period of time to reflect differences in writing performance measured through holistic evaluation (Pennington, 1993b, 1996b). It is possible that use of an analytic scoring protocol for examination of pretests and posttests might have revealed greater differences in writing performance than came out in the holistic scoring procedures of this study.

Students in the peer tutoring group wrote significantly more words across drafts as compared to students in the text analysis group. In an earlier case study comparing text analysis with process-oriented feedback, Pennington and Brock (1992) report similar findings. In that study, students using computerized text analysis to revise compositions wrote either fewer or only marginally more words across three drafts of three compositions completed during the study, while students receiving process-oriented feedback increased the length of their drafts markedly. In the present investigation, as in the previous on carried out by the authors, the use of text analysis as a revising aid resulted in either no increases or very small increases in the number of words written across three drafts of five assignments completed during the study, while the use of peer tutoring resulted in significantly greater increases in the number of words written across drafts compared to text analysis.

Quantitative differences in the performance of the two groups across drafts of the five assignments suggests differences in the writing process of students in the peer tutoring and text analysis groups. The increases in number of words and in sentences and paragraphs, especially in going from first to second draft, of the peer tutoring group suggests that they viewed their first draft not as a fixed text but as content to be developed further. The minimal variation in number of words, sentences, and paragraphs across drafts for the text analysis group suggests that their main strategy for developing their compositions after generating a first draft was a fine-tuning of what they had already written. Thus, it can be ar-

89

gued that the text analysis revision aids encouraged students to view their first draft as fixed in amount of content, whereas peer tutoring fostered a view of a first draft as material which could be enlarged and elaborated in a later draft.

3.3.2. Revision

Although there was no significant difference between the peer tutoring and text analysis groups according to the holistic measure of writing improvement from pretest to posttest, the two groups had substantially different profiles with respect to the types of revisions made on the three drafts of the five assignments completed during the course of the study. These differences can be assumed to reflect differences in the instructional treatments the groups received. It seems that use of word processing with peer input, i.e., as part of a traditional process writing approach, stimulated more revisions of different types in going from first to second drafts than did use of word processing with computer revising aids, which seem to have stimulated revision more in final than in intermediate drafts. In a later draft, the computer revisers changed their texts more on the surface level than did the traditional process group exposed to peer tutoring. In addition, they showed more content changes that replaced one piece of text by another. The peer tutoring group, in contrast, showed more content changes in the second draft of the sort that add or delete material. It is also of interest that while the bulk of the content changes made by the peer tutoring group occurred in the second draft, the text analysis group made more content-level changes in the third draft. Thus, the peer feedback group, which was the group exposed to word processing in the context of a traditional process approach to writing, made changes in the content of their work to a greater extent and at an earlier stage than did the text analysis group.

A main difference in the revising behavior of the two groups was in the number and type of content-level revisions completed across drafts of the five assignments. Members of the peer tutoring group made significantly more content-level revisions than members of the text analysis group. Consistent with the quantitative findings, the most common type of content-level revision made by members of the peer tutoring group was the addition of new information across drafts, whereas this type of revision was much rarer in the text analysis group, who tended to make changes by surface editing or substitution.

One explanation for the difference in content-level additions between the two groups relates directly to the manner in which students in the two groups revised their assignments. Members of the peer tutoring group exchanged hard copies of drafts with their peer tutors—at least hard copies of the first draft; a small number of students read and responded to their tutor's second drafts as they appeared on the computer screen. They read and responded to drafts based on revising protocols. The process of reading their peer tutors' drafts most likely provided a source of new ideas and information that students could then draw upon in revising their own drafts. Members of the text analysis group, in contrast, were more bound to the computer screen, most paying little attention to the hard copies of their drafts and preferring instead to read and revise their compositions with the aid of the computer. It is possible that because members of the peer tutoring group were less computer-bound, they were able not only to consult the hard copy of their tutors' first draft but also the student's course book, which contained the simulations on which assignments were based, resulting in the addition of new information in subsequent drafts. However, because members of the text analysis group focused more of their attention on the computer screen, they were less likely to consult the hard copy of their drafts and the simulation on which assignments were based. This lack of attention to input off the computer may have resulted in their adding less new information to their compositions across drafts as compared to members of the peer tutoring group.

A second explanation for this difference in the number of content-level revisions completed by members of the two groups lies in the very nature of text analysis itself. It is evident from the statistical analysis of first drafts that students in the text analysis group were unable to use *Writer's Helper* as a revision aid that prompted substantial content-level revisions in their texts. In fact, as the small number of content-level as well as surface-level revisions completed in going from first to second drafts indicates, members of the text analysis group made few revisions of any kind on first drafts of assignments. Furthermore, while the total number of revisions completed in going from second to third drafts revised with the aid of *Grammatik* increased markedly, the number of content-level revisions remained low, with text analysis students making a mean of only 2.2 total content-level revisions per assignment compared with an average of 5.0 total content-level revisions per assignment made by the peer-tutoring students. This is not an entirely unexpected finding and is similar to the results reported by Pennington and Brock (1992). What is somewhat surprising, however, is the almost complete failure of text analysis students to make use of the text re-formatting features provided by *Writer's Helper* to review and revise their texts. As the responses of four students interviewed from the text analysis group indicate, students in that group did not find the program helpful in revising texts, were unable to use the program's reformulation of the surface features of their texts to revise, and so made very few changes from first to second drafts.

The finding that students using text analysis as a revision aid made very few changes in content appears to refute suggestions made by

Kiefer (1987) and Reid (1986) that text analysis prompts students to make both surface- and content-level changes in their texts. Of course, their claims were made based on studies that combined text analysis with teacher and peer feedback, while this study attempted, as suggested by Logan (1988), to isolate the effects of text analysis on ESL student writing. The results of the present study indicate that when text analysis is used independently, as indeed it is designed to be used (Wresch, 1984), it does not prompt ESL writers to make content-level revisions, and the revisions students do make are primarily those suggested by the text analyzer itself. There is nothing very surprising in these results, as students generally perform in ways they are taught.

3.4.   CONCLUSION

The main results of the present investigation of computer-assisted writing with peer vs. computer input to revision are the following:

> 1. Over the period of one school term, no qualitative difference emerged in holistically scored pretest and posttest essays of student groups using computerized text analysis vs. peer tutoring as input to revision.
>
> 2. Students who used word processing within a traditional process approach with peer tutoring made more revisions of all types than students who revised word-processed compositions with the aid of two computerized text analysis programs.
>
> 3.Students in the text analysis group made few revisions in content, while students in the peer tutoring group made substantial changes in the content of their texts.
>
> 4. Students in the peer tutoring group made significantly more additions of new information compared to students in the text analysis group.
>
> 5. Peer tutoring promoted more revision in going from first to second draft than did text analysis. Students in the text analysis group made markedly more revisions to their compositions in going from second to third draft, when revising with *Grammatik*, than in going from first to second draft, when revising with *Writer's Helper*.

6. Students using text analysis made few changes that were not directly prompted by the feedback provided by the text analysis programs, though they were not always able to use the feedback given.

The results of this study suggest that computerized text analysis, contrary to some published claims, not only does not prompt content-level revision—particularly, the addition of new information across drafts—but may plausibly have the opposite effect, actually discouraging many types of revision and the addition of new information in written work produced on a word processor. In contrast, a combination of word processing and peer tutoring, even when it is only loosely guided through the use of revising protocols as was the case in the present study, does result in students adding more new information to texts, making more substantial changes in their texts, and writing progressively more words across drafts. The experience of engaging in peer tutoring during the study may also have had a significant effect on the number of words written by peer tutoring students on posttests, i.e., when they were not engaged in peer tutoring. This significant increase in the total number of words written by peer tutoring students on posttests possibly reflects a desire among these students to include as much relevant information as possible in their texts. On the other hand, the significantly smaller number of words written on posttests by members of the text analysis group may reflect less development, resulting from the use of text analysis during the study, in those subjects' ability to focus on and expand the information included in their texts.

While future developments in computer hardware and software technology will certainly increase the sophistication and accuracy with which text analyzers respond to text, it is unlikely in the near future that computerized text analysis will have the capability of addressing meaning-level concerns. Though the parsing ability of these programs will grow quickly, even exponentially, in the coming decade, this study suggests that any incorporation of this medium into the language or composition classroom should be approached with great caution. Not surprisingly, this study suggests strongly that students should not be left to their own devices in using text analysis as a revision aid for revising their writing. Furthermore, teachers who do consider incorporating text analysis into their composition curricula should consider whether the time spent directing student use of computerized text analysis is the most productive and effective use of their own and their students' time. As Sirc (1989) has warned, whenever we choose to allow computers to talk directly to our students, "we limit our pedagogy" (p. 187). It would appear from the results of this study that doing so may limit the potential of our student writers as well. This study suggests on the other hand that a combination of word processing and a process approach which incorporates a multiple draft requirement and peer tutoring can help student writers exploit the potential of the interaction between human and computer.

4. The Effect of Peer Feedback versus Self-Assessment on the Quality and Revision of Compositions Word-Processed by Advanced ESL Learners

Sultan Al-Hazmi and Phil Scholfield

ABSTRACT

This chapter reports on a study comparing the word-processed essays of two groups of Arab students enrolled in a London secondary school. One group revised their essays on the basis of peer feedback and the other on the basis of self-assessment. Subjects in the peer feedback group showed somewhat more improvement between drafts than those in the self-assessment group, whereas the self-assessment group had somewhat higher mean scores in their final drafts for mechanics, language use, vocabulary, organization, content, and length. The self-assessment group made more and higher level revision changes (i.e., involving larger structural units and content changes) to their drafts than the peer feedback group. This finding is consistent with the fact that the self-assessment group were judged to be of higher general writing ability than the peer feedback group. For the comparatively lower proficiency group, peer feedback seemed to assist them in improving content and vocabulary between drafts.

4.0.   INTRODUCTION

In these days of widespread ownership of computers around the globe, with more and more compositions, term papers, and theses being prepared by second language (L2) speakers in educational institutions by electronic means, clearly there is need for more research at the crossroads where writing meets computer. It is with this inspiration that the present study was undertaken, focusing on two different ways of implementing one aspect of the writing process—revision—specifically, in the context of the word processing of English compositions by students with Arabic as a first language (L1) in a London secondary school.

Proponents of CALL have striven over the years to associate this field with recognized movements in language learning and teaching, so as to demonstrate that the technological resources it provides have a pedagogical value beyond their acknowledged motivational potential. It was not difficult to make such a connection for the early drill-like exercises that clearly fitted the behaviorist/audiolingual paradigm, or the later simulation programs which could be made by the resourceful teacher to operate as key components of communicative tasks. Word processing, however, being inherently a generic, content-free utility, did not very obviously accord with any such learning-teaching paradigm. The truth is that word processing *could* be implemented with students by a teacher in a manner compatible with almost any approach to pedagogy.[1] The grammar translation teacher could enter a text in the learners' L1 for the learners to access and replace on screen with a target language equivalent, perhaps aided by an on-line bilingual dictionary. The audiolingual teacher could provide a target language text on screen with spaces to be filled more or less mechanically by the student user to produce a complete L2 composition, thus reproducing the classic guided writing task.

More recently, however, CALL has become influenced by the learner autonomy movement in language learning and teaching, and its interpreters have embarked on an exploration of the different roles that the computer can play relative to the user. Phillips (1986), for example, identifies a role where the computer is no longer conceptualized only as teacher-substitute but also on occasion as tool (or 'prosthesis'). This role very much fits the way L1 writers—and in many situations L2 learners—exploit a word processing program when writing more or less 'free' or 'communicative' compositions. In that case they do not so much employ word processing for *learning*, but as a part of *using* the language. Viewed in this way, word processing may be conceptualized as a self-access aid to the processing of language in the written form, with the Internet browser and hypertext mark-up language software of the World Wide Web providing a parallel aid to reading. Neither of these tools comes inherently with pedagogical content or intent, unless a teacher puts it there; but both have immense potential to support more or less communicative language practice within a language teaching program. Consequently, both invite research on how learners use them, how teachers may implement their use in relation to teaching English as a second or foreign language, and how effective these software-plus-implementation combinations are in aiding learners to write or read more successfully. It is within this conceptual framework that the present study finds its place, as a description and evaluation of two such imple-

---

[1] In fact, word processing is often nowadays simply assumed as background for writing, although Snyder (1993) argues that it is more effectively used if explicitly related to curriculum goals. For many suggestions regarding the implementation of word processing within a writing curriculum, see Pennington (1996b, ch 4). (Editor's note)

mentations of the word processing of compositions in the ESL classroom, one involving peer feedback and the other self-assessment.

Alongside the changing ideas about the role of the computer in CALL, research on writing has been exploring and unpacking the writing process, especially through observation and think-aloud studies with writers as they write compositions or undertake other normal writing tasks. Predominantly, the research has arrived at the present view of writing by studying English L1 writers working with pen and paper, though an increasing number of studies have centered on L2 writers as subjects. The influential Hayes and Flower (1983) model of the writing process, reflected to some degree in many process approaches to teaching writing (e.g., White & Arndt, 1991), distinguishes three central aspects of that process—**planning, translating** (turning thoughts into words, i.e., composing), and **reviewing** (in order to edit and revise). Word processing can be seen as a tool relevant to all three of the central aspects of writing. Writers may word process and manipulate on screen jottings and notes representing ideas for a piece of writing (planning). They may use the word processor and its facilities to actually type the draft text (translating). They may read and evaluate what they have written on screen and use the word processor's facilities to edit it (reviewing), including mechanical editing, revising, reviewing, redrafting, and correcting.

At the stage where writers review or revise what they have written, or any part of it—which may happen after very short or quite long intervals—several sources of feedback may be exploited to facilitate the evaluation that constitutes a key component of any such reviewing or revising process. First, there is self-feedback, or **self-assessment**. Though always an available option to the writer, in some older, product-focused methods of teaching writing, even self-assessment was not promoted, as when students were required to write one-draft essays under time pressure. Such an approach is still the prevalent one in many Arab countries (Halimah, 1991), in contrast to the situation of our Arab subjects, who were working more within a process approach to teaching writing (see Method section). Second, in a school context where a process or cooperative learning approach is being implemented, there may be **peer feedback** from one or more classmates. Further, when word processing, there is the availability of **computer feedback** in the form of spell-checking and (usually rather rudimentary) grammar- and style-checking, if the writer chooses to access it.[2] Finally, as in all classroom contexts of writing, there may be **teacher feedback**, if the teacher reads and

---

[2] A series of investigations of computerized text analysis by Brock (1990a, b; 1991; 1993; 1995), Brock and Pennington (this volume), Pennington (1992; 1993a), and Pennington and Brock (1992) strongly urge against making this computerized device a central part of a writing curriculum. (Editor's note)

comments on a draft before it is regarded as final and submitted. However, in many situations the teacher does not have time to provide such feedback on students' pre-final drafts, and teacher feedback is then given only on the final draft, frequently combined with some kind of formal assessment. In part it is this limitation of teaching time that gives rise to interest in whether peer feedback has value if the teacher cannot provide pre-final draft feedback: the basic premise is that any feedback beyond the writer's own may be of value, given the notorious difficulty anyone has in seeing their own shortcomings, compared with the ease with which they may identify others' deficiencies. Furthermore, there is the advantage Nystrand (1986) notes, from a study comparing peer review with teacher review, that "students increasingly viewed their peers not as judges of their writing....but rather as collaborators in a process of communication" (p. 184).

In terms of the field of writing research, then, the present study investigates one aspect of the writing process, looked at specifically in a computer rather than a traditional writing context, with ESL writers in a classroom setting. This precise combination is not one that has been very commonly researched (although see other chapters in this volume), and particularly not involving peer feedback as well as self-feedback. Nevertheless, this combination is of special interest for several reasons. The review phase is widely seen as crucial to success in writing. The word processor offers a number of features that should make it especially helpful in this phase. The ability to move, delete, and add text at any point without having to retype the whole text is the most obvious one. In addition, there is the availability of extra sources of feedback already mentioned, and of added referencing resources such as a computerized dictionary or thesaurus to supplement the personal mental lexicon which each writer brings to a writing task. In fact, the availability of computerized revision aids has not unambiguously been found to promote better revision (Daiute, 1986; Pennington & Brock, this volume; Phinney, 1989), but this is not our concern here. Rather, we focus on the effect of peer feedback versus self-assessment in the word processing context. Apart from the general interest today in word processing and peer feedback in their own right, a special reason to look at these together is the common observation that computer users working in a room together often develop a cooperative sociability that one does not see elsewhere (Jones & Fortescue, 1987; Snyder, 1993). Whether such cooperation arises from a 'let's beat the machine together' camaraderie, or as a consequence of the often less strongly supervised condition of a computer lab as compared to a traditional classroom, a socializing tendency might lead to a special advantage for peer feedback conducted in a computer setting.

There is a lack of studies, especially in the L2 writing literature, that examine the impact of type of educational treatment, such as the type of revision method or the use of word processing, on both revision and quality of students' written products (although see other chapters in this volume). In this chapter, we examine the effects of peer feedback and self-assessment in a word processing medium on both types of outcome, and in addition explore connections between these outcomes.

4.1. RESEARCH QUESTIONS

Based on the existing literature on revision and word processing, the following research questions were formulated. Each of these questions, formulated in lieu of null hypotheses based on the direction of findings in other studies, was generally hypothesized to have a 'yes' answer.

RQ1.   Will peer feedback, compared with self-assessment, lead to superior final draft quality?

RQ2.   Will peer feedback, compared with self-assessment, lead to greater overall improvement between drafts?

RQ3.   Will the peer feedback group improve more over successive writing sessions than the self-assessment group, both in final draft quality and in between-draft quality improvement?

RQ4.   Will the method of revision have a stronger effect on measures of final draft quality and between-draft quality change than the effect expected from general writing achievement grade of each student?

RQ5.   Will students, regardless of revision method, generally make more surface than high-level/meaning changes to their texts?

RQ6.   Will the peer feedback group make more changes of all types, and more meaning-related changes, than the self-assessment group?

RQ7.   Will high achievers make more changes of all types, and more meaning-related changes, than lower achievers?

RQ8.   Will the types of changes made between drafts match the aspects in which between-draft quality improvement is detected for the peer feedback group more than the self-assessment group?

RQ9.   Compared with pen-and-paper studies, will there be any apparent enhanced writing effect due to word processing?

RQ10.   Will there be any differences between the results obtained for the subjects of this study—L1 Arab students studying in a UK secondary school—and those recorded for other types of students in other studies?

In addition, the researchers were prepared to examine any points of interest that might emerge from further qualitative and exploratory analysis of the data collected.

4.2.   METHOD

4.2.1.   Students

The subjects were twenty students in two year 10 classes from the Boys' Upper School of the King Fahad Academy in London. Their mean age was 15. This institution was chosen both because the researchers had an interest in Arab learners and because there were classes regularly word processing their compositions in a process writing context in this institution. Furthermore, both the institution and a specific key teacher were interested in assisting in such a study. The subjects were predominantly from privileged families (e.g., with the father in the diplomatic corps) and from a variety of Arab countries. They had a level of proficiency and length of residence in the UK that qualifies them to be regarded as ESL or bilingual rather than EFL users of English. Hence, they cannot be regarded as completely typical of Arab learners around the world, but rather of a wider population of ESL learners.

The subjects were used to word processing and also had some familiarity with desktop publishing, drawing programs, literature support software, and electronic encyclopedias. The last were typically used in the planning phase of the process writing schedule of teaching implemented by the regular teacher. Many subjects used computers at home as well as at school. This was in accord with an aim of the study not to research computing novices, where various novelty and/or unfamiliarity effects must be considered. The subjects were regarded by their teacher as having problems with writing mainly in the areas of limited vocabulary, paragraphing, inadequate length, and failure to understand the task set.

Practical difficulties ruled out the possibility of using a comparable female group and also restricted the researchers in that intact classes had to be used for each of the two modes of revision being compared. As a consequence, the class randomly chosen for the self-assessment treatment proved to be more proficient in writing than the class selected for peer feedback. Although less than ideal for comparative purposes, this group difference helped to reveal some possible advantages of peer feedback for weaker writers.

4.2.2. Instruction

In the interests of maximizing naturalness in respects other than those where intervention was unavoidable, the treatments of peer feedback and self-assessment were implemented during classes held in the usual way by the regular teacher. Students' writing was also assessed in the normal way for school purposes as coursework, aside from drafts being gathered and copied for analysis by the researchers. Subjects used *Microsoft Word for Windows 6* in a school computer lab for word processing within process writing lessons. Spell-checking and other facilities of the word processing program were equally available to all subjects. One writing task on a single topic was continued over two periods of 80 minutes each on different days, and there were five such double-period sessions over the duration of the study.

The first period of any writing session, the same for both groups in our study, and unaffected by the study, always consisted of prewriting activities followed by writing and printing a first draft. The prewriting involved collective class discussion and search of *Microsoft Encarta* or other computerized and non-computerized resources for relevant material. The teacher generally directed the students to pay attention to content and organization at this stage. While producing the first draft, students worked individually and received help from the teacher only on technical computing matters. In general, the teacher was observed to cooperate in the research by behaving as far as possible uniformly across groups and writing sessions. In the second period, students worked on producing a final draft. Prior to the study, as we learned from interview, the teacher had provided some prompting and encouraged self-assessment. He had sometimes also organized peer feedback, by having students comment on each others' drafts, though not as a prominent feature of instruction prior to our research.

In the present study, the research intervention consisted of assigning 30 minutes at the start of the second period, depending on the class, to either individual revision or peer feedback in pairs. Peer revisers therefore had about 15 minutes for each student to examine and comment on the other's draft, either on screen or in printout form as they preferred. After the 30 minute review period, students worked again individually to complete and print their final drafts. The teacher generally directed the students to add material and examine the draft at all levels when revising at this final stage. The two conditions under which revision took place were therefore not so much peer revision versus self-assessment, as (i) peer revision plus self-assessment versus (ii) self-assessment alone, at greater length.

Feedback pairs were assigned by the teacher randomly, and stayed the same over the five sessions, except when a subject was absent and the pairing had to be altered (something that happened rather often).[3] Some thought was given to the possibility of using revision prompt sheets as part of the intervention. These typically list points for revisers to look for or questions to answer about what they have written. They have been shown to help students in revision (Dimento, 1988; Freedman, 1992). However, they have also been criticized for not allowing students to form their own responses to drafts, for employing the same questions regardless of the type of writing being attempted, and for asking students to assess a draft overall rather than on specific points (Beach & Eaton, 1984). While the latter two criticisms could be dealt with by producing a better revision sheet, the first was felt to be decisive, especially since these subjects were not unfamiliar with revising. As DiPardo and Freedman (1988) say, such sheets "lessen the extent to which small groups are truly peer-run collectives and, in the most extreme case, move toward a mere parceling of tasks traditionally completed by an instructor, with students attending so closely to teacher mandated concerns that groups no longer serve the function of providing a wider, more varied audience for student writing" (p. 127). Thus, the instruction given to students in the present study was simply to: "revise your composition (in collaboration with your partner [peer feedback group] / on your own [self-assessment group]) focusing on crucial aspects of your essay."

4.2.3. Writing Topics

The discourse type of the compositions was held constant, in that it was always argument, or advocacy. Students were set to argue for and/or against something, e.g., the statement, "Nature is too strong: people cannot really do any damage to the natural environment." The individual

---

[3] The method of deciding pairs is a complex issue, such as whether students of equal or different proficiency, or teacher- versus student-selected pairs, work most effectively together (for discussion, see Freedman, 1987).

topics were chosen by the teacher, as usual, since the researchers were interested in investigating school writing done in as normal a way as possible. It was hoped to avoid the criticism voiced by Butler-Nalin (1984): "Often the writing task has been artificial in the sense that students write to a specially designed task for an unusual audience (the researcher)..." (p. 122). Though research has shown that audience and purpose, as well as discourse type, are important variables affecting writing, they too were held constant across groups and sessions in this study.

Five topics were covered in writing sessions extending over twelve weeks: Nature, Pollution, Computer Technology, The Future, and The Issue of BSE (a cattle disease which may pass in deadly form to humans who eat beef). The intention was that this number of sessions would allow the subjects time to get used to the different revision regimes they were following, and provide some chance for us to estimate the learners' variability and progression. In addition, the product of a writing task completed immediately before the researchers began their intervention was gathered to provide baseline information. This task differed slightly in discourse type from the type used in the study itself, in that, rather than being an essay, it was a formal letter written to a local official about the need to raise safety standards on a motorway.

4.2.4. Measurement of Writing Quality

The drafts from the two main stages of the writing process provided the basis for all the measurements of quality and types of revision for each topic. Quality was measured by applying the *ESL Composition Profile* [ESLCP] (Jacobs, Zinkgraf, Wormuth, Hartfield, and Hughey, 1981) on final drafts, and between-draft quality change was assessed by subtracting the ESLCP scores for the first (pre-treatment) draft from those for the final one. The ESLCP provides a framework for separate rating of five aspects of writing quality for each draft: mechanics, vocabulary, language use (=grammar), organization, and content. Error counting methods were not used as it is hard to implement them for analysis of organization and content. Holistic rating instruments such as the ESLCP do suffer from some disadvantages. For instance, they rely on the rater having a clear mental picture of what good writing should be, with which the protocols to be assessed are compared; but as Kroll (1990) says: "There is no single written standard that can be said to represent the 'ideal' written product in English" (p. 141). However, the ESLCP has the advantage of building the assessment on all the main levels of writing skill commonly recognized, including five separate ratings rather than just one overall rating, which might well be less reliable and would not have the same demonstrable content validity. Furthermore, it provides clear descriptions of criteria for proficiency of writing within each of those five areas; and above all, it has been widely used in other studies. Inter-rater reliability was measured, using Kendall's coefficient of concordance, between the researchers and two experienced EFL teachers on one-third of the protocols. High values were achieved on all five aspects measured by the ESLCP, the lowest being 0.77 for content.

As an additional measure, length was calculated as a word count. Though not itself a measure of quality, length is a variable often found to be affected by revision (e.g., Stoddard & MacArthur, 1993), and to correlate with quality (Bangert-Drowns, 1993). Overall writing achievement level of subjects was quantified by using subjects' grades in the previous end-of-term writing skill examination.

4.2.5. Measurement of Revision Changes

Types of revision were quantified by comparing first and final drafts, using Faigley and Witte's (1984) classification scheme of changes. This scheme has the advantages of reasonably well-defined and mutually exclusive categories, and of making a major distinction between meaning-changing and 'surface' or non-meaning changing revisions. Moreover, the different operations performed (addition, deletion, substitution, etc.), and the size of structural element changed (word, phrase, etc.) and, to some extent, the levels of language involved (spelling, grammar, lexis, etc.) are distinguished in the scheme. There are some problems with the scheme, however, in that some changes not regarded as meaning changes (e.g., tense changes) arguably do change meaning. In addition, the distinction between micro- and macro-level changes in meaning can be hard to judge, and we had a few problems with this. Also, the coverage of specific types of grammatical and lexical changes is not very comprehensive, perhaps because it is a scheme designed primarily for L1 writing. Nevertheless, like the ESLCP, the Faigley and Witte taxonomy is widely recognized as the best available, and we were able to make reasonably effective use of it in the present investigation.

There are some limitations to the picture of revision changes that arises from our chosen method of data gathering. In particular, we did not study in-process revisions (Cochran-Smith, 1991)—i.e., as performed within the activity of producing a single draft (in our case, during class periods). We did not have access to any revisions made by subjects while writing the original draft in the first period; we had a view of revision changes in the second period from a before-after double snapshot, not as a blow-by-blow series of events. Revisions-in-process were not studied for two reasons: first, a keystroke recording facility to note such activity was not available to the researchers, and second, it has previously been reported that it is exceedingly difficult to extract a meaningful picture from the mass of detailed operations this method records (Hawisher, 1989). Neither was it possible for the researchers to observe every subject all through the writing process, which would have required them all to write out of class in special individual sessions. Apart from being very difficult to organize, such sessions would have been of quite a different type from the regular class writing sessions which we wished to study. Moreover, the distinction between between-draft and in-process revision is not so clear in a word processing as a pen-and-paper context. In the latter context, a new draft usually means a completely new version written afresh from the start, with reference to an earlier draft. Hence, revisions introduced at this stage may be different from those made in, and out of, writing new text within a draft. However, in the word processing context it is rare to start over in this way, as the very nature of word processing allows and encourages change to the existing text rather than retyping again from the start. To an extent, then, all revision by word processing is 'in process', and distinct drafts arise just as often or as rarely as the writers produce a printout (see discussion in Pennington, 1996b, chs. 2-3).[4]

An important additional source of information on the peer feedback was observation. This was carried out by the first author, an Arabic speaker, listening in on pairs during the treatment phase—i.e., for the first part of the second period in each of the five sessions. Apart from establishing that the subjects were indeed doing what they were supposed to do, this procedure provided valuable qualitative data on the kind of feedback being given by peers. To conduct the observation, the researcher visited each pair in rotation for a fixed time and noted down the kinds of things being talked about with the help of a nine-category observation sheet which listed aspects of language the subjects might be focusing on and other activities they might be engaged in (e.g., solving a computer problem or conversing off task).

Finally, to provide some further insight on the self-assessors comparable to the observation for the peer reviewers, a questionnaire was administered to them just after the final draft had been printed. This elicited responses about what the subjects had been doing in the immediately preceding session under the same headings as the observation sheet and took under ten minutes to complete. In addition, two subjects were in-

---

[4] Most experienced computer writers report expanding the number of drafts in the sense of full hardcopy text as a result of access to word processing and printing utilities. In pen-and-paper conditions, production of only one draft is probably the norm for most writers and even professional writers would be unlikely to generate more than three drafts, whereas in word processing conditions, product of two drafts is common even among novice writers, and professional writers might produce many more than this (e.g., in my own work for publication, 6-8 drafts is the norm, with up to 12 in some cases). (Editor's note)

terviewed after each session for five minutes, to obtain 'open' responses about the self-assessment that might be missed by a questionnaire.

4.2.6. Data Analysis

Some damage was done to the research plan by the extent of absenteeism, lateness, and computer problems, which meant that some subjects in some sessions produced only one draft. In none of the sessions did all twenty subjects attend and produce usable protocols, the worst occasion being session five, at the end of term, when only nine subjects completed the task. Forty-two pairs of peer feedback drafts, and 24 pairs of self-assessment drafts were available for analysis from the five sessions, i.e., just two-thirds of the planned 100 pairs of drafts, along with 14 baseline final drafts. Only one subject produced a complete set of five pairs of drafts and a baseline protocol. Hence, some planned repeated measures analyses comparing the five topics and looking for progress over sessions from the baseline were not feasible, and the following account depends largely on average scores for subjects over the five sessions.

Several tables present the counts and scores in their original form as recorded using the relevant instruments. For ease of comparison and display in graphs, we have re-expressed all the ESLCP scores as percentages for the five aspects measured (they are originally on scales with different maxima and minima). For convenience, we have similarly expressed length figures as a percentage of 550 words, which seemed to be the effective maximum achievable in the time available. Furthermore, for the graphic presentation, we have rescaled to a common form the questionnaire and observation results for the two groups. All statistics were calculated with *SPSS for Windows*, using, unless otherwise stated, independent groups t-tests, linear stepwise multiple regression, and Pearson *r* correlation coefficients.

4.3.   FINDINGS

We present here the primary results with brief discussion relating to research questions 1-8. Key findings are given a more comprehensive interpretation in a separate Discussion section.

4.3.1.   Final Draft Quality in Relation to Revision Mode

As can be read from Table 4.1, the self-assessors did better than the peer reviewers on all measures of final draft quality during the period of the study. However, the differences are far from significant, other than in length of text, which is borderline significant (i.e., actually slightly over 0.05). There is therefore no prima facie support for an advantageous effect of peer feedback on final draft quality during the period of the research (RQ1).

Group	Self-Assessment (n = 8)		Peer Feedback (n = 12)		Test of Difference	
	mean	*sd*	*mean*	*sd*	*t*	*p*
Mechanics	4.87	0.27	4.80	0.33	0.50	0.62
Grammar	20.14	3.12	18.28	3.04	1.33	0.20
Vocabulary	14.06	2.05	13.53	2.21	0.54	0.60
Organization	14.08	1.28	13.71	2.32	0.41	0.69
Content	21.45	2.33	20.02	3.37	1.04	0.31
Length	339.4	109.1	226.9	123.1	2.09	0.05

Table 4.1. Final Draft Quality, Averaged over Five Sessions

Group	Self-Assessment (n = 6)		Peer Feedback (n = 8)		Test of Difference	
	mean	*sd*	*mean*	*sd*	*t*	*p*
Mechanics	4.83	0.41	4.63	0.52	0.81	0.43
Grammar	21.83	1.72	20.13	1.81	1.78	0.10
Vocabulary	17.17	0.75	15.37	1.77	2.57	0.03
Organization	17.67	1.37	15.13	1.96	2.71	0.02
Content	26.17	2.64	22.00	2.73	2.87	0.01
Length	212.8	85.6	150.5	43.6	1.79	0.10
Total ESLCP Score	87.67		77.26			

Table 4.2. Baseline Final Draft Quality

As we see from Table 4.2, in the baseline task the group destined to be self-assessors again did better than the group destined to be peer reviewers on all measures. However, the differences are more marked than those in Table 4.1, with the groups differing significantly on three of the six quality aspects measured, and being far from a significant difference only on one measure (that of mechanics). On these three measures there are significant interactions between group (peer feedback versus self-assessment) and time of measure (at baseline versus over study) for the 14 subjects who provided baseline data: on final draft quality of vocabulary, organization, and content they differed at the baseline but not in the study (vocabulary: $F = 5.97$, $p = 0.03$; organization: $F = 10.32$, $p = 0.007$; content: $F = 7.63$, $p = 0.017$). Since on the baseline task the two groups revised in the same way, and differed only in writing ability, we feel this result has important implications relative to the performance recorded during the study itself (see discussion below).

4.3.2. Between-Draft Change in Quality in Relation to Revision Mode

The results for between-draft quality change show that the peer reviewers outperformed the self-assessors on all measures except length, but this difference is significant only in the category of mechanics. On length improvement the difference is in favor of the self-assessors, and not far from significance. Overall there is a small degree of support here for the superiority of peer feedback with respect to between-draft quality improvement (RQ2). As can be seen in Table 4.3, standard deviations for between-draft quality change on all measures are in many cases of the same order of magnitude as means, signaling considerable variation in individual performance within each group, and making significance hard to achieve.

Group	Self-Assessment (n = 8)		Peer Feedback (n = 12)		Test of Difference	
	mean	*sd*	*mean*	*sd*	*t*	*p*
Mechanics	0.09	0.19	0.45	0.42	-2.56	0.02
Grammar	1.29	1.39	1.39	0.76	-0.21	0.84
Vocabulary	1.49	1.23	1.54	0.76	-0.11	0.91
Organization	1.24	1.41	1.51	0.78	-0.55	0.59
Content	1.43	1.21	1.77	1.17	-0.63	0.54
Length	150.8	62.1	96.4	67.7	1.82	0.08

Table 4.3. Between-Draft Quality Change, Averaged over Five Sessions

4.3.3. Improvement over Time on Measures of Quality

RQ3 raised the question as to whether the peer feedback group would improve more than the self-assessment group over the five sessions on either final draft quality or between-draft quality change. In fact, an investigation of the figures for the individual sessions evidenced no clear progression within either group on any measures of quality, perhaps in part due to the slightly different membership of each group in each session (see, however, the further discussion below).

4.3.4. Writing Achievement Grade in Relation to Measures of Quality

Table 4.4 indicates that, as expected, the exam achievement grade of subjects correlates positively with measures of their writing quality other than between-draft quality improvement in mechanics. The correlations with final draft quality are mainly strong and significant, especially in the baseline task; but the correlations with between-draft quality improvement are not, other than those of achievement grade with length and, to a lesser extent, with improvement in mechanics.

Correlation of Achievement Grade with:	Final Draft Quality at Baseline (n = 14)		Final Draft Quality during Study (n = 12)		Between-Draft Quality Improvement	
	r	p	r	p	r	p
Mechanics	0.40	0.159	0.41	0.071	-0.41	0.072
Grammar	0.72	0.004	0.64	0.003	0.10	0.686
Vocabulary	0.76	0.002	0.56	0.011	0.27	0.246
Organization	0.81	0.001	0.42	0.067	0.06	0.791
Content	0.76	0.001	0.58	0.008	0.20	0.409
Length	0.78	0.001	0.53	0.017	0.65	0.002

Table 4.4. Relationship Between Achievement Grade and Three Quality Measures

As anticipated from the known levels of the classes in the study, there is a significant difference between the two groups in achievement grade on the prior end-of-term examination in writing skill (t = 3.46, p = 0.01). This difference is in favor of the self-assessment group (mean 27.75) affirming that, on the whole, there were better writers in this group than in the peer feedback group (mean 19.25).

In order to provide an answer to RQ4, concerning the relative strengths of the effects of the treatment (i.e., mode of revision) and subjects' achievement grade, the two between-draft change measures which exhibited the most prominent group differences and correlations—those for length and improvement in mechanics—were analyzed as dependent variables in stepwise multiple regression analyses, using a .05 threshold value, with grade and group as predictors. Opposite results were obtained for the two dependent variables. The result for mechanics is that group emerged as the sole dominant explanatory variable ($F = 4.93$, $p = 0.04$, $R^2 = 0.22$). By contrast, writing exam grade is the sole predictor isolated for length ($F = 12.8$, $p = 0.002$, $R^2 = 0.46$). Analyzing the final draft quality scores in the same way, achievement grade always emerged as the sole predictor. Thus, in most instances a subject's general level of writing skill appears to have a stronger effect on the quality of their writing than their mode of revision.

4.3.5. Types and Spans of Revision Change in Relation to Revision Mode

Tables 4.5 and 4.6 show that, on the whole, the peer reviewers made fewer changes affected meaning and large-size structures than did the self-assessors. Conversely, the peer reviewers made more non-meaning changing and small-size structure changes, e.g., at the levels of letters and words. However, due in part to the high variation within groups, none of the differences between groups is significant, though two are nearly so: the self-assessors outdid the peer reviewers in number of macrostructure additions and in number of changes at multi-sentence level (variables which are obviously closely related to each other). The greater text-span of revisions in the self-assessment group is against our expectation with respect to RQ6. Furthermore, peer reviewers made approximately three fewer changes per draft than the self-assessors—not more changes as expected (means 10.08 and 12.97)—but this difference is not significant ($t = 1.46$, $p = 0.16$). With respect to RQ5, not all subjects but only the peer reviewers consistently made greater improvements on surface aspects than on higher-level features of organization and content.

Table 4.7 summarizes the findings from the observation of the peer reviewers and the questionnaire administered to the self-assessors. The peer reviewers were observed talking most about content and mechanics, and spending a fair amount of time off task. Superficially this does not entirely accord with the findings for actual revisions made. The self-assessors claimed a much more even spread of attention over the various aspects of the task, and very little time off task. However, this result is suspect, as taken up in the discussion below.

Group	Self-Assessment (n = 8)		Peer Feedback (n = 12)		Test of Difference	
Change Type	*mean*	*sd*	*mean*	*sd*	*t*	*p*
FORM						
Spelling, etc.	1.00	1.23	1.40	1.55	-0.65	0.53
Tense, etc.	0.41	0.71	0.54	0.58	-0.45	0.66
Abbreviation	0.06	0.18	0.03	0.09	0.58	0.57
Punctuation	0.50	0.97	0.66	0.51	-0.48	0.64
Paragraphing	0.28	0.39	0.16	0.22	0.89	0.39
Format	0.95	0.79	1.02	0.61	-0.24	0.81
MEANING- PRESERVING						
Addition	0.28	0.52	0.56	0.52	-1.17	0.26
Deletion	0.25	0.38	0.52	0.71	-0.99	0.33
Substitution	1.01	1.50	0.74	0.61	0.58	0.57
Permutation, etc.	0.13	0.19	0.20	0.43	-0.46	0.65
Total surface/ non-meaning changing	4.87		5.83			
MICRO- STRUCTURE						
Addition	0.31	0.44	0.29	0.27	0.12	0.91
Deletion	0.06	0.18	0.05	0.13	0.12	0.90
Substitution	0.34	0.69	0.41	0.60	-0.24	0.82
Permutation, etc.	0.06	0.18	0.00	0.00	1.00	0.35
MACRO- STRUCTURE						
Addition	6.86	4.70	3.29	2.22	2.00	0.08
Deletion	0.16	0.35	0.03	0.09	1.01	0.34
Substitution	0.25	0.35	0.18	0.57	0.29	0.77
Permutation, etc.	0.06	0.17	0.00	0.00	1.02	0.35
Total meaning-changing	8.10		4.25			

Table 4.5. Revisions Classified by Type, Averaged over Five Sessions

Group	Self-Assessment (n = 8)		Peer Feedback (n = 12)		Test of Difference	
Span of Change	*mean*	*sd*	*mean*	*sd*	*t*	*p*
Graphic	2.95	2.03	3.92	2.29	-0.98	0.34
Lexical	0.95	0.98	1.26	1.03	-0.68	0.50
Phrasal	0.59	0.71	0.83	0.84	-0.64	0.53
Clausal	0.72	0.86	0.39	0.30	1.04	0.33
Sentential	0.72	1.05	0.36	0.70	0.93	0.37
Multi-sentential	6.61	4.19	3.44	2.89	2.00	0.06

Table 4.6. Revisions Classified by Text Span, Averaged over Five Sessions

Group	Self-Assessment self-rating of time (mins.) spent (n = 8)		Peer Feedback observed time spent (n = 12)
Activity	*mean*	*sd*	*Percent*
Presentation	3.05	0.51	7.50
Mechanics	3.10	0.84	15.70
Grammar	2.25	1.16	5.20
Vocabulary	3.25	0.59	3.75
Organization	2.95	0.33	3.00
Content	3.00	0.95	30.80
Working computer	2.60	1.53	6.70
Talking to teacher	1.38	1.13	0.75
Silence, off task, etc.	0.90	1.20	26.20

Table 4.7. Time Spent on Activities during Revision Periods of the Five Sessions

4.3.6.   Types of Revision Change in Relation to Writing Achievement Grade

Our expectation with respect to RQ7 was confirmed, in that achievement grade correlates significantly and positively with number of meaning-changing revisions ($r = 0.59$, $p = 0.006$), and negatively with number of non-meaning changing revisions ($r = -0.51$, $p = 0.021$). A more detailed analysis shows that the main contributor to the former result is a strong positive correlation between achievement grade and number of macrostructure additions ($r = 0.57$, $p = 0.009$), while the main contributors to the latter result are negative correlations of achievement grade with number of punctuation changes ($r = -0.53$, $p = 0.017$) and number of meaning-preserving additions ($r = -0.62$, $p = 0.003$). Multiple regression analysis with grade and group as predictors confirms that once grade is included, group (i.e., revision mode) has no significant additional explanatory power (for meaning-changing revisions $F = 9.82$, $p = 0.006$, $R^2 = 0.35$; for non-meaning changing revisions $F = 6.42$, $p = 0.021$, $R^2 = 0.26$).

4.3.7. Relationship between Types and Spans of Revision Change and Between-Draft Quality Change

RQ8 was examined through a study of the correlations between, on the one hand, numbers of revisions (classified into 18 types according to the Faigley and Witte categories) and, on the other hand, the quality change scores (in the five ESLCP categories plus length), as calculated for each group separately. There were striking differences between groups in the number of positive correlations of any size obtained. Out of 108 correlations between (i) the 6 quality change types and (ii) the 18 revision change types, 82 were negative for the self-assessment group, but only 43 for the peer feedback group. Out of 36 correlations examined between frequencies of change at the six levels of revision span (graphic, lexical, phrasal, clausal, sentential, multi-sentential) and scores on the six quality change categories, 21 were positive for the peer feedback group, while only seven were positive for the self-assessors.

This prima facie support for the existence of a much closer relationship in the peer feedback than in the self-assessment group between the revision changes made and the quality improvement obtained is supported by Tables 4.8 and 4.9, which display instances where the correlation in these two measures was +0.40 or greater for either group. The self-assessors register only three strong positive correlations, between (i) spelling revisions and mechanics improvement, (ii) macro-addition and length, and (iii) multi-sentential changes and length. In contrast, the peer reviewers exhibit many more (18) positive correlations above +.40 and with much higher p-values (other than for the correlation of spelling and mechanics, where both r and p are higher for the self-assessment group than for the peer feedback group). The results for the peer feedback group shown in the two tables reveal positive correlations between revisions, whether considered in terms of type or span, and all of the relevant categories of improvement. Furthermore, most of the correlations make sense as pairings where one would expect changes of the stated type to affect quality of the stated type, taking into account the general lack of simple correspondence between the Faigley and Witte categories and those of the Jacobs ESLCP.

	Group	Self-Assessment (n = 8)		Peer Feedback (n = 12)	
Type of Revision	Quality Change	r	p	r	p
Spelling	Mechanics	0.94	0.001	0.42	0.180
Punctuation	Mechanics	0.00	1.00	0.48	0.114
Punctuation	Organization	-0.31	0.460	0.71	0.010
Paragraphing	Organization	-0.55	0.162	0.46	0.132
Paragraphing	Length	0.35	0.398	0.54	0.067
Meaning-preserving permutations, etc.	Grammar	-0.12	0.769	0.59	0.015
Micro-deletion	Mechanics	-0.20	0.629	0.56	0.056
Macro-addition	Vocabulary	-0.27	0.522	0.71	0.010
Macro-addition	Content	-0.03	0.940	0.60	0.040
Macro-addition	Length	0.79	0.020	0.82	0.001

Table 4.8. Major Correlations Between Revision Changes of Different Types and Between-Draft Quality Change Score

	Group	Self-Assessment (n = 8)		Peer Feedback (n = 12)	
Span of Revision	Quality Change	r	p	r	p
Graphic	Mechanics	0.56	0.151	0.52	0.080
Phrasal	Mechanics	-0.21	0.614	0.55	0.062
Phrasal	Grammar	0.04	0.917	0.57	0.051
Phrasal	Organization	0.06	0.886	0.43	0.161
Clausal	Mechanics	-0.15	0.729	0.66	0.027
Multi-sentential	Vocabulary	-0.23	0.579	0.68	0.015
Multi-sentential	Content	-0.05	0.916	0.66	0.019
Multi-sentential	Length	0.79	0.020	0.83	0.001

Table 4.9. Major Correlations Between Revision Changes of Different Spans and Between-Draft Quality Change Score

4.4.   DISCUSSION

4.4.1.   Final Draft Quality

One can see from Figures 4.1 and 4.2 (based on Tables 4.1 and 4.2) that scores are generally better for both groups for the surface level aspects of text, being close to the maximum for mechanics, and go down to a relative low for the higher level aspect of content, where the scores are characterized by the ESLCP as 'fair to poor'. This not only confirms the teacher's prior judgment of the subjects' weaknesses, but also exhibits a common profile of writing ability, such that learners are successively less expert at aspects of writing the 'higher' the level of those aspects (assuming the ordering with mechanics as the lowest- or most surface-level concerns, and organization and content as the highest-level concerns). This is not necessarily a direct reflection of the amount of actual revision effort expended, however.

The general level of performance of both groups is somewhat better on grammar, vocabulary, organization, and content in the baseline task than in the five tasks of the study. This could well be due to the different discourse type of the baseline task (a letter rather than an essay), which also probably accounts for the much shorter length. What it is more important to consider, however, is the group contrast between the baseline and the study (the interactions).

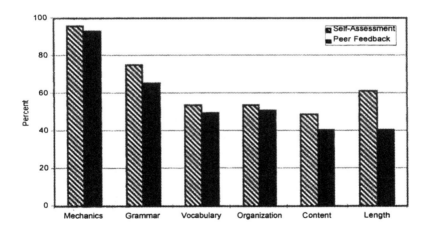

Figure 4.1. Overall Final Draft Quality

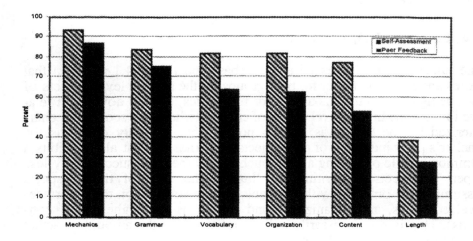

Figure 4.2. Baseline Final Draft Quality

Considering group differences, the fact the self-assessors outperformed peer reviewers during the study by only small and non-significant margins (on all measures except length) is important. The self-assessors did markedly better than the peer reviewers on most aspects of the baseline writing task, with a successively greater differential the higher the level of the aspect of writing involved. The three significant interactions reported in the Results section confirm the shift from a clear baseline difference to no difference in the study on three of the measures. Furthermore, the members of the self-assessment group were significantly better on the prior writing achievement exam than were the members of the peer feedback group. Consequently, the self-assessors might have been expected to do significantly better on most measures of final draft quality during the study, if the interventions of the study were having no effect. The results demonstrate that, during the time of the study, something—which we interpret to be the peer feedback treatment—had an effect on the peer reviewers that enabled them to improve their final draft performance to a level much closer to that of the higher grade self-assessment group in areas other than mechanics (where it was already close), grammar, and length (where it stayed considerably behind for the entire duration of the study).

The findings for the relationship between writing achievement level and final draft quality are compatible with this interpretation. It is reassuring rather than surprising to find that there are positive correlations between writing achievement grade as measured by the previous school exam and final draft scores on all aspects of writing (Table 4.4). The fact that the correlations are generally slightly stronger with the baseline final draft scores than with the final draft scores of the study could be a reflection of the effect of the differential treatments: peer feedback may be seen as reducing slightly the gross effect of subjects' writing skill level on their final draft performance. Nevertheless, the multiple regression analysis shows that a student's final draft quality was always related more strongly to their general level of writing skill than to their mode of revision.

We conclude, then, that using peer feedback has not been shown to enable writers of a slightly lower level of writing proficiency to outdo higher ability writers revising on their own, in terms of the quality of final drafts produced on a word processor. Possibly that is too much to expect of any revision method. However, there is some evidence that peer feedback in the context of word processing did enable the peer reviewers to close the gap on their higher proficiency schoolmates in the key areas of vocabulary, organization, and content (cf. RQ1).

4.4.2. Between-Draft Changes in Quality

Over the five sessions of the study, both groups made some improvement between drafts in all of the quality aspects measured. As seen in Figure 4.3, the improvements are on the order of 10 percent of the marking scale for the three areas that we highlighted in the discussion of the final draft quality results: vocabulary, organization, and content. This amount of improvement seems modest but would probably be regarded by most teachers as a worthwhile result for both types of focused feedback within a process approach where students do their writing on a word processor. Furthermore, the improvement scores do not tail off for successively higher level aspects of writing in the way the scores for final draft quality tend to. Still, there is substantial room for further improvement in all areas of composition quality except possibly mechanics (compare Figure 4.1).

We interpret the slightly greater amount of improvement achieved by the peer reviewers on most measures as a consequence of the peer feedback, and a reason for this group's final drafts approaching so close in quality to those of the self-assessors in many aspects other than length, when prior to the study they did not. The pattern of improvement varies depending on the aspect of writing, with improvement in mechanics and length showing a different pattern from other measured changes. The correlations of achievement grade with between-draft quality change scores (Table 4.4) mirror this difference in patterning in respect of the prominent, but opposite, relationships with improvement in length and mechanics.

In mechanics, the peer reviewers, of lower general writing grade, improved markedly more than the self-assessors, whose overall change score for this measure is very low (though we shall see they did spend some time revising this aspect). Indeed, the self-assessors' average mechanics score did not change at all in three of the five sessions. This result seems to be due to this group's first drafts having good mechanics already, thus leaving little room for improvement in this area (ceiling effect). By contrast, the peer reviewers exhibited a slightly greater improvement in mechanics than in the higher-level aspects of writing. This may be seen as consistent with what might be expected for relatively unskilled writers rather than for peer reviewers, but the multiple regression result shows that in fact group was the dominant factor over grade in predicting improvement scores in mechanics. We conclude, then, that peer feedback does reinforce the tendency of relatively unskilled writers to improve especially in the lowest- or surface-level aspects of writing (cf. RQ2, RQ4).

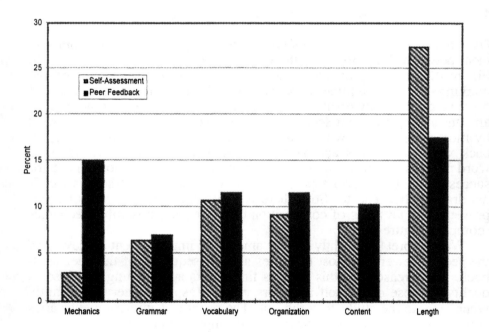

Figure 4.3. Overall Improvement in Quality between Drafts

The greater improvement in length, compared with the size of improvement in other measures, suggests that a lot of attention was paid in the second period of each session to adding material to the first draft, particularly by the self-assessors. It is possible that the teacher's encouragement to the subjects to add material while revising may have had some overall effect here. Moreover, the way the study was organized may have helped the self-assessors to improve the length of their texts more then the peer reviewers, and so to end up with final drafts of much greater length. This is because the peer reviewers, during the half hour when they were talking in pairs about each other's work, could not at the same time add text to their first drafts. During that time, however, the self-assessors were free, if they so wished, to spend the time adding text rather than going over the first draft making other revisions. Thus the length of the self-assessors' final drafts in the study exceeded those of the peer reviewers by a greater margin even than in the baseline task. Nevertheless, we cannot rule out that the higher grade self-assessors may have also been more fluent. In any case, the multiple regression result confirms that writing skill grade affects length improvement more than revision mode. For whatever reason, peer feedback did not help our lower level writers to write more (cf. RQ2).

The between-draft quality improvement scores for grammar are quite low for both groups, and this is perhaps reflected in the fact that the differential between the two groups in final draft quality for grammar remains much the same in the study as in the baseline task. By contrast, the improvement scores for vocabulary, organization, and content are a little higher, and show slightly greater (though far from significant) differences between the two groups, in favor of the peer reviewers. Despite the modesty of the amount of improvement made by the peer reviewers here, these three areas of improvement seem to have had the greatest impact on their final draft quality, since it is in these three areas that the peer reviewers reduce the gap between them and the self-assessors most markedly compared with the baseline. The weak or negligible correlations of achievement grade with improvement in vocabulary, organization, and content may simply reflect that some weaker students as well as some higher achievers may have been enabled through peer feedback to make some moderate between-draft improvements in these areas. However, given the extreme non-significance of our results in this area (Tables 4.3 and 4.4), we cannot claim to have shown conclusively that between-draft improvement in grammar, vocabulary, organization, or content is affected either by peer feedback or by general writing ability (cf. RQ4).

4.4.3. Between-Draft Revision Changes

In order to properly understand the effect of different modes of revision, it is necessary to look not only at effects on quality, but also at the between-draft revision changes, as distinct from but also in comparison to the between-draft quality changes. The subjects as a whole seemingly make relatively few between-draft changes, in proportion to the length of the drafts: 10-13 per draft on average, in drafts of several hundred words in length. However, a single change in the Faigley and Witte scheme, if it is a micro- or macrostructure addition, can actually contain many words. Furthermore, given our design, we do not know how much revision of the first drafts occurred while composing them within the first period. It was also observed that, especially in the last session, the students were not always taking the task as seriously as one would want.

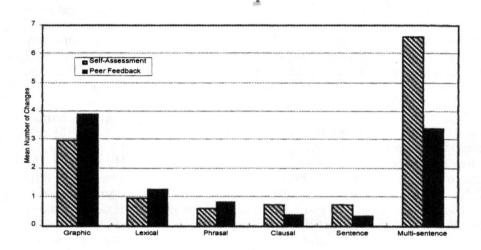

Figure 4.4. Text Span Revisions between Drafts

In terms of type of change, the changes are mainly of macrostructure addition, spelling, format, and meaning-preserving substitution (Table 4.5 and Figure 4.5). In terms of span (i.e., size of grammatical structure involved), they are predominantly at the highest and lowest levels (Table 4.6 and Figure 4.6). Several types of revision change in the Faigley and Witte scheme were made very rarely, especially ones involving abbreviation, and micro- or macrostructural deletion or permutation. The picture overall is of subjects concerned primarily with spelling, punctuation, and format, at the graphic level, and with addition of text, at the multi-sentential level, but relatively less with what lies in between these lowest and highest level extremes, or with moving material around.[5] The additions of text were observed to be often at the end of the first draft, though the Faigley and Witte scheme itself has no way of recording this. It is notable that formatting emerges as something focused on by both groups almost as much as spelling and capitalization. Formatting covers changes in spacing, choice of font, etc., and inserting things like pictures, date, and teacher information on the front page.

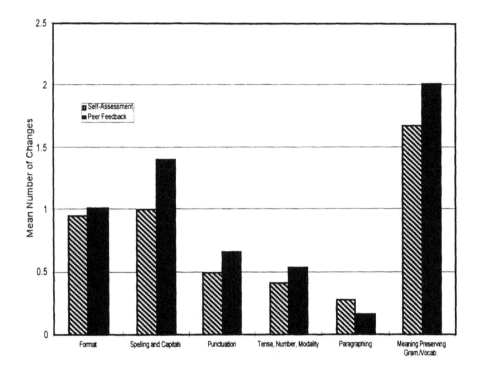

Figure 4.5. Non-Meaning Changing Revisions between Drafts

The differences between groups which come closest to significance are those for number of macrostructure additions and number of changes at the multi-sentential level of span. Macrostructure additions in the Faigley and Witte scheme are identified as additions which would alter the summary one would make of the whole composition, compared with

---

[5] Compare these results with those of Bisaillon (this volume), who found that with revision training, students made most improvement at a "middle" level of revision. (Editor's note)

microstructure additions which add details but not major ideas. Consequently, although 'structure' in these terms refers to semantic rather than grammatical structure, macrostructure additions tend to involve larger—multi-sentential—spans, and may often consist of entire added paragraphs. In the revision period, the self-assessors, compared with the peer reviewers, made about twice as many additions to their essays which expressed ideas radically different from those in the previous draft. However, general writing ability grade of student is related even more strongly (and significantly) than group to the frequency of these revision changes. We therefore conclude that the amount of revision of this span and type is due more to the fact that the self-assessors were of higher ability than to the fact that they were relying on self-assessment for feedback on their work. A similar line of reasoning applies to some of the revision types at the low- or surface-level end of the spectrum. Thus, punctuation changes and meaning-preserving additions are related to writing achievement grade rather than to revision mode, as lower level writers make more of these changes regardless of mode of revision.

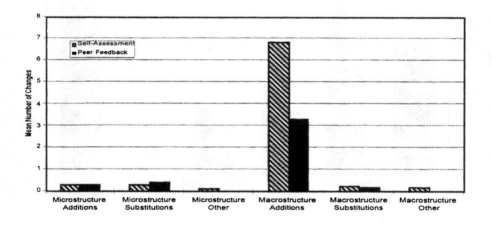

Figure 4.6. Meaning-Changing Revisions between Drafts

The overall pattern of difference between the groups can be described as one of the peer reviewers making fewer changes than the self-assessors. In addition, the peer reviewers revise more non-meaning changing aspects of their text, at a smaller size of structural span, up to phrase level, while the self-assessors revise more meaning-changing aspects, at the level of the clause or above. However, once again the evidence of the multiple regression analysis is that it is the ability level of the subjects more than their mode of revision that produces this profile (cf. RQ6, RQ7).

The relatively small overall numbers of revisions per essay has been noted by others for relatively proficient writers (Bridwell, 1980; Olson, 1990). With respect to the attention paid to format, it has been observed (e.g., Piper, 1989) that word processing tends to encourage writers to focus on such matters partly because it makes them easy to do and partly because such changes have a motivating effect of making the written product look attractive. The danger of course is that formatting may take up revision time and effort that would be better spent on more substantive matters. However, this does not seem to have happened in our study to any marked extent, given the evidence of the attention also paid to higher level changes.

The relative disuse of revision options such as permutation, deletion, and consolidation rather than addition has been also reported (e.g., Cochran-Smith, 1991; Faigley &Witte, 1981; Hawisher, 1987), and the wholesale addition of text specifically at the end of a first draft was noted by Piper (1996). Although word processing allows for great freedom of deletion, substitution, and permutation, writers do not always exploit the available options, e.g., the cut-and-paste and highlight-and-drag facilities. This phenomenon of ignoring other kinds of changes in favor of additions at the end of a text seems reminiscent of writing with pen and paper in a linear progression, in which additions at the end of a text are generally easier to make than other kinds of changes. It is discouraging that our subjects, who had the benefit of a teacher promoting the process approach and a medium which facilitated other sorts of revisions nevertheless still revised predominantly by adding text to what had already been written.

Finally, many studies show, as we also found, that higher proficiency writers revise more at higher levels of structure and meaning (Faigley & Witte, 1981; Piper, 1996; Sommers, 1980) than do those of lower proficiency. Overall it is noticeable how much the results of our study match those of pen-and-paper studies (RQ9) and those investigating most high-proficiency student groups of other nationalities (RQ10). Paradoxically, however, Al-Semari's (1993) Saudi students, though also claimed to be advanced, focused much more exclusively on surface changes. Our subjects instead compare well with the advanced or expert L1 writers described by Faigley and Witte (1981) as making on the order of 19-23 major meaning changes per 1000 words of text. If we calculate the number of macrostructural changes of our subjects per number of words of first draft and scale it to 1000 words we come out with 27 such revisions per 1000 words for the peer reviewers and 39 for the self-assessors. However, these figures may well be in part an artifact of the incompleteness of the 'first drafts' in our study.

4.4.4. The Distinction between Composing and Revising

The striking amount of macrostructure addition (and consequent between-draft changes in length) that we have reported draws attention to a
complex conceptual issue which is not entirely clear in the revision literature, let alone, no doubt, in the minds of students when told, as they all
were in that crucial half hour of every second period, to "revise". In
short, when is revision not actually revision, but rather composing new
text? The Faigley and Witte revision classification scheme can accommodate a large amount of added text as a single change under the heading of
'macrostructure addition'. However, the fact that any amount of addition
can be classified as revision does not mean that it is always appropriate
for it to be so classified. It is not by any means clear that all of what is
added to a first draft should be regarded as 'revising what has been
written' rather than 'doing more writing', or in Hayes and Flower's
(1983) terms, more 'translating' in the sense of putting thoughts into
words for the first time. Rather, it is possible to argue that there is a conceptual difference between (i) addition of material to a draft deemed by
the writer to be complete though provisional (a form of revision as seen,
for example, in Bridwell, 1980), and (ii) addition of material to a draft
deemed by the writer to be incomplete, or only 'half-written'. In the latter
case, later addition of material is not really revision of the first draft but
completion of it. In word processing, where the notion of a draft as a
distinct stage in the writing process does not in any case so naturally exist, since new drafts are not normally rewritten from scratch, these two
types of addition become particularly hard to distinguish.

In the last paragraph the criterion presented for distinguishing between addition that is a part of revising and addition that results from
further composing was the perception of the writer. However, even in a
think-aloud study, such perceptions may be hard to ascertain fully. In the
present study it did not occur to the researchers in advance to devise
some way of dealing with this, and consequently all additions made in
the second period were counted as revisions. However, the sheer quantity of addition leads us to suspect that a fair proportion of it is probably
not true revision. The students in this study seem in some measure to
have interpreted 'writing a first draft' as 'composing as much as possible
within the first period', and 'revising the first draft to produce a final
draft' in the second period in a broad sense to include 'completing the
composition' as well as 'reviewing what has been composed'. The
teacher's exhortation to add material in the second period may have enhanced this tendency.

As a percentage of the first draft length, on average the peer reviewers added 73% more words in the second draft, and the self-assessors
80%. We have already noted that this is high compared with some other
studies. Furthermore, a number of first drafts, on inspection, read very

much as incomplete, rather than complete but provisional. For example they are very short, break off in mid-sentence, or clearly lack a structural element, such as a conclusion, which will be present in the final version. The extreme case is that of the subject who by the end of the first period had produced a supposed 'first draft' consisting of no more than three lines of text.

A consequence of the above conclusions is that the moderate between-draft improvements in organization we found (Figure 4.3) may in part be an artifact of the incompleteness of some of the first drafts. An incomplete draft will inevitably score lower than a complete one on organization in the ESLCP, since among its specifications for grading of this aspect it refers to "not enough to evaluate" and "incomplete sequencing".

4.4.5. The Relationship between Revision and Quality Changes

As already noted, in principle the findings for numbers of between-draft revisions and the scores for between-draft quality change could be unrelated: writers might be doing a lot of revision but achieving no increase in quality, or the reverse (RQ8). A basic finding in our study is that the peer reviewers made fewer revision changes overall than the self-assessors, but, as the correlations reported in the Results section show (Tables 4.8 and 4.9), these revisions seem much more closely related to improvements in quality than do those of the self-assessors. This suggests that peer feedback stimulates more cost-effective revision changes than does self-assessment alone. On the other hand, since, on the whole, the peer reviewers wrote shorter essays, a given number of changes would have a greater impact on one of their essays than the same number of changes would have on an essay written by a member of the self-assessment group. In fact, on average, a final draft from a self-assessor would have been altered by 3.82 changes per 100 words of text, while one from a member of the peer feedback group would have undergone 4.44 changes per 100 words. However, we do not feel that this 'density effect' alone is enough to account for the much better relationship found between numbers of revisions and quality improvement scores for the peer reviewers than the self-assessors.

It is only with respect to improvement in quality of mechanics and length that both groups record substantial positive correlations between numbers of changes and quality of changes. These are also the areas where, as we have already seen, the two groups made the most changes and obtained the most marked improvements. At the lowest level of letters (i.e., graphic span), a greater number of spelling changes resulted in a higher quality improvement score for mechanics regardless of revision mode. This effect could be due to the use of the spell-checker by both groups (which they were indeed observed using). However, it is noticeable even here that there are further different types and spans of revision change which are related to improvement in quality of mechanics for the peer reviewers but which do not show any such connection for the self-assessors. Peer feedback seems to have enabled the peer reviewers to ensure that any changes they made in punctuation were beneficial, despite their generally lower writing proficiency level, while the self-assessors' changes in punctuation have no relationship with their improvements in mechanics whatsoever. Furthermore, for the peer reviewers, microstructure deletions at phrasal and clausal levels of span correlate with changes in mechanics. These are harder to explain, but it seems most likely that improvements in mechanics arose through punctuation changes made along with deletions of small stretches of text.

For both groups, an increase in multi-sentential macrostructure additions is related to an increase in length, but since these categories are connected by definition, this is not a very interesting result. What is much more telling is that the peer reviewers alone record a relationship between number of multi-sentential macrostructure additions and improvement scores for quality of vocabulary and content. Since the peer reviewers were of lower general writing proficiency than the self-assessors, it seems hardly likely that it was their general ability level that enabled them to make their macrostructure additions effective in these ways. We can only conclude that it was the peer feedback discussion that enabled them to make additions of text which contained high quality content and vocabulary, and not only added to the length of the text.

There are no types or spans of change which correlate strongly with between-draft improvements in grammar or organization for the self-assessment group. However, once again, the peer feedback group exhibits some clear relationships for these aspects of improvement. It seems entirely to be expected that, if changes to text were being made effectively, changes in punctuation and paragraphing would be reflected in improved scores for quality of organization. Yet this relationship seems to arise only when peer feedback is being used. It is also possible to see why meaning-preserving permutations, consolidations, etc., at the phrasal level of structure, though rare, should relate to improvement in quality of grammar. An example of such a change is when a subject revised *our country beauty* to *the beauty of our country*.

Despite the much more favorable picture for peer feedback in this area of our results, it must be noted that neither mode of revision seems to have given rise to relationships between some other pairs of variables which one might have expected to be related if revision were really effective. Examples are: number of macrostructure permutations with quality change score for organization; number of tense and modality changes with quality change score for grammar; number of lexical changes or meaning-preserving substitutions with quality change score for vocabulary. An example of the last is the revision of *they hold most of our records* to *they contain most of our records.* Still, these results provide some explanation for why it is that the peer reviewers, from rather fewer revision changes, the majority of which are, according to Faigley and Witte, 'non-meaning changing', might have improved slightly more than the self-assessors, especially in the key areas of vocabulary, organization, and content.

Olson (1990), in a pen-and-paper study with L1 writers, provides one of the relatively few comparable discussions of the relationship between revision changes and quality improvement. Students working with the help of peer feedback were found to be better able to revise, and improve quality, in the areas of mechanics, grammar, and vocabulary than those without peer feedback, just like our subjects. Olson found that self-assessors "made more content revisions than students who revised in pairs but showed a decline in rhetorical quality between rough and final drafts" (p. 28). This was not our finding exactly: our self-assessors did achieve an increase in quality of content, but not one commensurate with, or indeed related to, the quantity of meaning-changing revisions they made.

The effectiveness of the revisions made by the peer reviewers was further confirmed by an examination of the extent to which specific revision changes they made actually improved the text, when there was an identifiable error in the first draft. This is not something captured by the Faigley and Witte classification, which does not distinguish revision changes that are corrections from changes that result in error, nor deal with instances where changes were needed but not made at all. Changes made by our subjects were mostly correct. There was, however, a scattering of changes that made a student's text worse, i.e., introduced errors, such as *It's theirs....* changed to *Its theirs....* There were also instances of text left unchanged that needed correcting such as *from there own environment* which was left uncorrected by a writer in the peer feedback group who was clearly unable to spot this error either with the help of peer or spell-checker.

4.4.6. Observation and Questionnaire Evidence on the Revision Process

Figure 4.7 (based on Table 4.7) summarizes the findings of the observation and questionnaire over the five sessions. The graphs for the self-assessors are derived from the ratings they gave in response to questions about how much time they spent on each category of activity when revising. The graphs for the peer reviewers reflect the percentage of time that they were observed talking about each category, during the half hour of peer review when their behavior was sampled by one of the researchers listening in to them in turn. Clearly, there are several differences between the graphs of the two groups, and it is a matter of judgment how far they reflect different actual behavior in the groups or are an artifact of the different data gathering methods employed.

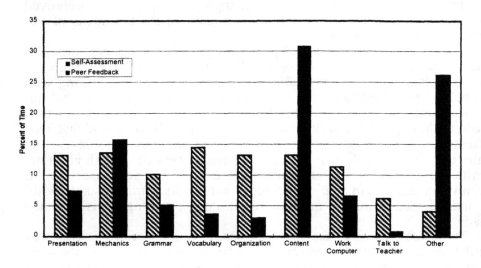

Figure 4.7. Use of Revision Time (Self-Assessment, Claimed; Peer Feedback, Observed)

The picture of the peer feedback group is largely compatible with our other findings. The relative high points for mechanics and for content are consistent with the number of changes we have seen in spelling and punctuation (Figure 4.5), the number of macro-additions (Figure 4.6), and the improvements recorded in mechanics vocabulary, organization, and content.[6] Furthermore, the amount of 'other' activity in the peer feedback group (e.g., silence or off task) is entirely realistic for the relatively unsupervised context in which the revision was taking place.

The fact that the amount of talk by the peer feedback group directly about grammar, vocabulary, and organization is small accords with the finding above that the improvements they achieved in these areas were not always related to changes made in the most obviously related aspects of the text. Thus, for example, it was the number of punctuation changes

---

[6] The dual focus on content and mechanics seems to be a consistent effect of peer feedback whether in the context of word processing or not, and whether in the context of explicit training or not (see Bisaillon, this volume; Brock & Pennington, this volume). (Editor's note)

that correlated most strongly with improvement score for organization, and discussion of punctuation would have been recorded in the observation schedule as discussion of mechanics. There is much to do in future studies to establish better the correspondences between the categories in these different evaluation schemes. Similarly, we saw that vocabulary improvement came on the back of macrostructure addition rather than representing simple lexical changes made to the text, and talk about such additions would have been recorded as discussion of content in the observation schedule. Furthermore, it is always possible that some changes we observed were not actually talked about directly during peer feedback, but were made in the remaining time of the second period when the students worked alone again and were consequent upon content changes that *were* talked about with peers. Talk about content may secondarily draw attention to instances where not quite the right lexical item was used.

On the other hand, the self-assessors' responses have the hallmarks of the kind of self-report that they are. The claimed 'other' activity is face-savingly low. And the profile of claimed attention to types of revision activity is relatively consistent across categories, suggesting that respondents were either unable or did not bother to recall what they really did, but rather gave a middling response in general. Certainly, the pattern does not seem to fit what those subjects actually changed in their texts. We believe there is some evidence here of just how misleading questionnaire data can be. What we get probably is, if anything, evidence of what these subjects think they *ought* to be doing rather than what they did. In the brief open interviews the self-assessors showed good awareness of a wide range of 'good composing' meta-knowledge. Alternatively, if the questionnaire evidence is valid, we can only really make sense of much of it by assuming that it captures revision which subjects worked on in their minds but which never found its way into actual changes in their texts (e.g., all the claimed work on organization). Put another way, if the self-assessors really were doing the much greater work they claim on vocabulary, organization, etc., they did not gain much by it in actual improvements in these areas (Figure 4.3).

The observations provided other evidence of the relationship between peer activity and students' written products. For example, use of the computerized thesaurus was observed during work on topic 1, and quite a high between-draft improvement in vocabulary quality was found that week. These were high proficiency subjects who could approach the somewhat impoverished information provided by a computer thesaurus with better success than other L2 learners. As a contrasting example, organization was the least common matter for direct discussion (Figure 4.7), and it is one of the things least changed (e.g., little permutation in the analysis above via Faigley and Witte's scheme). The observations also revealed some problems in type of feedback given and in some students' ability to translate feedback into substantive changes.

4.5. CONCLUSION

The fairly proficient ESL writers in the present study behaved much like those from other countries in other studies, and in some ways more like L1 than L2 writers. Differences of writing ability revealed themselves in the kinds of revision focused on, in the extremes of mechanics on the one hand and the large scale addition and alteration of content on the other. And the benefits of peer feedback in the revision phase of writing in the context of word processing are similar to those found in studies where traditional writing implements were employed. Thus, there is little evidence from the present study for a greatly enhanced benefit associated with writing on computer. The potential often referred to for moving material around, for example, remained largely unexploited by those subjects revising with peers as well as on their own.

At the same time, this investigation has helped to delineate how peer feedback can help the L2 writer, and particularly the complex connection between what is talked about with peers, what is actually changed in the text, and the resulting improvement between drafts. In essence, it seems that the number of revision changes subjects make, and the level of final draft quality they achieve, are more a function of their general writing level than the revision mode they employ. However, the extent to which the revision changes they make are realized as actual between-draft quality improvements, and probably the amount of that improvement, seems more directly related to revision mode, with an apparent advantage to peer feedback. This is true especially in the area of mechanics, but also to some extent in the areas of vocabulary, organization, and content. In particular, we have shown how in these aspects of writing, relatively lower level writers can exploit peer feedback to close the quality gap in final drafts between their work and that of slightly better writers who are revising on their own.

The messages for the writing teacher are clear. Multi-draft writing with peer feedback has value, and, as Chaudron (1983) notes, the saving in teacher time provides a motivation to make peer feedback as effective as possible. Effort must be made to get peers talking about organization as well as content and mechanics, and so to motivate them to exploit more of the capabilities of the word processor for making changes of different types. Above all, teachers need to be aware of the differences dependent on the overall ability or proficiency level of the students involved.

5. Effects of the Teaching of Revision Strategies in a Computer-based Environment[1]

Jocelyne Bisaillon

ABSTRACT

This chapter reports a quasi-experimental research study conducted with three classes of undergraduate students at an advanced level of French as a second language. The purpose was to investigate the effects of the teaching of revision strategies in a computer-based environment on revision and on the quality of texts. The findings of the study show that the three groups of students significantly improved both revision and quality of texts, not only at the surface level but also in organization and content.

5.0.   INTRODUCTION

Since the 1980's, new technologies have been increasingly applied in language teaching. The use of word processors in second language (L2) writing classes is one of the most widespread and well-accepted technologies (Pennington, 1993b). However, as findings on the quality of written work produced with the aid of word processors are controversial (Cochran-Smith, 1991; Hawisher, 1989; Pennington, 1993b), and as quality of writing is the main interest of writing teachers, more research is needed in this area. Based on numerous research studies on the use of word processors in writing classes, Pennington (1993b, this volume) reports that the pedagogical context in which the medium is integrated influences the results of its application as far as the quality of the written work is concerned.

It appears that word processors are productively used within a process-oriented instructional context (Hawisher, 1989; Kurth, 1986; Williamson & Pence, 1989). Furthermore, as revision is central to the process approach, the teaching of writing on computer must give a central role to revision. In the view of Williamson and Pence (1989), "if re-

---

[1] Funding for the research reported in this chapter has come from the Fonds pour la Formation de Chercheurs et l'Aide à la Recherche, Ministère de l'Éducation du Québec (1993-1996).

vision is not directly manipulated as part of the instructional procedures, there is little chance that any differential effects of word processing on student writing will emerge, given the complexity of revision as it has emerged in the previous research" (pp. 102-103).

Moreover, given that strategy teaching supports students' cognitive growth and learning overall (Tardif, 1992), combining the teaching of revision strategies with the use of word processors in a favorable pedagogical context might help students in an L2 writing course to improve both their revision behavior and ultimately the quality of their texts. A revision strategy is a means, an action or technique, taken by a writer which increases efficiency when revising a text; it involves a particular way of reading and making changes to improve a text in content, organization, and language.

If teachers want to use word processors effectively in their teaching of writing in L2 (foreign or second language) classes, the pedagogical context needs to be investigated in more detail. The research reported in this chapter, taking into account what previous research reveals about favorable pedagogical contexts for integrating word processors into instruction and emphasizing the teaching of revision strategies, seeks to determine the effects of the electronic medium on the revision and the quality of texts of advanced-level undergraduate students studying French as L2.

5.1. BACKGROUND

5.1.1. Writing and the Importance of Revision

Research into the composing process using the procedure of having subjects think aloud while composing (Emig, 1971; Sommers, 1980; Zamel, 1982, 1983) shows that writing is not a linear process moving from collecting ideas and outlining to revising. Rather, writing is a recursive process involving cycles of planning, translating (of ideas into text), and reviewing (Hayes & Flower, 1980). This process takes place in a context, is oriented to a task, and requires many different kinds of knowledge (of subject, schemas, audience, and language). In an L2, the writing process is more difficult than in a first language (L1) context because of the greater linguistic constraints (Whalen, 1988). As writing is complex, so is the teaching of writing, particularly in a process approach.

Numerous studies have suggested that revision plays a central role in writing (e.g., Gaskill, 1986; Sommers, 1980). For Steelman (1994), "it is the essence of the writing process itself" (p. 143). In fact, writers tend to revise almost right from the start and continue throughout the composing process (Lam, 1991). Hayes, Flower, Schriver, Stratman, and Carey (1985) have elaborated the most complete revision model, as I have discussed elsewhere (Bisaillon, 1991). Here, I would like to emphasize that reading plays a predominant role in revising. Hayes (1995) recently redefined his model of writing to give a central role to reading in order to understand, to find new ideas, to evaluate, and to look for errors.

Good writers are those who revise a lot, an idea which is supported by the experience of professional writers. Sartre, for example, said that when someone writes it is necessary to look at the text as if it were an "illegible scribble" (Vigner, 1982, p. 21). Only then does the writer make changes, reread the text, and make still other changes. Consequently, if writing means rewriting, then teaching writing means teaching rewriting. In fact, revising *must* be taught. Steelman (1994), reporting an idea of Arms (1982), wrote that "the quality of writing could be improved dramatically if revision were made as integral to writing as debugging is to programming" (p. 143). As research shows, inexperienced writers do little revising, and when they do, they often correct only surface level errors such as those involving punctuation, spelling, and vocabulary (Cochran-Smith, 1991). Many students indeed do not control the revision strategies that could help them to improve their texts at higher or deeper levels of content and organization. Another reason why students may not revise is that they find revising a tedious task of recopying in a pen and paper mode. This is the reason why word processors, which facilitate deleting, replacing, adding, and moving text, are perceived by many people as a panacea to the problem of revising. However, as research reveals, the reality is often quite different from this ideal.

5.1.2. Revision and Word Processing

Much research has been carried out on revising in an L1 or L2 with a word processor. According to some researchers (e.g., Bean, 1983; Collier, 1983), writers revise more often when using a word processor; nevertheless, they tend to make changes at the surface level and not necessarily at the deeper levels of their texts (Cochran-Smith, 1991). In addition, the texts produced by computer means are not necessarily of better quality than those written with pen and paper (Pennington, 1993b). It appears that using a word processor per se does not automatically lead to improved writing. As Steelman (1994) argues, "the research reported to date does not give evidence to support the use of word processors alone for the improvement of writing or revision strategies" (p. 144). We must also take into account many variables of the pedagogical context such as the writer's degree of skill at keyboarding or with the text editor, the approach to writing in which the word processor is integrated, and the teacher's preparation (Pennington, 1993b, this volume).

Steelman's investigation (1994) combining the teaching of revision strategies and the use of word processors produced noteworthy results. The study used a pretest/posttest non-equivalent control group design with two treatment groups and one control group of grade 6 students in a racially mixed American school. Various revision strategies were taught to the two treatment groups, though no details were provided on the way they were taught. Treatment group 1 was taught revision strategies systematically, and wrote with a word processor. Treatment group 2 was also taught revision strategies systematically, but did not use a word processor for writing. The control group, which wrote in pen and paper mode, was exposed to some revision strategies but this was not done systematically.

The researcher divided the strategies into four categories, ranging from low level to high level: **manuscript** strategies (e.g., legibility), **mechanical** strategies (e.g., punctuation, grammar), **language** strategies (e.g., vocabulary, varying sentence structure) and **organization** strategies (e.g., moving information, grouping ideas, expressing one main idea). Differences were found between the three groups with respect to revision strategies. Group 1, those writing on a word processor, tended to use higher level revision strategies (organization) to a greater extent than those who did not use a word processor. Similarly, Group 2, which received systematic strategy training, revised at a higher level than Group 3, which was exposed to strategies only sporadically. This last group tended to use more lower level revision strategies (mechanical) than the two others, probably because the focus of the teaching was not on higher level revision strategies. Students in the third group tended to concentrate on the appearance of the written texts, as is the usual practice of student writers.

This study indicates that the teaching of revision strategies positively influences revision in the middle grades; moreover, when such teaching is combined with the use of a word processor, it produces even better results. Nevertheless, more research is needed in order to be able to generalize the results to undergraduate students and to students writing in an L2.

In another study (Silver & Repa, 1993), word processors were again integrated in a process approach to writing. The researchers wanted to measure the effects of using word processors on self-esteem and the quality of writing. Sixty-six beginner-level ESL students in a secondary school were involved in the study. They were randomly assigned to a treatment group which used word processors and a control group which did not use the computer in their writing. The findings established that the students who used word processing wrote better texts and that the difference between treatment and control groups was statistically significant. However, once again, more research is needed with undergraduate students and with students at other levels of language proficiency in order to generalize on these findings. As for the improvement of self-esteem in relation to word processing, the hypothesis was not supported.

These two research studies highlight the importance of the pedagogical context when implementing word processors in the teaching of writing. In the next section, I take a more in-depth look at important aspects of this issue.

5.1.3.   Pedagogical Context

5.1.3.1.   Learner

It appears that writers will not benefit from using word processors if they are not at ease with keyboarding and word processing operations. Being at ease with the keyboard does not necessarily mean having used a word processor for a long time, but being able to type comfortably with all ten fingers. The research I conducted on writing strategies (Bisaillon, 1995a, p. 10) with four students writing academic papers without training in keyboarding revealed that these students wrote an average of only 4.10 words before stopping to correct their text. This lack of keyboard fluency prevented them from expressing their ideas smoothly; most of their revision time was spent correcting typing errors. In fact, 75% of their corrections were due to ineffective keyboarding (Bisaillon, 1997).

Other writers have confirmed the importance of keyboard fluency when using word processors to write. Dowling (1994) reported that writers who switched from pen and paper to word processors claimed that "writing does not appear to have become any easier" (p. 227). This is not surprising because the same writers admitted that their typing ability was inadequate.

In my own case study research, I found that students do not use word processing commands to execute functions such as 'cut' and 'paste' which would enable them to change the meaning of their texts, even after they have been instructed in how to use them. The same results regarding word processing operations were obtained by Joram, Woodruff, Bryson, and Lindsay's (1992) research. According to these authors, because poor editing ability interfered with their composing process, students preferred to use word processors for their final draft only.

To summarize, adequate technical skills are a prerequisite to an effective use of word processors in a writing class. Students who master keyboarding and editing skills will reap more benefits from using a word processor (Wenrich, 1991).

5.1.3.2. Laboratory

The computer laboratory or classroom also influences the successful use of word processors in writing classes. A computer laboratory must be easily accessible, open long hours, and staffed by at least one person to help students with technical problems. Too many technical problems can discourage students, as well as teachers (Bisaillon, 1995b; Williamson & Pence, 1989), from using computers to write.

5.1.3.3. Teacher

As in all pedagogical approaches or methods, as regards the use of word processors in a writing class, student improvement in writing depends greatly on the teacher. In her review of word processing research, Pennington (1993b, p. 234) stresses the importance of the individual teacher in student outcomes. Pennington (1993b) maintains that "differential effects for word processing in both first and second language environments are promoted by differences in teachers' views, or subjective theories, of computer-assisted writing, and in their individual responses to the constraints operating on them in their teaching contexts" (p. 234). Thus, teachers' skills with word processors, along with their attitude to the use of word processors in writing, is of central importance in using them for instruction.

5.1.4. Need for the Present Investigation

From the review of the literature reported briefly here, there would seem to be a need for further research on the effectiveness of teaching revision strategies combined with the use of word processors to undergraduate students at an advanced level of language proficiency. There is also a need for more research on teaching writing in French as L2, as current research has mostly concerned English as L2 (Pennington, this volume).

As maintained by Pennington (1993b, p. 245), for the best results in terms of improvement in the quality of written products, word processors should be used with students who type well and who will be using the computer for an extended period of time—at least three months—under the guidance of an experienced and motivated teacher employing a process approach to writing. These were the conditions in which the present investigation took place.

5.2. HYPOTHESES

The hypotheses of the study are formulated as follows:

H1. After the teaching of revision strategies combined with the use of a word processor, students will revise their text significantly better in content and organization, that is, they will make more meaningful changes in a posttest than in a pretest.

H2. After the teaching of revision strategies combined with the use of a word processor, students will revise their text significantly better at all levels of the text.

H3. After the teaching of revision strategies combined with the use of a word processor, students will significantly improve their text in content and organization, that is, they will have higher scores at these levels on a posttest than in a pretest.

H4. After the teaching of revision strategies combined with the use of a word processor, students will significantly improve their text at all levels, that is, they will have higher scores at all levels on a posttest than in a pretest.

5.3. METHOD

5.3.1. Design

In educational contexts, it is difficult for researchers to have the liberty to choose the conditions in which they desire to conduct their research. Groups already exist and teachers have a program to respect. For this reason, researchers often opt for quasi-experimental designs. Seliger and Shohamy (1990) explain that "quasi-experimental [research designs] are constructed from situations which already exist in the real world, and are probably more representative of the conditions found in educational contexts" (p. 148).

Since two teachers were involved in the classes of the present investigation, both different in their experience of teaching French and of teaching writing, it was not possible to apply a control group pretest/posttest design for the research. In order to assure reliability, I decided to repeat the same treatment with three groups at different times; this is known as the "separate sample pre-test/post-test design" (Seliger & Shohamy, 1990, p. 149).

As in a previous research study on revision (Bisaillon, 1991), I have added a revising test to a writing test. The design of the investigation is presented in schematic form in Table 5.1.

Group A	Revising Pretest Writing Posttest	Treatment	Revising Posttest Writing Posttest
Group B	Revising Pretest Writing Posttest	Treatment	Revising Posttest Writing Posttest
Group C	Revising Pretest Writing Posttest	Treatment	Revising Posttest Writing Posttest

Table 5.1. Separate Sample Pretest/Posttest Design

5.3.2. Students

The subjects were 60 French L2 students enrolled in *Rédaction II*, an advanced writing class, in the BFLS (Baccalauréat en français langue seconde) program at Université Laval, Québec (Canada). Two groups of students (Group A and Group B) were enrolled during the 1995 winter term and one (Group C), during the 1995 autumn term. Group A was composed of 26 students, Group B of 25 students, and Group C of 24 students. However, only 21 subjects in Group A, 20 subjects in Group B, and 19 subjects in Group C were selected for the study because they respected the following requirement: to write the four tests necessary for analyzing the results of the treatment. Groups A and C were taught by an experienced teacher who had been teaching writing in French as L2 for 15 years while Group B was taught by a younger teacher who was teaching the class for the fourth time.

5.3.2.1. Group Characteristics

A background questionnaire as developed by Perl (1979) and Sommers (1982) that included information on students' individual characteristics in terms of age, language background, and writing habits was filled out by participants in the investigation. Table 5.2 summarizes the students' individual characteristics in each group.

Table 5.2 shows that the three groups of students are similar in characteristics. The average age is 25 for Groups A and C and 27 for Group B. The predominant mother tongue is English; this is the case for 86.5%

of the students in Group A, 70% of those in Group B and 74% of those in Group C. Moreover, the majority of the students have French as L2 or as L1 (A, 100%; B, 80%; C, 79%). In addition, nearly all of the students (A, 84%; B, 90%; C, 89.5%) have completed the prerequisite to *Rédaction II* (i.e., *Rédaction I*). The others have taken an equivalent course at another university. Finally, almost all of the students are enrolled in a French language program (A, 88%; B, 100%; C, 89.5%). It can thus be concluded that the subjects of the three groups have comparable characteristics.

CHARACTERISTICS	Group A n = 21	Group B n = 20	Group C n = 19
Average Age	25	27	25
Mother Tongue			
Chinese	5%	---	---
English	86%	70%	74%
German	---	---	5%
Japanese	---	10%	---
Polish	---	5%	---
Spanish	4.5%	10%	21%
Swedish	4.5%	5%	---
L2			
English	---	20%	21%
French	100%	80%	79%
Rédaction I	84%	90%	89.5%
Studies in			
L2 French	88%	100%	89.5%
Other	12%	---	10.5%

Table 5.2. Group Characteristics

5.3.2.2. Writing Profile

The writing profile of the students in the three groups was taken from the answers to the questionnaire. Students were asked about their writing practices in their L1 and L2, problems in the L2, their perception of a good writer, their writing process, and their skill in using a word processor. The results are described in the following sections.

Writing Practices. More than half of the students (A, 56%; B, 53%; C, 53%) related that they write 'rather often' or 'very often' for pleasure in their mother tongue; for example, they write letters, poems, or in diaries. They write much less often in their L2. In fact, nearly half of the students in Group A (48%) and approximately three-quarters of the students in Group B (71%) and Group C (79%) responded that they 'never' write or 'rarely' write for pleasure in their L2. Finally, most of them perceived themselves as good writers in their mother tongue (A, 68%; B, 68%; C, 63%).

Writing Problems in the Second Language. Problems in the L2 mentioned by students are mainly linguistic problems. Students have difficulty translating their ideas into French, so they use structures in French that are parallel to structures in their mother tongue. They wrote that they also have problems with vocabulary, grammar, and spelling.

Perception of Good Writers. For the students in all three groups, good writers are characterized as those who are able to express their ideas with clarity and to keep the attention of a reader. Moreover, their ideas are well-chosen and well-organized. Finally, good writers are those who do not make errors in their texts.

Writing Process. The majority of the students said they planned what they wanted to say before starting to write in both their mother tongue and in French (A, 58%; B, 68%; C, 58%). Most of the students said they used their mother tongue when they wrote in French (A, 68%; B, 65%; C, 74%), but most of them also said that they used the mother tongue in thought only (A, 75%; B, 85%; C, 71%). In other words, they use their L1 to help them translate their ideas, but not as a compensatory strategy for writing.

Half of the students or more said they had not been taught revising at school in either L1 or L2 classes (A, 45%; B, 60%; C, 89.5%). When asked if they have a particular method for revising, nearly all of them simply answered that they read or reread their texts many times. They did not identify a special way of reading for revision.

Word Processors. Before the writing class, 62% of Group A, 65% of Group B, and 63% of Group C were already using word processors for their assignments. However, few students said they had mastered keyboarding (A, 25%; B, 50%; C, 32%).

5.3.3. Strategy Selection and Instruction

Revision strategies, as presented by Oxford (1990) are one of the main cognitive strategies used in developing skilled writing. These strategies help students detect and correct deficiencies in previously written text. In the present study, students were first trained to use revision strategies with imperfect texts written by others using pen and paper. These were texts written by students enrolled in the same writing course in a previous year; they were selected because of their deficiencies in content and organization, and they were slightly modified to be clear of all language errors. After working alone on a text, the students compared their ideas in class and learned to justify the changes they proposed. They also did the same exercise in a computer-based environment. Then they practiced revision strategies with their peers' texts. Finally, they applied these strategies to their own texts. For all these revising activities, students were provided with a list of questions on a sheet of paper to help them in the revising process (Appendix 5.1).

Revision was associated with selective attention related to two aspects of text: content and organization. These features of writing must be emphasized if improvement in overall writing quality is to be shown. The teaching of revision strategies and revising activities focused on content are based on Charolles' (1978) coherence theory. According to this theory, writing for coherence means applying four rules: repetition, relation, progression, and non-contradiction. In other words, writers have to avoid errors due to the non-repetition of an idea (misuse of a pronoun, for example), the non-relation of an idea to others, the non-progression of meaning, and the contradiction of an idea with others in the text.

After the explanation and illustration of the four rules, students were trained to recognize errors in texts when these rules were not applied. At the beginning of the training, it was difficult for students to detect these sorts of errors because they were not used to revising texts for the content. After a while, students were asked not only to detect, but also to correct coherence errors. Then, nearly all revision activities were linked with using the word processor. Moreover, all of the writing assignments, from the first to the final draft, were accomplished with a word processor.

5.3.4. Tasks and Data Collection

The data for this study were collected in the three groups at the beginning and at the end of two school trimesters. During the second week of the trimester, the students had to fill out a questionnaire and revise a text with errors in it (pretest 1); in third week, they wrote a descriptive composition (pretest 2). In the fourteenth week, they revised a text (posttest 1); and in the last week, they wrote another descriptive composition (posttest 2). The revision of the text was limited to two hours, and the writing of the description, to four hours. The tasks took place under natural instructional conditions in a computer laboratory.

The tasks were the following: a description of a person to revise (pretest 1 and posttest 1) and a description of a person to write (pretest 2 and posttest 2). The text to revise was a description written by a student during an earlier term, slightly modified in order to include errors at all levels of the text (content, organization, and language). The errors selected were those most frequently encountered in student texts at that level of proficiency. The errors in content and organization had been seen by the instructor previously when students practiced the revision strategies. The introduced errors were distributed as follows: 6 errors in content, 5 in organization, and 10 in language. The students could use the spellchecker to correct four out of the ten language errors. The students did not know the number of errors in the text, but they knew that the text had errors at the three levels mentioned.

The writing assignment was similar for pretest 2 and posttest 2. Students taught in a process writing approach were asked to follow that approach for the writing of a 300-350 word description of a person. At the end of the test, according to the process approach procedures used, they had to give the teacher their outline, their first draft, their written evaluation of that draft, and the final draft.

5.3.5. Data Analysis

The data were collected and entered on a grid by one person and reviewed by an another one for reliability. The 21 errors were classified into levels (content, organization, and language) and categories (non-repetition, non-progression, non-relation, and contradiction). Each error was identified for the analysis as: (i) error detected only, (ii) error detected and corrected inappropriately, or (iii) error detected and corrected appropriately.

To analyze subjects' writing performance, Jacobs, Zinkgraf, Wormuth, Hartfiel, and Hughey's composition profile (1981), which has been used in many research studies on writing, was adapted to meet the needs of the present study. Since it was constructed to evaluate an expository text, changes were made in the composition profile to take into account the characteristics of a description of a person as well as the revision strategy being taught. The highest possible score was 100, with the following maximum possible marks in each category of the rating scheme: content, 30; organization, 10; vocabulary, 20; syntax, 30; spelling and punctuation, 10 (Appendix 5.2). To ensure the reliability of the instrument, the profile was tried out on other texts, and the results compared with those obtained with the rating profiles currently in use in the class. The similarity of the results (a difference of rating of 2-4 marks) attests to the reliability of the instrument.

Two judges were trained through a process of assessing descriptive essays which were not part of the data. The judges and researcher then made many evaluations of student essays using the revised composition profile until they came to the same results many times in sequence. The judges were then considered to be ready to evaluate the compositions of the investigation. Pretests and posttests were mixed to avoid influencing the judges' assessment. The results of all the tests were analyzed statistically by an experienced statistician[2], who advised that the researcher employ a 'split-plot design' with analysis of variance.

5.4.   FINDINGS

Of the four hypotheses formulated, two concerned revision and two concerned the quality of writing. We will look first at the results for revision and then at those for writing quality.

5.4.1.   Revision of Texts

Table 5.3 presents the results for the three groups on pretest 1 and posttest 1 for the three levels of revision.

Level	Tests	A (n = 21)	B (n = 20)	C (n = 19)	Group Average
Content /6	pre-test	1.50	0.83	1.17	1.17
	post-test	3.43	2.30	3.18	2.97
	change	+1.93	+1.47	+2.01	+1.80 (30%)
Organization /5	pre-test	1.00	0.30	0.98	0.76
	post-test	2.95	2.15	2.38	2.50
	change	+1.95	+1.85	+1.40	+1.73 (34.7%)
Language /10	pre-test	3.53	2.40	1.22	2.38
	post-test	4.52	4.80	5.04	4.79
	change	+0.99	+2.40	+3.82	+2.40 (24%)

Table 5.3. Pretest 1 and Posttest 1 Text Revision Means for Groups A, B, and C

---

[2] Gaétan Daigle, consulting statistician from the *Service de Consultation Statistique* at Université Laval (Québec).

143

5.4.1.1.   Content Level

Even though the teachers were not the same (Groups A and C, experienced teacher; Group B, inexperienced teacher), and the time of the experiments was not the same (Groups A and B, winter term; Group C, fall term), each group improved in revision at the content level. Students in Group A detected and corrected an average of 25% of the errors at the content level in the pretest as against 57% in the posttest. Those in Group B detected and corrected an average of 14% of the errors at the content level in the pretest as against 38% in the posttest. Those in Group C detected and corrected an average of 19.5% of the errors in the pretest and 52% in the posttest. The improvement of each group can be seen in Figure 5.1.

At the content level, the statistical analysis revealed a significant effect for Test, $F = 75.10$, $p = 0.0001$, and no significant Group x Test interaction, $F = 0.64$, $p = 0.5312$. These results can be taken to mean that the sample as a whole improved from pre-test to post-test in their ability to correct content errors, with the improvement being roughly equivalent, from a statistical point of view, in each group. In addition, post hoc comparisons revealed that each group's improvement in content revision was significant at the $p = 0.0001$ level of significance. We can therefore postulate that the treatment had an effect on revision at the content level because treatment was the common feature of the three groups.

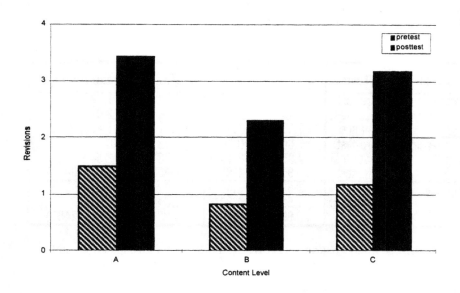

Figure 5.1. Revisions at the Content Level (maximum: 6) for Groups A, B, and C

144

If we combine results of all three groups, we see that the students improved in their content-level revisions on average by 30%. Although the results were positive and the teaching of revising strategies at the content level had an effect on the revision results, there is obviously still room for improvement. In fact, after three months of training on content revision, students were able to find only half of the errors in the text (i.e., 2.97 out of 6).

A detailed analysis of the results provides a view of students' strengths and weaknesses. Content-level errors are coherence errors. Charolles' (1978) coherence theory identified four categories of errors at the content level: errors due to the non-repetition of an idea, the non-relation of an idea to others, the non-progression of meaning, and the contradiction of an idea with others in the text. In the text to revise, there were errors of these four types. An examination of the posttest results showed that students were good at detecting and correcting errors involving ideas that were not in relation to others in the text (i.e., non-relation of an idea to others) or ideas that did not add meaning to the text (i.e., non-progression in meaning).

The following paragraph, extracted from the text the students were to revise, gives examples of two errors—one due to the non-relation of an idea to others and one due to the non-progression in meaning. The author, a mother, describes her teenager's clothes.

> *Son habillement attire mon attention. Comme ses amies, elle porte de vieux jeans noirs, déformés et, sans doute, très confortables et une vieille chemise en flanelle à carreaux, trouée, déboutonnée et ouverte aux poignets. Sous cette dernière se cache un vieux "t-shirt" blanc, très usé. Elle a donc besoin d'aller s'acheter des vêtements* (**non-relation to other ideas**). *Elle ira sûrement ce soir* (**non-relation to other ideas**). *Ses jeans aussi sont vraiment vieux* (**same idea as in the first line, that is old jeans, i.e., non-progression in meaning**). *De gros bas de laine gris et blancs trop grands pendent de ses pieds.*

Students had difficulties with ideas in contradiction and the use of anaphoric reference (non-repetition). These two aspects showed improvement from pretest to posttest, but this improvement was not statistically significant. One example of an error due to contradiction of an idea to others is the use of the word *bruyant* ('noisy') in the following paragraph, which introduces the person who will be described by the author.

> *Souvent, à la brunante, quand j'entends, affairée dans la cuisine, les notes aigres-douces de la musique des années soixante qui*

coulent dans l'escalier, je m'en vais d'un pas rapide et <u>bruyant</u> vers la chambre de ma fille.

The students should have replaced *bruyant* by *silencieux* ('silent') because the author, the mother, was saying that she was trying to walk to her daughter's room in order to listen to her play the guitar. She did not want to be seen or heard by her daughter. Some students did not see the contradiction, possibly because they did not know the meaning of the word *bruyant* and did not look it up in the dictionary.

An error in anaphoric reference often missed by the students was the use of a pronoun instead of a noun. In such a case, a reader will not know which word a pronoun refers to, and so the writer should replace it by a noun. This type of error (non-repetition of a noun) is also often made by L1 speakers of French (or any language).

5.4.1.2.   Organizational Level

Each group improved from pre-test to post-test in revision at the organizational level. Students in Group A detected and corrected an average of 20% of the errors in organization in the pretest as against an average of 59% in the posttest. Students in Group B detected and corrected 6% of the errors in organization in the pretest as against an average of 43% in the posttest. Students in Group C detected and corrected an average of 20% of the organization errors in the pretest and 48% in the posttest. The improvement is apparent in Figure 5.2.

At the organizational level, the statistical analysis again revealed a significant effect for Test, $F = 108.78$, $p = 0.0001$, with no significant Group x Test interaction, $F = 1.00$, $p = 0.3745$. These results can be taken to mean that the sample as a whole improved from pre-test to post-test in their ability to correct organizational errors, with the improvement in each group being roughly the same. In addition, each group improved significantly at the $p = 0.0001$ level according to the post hoc comparisons. It would therefore appear that the treatment had an effect on revision at the organizational level as well.

The revision strategy of focusing on the organization of the text was repeated as many times as the revision strategy of focusing on the content of the text. Even though the results were positive, and the teaching of a revising strategy at the organizational level had an effect on revision, once again the improvement could have been greater, possibly as a result of adding more revision activities. Perhaps word processing screen revision activities could usefully be complemented by hardcopy revision activities, as students were able to find only half of the errors (an average of 2.5 out of 5), despite three months of training in organizational revision.

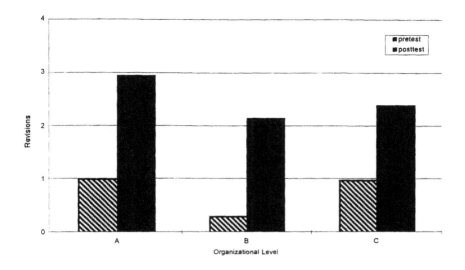

Figure 5.2. Revisions at the Organizational Level (maximum : 5) for Groups A, B, and C

A detailed analysis of the results showed that all of the students were good at detecting and correcting sentence-order errors in a paragraph, but they were less skillful at changing the order of paragraphs in a text. They were more proficient at a 'medium-level' of sentence-order errors than at the most macro-level of text order, i.e., that of paragraph arrangement. In terms of organization, these students were least adept at the most micro-level revisions.[3] Their biggest difficulty was in the use of connective words or phrases to link ideas between two sentences. More research needs to be carried out in regard to this aspect of composition, which even L1 writers have difficulty with.

5.4.1.3.   Language Level

At the language level, the results show a significant effect for Test, $F = 59.71$, $p = 0.0001$, but in this case with a significant Group x Test interaction, $F = 6.73$, $p = 0.0024$. Post hoc analysis indicates that Group B and C improved significantly, with Group A's improvement nearly

---

[3] It may be that the treatment offered or word processing in general focused attention on improvement at neither the most macroscopic level of the text nor the most microscopic, where reading a word processing screen may be least efficient. (Editor's note)

achieving significance at $\alpha = 0.05$ (B and C, p = 0.0001; A, p = 0.0576). This improvement is shown in Figure 5.3.

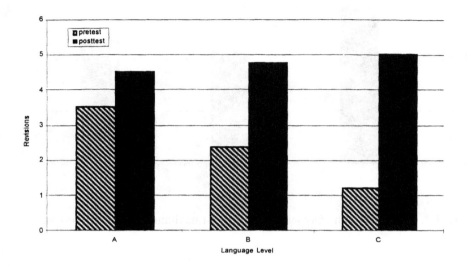

Figure 5.3. Revisions at the Language Level (maximum: 10) for Groups A, B, and C

Even though the teachers did not focus on revision strategies at the language level, students learned to use the spellchecker and were able subsequently to correct four out of the ten errors in language. The details of the analysis show that spelling errors were indeed the type of errors most often corrected by students. These results can probably be explained by the use or non-use of a spellchecker.

5.4.1.4. Summary of Results for Revision

The results for revision support the two first hypotheses: after the teaching of revision strategies combined with the use of a word processor, students revise their text significantly better not only in content and organization, but also in language. The students made significant progress in revision at the organizational level (35%) and at the content level (30%)—the two levels of most concern in the teaching of revision strategies. They also improved at the language level (24%), probably because of the use of a spellchecker, but also possibly because they were trained to pay attention to the content and the organization of the text as a result of the training provided: they became used to questioning them-selves about different aspects of the text and looking at it in depth and in detail.

5.4.2. Quality of Compositions

Because two judges had been asked to rate the students' descriptive compositions, an inter-rater reliability coefficient was calculated. A high correlation was found for all pretests and posttests, with the exception of the posttest of group B. The correlation of both raters on pretest and posttest, respectively, for each group was as follows: Group A, 0.92643 and 0.94092; Group B, 0.96226 and 0.66460; Group C, 0.85097 and 0.88169. The average of the two judges' scores is given in the presenta-tion of the results. Table 5.4 presents the results of the three groups for pretest 2 and posttest 2 at the three levels.

Variable	Test	A (n = 21)	B (n = 20)	C (n = 19)	Average	%
Content /30	pretest	20.83	20.03	19.89	20.25	67.5%
	posttest	23.21	22.68	22.37	22.75	75.8% (+8.3)
Organization /10	pretest	6.29	6.17	6.21	6.22	62.2%
	posttest	7.96	7.31	7.45	7.57	75.7% (+13.5)
Language /60	pretest	41.99	39.59	40.63	40.73	67.9%
	posttest	46.76	45.45	43.47	45.22	75.4% (+7.5)
Total	pretest	69.11	65.79	66.73	67.21	67.2% /100
	posttest	77.93	75.44	73.29	75.55	75.6% (+8.4)

Table 5.4. Pretest 2 and Posttest 2 Composition Ratings Means for Groups A, B, and C

5.4.2.1. Content Level

At the content level, all three groups improved from pretest to posttest, with an average improvement of 8.3%. Statistical analysis confirmed that the improvement was significant ($F = 28.18$, $p = 0.0001$), and post hoc comparisons showed that this was significant for each group. This result suggests that the treatment had an effect on the students' writing at the content level. Once again, despite the fact that the teachers were different and the time of the administration of treatments was not the same, all three groups improved significantly.

A comparison of these results with those obtained from the text which students revised shows that improvement is greater when students do not have to revise their own text. Students seem to see someone else's text more objectively. In fact, to help students be more objective with their own texts, teachers need to give them 'time distance', so that revision does not have to take place immediately after writing of the text. In the investigation, students had to revise their texts immediately after writing; this may explain why they did less well in revising their own texts.

5.4.2.2. Organizational Level

Once again, at the organizational level, Table 5.4 shows that the three groups progressed from pretest to posttest. The improvement here is the greatest of all three levels, as the combined results show a change of +13.5%. Statistical analysis confirmed the significance of this effect ($F = 34.21$, $p = 0.0001$), and post hoc comparisons showed that the result was significant for each group. As a result, we can conclude that the treatment had an effect on the students' writing at the organizational level.

5.4.2.3. Language Level

At the language level, the table shows that all three groups progressed from pretest to posttest. The combined results for all subjects show that there was an 8.4% improvement, which is very similar to the result at the content level. The statistical analysis confirmed significant improvement in the groups from pretest to posttest ($F = 22.70$, $p = 0.0001$), with the post hoc comparisons again indicating that the individual groups improved significantly.

The results support the last two hypotheses: after the teaching of revision strategies combined with the use of a word processor, students revise their text significantly better not only in content and organization, but also in language. The students made significant progress in organization (34.7%) and in content (30%), both of which are the focus for the teaching of revision strategies. They also improved in language (24%), once again probably because of the use of a spellchecker but also because they were trained in self-assessing their text.

5.5.   DISCUSSION

The findings in support of the four hypotheses suggest that using revision strategies combined with word processing may be a significant pedagogical means to improve the quality of revision, as well as the quality of writing in all aspects of a text—content, organization, and language.

In both types of test, revising and quality of writing, the most substantial improvement observed was at the organizational level. These results can be explained by the fact that this is possibly the easiest level to improve, particularly, when it involves the 'medium-level' concerns of sentence order. To detect a problem of sentence order, students must identify the order of sentences in a paragraph and decide if it is the best order required to facilitate the meaning of the text. In addition, to make corrections at this level of text, students need to reorganize the sentences or the paragraphs. At the micro-level, a particularly difficult aspect to improve for both L1 and L2 writers is the use of linking words, an aspect where improvement was not statistically significant in the present study. Further work focusing on this aspect of the text is needed in order to foster greater improvement among student writers.

In other respects, detecting and correcting errors in content requires a greater knowledge of language use. The contradiction or the non-progression of ideas, for example, is often subtle and difficult to discover in a text. It possibly requires more practice first on the detection of problems, and then on the correction of those problems which are detected. More research is needed to increase our understanding of content-level revision and the ways in which it may be taught.[4]

Finally, the level showing the least improvement in the present study, even though the improvement was statistically significant, was that of language. This is not very surprising because the students in this study were not trained to use revision strategies to focus on detection and correction of language errors. Nevertheless, since this level is usually emphasized in traditional writing classes, students are used to looking for

---

[4] Indeed, there is a need for more attention to instructional interventions aimed at improving students' skill at detecting and revising problems in their written work, with particular attention to training the revision process in the context of word processing. (Editor's note)

these kinds of errors. Moreover, the use of a spellchecker, which was provided to these subjects, is useful in correcting some of these errors.

In the research conducted by Williamson and Pence (1989), university students in word processing sections of English composition showed significantly greater improvement in the quality of their texts than those in handwriting sections. In other respects, students in the word processing sections did not revise to a greater extent than those in the handwriting sections, except at the surface level. An explanation for the difference observed in that study as compared with the present study is the focus put on revision of content and organization. It can be claimed that if students are not trained to detect and correct weaknesses concerning content and organization of their texts, they will be less likely to notice them. It is difficult for students to improve with training, and even more difficult without the training.

5.6. CONCLUSION

The effectiveness of the combination of strategic teaching with the use of a word processor no longer needs to be proven. Several previous research studies have shown that the use of a word processor alone is not necessarily effective; others have shown that strategic teaching combined with word processor use is more effective than strategic training alone (Silver & Repa, 1993). Sufficient data comparing students writing with pen and paper and with a word processor is currently available.[5] What is needed now is more research providing detailed examination of the pedagogical conditions in which word processors are used effectively. There is also a need to investigate more about the teaching of revision strategies. It is hoped that the present report makes a contribution in each of these areas.

---

[5] This is perhaps somewhat of an overstatement: there are in fact not very many such studies with L2 writers, even fewer for languages other than English; and the instructional input given varies widely from one study to the next, so that findings may not be generalizable. (Editor's note)

APPENDIX 5.1.

Students' Revising Questions

ÉVALUATION DU PORTRAIT DE _____

CONTENU ET ORGANISATION (50 points)

Nom de L'évaluateur/trice: _____

Lisez le texte du pair pour votre plaisir. Ensuite, répondez aux questions suivantes pour l'aider à en améliorer le contenu et l'organisation. Encerclez la bonne réponse et complétez quand c'est nécessaire.

1) Le **titre** traduit-il bien le contenu?   **OUI   NON   EN PARTIE**

2) INTRODUCTION
   - a) Le texte comporte-t-il une introduction?   **OUI   NON**
   - b) Y a-t-il **un point d'ancrage** au portrait?   **OUI: L'identifier   NON**
   - c) L'introduction est-elle complète (temps, lieu, personnage)?   **OUI   NON**
   - d) L'introduction est-elle trop longue?   **OUI   NON**

3)
   - a) Le texte contient-il au moins 3 éléments différents (physique, vêtements, comportement, etc)? **Les identifier.**
   - b) Sont-ils suffisamment développés?   **OUI   NON**
   - c) Le texte a-t-il de l'unité?   **OUI   NON**
     Si oui: Sur **quel aspect du personnage** porte l'unité du texte?
     Si non, pourquoi?

4) COHÉRENCE
   - a) Est-ce que le texte contient des idées en contradiction avec d'autres?
     NON   OUI: Indiquer 4a dans la marge à côté du mot ou de la phrase incohérente.
   - b) Est-ce que le texte contient des idées répétées (= manque de progression)?
     NON   OUI: Indiquer 4b dans la marge à côté des idées répétées en tout ou en partie.
   - c) Est-ce que le texte contient des idées non en relation avec le reste du texte ou non nécessaires, c'est-à-dire non pertinentes?
     NON   OUI: Indiquer 4c dans la marge à côté des idées non pertinentes.
   - d) Est-ce que les idées s'enchaînent facilement grâce aux reprises (reprise nominale, substitution lexicale ou pronom personnel)?
     OUI   NON: Indiquer 4d dans la marge à côté des phrases où il n'y a pas de reprise.
   - e) Est-ce que le texte comprend des idées qui ne sont pas claires, c'est-à-dire dont tu en comprends mal le sens?
     NON   OUI: Indiquer 4e à côté de l'idée qui ne semble pas claire.

f) Est-ce que le texte comprend des idées incomplètes, c'est-à-dire non développées suffisamment pour en comprendre le sens?
NON OUI: Indiquer 4f à côté de l'idée incomplète.

5) CONCLUSION
   a) Le texte se termine-t-il par une conclusion ? **OUI NON**
   b) La conclusion est-elle assez originale? **OUI NON**

6) ORGANISATION
   a) Est-ce que chaque paragraphe contient une idée? Laquelle? **Soulignez la ou les idées intruses. Écrivez 6a dans la marge.**
   b) L'ordre adopté entre les paragraphes est-il justifiable? **OUI NON** Pourquoi?
   c) L'ordre adopté *à l'intérieur des paragraphes* ou entre les phrases est-il correct? **Soulignez les problèmes relevés.**
   d) Identifiez les mots-liens ou les idées-liens (éléments récurrents) entre les paragraphes et entre les phrases. **S'il en manque, indiquez-le à l'endroit en question par un 6d.**

APPENDIX 5.2.

Adapted Writing Profile (Grille D'Évaluation du Portrait)

CONTENU (choix et cohérence des idées)

30-27 **Excellent à très bon:**	1) l'introduction est complète = point d'ancrage + temps, lieu et personnage 2) le texte a de l'unité = il veut faire ressortir un aspect du personnage 3) les idées sont cohérentes = il n'y a pas d'idée en contradiction, d'idée répétée ou d'idée non en relation 4) les idées sont clairement exprimées 5) les trois aspects du personnage sont suffisamment développés 6) la conclusion assez originale
26-22 **Bon à moyen:**	1) l'introduction est presque complète = il manque un des éléments 2) le texte a de l'unité, mais quelques idées sont inutiles ou non pertinentes 3) certaines idées manquent de cohérence = il y a quelques idées en contradiction / répétées / non en relation 4) certaines idées manquent de clarté 5) l'un des trois aspects du personnage n'est pas suffisamment développé 6) la conclusion n'est pas originale
21-17 **Faible à pauvre:**	1) l'introduction est incomplète = il manque plusieurs éléments 2) il y a peu d'unité = il y a beaucoup d'éléments qui ne sont pas pertinents par rapport à l'unité du texte 3) les idées manquent de cohérence = il y a plusieurs idées en contradiction / répétées / non en relation 4) plusieurs idées ne sont pas claires 5) plus d'un aspect du personnage est insuffisamment développé 6) la conclusion est absente ou très faible
16-13 **Très pauvre:**	1) il n'y a pas d'introduction ou l'introduction est très faible 2) il n'y a aucune unité dans le texte 3) le choix des idées n'est pas adéquat 4) les trois aspects du personnage ne sont pas suffisamment développés
OU	l'information est insuffisante pour évaluer

ORGANISATION

10-9 **Excellent à très bon:**	1) chaque paragraphe contient une idée principale 2) le texte est bien organisé = ordre correct entre les paragraphes 3) l'ordre entre les phrases est correct 4) le texte contient suffisamment de mots-liens et ils sont correctement utilisés
8-6 **Bon à moyen:**	1) l'un des paragraphes contient plus d'une idée principale 2) le texte est plutôt bien organisé = l'un des paragraphes n'est pas à l'endroit le plus logique 3) il y a peu de problèmes d'ordre entre les phrases 4) le texte contient suffisamment de mots-liens mais quelques-uns des mots sont mal utilisés en contexte
5-3 **Faible à pauvre:**	1) plusieurs paragraphes contiennent plus d'une idée 2) les idées sont confuses et ne se suivent pas 3) le texte contient très peu de mots-liens et il y a des erreurs
2-1 **Très pauvre:**	1) il n'y a pas de paragraphes 2) il n'y a aucune organisation 3) il n'y a aucune utilisation de mots-liens ou mauvaise utilisation de mots-liens
OU	insuffisant pour évaluer

VOCABULAIRE

20-18 **Excellent à très bon:**	1) vocabulaire sophistiqué = recherché 2) vocabulaire très diversifié = pas de répétitions 3) choix adéquat des mots en contexte = registre approprié + sens précis
17-14 **Bon à moyen:**	1) vocabulaire approprié le plus souvent, mais les erreurs des mots en contexte n'entrave pas la compréhension du sens de la phrase 2) vocabulaire assez diversifié = peu de répétitions
13-10 **Faible à pauvre:**	1) vocabulaire qui contient quelques erreurs qui entravent la compréhension 2) signification des mots confuse et obscure 3) vocabulaire peu diversifié = beaucoup de répétitions
9-7 **Très pauvre:**	1) peu de connaissance du vocabulaire français et de l'utilisation des mots 2) beaucoup de répétitions
OU	insuffisant pour évaluer

GRAMMAIRE ET SYNTAXE

30-27 **Excellent à très bon:**	1) constructions complexes de phrases 2) quelques erreurs de structures de phrase (ordre, formulation) 3) quelques erreurs d'accord (verbe, nom et adjectif), de temps de verbes, d'articles, de pronoms et de prépositions
26-22 **Bon à moyen:**	1) constructions simples de phrases 2) problèmes mineurs dans les constructions complexes 3) plusieurs erreurs d'accord (verbe, nom et adjectif), de temps de verbes, d'articles, de pronoms et de prépositions
21-17 **Faible à pauvre:**	1) problèmes majeurs dans la construction des phrases 2) erreurs dans les structures de phrase (ordre, formulation) 3) plusieurs erreurs d'accord (verbe, nom et adjectif), de temps de verbes, d'articles, de pronoms et de prépositions
16-13 **Très pauvre:**	1) aucun respect dans la construction des phrases françaises 2) texte dominé par les erreurs d'accord (verbe, nom et adjectif), de temps de verbes, d'articles, de pronoms et de prépositions
OU	insuffisant pour évaluer

ORTHOGRAPHE ET PONCTUATION

10-9 **Excellent à très bon:**	très peu d'erreurs d'orthographe et de ponctuation
8-7 **Bon à moyen:**	erreurs occasionnelles d'orthographe et de ponctuation
6-5 **Faible à pauvre:**	erreurs fréquentes d'orthographe et de ponctuation
4-3 **Très pauvre:**	texte dominé par les erreurs d'orthographe et de ponctuation
OU	insuffisant pour évaluer

Droits réservés de Jocelyne Bisaillon (Université Laval, 1995)

158

6. Investigating Academic Writing On-Line: A Study of Temporal Aspects of Text Production

Kristyan Spelman Miller

ABSTRACT

This chapter reports on a study of the temporal features of written text production of writers using a word processor. The on-line methodology used, known as *keystroke logging*, involves the recording of all keyboard operations including keypresses, cursor movements and periods off writing (pauses). The information stored electronically in logfiles can then be analyzed in order to reveal, among other things, aspects of fluency and non-fluency in writing. In the part of the study reported on here, pause behavior is considered principally from the point of view of location in the text string. Location is interpreted not only in terms of grammatical position, but also from a discoursal perspective, and the notion of a topic-related 'framing device' is introduced. Results are presented concerning the writing behavior of the students, who come from both English as a first language and English as a foreign language backgrounds, as they write on two academic essay tasks.

6.0.   INTRODUCTION

The starting point for work reported in this chapter is a pedagogically driven interest in the writing behavior of students operating within the academic discourse community. Focusing on the real-time production of text, the investigation seeks to explore temporal features of writing behavior as student writers perform academic tasks using a word processor. By focusing on the temporal aspects of pausing and fluency, this work picks up on and develops the area of interest traditionally handled within psycholinguistics, that of performance phenomena as evidence of language processing, but extends this to the less widely discussed written modality.

6.1.   THE STUDY OF NON-FLUENCY IN LANGUAGE

6.1.1.   Non-Fluency and Planning

The issue of non-fluency is well established in research into spoken language production. A number of early studies (e.g., Beattie, 1983; Butterworth, 1980; Garrett, 1982; Goldman-Eisler, 1968, 1972; Rochester, 1973) discuss the occurrence of performance features in speech, namely, filled pauses (*er, um*), partially filled pauses (*well, I mean*), and silent pauses, as evidence of the processing demands on the speaker. These phenomena are associated with the functional and situational characteristics of typically spontaneous, interactive speech, which impose processing demands on the producer, both to plan the message and produce the string of sounds between breath groups, and to accommodate the needs of the receiver by chunking the message for the listener to process.

In these studies on speech, non-fluency has been seen, at least in part, as evidence of planning processes in speech, and this planning has been acknowledged as occurring at a number of different levels. Levelt (1989) talks of a distinction between macro- (long-range) planning and micro- (or local-level) planning. The occurrence of non-fluent phases in speaking, it is suggested, coincides with major planning points where macroplanning, or forward, conceptual planning, seems to occur (Beattie, 1983; Butterworth, 1980). Local-level planning or microplanning, which in Levelt's terms involves the assignment of informational and propositional shape to the intended message, may take place during more fluent phases of production. In reality, however, the distinction between types of planning may not be so clearcut, as different types of planning may co-occur at particular points.

6.1.2.   Non-Fluency in Writing

The occurrence of pausing, then, may be seen as a measure of writing fluency and as indirect evidence of cognitive activity associated with planning, and as such may provide valuable insights into the processes involved in the production of spoken language. In the case of written language production, it may be argued that similar insights can be drawn from evidence of temporal aspects of production. De Beaugrande (1984) justifies the interest in non-fluency for investigating "such mental events as phrasing, memory search, decision, feedback, conceptual integration, and so forth" (p. 166) associated with written text production. However, because of the functional and situational characteristics of writing as a typically non-interactive activity in which writer and reader are normally spatially and temporally distanced from one another, these temporal features are generally not in evidence in the written product. In other words, indices of the covert processes which underlie text production, the concealed 'seams' of the writing process, "the false starts, the dead ends, the deletions, and the rearrangements", as Smith (1982, p. 2) describes them, are typically untraceable from the surface product of the text. Unlike the analysis of off-line speech (for example, using the transcription of a stretch of spoken language), the off-line analysis of written text typically operates on a polished, rarefied product in which evidence of points of hesitation, retracing, false starts, and reformulations is not normally available (Pennington, 1993, 1996b, ch. 2). In this way, text product and writing process may be seen as quite distinct, with process largely uninferrable on the basis of product. Murray (1980) sums up this idea by claiming that "process can not be inferred from product any more than a pig can be inferred from a sausage" (Murray, 1980, p. 3).

In adopting process approaches to writing research, pioneering researchers such as Emig (1971), Sommers (1980), Perl (1979), Flower and Hayes (1981), Raimes (1985), among others, sought in the 1970's and 1980's to open up the otherwise unobservable processes of production. The methodology largely favored in this real-time (or on-line) process research involves elicitation and analysis of verbalizations (or think-aloud protocols), whereby the thoughts expressed by the writer as they participate in the writing activity are recorded and later coded by the analyst (see Ericsson & Simon, 1993, for a discussion of the principles of the think-aloud method).

This method of data elicitation is not uncontroversial, however. As a so-called direct method of eliciting subject-generated data, it has the advantage of offering a wealth of on-line data of thought processes during writing. However, as many have pointed out (see Smagorinsky, 1994; Stratman & Hamp-Lyons, 1994, for overviews), there are both theoretical and practical problems associated with using this type of methodology. For example, arguments have been raised that the picture of the writing activity available through protocols is incomplete, that there is a need for the analyst to infer processes rather than those processes being directly accessible through the subjects' verbalizations, and that the intrusive, *reactive* nature of the think-aloud method potentially interferes with or disrupts the very behavior it is intended to expose.[1] Such arguments lead to strong condemnations of the method by

---

[1] This issue of *reactivity* (Russo, Johnson, & Stephens, 1989), that is, the disruption of the writing process by the think-aloud method, is itself the subject of empirical investigation by Janssen, van Waes, and van den Bergh (1996). They report that the method does indeed have an effect, i.e., of increasing pause length at all planning levels. However, this effect seems to be sensitive to task type, with a greater effect in evidence on more complex tasks.

some such as Kowal and O'Connell (1987) who claim that "protocol analysis must be said to generate a great deal of data about something other than the process of writing" (p. 125).

As an alternative real-time method of observing the writing process, pause analysis has been proposed as an appropriate method of writing research. Despite limitations due to the fact that pauses offer indirect (and hence only partial and speculative) insights into the writing process, it is suggested that these visible indices of cognitive processes "are fundamental moments of conceptualization, formulation or control of the message production of language" (Chanquoy, Foulin, & Fayol, 1996, p. 37).

Matsuhashi's early work (1981, 1987) in exploring cognitive planning is perhaps the best known example of exploratory pausological research in writing. Through her observational studies of writing behavior, she points to the potential importance of pause analysis in providing a window on the writer's thinking processes. In Matsuhashi's methodology, data from video-recordings of writing sessions are annotated so as to identify the point at which a break occurs in the flow of production (pausing) and also the type of alteration made to the existing text (deletion or insertion). This allows access to measures of fluency of production (time spent on and off writing), as well as to features of the revision (type and level, and distance from the point of inscription). Pause location is interpreted principally in terms of position prior to certain grammatical units (more specifically, prior to certain types of t-unit, or main clause plus any subordinate clauses). The important outcome of this research for the present work is the suggestion that pausing at these t-unit junctures reflects important macro-level planning. However, the lack of further specification of pause location beyond this notion of inter-clause/sentence position leaves open the challenge for a more detailed linguistic characterization of pausing behavior.

Later temporal studies of writing (e.g., Chanquoy, Foulin, & Fayol, 1996; Hadenius, 1991; Phinney & Khouri, 1993; Sanders, Janssen, van der Pool, Schilperoord, & van Wijk, 1996; Schilperoord, 1996; Stromqvist & Ahlsen, 1998; Warren, 1996) to some extent begin to address notions of a variety of other potential locations for pausing, such as at word boundaries and word-internally; but in general these are rarely specified further, with the result that most discussion remains focused on the sentence/clause boundary location as the most significant locus of pausing.

In the design of the procedure for pause analysis of the present study, I intend to respond to this gap in previous studies of non-fluency in writing by developing a more finely specified set of categories of pause location. In attempting to do this, I draw to some extent on work on spoken language production which attempts to throw light on the relationship between pausing and grammatical structure. Through the analysis of pausing during reading aloud and from parsing sentences, Grosjean, Grosjean, and Lane (1979) and Gee and Grosjean (1983), for example, consider the coincidence of grammatical units such as noun phrases and complement clauses with production spans between pauses. Their analysis uncovered a partial correspondence between these units, while acknowledging the significance of other influences (such as length of output string) as determiners of pause location. In the discussion below, the location categories devised for use in the current study are outlined. The categories presented correspond in the first place to traditional grammatical categories, but then, in addition, a proposal is made to introduce a discourse interpretation of certain pause locations.

So far, I have justified the real-time indirect approach to writing research taken in the current study using pause analysis, and have furthermore suggested the need for the elaboration of categories of pause location. We should turn now to the methods of data collection available within pause analysis research, and introduce the specific tool selected for the study.

6.1.3. Computer-Based Pause Analysis

In contrast to the use of video recording in the Matsuhashi (1981) study, the advent of computer-based writing tools has made available more sophisticated and less intrusive tools for the observation of the writing process. One such example is given by Levy and Ransdell (1996), who use an unobtrusive video-recording technique as subjects write on a word processor. This involves using a signal splitting and converting device, so that without the physical presence of a video camera, a real-time recording could be made of the text production process. In their study of undergraduates, the researchers combine this method with the recording of verbal protocols provided by the subjects as they write. These two sources of data, then, allow the researchers to build up a more complete picture of the writing event, with fine-grained analyses, for example, of pause location and duration, complementing insights into identified writing behaviors such as rereading, evaluating, planning future topic content, and so on.

Another significant and potentially more versatile computer-based tool for pause data elicitation is provided through the availability of software for recording keyboard activity. A resident program unobtrusively records all operations (including keypresses, editing functions, and cursor movements) made by the writer while writing using a word processor. This information is stored electronically as a logfile, and may be retrieved for subsequent analysis concerning the fluency of the writing (where and when pauses occurred, and their duration) and the sequence of all actions including text production and commands (such as scrolling, navigating with the cursor and deleting). The output of the logfile, an example of which is provided in Figure 6.1, is a highly detailed record of the temporal features of the writing activity which provides a rich source of data for analysis. Pausological information is presented as bracketed numbers (e.g., <3.2> representing a pause of 3.2 seconds); cursor movements are indicated by the left/right and up/down arrows; backspace deletions are indicated by the crossed arrow symbol; space bar presses are indicated by the underline ('_') symbol; and all other characters (letters and punctuation marks) are also shown. The running time of the writing event (in seconds) is given down the left-hand margin.

Figure 6.1. Sample From a Keystroke Logfile

This robust data collection tool, keystroke logging, which is currently being exploited by researchers in a variety of contexts and with a variety of research aims (Flinn, 1987a, 1987b; Severinson Eklundh, 1990; Severinson Eklundh & Kollberg, 1995; Sullivan, Kollberg, & Palsson, 1997; van Waes, 1991), has been selected for use in the study reported here. In the section which follows, details of the present study are outlined in terms of the research context, the research questions posed, and the specific software used.

6.2.   METHOD

6.2.1.   Purpose

The project is concerned with students studying in a Faculty of Letters department of a British university. As a lecturer and examiner in the department concerned, I am interested in investigating our students' writing processes as they produce genuine academic tasks. The data collection involves recording the writing behavior of a number of students who are studying within the same curriculum area. The study aims to investigate the writing behavior of the students as they produce two standard academic essays. The design of the research allows investigation of potential task differences which have been suggested elsewhere in the literature.

6.2.2.   Research Questions

Matsuhashi (1987), in her investigation of the writing process in generalizing and reporting essay tasks, reported differences in pause duration associated with attention to different aspects of planning—conceptual, "the network of underlying concepts and relations" (p. 206), and sequential, "the arrangement of elements in the surface text" (ibid.). In her investigation, the longer periods of pausing on the generalizing essay are interpreted in terms of revisions reflecting conceptual plans, whereas on the reporting task more time appeared to be spent on revisions reflecting sequential plans. Overall, the subject in her study spent the highest percentage of time revising the generalizing essay. In other words, the writer appeared to adjust her writing behavior according to the demands of the two task types.

Following this line of research, one question for the present study is whether an evaluative, interpretive task, which requires the synthesis of various viewpoints and their evaluation in a way similar to Matsuhashi's generalizing essay, might be more demanding than a descriptive, reporting task, and will therefore give rise to different features of production. An evaluative task might be associated with such features as longer, more frequent pauses; lower quality judgments of the text produced; and a shorter length of text produced. Also, the revision behavior in terms of the kind of changes made to the text (frequency of revisions at higher and lower levels) is likely to vary across tasks, with an evaluative task involving the writer in struggling with the text to a greater degree and at a higher conceptual level than a descriptive task.

Other research, however, suggests a less straightforward association between task type and process features. Ruth and Murphy (1988), for example, have looked at the interaction between topic wording (potentially signaling different discourse type) and writing processes, in particular, planning time and rereading. Although apparently clear differences in planning are reported, no significant difference was found in the mean holistic scores across topic versions varying in task types. What is more, the complexity of interactions between processes among writers leads to the suggestion that this is an issue of individual response to different task demands. Ruth and Murphy (1988) call for more research "to determine whether students' composing processes are influenced by different topic versions, whether or not these processes are natural to the students who adopt them, and whether or not these processes are optimal for successful performance" (p. 148). The current research seeks to respond at least in part to such an invitation, by providing a fine-grained analysis of individual performances under the two task conditions, evaluation and description. The first research question therefore concerns task demands:

RQ 1.   Do writers respond differently to different task demands (descriptive versus evaluative) in terms of their pausing behavior when writing on a word processor?

The second research question concerns the potential differences in writing behavior across writers with different language backgrounds. There has been substantial research into characterizing the nature of second language (L2) writing behavior in comparison to that of first language (L1) writers (for overviews, see Grabe & Kaplan, 1996, and Krapels, 1990). The result is a complex picture of similarities and differences, particularly with respect to writing processes. L2 writers' difficulties, it is argued by some (e.g., Zamel, 1983, 1985), are principally a matter of composing competence rather than linguistic competence. This issue is linked by some (Edelsky, 1982; Gaskill, 1986; Jones & Tetroe, 1987) to the notion of transfer of L1 writing processes to L2 writing. In contrast to much discussion of similarities in processes, Raimes (1985) and Arndt (1987), most notably, point to significant processing differences between L1 and L2 writers.

These process studies, which typically involve small numbers of subjects in uncontrolled research contexts using protocol or observation methods, are in fact limited in their power to offer insights into differences between writing in L1 and L2 (Grabe & Kaplan, 1996, pp. 141-143). The wealth of studies cited by Silva (1993), for example, suggests that both in terms of composing processes and product features, there is considerable scope for renewed attention to the distinct nature of L2 writing. Against this substantial background of research into L2 writing behavior, the second research question for this study is proposed as one related to L1-L2 writing differences:

> RQ2.   Do L1 and L2 writers of English respond differently to descriptive and evaluative writing tasks in terms of their pausing behavior when writing on a word processor?

6.2.3.   Students

The subjects are 21 students who had been following the same lecture course in Applied Linguistics. They include both L1 writers of English (n = 10) and mixed nationality L2 writers of English (n = 11), of whom seven share the same first language background, Greek. Given the larger number of this Greek group, and the similarity of their backgrounds in terms of educational and linguistic experience, attention is focused in particular on this subset of L2 writers. All subjects were self-selecting volunteers, roughly matched in terms of academic achievement, age (20-23 years), and familiarity with word processing. All were female except for one male in the L1 group.

6.2.4.   Writing Tasks

The subjects produced two academic examination-type essays, both under timed conditions, each involving a differently formulated prompt: one a descriptive or reporting task and the other an evaluative or interpretive task. The prompt for the descriptive task was: "What is known about individual differences in the acquisition of a second language?" For the evaluative task, the prompt was: "Evaluate the contribution of research to our understanding of individual variation in second language acquisition."

6.2.5.   Research Tool

The selection of a keystroke logging software program, *JEdit*, which has been developed at the IPLab, Royal Institute of Technology, Stockholm (for details, see Severinson Eklundh & Kollberg, 1992, 1996a, 1996b), was made on the basis of its ease of use, flexibility, and versatility as a research tool. This specially designed text editor appears to users as a familiar word-processing package running on a Macintosh machine, with operations such as cut, paste, and cursor movements using a mouse or arrow keys. The information recorded in *JEdit* may also be converted using a further piece of software called *S-notation* (Severinson Eklundh & Kollberg, 1992, 1996a, 1996b) to reveal the effect of revision operations (i.e., insertions and deletions) on the emerging text, and a further interactive program called *Trace-it* (also designed by Severinson Eklundh & Kollberg) allows the writing session to be replayed revision by revision. This replay facility was used in a related study to elicit retrospective commentary by subjects on their motives for revisions.[2]

6.2.6.   Data Analysis

6.2.6.1.   Pause Location Categories

A first step in defining pausing behavior is to establish categories of pause location. As has been suggested above, the definition of location in previous studies has often lacked linguistic specificity. For example, a word-level unit does not sufficiently distinguish different word classes such as function words from content words (e.g., determiner vs. noun) or auxiliaries from main verbs. The categorization proposed in the present study involves a number of linguistic units, corresponding to sentence, clause, intermediate constituent (including phrases, 'container' structures for complements, conjuncts and disjuncts), word, and character.

A further feature of the categorization presented here responds to the need to account for pause location in terms of potential rather than definitive linguistic units. The dynamic nature of the on-line data, in which the form of constituents is open to change or replacement during later operations on the text, requires the characterization of location in the text string in a flexible way, to reflect the status of the unit at that particular moment in the construction of the text. In response to this re-

---

[2] This chapter draws on a larger study which includes analyses of fluency and revision behavior displayed by the same subjects.

quirement, the locations identified are referred to as 'potential completion points' at the following levels:

- character completion point (XCP)
- word completion point (WCP)
- intermediate constituent completion point (ICP)
- clause completion point (CCP)
- sentence completion point (SCP)

The sample of text given in Figure 6.2, simplified from a logfile, illustrates the application of these categories to pauses in the data.[3] Analysis of variance (ANOVA) was applied to mean pause values with tasks and subject groups as factors, using *Minitab 11.2*. A General Linear Model was used since the subject groups were unbalanced.

It has been stated that <*ICP*> learners' individual differences <*ICP*> have effective role in the acquisition of <*WCP*> a second language <*CCP*>. <*SCP*> <*SCP*> There are a number of variables <*CCP*> which can be <*ICP*> illustrated <*CCP*> such as learners' age, <*CCP*> aptitid<*XCP*>e, motivation, attitude, personality and purpose of <*WCP*> L2 learning. <*SCP*> <*SCP*>

Figure 6.2. Illustration of Pause Locations in a Data Sample [NGK: A_D]

6.2.6.2.   Discourse Perspective on Pause Location

A further development in the definition of pause location has involved the specification of the function of certain locations in terms of their potential discourse function. It is proposed that certain units or elements produced on-line serve functions related to the presentation or development of the topic of the discourse. In the light of this proposal, the notion of pause location has been expanded to include the identification of such units, which appear to be associated with the establishment or framing of the topic. These constituents, which include such items as nominals in subject or adjunct position, initial clause structures, and disjuncts and conjuncts, are referred to in the analysis as

---

[3] As can be observed from the sample, the location of the pause is labeled in terms of the highest level unit which has been completed up to that point. It can also be observed that the writer in this sample paused twice at the end of each sentence, once before and once after typing a full stop. (Editor's note)

framing devices. The selection of these devices is informed by various discussions in the literature on the notion of topic in discourse and corresponds most closely to the definition given by Goutsos (1997) of certain devices or elements which serve to signal topic shift—introduction of a new topic or topic closure—or topic continuation. It also draws on Halliday's (1985) notions of theme in defining 'what the message is about'.

The framing devices employed in the present investigation as a means of interpreting pause location from a discourse perspective comprise the following thematic elements (with examples from the data):

1: Subject theme
Research on SLA <>
This paper <>

2: Adjunct/complement theme
At the same time <>
By the term affective states <>

3: Non-experiential theme
On the other hand <>
Historically, <>

4: Empty theme (*it*, existential *there*)
It has been stated that <>
There are <>

5: Thematized structure (initial clauses)
When we say that learners of a SL vary in their beliefs, <>
Although these claims are countered by evidence, <>

6.3.   RESULTS

6.3.1.   Pause Duration

The results for the 21 subjects on the two tasks taken together confirm the expectation that pause duration (measured in seconds) increases as text unit level increases (Figure 6.3). As anticipated, the longest pauses (and the greatest variation as shown by high standard deviations) occur at CCP and SCP locations, and the shortest pauses occur word-internally (at XCP location).

When pause duration by location is considered for the two tasks individually, a similar set of results emerges. Table 6.1 presents the mean values (in seconds) and standard deviations for all subjects by task. These results show the same general tendency for pause duration across location categories for the two tasks, which suggests that pausing behavior may not be affected by task differences.

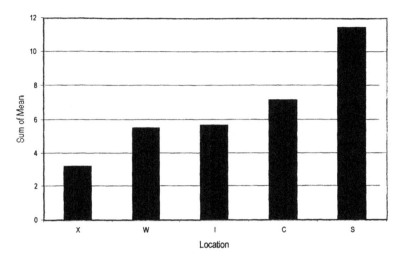

Figure 6.3. Mean Pause Duration by Location

Task		XCP	WCP	ICP	CCP	SCP
D	mean	3.24	5.55	5.66	7.1	11.41
	sd	0.69	1.23	1.56	6.68	5.45
E	mean	3.78	5.52	5.99	6.66	11.09
	sd	0.87	1.49	1.14	1.86	4.35

Table 6.1. Mean Pause Duration by Location and by Task (D = Description; E = Evaluation)

Table 6.2 presents ANOVA results for task (D/E) and group (L1/L2). The statistical analysis confirms no difference between tasks for pause duration in each category, other than at the level of XCP (i.e., word-internally), where there appears to be some evidence of significant task difference, (F = 5.58, p < 0.05). At other text unit levels, task difference did not have an effect on pause duration. Thus, research question 1, which asks whether writers respond differently to different task demands (descriptive versus evaluative) in terms of their pausing behavior when writing on a word processor, must for the most part be given a negative answer.

Location	Source	F	P
XCP	Task Language Task/Language	5.58 7.63 1.10	0.023* 0.009** 0.302
WCP	Task Language Task/Language	0.02 5.65 2.69	0.894 0.023* 0.110
ICP	Task Language Task/Language	0.76 10.86 0.10	0.390 0.002** 0.750
CCP	Task Language Task/Language	0.07 1.99 0.36	0.794 0.166 0.552
SCP	Task Language Task/Language	0.04 5.17 0.22	0.848 0.029* 0.640

*$p < 0.05$ **$p < 0.01$
df $= 1$ for each source

Table 6.2. ANOVA Results for Task (D/E) and Group (L1/L2)

Group		XCP	WCP	ICP	CCP	SCP
L2	mean sd	3.81 0.76	5.98 1.3	6.42 1.39	7.9 6.53	12.84 5.61
L1	mean sd	3.18 0.79	5.05 1.25	5.16 0.99	5.77 1.00	9.51 3.22

Table 6.3. Mean Pause Duration by Location and by Group (L1/L2)

With regard to the second research question, whether L1 and L2 writers of English respond differently to descriptive and evaluative writing tasks in terms of their pausing behavior when writing on a word processor, mean pause duration (in seconds) by location and subject group are presented in Table 6.3. According to Table 6.3, the L2 group appears to produce longer pauses across all locations. The statistical results shown in Table 6.2 confirm a difference between the L1 and L2 groups for all pause locations (SCP: $F = 7.63$, $p = 0.009$; WCP: $F = 5.65$, $p = 0.023$; ICP: $F = 10.86$, $p = 0.002$; SCP: $F = 5.17$, $p = 0.029$) other than at the clause-completion point (CCP: $F = 1.99$, $p = 0.166$).

Table 6.4 presents the L2 writers as consisting of two subgroups, the Greek students (GK, $n = 7$), who share the same language background and similar language learning experience, and a mixed non-Greek group (NGK, $n = 4$) consisting of L1 speakers of Russian, German, Japanese, and Portuguese.

L2 SubGroup		XCP	WCP	ICP	CCP	SCP
GK	*mean*	3.85	6.43	6.8	9.18	14.95
	sd	0.84	1.24	1.51	7.94	5.68
NGK	*mean*	3.73	5.19	5.76	5.65	9.13
	sd	0.65	1.06	0.88	1.35	3.15

Table 6.4. Mean Pause Duration by Category and by L2 SubGroup (GK/NGK)

It is clear from this information that although the groups follow the same general tendency with regard to pause duration by location, there appear to be differences between the Greek students and the mixed L2 group. This difference is greatest at the higher text unit levels. It appears that much of the difference in the L1 and L2 students' performance arises from the performance of the Greek L2 subgroup. Greek subjects' average pause lengths are longer at all levels than those of the L1 group, and are particularly so at CCP and SCP locations (although the higher standard deviations at these levels suggest wide individual variation). The non-Greek subgroup also produces average pause lengths at XCP longer than those of the L1 group, but at the higher text level locations (CCP and SCP) they produce on average shorter pauses than the L1 group.

Table 6.5 presents ANOVA results for task and group, where the latter category is subdivided into L1, Greek, and Non-Greek groups. As can be seen in Table 6.5, the statistical analysis supports the notion of variation in pause duration according to language group. In particular, there is evidence of significant differences according to language group at XCP ($F = 3.77$, $p = 0.03$), WCP ($F = 5.71$, $p = .0007$), ICP ($F = 7.79$, p = 0.002), and SCP (F = 7.77 , p = 0.002) locations. The observation that L2 writers of English will pause for longer at all locations may be supported in general, although I recognize the need to refine the definition of the L2 group in a way which distinguishes the Greeks as a group. The Greeks produce longer pauses at all locations, and only at the XCP location does the pause duration behavior of the non-Greek students appear similar to that of the Greeks. In all other cases, it is the Greeks which account for most of the group differences.

Location	Source	F	P
XCP	Task Language Task/Language	5.22 3.77 0.89	0.028* 0.033* 0.418
WCP	Task Language Task/Language	0.24 5.71 1.54	0.624 0.007** 0.229
ICP	Task Language Task/Language	1.02 7.79 0.66	0.320 0.002** 0.523
CCP	Task Language Task/Language	0.05 2.43 0.60	0.828 0.103 0.553
SCP	Task Language Task/Language	0.03 7.77 0.41	0.860 0.002** 0.664

*p < 0.05   **p < 0.01
df = 1 for task, df = 2 for language

Table 6.5. ANOVA Results for Task and SubGroup (L1/GK/NGK)

As we saw in Table 6.3 for the L1 and L2 group as a whole, we can see in Table 6.5 that task does not yield significant differences in pause duration, except at XCP location (F = 5.22, p = 0.028), for groups defined as L1, Greek, and non-Greek. It is also clear from these two tables that there are no significant interaction effects of task and language on pause duration.

6.3.2.   Framing Devices

As can be seen in Table 6.6, the most commonly occurring framing device is the subject theme. Although it might be anticipated that occurrence of these devices will be affected by task—e.g., that the descriptive task, which involves more sequential treatment of the topic, may give rise to more use of subject theme devices—there is no evidence for such a claim. As shown in Table 6.7, the different types of framing devices occurred with similar frequency in the descriptive and evaluative tasks, with no significant differences.

	1 Subject	2 Adj/Cmp	3 Non-Exp	4 Empty	5 Them Str	Total
N	528	37	154	61	80	860
mean	12.57	0.88	3.67	1.45	1.90	20.47
sd	5.07	1.35	2.35	1.78	2.26	7.82
%	61.4	4.3	17.9	7.1	9.3	100

Table 6.6. Occurrence of Framing Device Categories 1-5

Task		1	2	3	4	5
D	*mean*	12.90	0.88	3.67	1.67	1.76
	sd	4.96	1.46	2.54	2.24	1.73
E	*mean*	12.24	0.90	3.67	1.24	2.05
	sd	5.27	1.26	2.22	1.18	2.73
Difference (df = 1)						
F value		0.17	0.01	0.00	0.60	0.16
p value		0.68	0.90	1.00	0.44	0.69

Table 6.7. Occurrence of Framing Device Categories 1-5 by Task (D/ E)

Table 6.8 presents the frequency of each framing device in each of the subgroups, with the statistical comparison in each category showing no significant differences. Since raw frequencies of occurrence are small, no specific pattern of framing device pause occurrence emerges. However, it can be noted that in all categories the L1 group produces fewer pauses at framing device boundaries, in line with this group's generally lower mean pause frequency, especially at ICP locations. Another interesting observation concerns the Greek students, who appear to pause less frequently at framing device boundaries than might be expected, given their higher overall frequency of pausing—in particular, at ICP locations.[4] It may be that the coincidence between framing device and pause occurrence is less strong in the case of this subject group.

Subject		1	2	3	4	5
L2	*mean*	13.23	1.18	3.95	1.68	2.23
	sd	5.64	1.37	2.82	1.96	2.33
GK	*mean*	12.33	1	3.5	1.14	2.57
	sd	7.06	0.88	2.71	1.03	2.62
NGK	*mean*	13.75	1.5	4.75	2.25	2.07
	sd	2.96	2	3.01	2.66	2.16
L1	*mean*	11.85	0.55	3.35	1.2	1.55
	sd	4.38	0.28	1.73	1.58	2.19
Difference (df = 3)						
F value		0.43	1.50	1.04	1.01	0.41
p value		0.65	0.23	0.36	0.37	0.42

Table 6.8. Occurrence of Framing Device Categories 1-5 by Subgroup

When subject theme in particular is considered, it appears that statistically significant group differences emerge in the duration of subject theme pauses, $F = 9.29$, $p = 0.001$. Consideration of the means by subject group makes it possible to interpret the nature of this significant effect. In the case of the L1 group, means for subject theme and non-subject theme pause duration is very similar (5.13 and 5.24, respectively). For non-Greek students, the means for pause duration for subject themes are somewhat longer than for non-subject themes (6.07 vs. 5.49); in the case of the Greeks, the differences are more marked (7.97 vs. 6.47). This suggests that L1/L2 group differences may once again be accounted for largely in terms of the behavior of the Greek sub-

---

[4] As in studies of pausing in spoken discourse, the L1 group in this study paused less in frequency and duration than the L2 group, especially as compared to the Greek L2 writers. This finding lends support to the view that writing (and in general, language production) in an L2 is more cognitively demanding than writing in an L1. (Editor's note)

176

group. With respect to pausing and framing devices, it appears that the Greek subjects in general may make use of the subject theme framing device location to produce pauses of greater duration than the mean for the equivalent structural unit of ICP. This tendency is less strong in the non-Greek subgroup of L2 students, but the pausing behavior of both L2 writer groups contrasts with that of the L1 student writers, who appear in general not to share this strategy of producing substantially longer pauses at subject theme locations than at ICP boundaries. A finer grained exploration of individual writing episodes will help to examine this observation further.

Another noteworthy finding concerns the tendency for subject theme pauses to occur following a full noun phrase rather than a pronoun.[5] Of the 528 instances of subject theme pausing, the vast majority (458, or 86.7%) involve full noun phrases rather than pronoun subjects.

In sum, the analysis of framing devices has led to some potential insights into the function of subject theme units in establishing and introducing the topic. In the following section, the potential usefulness of the notion of framing device is explored further as a way of accounting for individual differences in pausing behavior

6.3.3. Framing Devices in Case Study Data

For this section of the analysis, the pausological data from three subjects—one non-Greek (NGK: A), one Greek (GK: Ya), and one native speaker (L1: E)—have been selected for closer examination. An initial question concerns the uptake of the framing device location for pausing in production of the string. Table 6.9 suggests that approximately one-third to one-half of all available framing device slots are taken up as opportunities for pausing. When only subject theme framing devices are considered (Table 6.10), a similar picture emerges, with approximately one-quarter to one-half of available framing device slots associated with pausing.

---

[5] This finding can be interpreted as evidence of the writer's greater degree of 'forward momentum' in writing (and hence fluency of text production) in relation to old or continuing subject themes than in relation to new or reinstated ones. The finding further suggests that subject pronouns are generated in relation to larger units of discourse whereas subject nouns may be generated to some extent as autonomous units. (Editor's note)

Subject	Task D	Task E
NGK: A	0.45	0.41
GK: Ya	0.48	0.31
L1: E	0.27	0.37

Table 6.9. Proportion of Framing Device Locations Where Pauses Occurred

Subject	Task D	Task E
NGK: A	0.49	0.51
GK: Ya	0.35	0.27
L1: E	0.25	0.31

Table 6.10. Proportion of Subject Theme Locations Where Pauses Occurred

It is interesting to note, for each individual, a general consistency of pauses at framing device locations across the two tasks. When the uptake of pausing at clause and sentence locations is compared as a proportion of available slots (Table 6.11), it is clear that the CCP/SCP locations are more consistently associated with pausing, with 54% to 79% of these slots attracting pauses, than are the discourse framing devices.[6] However, for one of the individuals (NGK: A), the occurrence of pauses in framing device slots is similar to their occurrence in inter-clause/sentence locations. These findings suggest the possibility that individuals make differential use of the availability of these framing device slots as locations for pausing, and that this may perhaps be related to their language background or proficiency.

When relative frequency and duration of pauses at framing device locations are considered (Table 6.12), further confirmation of differences between individuals emerges. For all three subjects in this analysis, pauses at framing device locations account for a similar proportion of all pauses produced (14% to 26%). However, it appears that the length of the pauses at these locations differs according to individual.

---

[6] That the structurally identified (inter-)clause and sentence locations are more consistently associated with pausing than are the functionally identified framing devices tends to reinforce an interpretation of writers' pausing behavior as indicative of macro-planning in terms of complete 'thought units' rather than in terms of topical themes. (Editor's note)

178

Subject	Task D	Task E
NGK: A	0.54	0.54
GK: Ya	0.60	0.79
L1: E	0.60	0.60

Table 6.11. Proportion of Inter-Clause/Sentence Locations Where Pauses Occurred

In the case of the non-Greek L2 writer A, pauses are shorter than for the other two subjects. The Greek student Ya, however, produces high mean pause durations at these framing device slots, suggesting a different strategy of writing production from her non-Greek counterpart. Although the uptake of these potential pause slots may be less regular in the case of the Greek writer Ya than for both the non-Greek writer A and the L1 writer E, it seems that she makes use of the slots when taken up for particularly long pauses. This close analysis of individual pausing behavior offers insights into potentially significant differences in text production strategy, which may be complemented by more extensive study of pausing behavior in relation to framing devices to provide a detailed picture of the complexities of individual processing styles.[7]

Subject	All Framing Devices (secs)	Subject Themes (secs)	Proportion (%) of Pauses at Framing Device Locations
NGK: A_D	4.99	4.12	0.26
NGK: A_E	5.25	3.84	0.21
GK: Ya_D	6.66	5.92	0.26
GK: Ya_E	7.00	9.43	0.16
L1: E_D	6.11	4.16	0.14
L1: E_E	6.35	4.26	0.22

Table 6.12. Mean Duration and Proportion of Pauses at Framing Device Locations

---

[7] Within the larger study, a number of other issues have been considered, including the coincidence of framing device pausing and productivity (subsequent flow of text string), and the occurrence of revision behavior (insertions and deletions) following framing device pausing.

6.4.   DISCUSSION

The insights drawn from the analysis of pause location and duration suggest potentially important differences in subjects' writing behaviors. However, when both individuals and subject groups are considered, a consistency is apparent in pausing behavior across a descriptive and an explanatory task. Analysis of frequency as well as duration of pausing further confirms this observation: subjects appear to react in a similar way to the two tasks, despite a supposed difference in rhetorical purpose. Given the context of the writing event (a timed examination-type essay), it may be that sensitivity to rhetorical demands is lost, or less in evidence, and little adjustment is made to the directives given in the essay prompts. Further research varying the conditions of writing and the type of task demands may provide more insight into the issue of task effect on performance.[8]

The pause data clearly shows the significance of the inter-clause/sentence location as a locus of time off writing. As has been suggested, the association between pausing and planning can only be inferred, since non-fluencies in writing may be due to other activities, such as rereading the text produced so far, consulting notes, and even non-task related activities such as daydreaming, responding to interruptions, and so on. On the basis of the findings of the present investigation, it appears that grammatical locations vary in the extent to which they attract pauses. Major boundaries in the text, coinciding in particular with paragraph, sentence, and clause junctures, are clearly powerful

---

[8] Studies of task differences in spoken production "suggest that pausing behavior varies with task and that speakers operating at or near their information-processing capacity will pause more than those who are having no difficulty managing cognitive load" (Pennington & Doi, 1993, p. 70). Assuming that different task constraints produce different pausing behavior in written as well as spoken language production, the implication for the present study is that the task constraints were similar for both types of task. It is possible that the lack of task differences is a consequence of the fact that the two essay prompts of the present study may have been perceived by the students as similar academic tasks of *expository analysis*. Thus, the descriptive intent of "What is known about individual differences in the acquisition of a second language?" may have been overridden by a tendency among students to frame academic writing tasks—and this may be especially the case in examination conditions—as requiring a critical or argument type of response. It would be worthwhile to carry out similar investigations with other, perhaps more extreme, types of task contrasts. It is also possible that the use of a word processor tends to 'even out' differences in task constraints that would be more apparent in pen-and-paper composing conditions, perhaps as a result of, or in interaction with, its own technological constraints or task characteristics having to do with machine operations or the affective context of word processing (as discussed to some extent in the introductory chapter to this volume and more fully in Pennington, 1996b, esp. ch. 3). (Editor's note)

in attracting pauses, whereas the smaller (e.g., word-internal) locations are infrequently associated with pausing. Although the explanation for this may only be speculative, it seems possible, in line with expectations from the literature, that significant macro-planning activity does occur at these major grammatical boundaries.[9]

Where the current analysis attempts to go further is in the interpretation of certain grammatically defined locations from a topic-related discourse perspective. The notion of 'framing device' is introduced as a way of identifying certain elements in the text string which potentially serve the function of establishing or highlighting the topic of the discourse. It seems that both uptake of pausing opportunities at these framing device locations and the duration of pauses when pauses do occur may vary across individuals and potentially also across language groups. This tentative observation needs to be explored further in future research.[10]

In the present analysis, the focus has been on the occurrence of pauses in computer-generated text at the boundaries of certain discourse-oriented constituents, since this offers a new approach to the traditional grammatical categorization of pause locations in written text. It is clear, however, that the notion of framing device offers only a partial explanation of the occurrence of pauses at non-clause/non-sentence boundaries. Further fine-grained analysis of pause data may reveal other reasons for extended or frequent pausing, such as to retrieve a lexical item or to focus on a spelling issue. The picture which emerges from such detailed examination of the temporal features of writing activity is a complex one that can supplement other sources of insights into writing processes carried out by different individuals or groups, both L1 and L2, and under different conditions.[11]

---

[9] The relationship of pausing to planning can be further investigated by studies that combine keystroke analysis with subjects' think-aloud record or immediate recall of composing sessions, such as in the *Writing Environment* computer tools and procedures described by Lansman, Smith, and Weber (1993). "However," as I have remarked elsewhere, "it is by no means an easy matter to operationalize and to measure the higher order processes of composing—which may in fact not be identical when composing with and without the computer medium, and so not properly identified by the same coding and classification schemes" (Pennington, 1996b, p. 63). (Editor's note)

[10] Similarities and differences in pausing behavior for individuals, language groups, and L1 vs. L2, which have been explored for spoken text production (see, e.g., Dechert & Raupach, 1980; Dechert, Mohle, & Raupach, 1984; Siegman & Feldstein, 1978), can now be productively investigated for (manual or computer) written text production. (Editor's note)

[11] It is worth investigating further the effect of medium on pausing behavior, by comparison of the same subjects' writing in word processing and pen-and-paper conditions, the former captured on computer as in the present study or in the system

181

6.5. CONCLUSION

This chapter has presented pause analysis through keystroke logging of electronically produced text as a means of generating a detailed object record of writing behavior. Although only indirect evidence of cognitive processes associated with planning, these data concerning the temporal features of writing offer the researcher a rich source of information for the investigation of the real-time activity of writing from a number of perspectives, both grammatical and discoursal. As such, this type of approach may allow us to move closer in the future towards the goal of integrating analyses of text form and text production processes.

---

described by Lansman, Smith, and Weber (1993) and the latter by direct observation (e.g., Pennington & So, 1993) or video recordings of the composing process of individual writers (e.g., Levy & Ransdell, 1996; Matsuhashi, 1981; Williamson & Pence, 1989). (Editor's note)

7. Patterns of Adaptation to a New Writing Environment: The Experience of Word Processing by Mature Second Language Writers

Ruru S. Rusmin

ABSTRACT

This chapter examines individual differences in the responses of mature second language students to using the computer as a writing tool. A group of mature students in a Hong Kong tertiary institution were taught to write academic essays on computer, and data were gathered from four assessments of attitude and writing processes over a 14-week time span, supplemented by in-class observations and ratings of written work. Findings indicate that subjects with the most positive attitudes about the computer tended to be the most positive about their own writing, and possibly wrote better quality essays. Other subjects exhibited different patterns of adaptation, including increasingly strong convictions in some cases and growing skepticism in others about the usefulness of the computer as a writing tool, accompanied by corresponding positive and negative attitudes towards writing. Identification of different patterns of reaction to word processing may help teachers of computer composition find different ways of motivating students to improve their writing skills.

7.0.   INTRODUCTION

Adaptation, defined by the Oxford dictionary as the "process by which [an] organism or species becomes adjusted to its environment," is a defining feature of human life. Today, the accelerated pace of change caused by technological development places increasing demands on our adaptive capabilities. As writers and teachers of writing and language, we too have had to adapt, especially to the new writing environments created by the introduction of word processing, "perhaps the most accepted and universal use of computers in education today" (Hyland, 1993, p. 21). The way writers adapt themselves to this new writing tool has been the focus of much research with first language writers, and more recently with second language (L2) writers as well.

183

The most commonly reported effect of transferring from writing with pen and paper to writing on computer is an improvement in attitude. Although some L2 writers may feel that the writing task is complicated by the addition of an "unfamiliar, intimidating" machine (Berens, 1986, p. 13), and others may be 'turned off' to writing because of technical problems (Piper, 1987), many students do not experience technical difficulties nor feel nervous in the computer lab (Neu & Scarcella, 1991). Anecdotal reports maintain that students enjoy writing on the computer, possibly because they have less fear of errors and illegibility (Phinney, 1989), and they feel a sense of pride in their written product due to the attractiveness of the printout (Huffmann &Goldberg, 1987; Piper, 1987). Furthermore, students may find drafting and revision faster and easier in a computer writing environment (Hermann, 1986; Phinney & Mathis, 1990; Piper, 1987).

Questionnaires on users' reactions confirm that students find writing easier and more enjoyable on the computer (Chadwick & Bruce, 1989; Neu & Scarcella, 1991; Piper, 1987; Reid, 1986), and that students writing on computers show some decrease in apprehension and improvement in their attitude towards writing (Phinney, 1991a; 1991b). Students may also believe that word processing can help improve the quality of their writing (Li, 1990; Phinney & Mathis, 1990; Reid, 1986), some saying that it helps them pay more attention to grammar, word choice, organization, and use of transitions (Neu & Scarcella, 1991). Improvements in attitude could be especially important for L2 writers, who often have even greater writing anxiety than first language writers (Phinney, 1991; Pennington, 1993b, this volume). Furthermore, improved attitudes may have positive effects on the quality of writing, since "[i]f the computer makes writing a less onerous, more satisfying experience for many students, there is at least the possibility that improvement in writing will follow" (Teichman & Poris, 1989, p. 100). Such a possibility may also be confirmed by Bangert-Drowns' (1993) meta-analysis of studies comparing first language writers who used computer and pen and paper, which concludes that there may be "a strong linear relationship between attitude toward writing and writing quality" (p. 83). Specifically, Pennington (1996b) speculates that greater enjoyment of writing can lead to more writing and revision, which may lead to improved quality.

Holistic measures of computer vs. pen and paper writing generally indicate higher scores for computer writing (Bangert-Drowns, 1993; Li, 1990; Williamson & Pence, 1989) though sometimes no significant difference is reported (Chadwick & Bruce, 1989; Reid, Lindstrom, McCaffrey, & Larson, 1983). Discrete assessments may also show improvements in certain aspects of computer writing (Lam & Pennington, 1995; Bradin & Davis, 1995). Improved quality may also be implied by increased or improved revision, and increased writing activity or longer texts, which might be short-term indications of a longer term improvement in quality (Pennington, 1993b, 1996b). Increased revisions on both the macro and micro structural levels have been reported for word processing students (Chadwick and Bruce, 1989), while longer essays have been noted for both first language writers (Bangert-Drowns, 1993; Hawisher, 1989) and L2 writers (Hanson-Smith, 1990; Li, 1990) on computer.[1]

Despite the apparent benefits of word processing, it can be difficult to draw precise conclusions about the nature of changes in attitude or quality when writing on computer because of the many variables involved in the process of writing. For example, a sufficient time span, possibly more than one semester, is needed for students to adapt their writing strategies or create new ones for writing on computer (Phinney & Khouri, 1993) since it takes time not only to acquire writing skills but also to master new technology (Phinney, 1989). In fact, positive results, apart from some improvement in attitudes, may come only after a certain level of competence and automatization with equipment and programs are reached (Hermann, 1986; Pennington, 1993b, 1996b).

It is also clear that the computer is simply a tool, and as such, may not in and of itself lead to any changes in learners or in their writing. The instructor can be an important influence in shaping students' attitudes to, and use of, the computer; for example, the enthusiasm of a teacher who is a convert to computers may rub off on students and help improve their attitudes (Thiesmeyer, 1986). The instructor's intervention is also required for learners to make good use of the computer for writing (Phinney, 1989; Hyland, 1993). Pennington (1996b), for instance, suggests that a type of instruction which, among other things, "aims to increase the sense of flexibility and experimentation in composing" (p. 154), and makes "composing processes more explicit" (*ibidem*), can best help learners develop a writing style that takes advantage of the computer's particular strengths.

Another important element that affects learners is the environment of a computer writing lab, which is very different from a classroom in that the layout of the workstations and the visibility of the screens can make it a public space. This may be a disadvantage for those students who prefer to work privately (Piper, 1987) but an advantage in the sense that it allows both peers and teachers to easily give immediate and extensive feedback (Herrmann, 1986; Phinney, 1989; Piper, 1987). The public nature of the lab can also provide a perceived or even real audience for novice writers (Davidson & Tomic, 1994; Pennington, 1991; Piper, 1987). Moreover, the kind of small group work or collaborative writing that can be conveniently implemented in computer labs

---

[1] See also papers in this volume by Akyel and Kamıslı, Bisaillon, and Brock and Pennington. (Editor's note)

helps to extend the sense of audience, and to reduce fears of writing since one's identity can be subsumed into that of the group (Dam, Legenhausen, & Wolff, 1990). The emphasis on group work, the increased interaction among students, and the physical nature of the computer lab, which requires the teacher to circulate among the students, can all contribute to make instruction in a lab setting more learner-centered and more individualized (Davidson & Tomic, 1994; Pennington, 1993c; Piper, 1987).

Finally, the characteristics of the students themselves might be more important than the machine they use. For example, if learners are insecure about themselves and their writing, they may be less apt to take advantage of the potential of the computer (Benesch, 1986; Hawisher, 1989; Pennington, 1993b, this volume). There may be students who do not like computers or the computer lab environment (Piper, 1987). Computer anxiety can greatly affect the student's mastery of computer skills, and greater exposure, or experience, may only go some way towards improving such negative attitudes (McInerney, McInerney, & Sinclair, 1994).

Not only the attitudes of the students but also their writing habits and strategies can take precedence over the influence of the computer (Gerrard, 1989; Poulsen, 1991). Again, however, it may be only after a certain period of time working with the computer that writing attitudes and habits can change. Longer experience with computers may lead to more positive attitudes (Neu & Scarcella, 1991), more efficient computer revision strategies, and greater revision (Phinney & Khouri, 1989).

Other user characteristics such as age and gender may be important. Daiute (1985), for example, suggests that while "most children approach the computer with confidence and delight, many adults are cautious" (p. 138). In terms of gender, various studies have found less anxiety, higher interest, and greater confidence among boys (Fetler, 1985; Miura, 1987; Okebukola, 1993; Todman & File, 1990), as well as among college age males using computers (Badagliacco, 1990; Colley, Gale, & Harris, 1994; Ogletree & Williams, 1990; Wilder, Mackie, & Cooper, 1985), although other studies have found more positive attitudes for females (Loyd, Loyd, & Gressard, 1987). Often, males have greater experience and exposure to computers than females (Badagliacco, 1990; Fetler, 1985). Furthermore, studies of computer experience and gender-typing, or the identification of subjects with female and male personality characteristics, seem to indicate that these two variables are more important than biological sex in determining computer attitudes (Colley, Gale, & Harris, 1994; Ogletree & Williams, 1990).

In light of the fact that variables in the environment and among students are of such consequence, it is difficult to state categorically that the introduction of a new writing tool such as the computer will have certain universal effects on writers. The interaction of various elements also makes it important to fully describe the contexts and subjects when investigating student writers' processes of adaptation. Hawisher (1989), in a review of sixteen case studies and ethnographies, comments that for both the quantitative and qualitative studies, "[w]hen we look to the description of the context in which the research was conducted, there is often a decided lack of detail" (p. 56). Similarly, Curtis and Klem (1992) state that "[o]ur own readings have found a corresponding absence of *teachers* and actual *teaching* from the bulk of computer research, even from examinations of the computer's relationship to teaching methodology; the focus, rather, seems inevitably to shift to the presence of the machines" (p. 157). Thus, one aim of the research reported in this chapter is to offer a more detailed (though not exhaustive) description of the context of computer use and the nature of its subjects, with a view to exploring not only the different ways that writers adapt to the computer, but also some of the factors that contribute to their different patterns of adaptation.

Furthermore, in place of formulating and testing set hypotheses, the investigator in the present case selected a group of L2 students and taught them composition using word processing as a tool. Then, the students' attitudinal reactions, changes in writing quality, and shifts in writing patterns served as a basis on which to construct explanations as to why they adapted the way they did. This method corresponds to the ethnographic approach and its development of *grounded theory*, that is, theory generated from the data, in contrast to the testing of predetermined hypotheses, as is the nature of a 'top-down', theory-driven research approach (Watson-Gegeo, 1988).

7.1.   METHOD

7.1.0.   Students

The twelve male and fifteen female subjects in this study were adult students ranging from 34 to 57 years of age, all native Cantonese speakers who had lived most of their lives in Hong Kong. Like the majority of Hong Kong students, they had studied the English language from elementary school, and most of them had to use English for part of their tertiary studies. However, these subjects had all finished their tertiary studies at Hong Kong Baptist College (now University) 15-30 years before. At the time of the investigation, they were enrolled in a 'conversion' study program at the university. The purpose of the program, which consisted of evening classes held after students finished their full-time day jobs, was to convert their previously earned graduate diploma into a Bachelor's degree. The English for Academic Purposes course which was the context for the investigation was compulsory for conversion students scoring below a certain level in an English language examination set by the university's Language Centre. Therefore, the subjects can be considered to have had a fairly low standard of English, especially given the fact that they did not use much English in their working lives as primary or secondary school teachers and middle grade civil servants. Their major subjects of study were History (11), Chinese (7), English (4), Geography (3), and Sociology (2).

Students registered for the two out of eight sections of the English for Academic Purposes course chosen for the study without being aware of the added computer component in these particular sections; their only criterion for selection was timetabling convenience. In the first class meeting students completed a questionnaire about the extent of their experience with word processing and computers (Appendix 7.1). According to their response, nine of the twenty-seven students, or one-third of the class, had prior word processing experience. Although their experience with computers ranged from one month to nine years, only two subjects had word processed for more than a year. A noticeable difference in gender and computer experience was apparent at the outset: six (one-half) of the male students had used word processing in contrast to only three (one-fifth) of the female students.

7.1.2. Course Structure and Activities

The English for Academic Purposes course was offered in the second semester of a program that concentrated on writing. Although writing constituted the bulk of the course, reading comprehension, structural analysis of texts, and grammar exercises also formed part of the coursework.

In the first semester, students, under different instructors, learned to write paragraphs. In the second semester, students learned various rhetorical modes and wrote four assignments over fourteen weeks of class. The first two assignments were of paragraph length while the last two were essays of three to six paragraphs. The only other constraint on the assignments was the rhetorical mode used: generalization and exemplification (Assignment 1), description (Assignment 2), comparison and contrast (Assignment 3), and classification (Assignment 4).

For the class under study, students worked on each assignment over three class sessions, with both peer and teacher feedback. The students divided themselves into small groups of two to four for peer feedback and other group work, and they chose to stay in the same groups throughout the course. They were informed that peer feedback was useful for giving a different perspective from teacher feedback, and were given a set of questions (Appendix 7.2) to answer in writing at home before peer discussion in class. Apart from this, no other training such as a sample feedback session was given. Teacher feedback was given in a different session. The teacher/researcher, who had limited knowledge of Cantonese, carried out all instruction in English. The students responded to the teacher in English but otherwise generally used Cantonese.

Students were taught to use *Microsoft Word for Windows*, the most popular word processing program among daytime university students, and the program students were most familiar with by far, according to a previous informal survey conducted among incoming freshmen. All in-class writing sessions were held in the writing laboratory, where students each had access to their own computer. The lab was reserved for the exclusive use of the class and no one else was present apart from the students and the instructor.

At the first class meeting, the instructor (the researcher) explained that students would be taught how to use the computer to write, although they would not be required to use it if they did not want to do so. The instructor further clarified that students could use the computer as much or as little as they wished in developing their written assignments. In other words, if they felt more comfortable using pen and paper to outline, to revise, or to write the whole paper, this would be acceptable. During part of the first two classes, students learned the rudiments of word processing, including turning on the computer; accessing, starting, and quitting the program; opening, saving, and closing files; and inputting and deleting text. Students were also shown how to select, cut, and paste blocks. Use of the spellchecker was left to the fifth meeting. Other functions such as the thesaurus and formatting were mentioned to the entire class, but only taught to individual students upon request.

After the first two training sessions, students wrote each assignment, using whichever writing tool they preferred, computer or pen, over a three-week period. In the first week, students had one hour in the lab to compose their first draft. One of the two sections, Group A, then submitted their drafts on diskette to the teacher for feedback. The other section, Group B, printed out copies of their papers for peers to take home and read. In the second week, Group A had one hour to consider the teacher feedback and to finish a second draft, which they then printed out for their peers to take home. Group B spent 30-45 out of 90 minutes on peer discussion and the rest of the time on writing the second draft to be submitted to the teacher for feedback. In the third week, the feedback process was reversed for the two groups, so that Group A now received peer feedback and Group B teacher feedback, after which they completed a final draft submitted on diskette at the end of the period. Assessment and grammar comments from the instructor were then returned to the students the following week. At that time, students were also given a questionnaire designed to elicit information about their experiences in that assignment (Appendix 7.3), to be returned the following week. Each of the four assignments was completed in this way over a three-week period. The four completed questionnaires from each student for each assignment constituted the bulk of the data for the study.

7.1.3.   Questionnaire on Assignments

The first section of the questionnaire required students to complete statements by indicating their responses on 6-point scales with labeled endpoints. The first three items asked students how easy it was in each assignment to develop content, to organize their ideas, and to express their ideas, with endpoints marked 'very difficult' and 'very easy'. The purpose of these statements was to uncover changes in students' perceptions of writing difficulty. The second three items were related to helpfulness of peer feedback, teacher feedback, and grammar feedback, with endpoints of 'not at all helpful' and 'very helpful'. The objective of these items was to assess students' attitudes towards different types of feedback and changes in these attitudes over time. The third set of three items attempted to assess the quantity of changes students made after each type of feedback, with endpoints of 'none at all' and 'very many'. The responses to these items could indicate whether students made more or fewer revisions over time. Finally, for each of the three revision items, students were asked what kinds of changes they made—content, organization, expression, or grammar—thus giving a more detailed picture of students' revision patterns.

A second section of the questionnaire attempted to analyze students' use of the computer. Given a list of the various stages in writing such as outlining, drafting, revising, etc., students were asked to indicate which tool (word processing or pen and paper) they used to complete these steps. They were also asked to indicate whether they completed these steps when writing the first, second, and/or third drafts of each assignment. The purpose of this question was to capture the interplay of computer and pen and paper in the various stages of writing, and to detect any changes in the quantity or pattern of use of the two writing tools.

The third section of the questionnaire consisted of sentence completion items with responses on 6-point scales with marked bipolar endpoints as above (Appendix 7.3). Q11 assessed students' attitude towards the usefulness of the computer for writing. Students' answers to this question at different points in their course were considered to be a key indicator of their response to word processing. The next two questions examined their affective responses to writing in the lab and home environments. Questions 14-17 asked students to report any changes they perceived in the quality, speed, quantity, and ease of their writing. Questions 18 and 19 attempted to measure the level of subjects' anxiety towards writing. Finally, the last three open-ended sentence completion items asked students to report what they found easy and difficult about the written assignment, and what changes they felt were occurring in their writing.

7.1.4. Other Sources of Data

Students' marks for the four assignments were recorded in order to assess the quality of their written work. Since these marks were awarded by the instructor, who may have been influenced by personal knowledge of the students, six of the assignments which showed a range of marks were assessed a second time by the instructor and by two independent raters using the *ESL Composition Profile* designed by Jacobs, Zinkgraf, Wormuth, Hartfiel, and Hughey (1981). The two independent raters were experienced ESL teachers working in the same institution as the researcher; they had no previous experience with the *ESL Composition Profile*. Finally, the instructor/researcher made and recorded observations during the class periods, and also attempted to discuss with students their thoughts and concerns about writing.

7.1.5. Data Analysis

Data gathered from the four questionnaires (one per assignment) completed by each subject were analyzed in order to identify patterns of similarity among subjects and patterns of change over time. For changes over time, somewhat more weight was given to subjects' final answers, as these could be interpreted as a final or summative judgment on each question. Patterns were assigned colors—e.g., one color for consistently positive choices on a question and another for choices showing an increase on that scale over time. After the color coding was completed, the researcher observed whether certain colors, or patterns of response, in each question tended to relate to the patterns in other questions. In addition, means and standard deviations for the responses to each question were calculated as an aid to identifying patterns in the data.

The assignment marks for each student were examined in terms of mean scores and changes over time. These data were then compared to students' responses from the questionnaire in order to determine whether patterns of computer attitudes or use appeared to be related to writing quality. In addition, since the two sections of students differed in which type of feedback, teacher or peer, they received first, mean responses of the two groups for each item on the questionnaire were compared in order to determine whether the order of feedback might have led to different results.

7.2. FINDINGS

7.2.1. Questionnaire

7.2.1.1. General Perception of the Computer's Value for Writing

Analysis began with the item in Q.11: "I find the computer useful for writing", as the subjects' general attitude towards writing on the computer offered a framework for interpreting their responses to other items. Patterns of responses to this item were identified as subjects' overall orientation to or enthusiasm for the computer in writing, and students with similar patterns of response were grouped into categories (see Table 7.1).

Item 11: I find the computer useful for writing (1 = not at all ... 6 = very much)

	Assignment Mean										
	#1	#2	#3	#4	No.	Male	Female	Exp.	%	No Exp.	%
Devotees	6.00	6.00	6.00	6.00	5	4	1	4	80	1	20
Enthusiasts	6.00	5.00	5.40	5.40	5	2	3	2	40	3	60
Rededicateds	5.17	3.80	4.00	2.17	6	3	3	2	33	4	67
Positives	4.67	4.33	4.67	4.67	3	1	2	1	33	2	67
Converts	3.50	4.60	4.83	5.33	6	1	5	0	0	6	##
Skeptics	4.50	4.50	3.00	3.00	2	1	1	0	0	2	##
Overall	5.00	4.76	4.82	5.19	27	12	15	9		18	

Table 7.1. Classification of Subject Responses, Sex, and Computer Experience.

The first group, who responded to this item with consistent maximum scores of 6, we may call computer **devotees**. These students began the course with a high evaluation of the usefulness of the computer for writing, and maintained their very positive assessment

192

throughout the semester. All but one of these subjects had previous experience with word processing, indicating that strong enthusiasm for word processing is probably related to previous experience. Of these five individuals, four were male and one was female. Although on the surface gender seems to be an influence on attitude, it may rather be that gender predicts to computer experience.[2] Out of a total of nine experienced word processing subjects in the entire pool, six were male and three were female. That four males and one female out of this subgroup of nine experienced computer users were **devotees** suggests computer experience as a key factor determining users' positive responses to computer-assisted writing.

The second group consists of those five students who began with maximum scores of 6 ('very much') in response to the question of whether they found the computer useful for writing, but then occasionally dropped their assessments to 5. These subjects we may call computer **enthusiasts**.

The third group were identified not so much by their actual scores, but by the pattern of the shift in their scores. These were six students who began with a high regard for the computer which then fell off. Towards the end of the semester, however, their assessments rose again. These computer **rededicated** students seem to have been subject to an initial novelty effect, and when this effect wore off their assessment dropped, although they still remained generally positive. However, their resurgent later ratings would seem to indicate that they began to feel more positive about using the computer for writing as time passed.

The fourth group consists of three subjects with consistent positive scores of 4 and 5 on the question of computer usefulness; we may call them computer **positives**.

The fifth group consists of six students who began with relatively neutral scores of 3 and 4, but then later raised their assessments to 5 or 6. These computer **converts** clearly became more positive towards the computer as they began to use it more.

The last group consists of two computer **skeptics**, who began positively but then ended the term with an assessment of 3 as regards the computer's usefulness for their writing, slightly on the negative side.

Overall, it can be seen that twenty-five of the twenty-seven subjects, an overwhelming majority of over 90% of the class, ended the

---

[2] The fact that more males than females had computer experience at the beginning of the course may be related to pre-existing, commonly reported differences in gender-related attitudes and other characteristics that predict to computer use. Any attempt to disentangle the gender factor from the experience factor in terms of pre-existing differences among the subjects would therefore seem to be a relatively fruitless exercise. (Editor's note)

semester with positive attitudes towards the computer's usefulness for their writing. Interestingly enough, the mean responses for the last assignment, which as noted previously may be considered a kind of final of summative judgment, indicate that the **converts** reached almost the same level of positive regard for the computer as the **enthusiasts,** and both they and the **rededicateds** looked more favorably upon the computer for writing at the end of the course than the **positives** (see Figure 7.1).

Item 11: I find the computer useful for writing (1 = not at all ... 6 = very much)

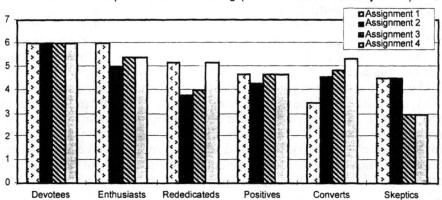

Figure 7.1. Assessment of Usefulness of Computer for Writing over Time.

It also seems clear that experience is an important factor in determining the strength of subjects' positive attitudes. Those with experience tended to be the most enthusiastic, as can be seen by the percentages of experienced subjects in each category (Table 7.1). Those with no experience tended to start with lower evaluations, but then changed their assessment more, which is not surprising since they had no basis on which to make their first assessments. Again, gender is probably eliminated as an independent factor after taking into account the initial imbalance in experience between the sexes *(but see footnote 2—Ed.).*

7.2.1.2.   Responses to Other Questionnaire Items

On the whole, the response pattern to items 12-19, given in Appendix 7.4, reflects the response to Q11, though some individual points in relation to these other items can be raised.

Q12: "I like writing in the computer lab." Students generally liked writing in the lab; the overall mean response of 5.0 was one of the highest among all of the questionnaire items. The means for each of the six groups identified tend to indicate that greater enthusiasm for the computer corresponds to greater enthusiasm for the lab[3]; as in Q11, the **devotees** responded most positively, followed by the **enthusiasts**. The **rededicateds**, **positives**, and **converts** then followed. The responses of one of the **skeptics** was low, which accounts for the low average for the subjects in that category.

Q13: "I like writing alone, at home." Students had strong feelings both for and against writing at home, as indicated by a relatively high standard deviation (1.4) for this item. The mean response to this item for each group, with one exception, shows an inverse relationship with the mean group responses to Q11. In other words, lesser enthusiasm about the computer's usefulness tended to be related to liking to write alone, at home.[4] The exception to this pattern occurs with the **skeptics**, one of whom greatly disliked writing at home, as revealed by her consistent responses of 1 to this item. One can assume that the home environment represents many different circumstances, some of which may not be conducive to writing.

Q14: "I feel my writing has improved." For this item, responses were positive, with an overall mean rating of 4.2. The **devotees** were more sanguine about their own improvement, with ratings from 4-6 and a group mean of 4.85. The other groups—the **enthusiasts**, **positives**, **rededicateds**, and **converts**—were somewhat less positive, with mean group ratings all clustering just above scale point 4. Interestingly, the means for final assessments show that the **converts** were more certain than all of the other groups except for the **devotees** about improvements in their writing.[5] Of the **skeptics**, one felt there was quite a lot of improvement and the other, little improvement.

Q15: "I write faster now than I used to." In terms of writing speed, or fluency, ratings were again in a positive direction, with a mean of 4.1 for all subjects. As in the responses to other items, the **devotees** had

---

[3] This result underscores the significance of a favorable setting in ensuring positive outcomes of computer use. (Editor's note)

[4] This tendency may indicate that 'loners' benefit less from computer use in a setting with other learners, thus illustrating the effect of individual differences on adaptation pattern and computer effects. (Editor's note)

[5] Thus, like converts in other types of circumstances, these computer writing converts show an even higher level of commitment than other supportive groups. (Editor's note)

much higher ratings than the other subjects, with a group mean of 4.85 and a preponderance of responses in the 4-6 range. The only negative score of 1 was from a **skeptic**.

Q16: "I write more than I used to." In terms of quantity, although again the **devotees** were much more positive than the other categories of respondents, most subjects believed they were writing more, with an overall mean response of 4.2. For this item, again, the **converts'** final assessments are second only to those of the **devotees**.

Q17: "I find writing easier than I used to." Somewhat similar patterns emerge for the question of writing ease. The **devotees** had by far the highest scores of all respondent categories, but subjects were generally positive, with an overall mean for all respondents of 4.0. Only two students felt that writing was becoming less easy over time. One was a **skeptic**, whose response corresponds to her negative reactions to most of the other items. The other was a **rededicated**, who had responses for this item across the four assignments of 5-2-3-2. The inconsistency of this response pattern, which stands out from the usual **rededicated** pattern, could suggest that this individual was subject to a novelty effect, but otherwise did not find that the computer, though useful, made writing less of a chore.

Q18: "I enjoyed this assignment." Subjects' enjoyment of the assignments seems to be related to their enthusiasm for writing on the computer, as mean group responses to this item echo responses to Q11. No clear patterns of change over time emerged, and no preferences for particular assignments appeared for any category of respondents.[6]

Q19: "I feel nervous about writing." Although the mean of students' responses to this item was at the median point on the scale of 3.5, the responses also showed more variation in ratings, with a standard deviation of 1.2, than in most of the other items. On the whole, the **devotees** showed the least nervousness, averaging a rating of 2.7 on this item across the four assignments. One **devotee** was not at all nervous, with consistent responses of 1. One of the **skeptics** seemed to be most nervous about writing as her responses of 6-6-6-5 to this item indicate high levels of anxiety. All of the other groups show great variation, both

---

[6] It would appear that a positive attitude to the assignments given for the course is part of a global positive effect on attitudes (a 'halo effect') of computer use. As a generalization, it may be suggested that a preset topic for a writing assignment will elicit a relatively weak affective response from students and thus show a less distinctive or independent pattern of attitudes than a self-selected topic, to which a writer will naturally have a greater commitment. (Editor's note)

among subjects and in patterns of change over time. However, in the final administration of the questionnaire, the **converts** claimed a low level of nervousness about writing, approaching that of the **devotees**.

In the items discussed thus far, levels of enthusiasm about the computer as a writing tool, as classified by responses to Q11, seem to correspond to: liking to write in the lab, not liking to write at home, and enjoying the assignments. The **devotees** are consistently more positive than all of the other categories of respondents about the computer, about writing in the lab, and about improvements in the quality, speed, quantity, and ease of their own writing. They also show the highest levels of enjoyment and the least nervousness. The **converts** completed the study with very positive responses, coming second to the **devotees** in their final assessments of quality, speed, quantity, and lack of nervousness about their own writing. It is difficult to draw conclusions about the **skeptics**, as one of the two subjects in this group was consistently negative in her responses to all items, while the other was somewhat more positive.

Qs 1-3: 1 = very difficult ... 6 = very easy

	developing content	organizing	expressing ideas
Devotees	3.90	3.85	3.85
Enthusiasts	3.95	4.05	3.80
Rededicateds	3.47	3.47	3.55
Positives	3.08	3.17	3.33
Converts	3.35	3.35	3.52
Skeptics	2.88	3.25	3.00
Overall Mean	3.55	3.56	3.58
sd	0.90	0.89	0.84

Table 7.2. Perceptions of Ease of Writing.

Qs 1-3: "Developing the content/organizing/expressing my ideas in this assignment was very difficult-very easy." In these three items (Table 7.2), the group means show that the **devotees** and **enthusiasts** tended to find writing easier. They are followed by the **rededicateds**, and then the **converts**. The **positives** and the **skeptics** found writing most difficult. The fact that the same response patterns found in the previous items do not emerge here may be because this set of items is more assignment-specific: instead of general attitudes towards writing, these ratings show particular responses to each assignment. On the other hand, the responses may indicate the different focus of individuals on different aspects of their writing.

With regard to changes over time, only a few subjects for each of these questionnaire items found writing becoming easier, and these subjects were from various respondent categories. Only one subject perceived a clear decrease, and that was in ease of expressing ideas. There does not seem to be any clear relationship between ease of writing for specific assignments and particular respondent categories or individual subjects. It could be that attitudes toward the computer as a writing tool do not necessarily translate—at least not in the short period of this study—into a sense of ease in developing content, organizing, or expressing ideas in writing, contrary to what some studies seem to suggest.[7] Rather, computer users seem to develop an overall attitudinal stance towards the electronic medium.

Qs 4-6: "The peer/teacher/grammar feedback was not at all helpful-very helpful." It was difficult to determine how the various groups reacted to the question of feedback (Table 7.3) as there were no clear patterns of response in terms of the categories derived from the Q11 responses. Some subjects found some types of feedback less useful over time, while others either showed stable patterns in relation to the different types of feedback, which may be an indication that they had a fixed idea of how useful feedback was, or a lack of patterning in the responses, which may indicate that the usefulness of feedback varied according to the assignment.

Overall, of these three types of feedback (in-process peer feedback, in-process teacher feedback, and final grammar feedback and comments on marked assignments), ratings indicate that subjects found grammar feedback and comments made after marks were given to be most useful. The same was found for the individual group means, with the exception of the **converts**, who found teacher feedback at an earlier stage of writing slightly more useful than the other types of feedback. The tendency to value grammar feedback and final comments highly may be due to the students' concern with language as a result of their previous language studies. Additionally, they may have valued this post-writing feedback more since it was the only grammar feedback they received from the instructor.

---

[7] Computer users may gain a sense of the computer's facilitation of mechanical aspects of production and revision, but not of the higher level operations of writing. (Editor's note)

Type of Feedback	Qs 4-6: 1 = not at all helpful ... 6 = very helpful			Qs 7-9: 1 = none at all ... 6 = very many		
	Peer	Teacher	Grammar	Peer	Teacher	Grammar
Devotees	4.25	5.05	5.50	3.85	4.45	4.25
Enthusiasts	3.90	5.10	5.30	3.30	4.40	4.40
Rededicateds	4.14	4.86	4.91	3.72	4.34	4.00
Positives	4.75	5.08	5.17	4.50	4.75	4.42
Converts	4.09	4.83	4.74	3.86	4.05	3.62
Skeptics	3.38	4.38	4.75	4.14	4.75	4.00
Overall Mean	4.06	4.86	5.01	3.75	4.31	3.01
sd	1.03	0.86	0.87	1.07	1.05	1.00

Table 7.3. Usefulness of Feedback and Number of Post-Feedback Revisions.

Qs 7-9: "I made changes in my assignment after peer/teacher/ grammar feedback." The self-report data do not show that any category of subjects tended to make more changes than others (Table 7.3). In terms of individual students' trends over the four assignments, ten subjects showed a pattern of making fewer changes after peer feedback over time (Q7), with only four subjects indicating that they made more changes after peer feedback as time passed. In addition, the individual response pattern for Q7 about number of revision changes resulting from peer feedback shows no relationship to the response pattern for Q4 about the perceived helpfulness of peer feedback. With teacher feedback, ten subjects reported some increase in the number of changes they made from first to last assignment, while five reported some decrease (Q8). For only two subjects in each group did there appear to be a relationship between their responses to Q8 on number of revision changes and those to Q5 on helpfulness of teacher feedback. Finally, six subjects showed a self-reported increase over time in the number of changes they made after grammar and marking comments (Q9), with only one claiming to have reduced the number of changes made as a result of the teacher's grammar feedback and marking comments. Only one subject's pattern of response showed any relationship over time between Q9 (number of revision changes after grammar and marking comments) and Q6 (helpfulness of grammar feedback).

199

In general, the lack of connection between the two sets of items regarding the helpfulness of feedback and the number of revision changes made, and the lack of any clear pattern of change for subjects over the three areas of feedback, would seem to indicate that perceptions and outcomes related to feedback occur at the individual level rather than as an effect of the computer or of attitudes towards the computer.[8]

Q10: "In this assignment, I used the computer/pen and paper to jot down my ideas, organize, etc." Some patterns emerge from the analysis of which tool was utilized during which stage of writing. In terms of the tool that was used more, not surprisingly, the **devotees** tended to use the computer almost exclusively, employing pen and paper for, at most, the initial steps of developing the first draft. The **enthusiasts** and **rededicateds** tended to use both tools, but employed pen and paper mainly for the first and sometimes the second drafts. Of the three **positives**, two used the computer almost exclusively throughout the writing process. Five of the six **converts** used both tools, employing pen and paper either mainly for the first draft (two subjects), or throughout all three drafts (three subjects) in conjunction with the computer. Finally, one of the **skeptics** used pen and paper exclusively and the other, the computer almost exclusively. In general, those who used pen and paper employed it mainly for the first draft, for jotting down ideas, organizing, outlining, and drafting. It seems, then, that the majority of subjects used both tools, but the greater the reported level of positive orientation to the computer, the greater the use of the electronic tool.[9]

There were no general patterns of change in the different types of use made of computer vs. pen and paper tools for the various respondent categories. Some subjects experimented with using only the computer for the first assignment but then returned to pen and paper for certain tasks. Others gradually began to use the computer more. Still others wrote by hand at first, then changed over to the computer, later returning to pen and paper for steps such as revision. Many subjects, however, had unidentifiable or non-existent patterns of change. This may be in part because the self-reports were not accurate. On the other hand, it may be because writing habits take time to change, and stu-

---

[8] Alternatively, the findings for these two sets of items may indicate that students were unable to reliably report their revisions or to reliably relate revision changes to the type of feedback received. (Editor's note)

[9] It is interesting to speculate as to whether this positive orientation is cause or effect of greater use, or whether this relationship represents the sort of mutually reinforcing bidirectional causality I have posited for writing outcomes in relation to attitudes and the computer's facilitating effects (Pennington, 1996b, ch. 3; 1996c-d; 1999; this volume). (Editor's note)

dents were still experimenting and needed more time to find a combination of the two tools that they felt comfortable with.

In terms of the amount of writing activity, it is clear that some subjects began to repeat composing operations throughout the three drafts, i.e., to write in a recursive fashion. For example, although initially they revised content in the first draft only, later they revised content in all three drafts. Of the students who reported writing more recursively as the course progressed, two were **devotees**, one an **enthusiast**, three **rededicateds**, and two **converts**. A total of nine subjects out of twenty-seven, i.e., one-third of the entire subject group, reported increased recursivity in writing.[10]

7.2.2. Writing Quality

The generally positive response to the computer of all but two of the subjects is reflected (Table 7.4) in a general increase across all subjects in marks from first assignment (mean 6.29 out of 10) to last assignment (mean 6.64 out of 10), with average marks in each group ranging from 5.61 (**positives**) on the first assignment to 7.33 (**devotees**) on the last. In addition, consistent with their most positive overall response to the computer, the **devotees** received the highest average marks across all four assignments, with an overall mean of 6.86 out of 10, as well as on all of the individual assignments except the second. The *ESL Composition Profile* scores given by the independent raters to the assignments of six of the subjects reflect almost the same ranking, from best to worst, as the ranking obtained from the class marks. This finding gives some confidence in the value of class marks as an indicator of the comparative rank and progress of individual students.

7.2.3. Teacher vs. Peer Feedback First

The two sections underwent different treatments in that Group A received teacher feedback after the first draft and peer feedback after the second draft, and Group B the opposite order of feedback. In a comparison of the mean ratings, some differences emerged between the two groups. Group A had higher means for most of the items. In particular, Group A gave higher ratings on Q4-6 regarding helpfulness of feedback, and on Q11 and Q12 regarding finding the computer useful for writing and liking the computer lab. In general, then, Group A, who re-

---

[10] This is one of the more interesting findings of the study, as it suggests a general change in writing approach in relation to the computer context (e.g., as described in Pennington, 1996b-d; this volume). (Editor's note)

ceived teacher feedback before peer feedback, seems to have been more positive overall.

Class marks: 1 = minimum ... 10 = maximum score

Assignment	mean 1	mean 2	mean 3	mean 4	mean All Assigns.
Devotees	7.17	6.10	6.83	7.33	**6.86**
Enthusiasts	6.63	6.37	6.43	6.87	**6.58**
Rededicateds	6.42	6.64	6.89	3.72	**6.67**
Positives	5.61	5.89	6.00	5.72	**5.81**
Converts	6.25	6.67	6.69	6.75	**6.59**
Skeptics	5.67	6.33	5.83	6.42	**6.06**
Overall Mean	6.29	6.33	6.45	6.64	

Table 7.4. Marks on Writing Assignments

Grp A = Teacher feedback first
Grp B = Peer feedback first

Q	1	2	3	4	5	6	7	8	9
Grp A	3.49	3.57	3.63	4.16	5.06	5.21	3.80	4.43	4.07
Grp B	3.63	3.53	3.51	3.91	4.56	4.72	3.69	4.12	3.93

Q	11	12	13	14	15	16	17	18	19
Grp A	5.14	5.25	3.29	4.18	4.06	4.23	4.02	4.61	3.44
Grp B	4.65	4.63	3.70	4.12	4.14	4.07	3.98	4.21	3.60

Table 7.5. Comparison of Responses for Order of Feedback

7.3. DISCUSSION

7.3.1.   Attitude

This 14-week study has been a brief period in which to assess subjects' attitudes as they adapt to a new writing tool and a new writing environment. It is clear that at the start of the investigation almost all of the subjects had a positive regard for the computer as a useful writing tool. Some subjects, such as the **devotees**, the **enthusiasts**, and the **positives**, did not change their assessment over time. The **rededicateds**, however, began with a high initial assessment which they later revised downward. Toward the latter half of the course, however, they either returned to their initial high assessment or rated the computer even more useful than at first. These **rededicated** students may have been attracted at the start by the novelty of using the computer. After this novelty effect had faded, their assessment fell; but as they began to master computer skills and adjust their writing habits to the new tool, they reconfirmed or reasserted their previous belief in the computer.[11]

Other subjects, the **converts**, began with more neutral assessments of the usefulness of the computer for writing, but then revised their assessment upwards. Since these **converts** had had no previous experience with word processing, the improvement in their attitudes may be due to their exposure to word processing and their growing mastery of the tool for their own writing. Finally, of the two **skeptics**, who revised their assessment of the computer downwards, one seems to have been prone to computer phobia, perhaps worsened by the lack of typing skills, and the other suffered high levels of anxiety about writing.

On the final evaluations, twenty-six out of the twenty-nine students recorded positive ratings of 5 or 6 regarding the computer's usefulness as a writing tool. Furthermore, in the addendum to the final questionnaire, all of the subjects indicated that they would recommend that their classmates take a computer rather than a non-computer section of the course, and all but one, the computer-phobic **skeptic**, declared that they would have chosen a computer section for themselves. These results tend to confirm findings of previous studies that a majority of students have a positive reaction to writing on the computer.

---

[11] On the analogy of the patterns over time of the 'culture shock' syndrome (e.g., as reviewed by Brown, 1987, ch. 7), the *rededicted* pattern of adaptation can be seen as going from a 'honeymoon period', through a period of 'computer shock' or 'computer stress', and then gradually emerging into a period of 'recovery' and positive adjustment. (Editor's note)

On the whole, those subjects who demonstrated the strongest positive orientation to the computer were also those who believed most strongly that they were writing better and faster, writing more, writing more easily, and with greater enjoyment. The **devotees** consistently scored highest of all of the groups in the attitude items, and the **converts**, whose final assessment of the computer for writing was third among the respondent categories, had correspondingly high final ratings on the attitude items. This would seem to indicate that positive attitudes about the computer are linked to positive attitudes about writing. However, the exact nature of the relationship between the two is probably not one of simple, one-way causation. Those writers with previous word processing experience like the **devotees** of this study may have found that the structure of the course, with its in-class writing on computers in the lab, was fitted to their habits; thus, they had a positive sense of improvements in their own writing. Reciprocally, for those students without previous word processing experience, good attitudes or strong motivation may have made them more open to and more positive about learning to write on the computer.

Given a favorable initial attitude towards writing and a positive or neutral regard for the computer, as posited by Pennington (1996b, ch. 3; 1996d), these attitudes may then reinforce each other. For example, in terms of quantity of writing, the belief that the computer can help a writer to write more may actually lead a writer to produce more, thus confirming the initial belief. Similarly, the experience of writing and revising three drafts more quickly on the computer than with pen and paper may lead to a faith in the potential of the computer to increase writing speed, which may then encourage the writer to write with increasing facility (Pennington, this volume). Furthermore, attitudes towards the different aspects of writing may also influence each other reciprocally. For example, a conviction that the computer can help one to write faster might lead to a 'self-fulfilling prophecy' of writing more or of spending more time at the computer (*ibid.*)

On the other hand, the lack of a favorable initial attitude may mean that negative attitudes towards writing and towards the computer will reinforce each other.[12] In the present study, while the most computer-enthusiastic students, the **devotees**, reported by far the lowest levels of writing nervousness or anxiety, the students who were least positive about the computer, the **skeptics**, had by far the highest self-reported anxieties. For one of the **skeptics**, his apparent computer phobia and difficulty with typing may have increased his anxiety about writing; for the other, who in fact seemed to learn word processing quite easily,

---

[12] See Pennington (1999) for a detailed discussion of the importance of attitudes as a causal factor in computer writing outcomes. (Editor's note)

anxiety about writing perhaps led to skepticism regarding the computer as a useful writing tool.

While attitudes towards the computer and towards writing may re-inforce each other, it is also possible that attitudes and skills are related. As Pennington and So (1993) comment in their study on Singaporean writers, it is difficult to pinpoint how a writer's level of process writing skill is related as cause and/or effect to interest and experience in writing. Writers' initial attitudes and writing skills may over time interact in a reciprocal fashion. Or, as Pennington (1996d) suggests, learners with a less positive attitude and/or weaker skills, or those who have to contend with external factors that make writing difficult may find that their "starting affective state may or may not be able to provide sufficient energy in the way of enthusiasm and drive to override other influences" (p. 137).

It is also clear that other factors can contribute to the determination of attitudes. As Pennington (1996c) suggests, the writer's attitude not only towards writing and the computer, but also towards "language and the educational enterprise more generally, are not easily disentangled from the effects of writing on computer in a particular educational environment" (p. 102). In the Hong Kong context, for example, concern about marks may cause students to have higher anxiety levels. However, anxiety does not necessarily have to be a negative factor. Though students like the **skeptics** may have been subject to what Brown (1987, p. 106) describes as 'debilitating' anxiety, 'facilitative' anxiety that offers just enough stress to impel writers to put substantial effort into writing can be helpful. Writers like the **positives**—who exhibited the lowest levels of anxiety according to Q19 and the lowest scores in the class marks—may not have had enough motivation to work seriously on their writing.

In fact, the concept of 'facilitative' anxiety may help to explain why subjects believed that writing was becoming easier (Q17) but did not find developing content, organizing, or expressing ideas as becoming easier (Q1-3). While subjects felt that their writing skills were becoming generally stronger in the context of computer use, they could also have felt that the demands upon them in each assignment had increased. Although they may have perceived these demands to be external, they may also have had higher expectations of themselves—i.e., they might have developed 'facilitative' anxiety—as they improved their writing skills. As Pennington (1996b) speculates, it is possible that during the writing process the motivated writer "continually adjusts the goalpost for communication slightly beyond what he or she can attain or has already attained" (p. 86).

7.3.2.   Adaptation to Writing on Computer

The majority of subjects used both computer and pen and paper to
write, and the choice of tools is not predicted by previous computer
writing experience: there were cases of experienced word processing
subjects who used pen and paper as well as inexperienced computer
writers who used word processing exclusively. It is also clear that some
experimentation took place as participants tried to find a comfortable fit
between their writing habits and the available writing tools. The
essentially positive reactions to writing on the computer in the present
investigation could in fact have been due in part to the choice students
had of which tool to use. Such freedom of choice not only avoided
problems such as those reported by Piper (1987) of disgruntled students
who dropped out of an EFL class with a word processing component,[13]
but may also have led students to feel less threatened by the computer.
The lack of obligation to use the computer may have been why, given
the technical difficulties some of the novices experienced, they showed
an admirable persistence in wanting to write on the computer.[14] The
other change observed was an increase in writing activity for some
subjects. However, since these subjects were from various groups, it is
difficult to conclude that this increase in writing activity is related to
computer enthusiasm. Overall, it is probable that the process of
adaptation and the increase in writing activity were not concluded
within fourteen weeks; writing habits were still changing at the close of
the investigation.

7.3.3.   Writing Quality

Although the most computer-oriented students perceived the greatest
improvement in their writing, and in fact received the highest class
marks on their assignments, the differences among the groups' assignment marks were small. Furthermore, the measurement instruments
used in the research were insufficient to assess whether participants in
the study were, in fact, writing better. The assessment using the *ESL
Composition Profile* generally confirmed the level of quality assessed
by the holistic marks on assignments; but class marks, especially when
assigned by a researcher who is also the class teacher, are not sufficiently reliable to be a basis for theorizing about adaptation and quality.

[13] As discussed elsewhere in this volume (ch. 1, ch. 8) in relation to the selection of
topics in e-mail communication, freedom of choice may be an important factor predicting to students' success in computer use. (Editor's note)
[14] These students' computer use illustrates the personal commitment of intrinsic, self-
imposed motivation in contrast to externally imposed motivation or sanctions.
(Editor's note)

Finally, the amount of revision reported by students as self-report data is also not reliable. In any case, the levels of revision reported by the students in this investigation showed no obvious positive or a negative relationship to subjects' degree of enthusiasm for writing on the computer.

The holistic scores given as class marks do, however, provide some evidence that strong or increasing enthusiasm for the computer over time may be accompanied by increasing quality of writing. The improvement in marks for some of the **devotees** and **enthusiasts**, and for most of the **converts**, corresponds to Bangert-Drowns' (1993) conclusion about computer use from his meta-analysis of comparative studies of word processing and pen-and-paper composing, that "as the attitude becomes more positive, the writing quality improves" (p. 83). Even with evidence of a relationship between enthusiasm for the computer as a writing tool and writing quality, it is difficult to determine the direction of the influence. For example, in the case of the **converts**, whose increase in enthusiasm was matched by an improvement in class marks, greater mastery of word processing skills may have led them to be able to spend more time and to pay more attention to their writing. On the other hand, as the only group that found in-process teacher feedback to be more useful than grammar and final feedback, the **converts** may have tried harder to adjust to teacher expectations and have gotten better marks as a result, which may have led them to be more positive about using the computer.[15]

7.3.4.   Influencing Factors and Limitations

In the process of adapting to writing on the computer, attitudes, writing processes, and writing quality may change, but clearly it is difficult to separate these changes from the many variables in the environment and among the writers themselves. In other words, although we have discussed possible effects of word processing, "when students make progress, much more than just the computer is involved" (Hermann, 1986, p. 6). In her review of word processing studies, Pennington (1993b; 1996b, ch. 2) suggests that the different and sometimes contradictory findings reported may be due in large part to different situational and methodological variables in subjects, teachers, setting, time span, instruction, software and hardware, and effectiveness measures. It will be useful, then, to discuss at least some of these variables in relation to the present study.

---

[15] It is perhaps worth noting in this connection that the *converts* are a wholly inexperienced group, and their lack of prior experience may have made them work harder to 'catch up' to those with more computer experience. (Editor's note)

7.3.4.1.   Time

Fourteen weeks is a limited time in which to examine subjects' attitudes and adaptations to using the computer for their writing. Another semester would help to reveal whether the patterns of adaptations and changes identified would continue or shift. In light of the few changes observed, however, it is possible to speculate that there exists a cycle of attitude changes as students master word processing skills and alter their writing process. Each gain in new skills and each adjustment in writing habits is linked to an increase in positive attitudes, which may then fall slightly or be maintained on a plateau for some time. Within a pattern characterized by small rises and dips or plateaus, there may be a gradual improvement in attitudes towards use of the computer for writing. Although the opposite scenario may occur—**rededicateds** and **converts**, and other subject groups with positive attitudes, may find the computer less useful over time—the fourteen weeks of the study were probably a sufficient time period to account for such a decline in positive attitudes as related to the novelty effect of the machine. Also, as Piper (1987) has observed, few people who have learned word processing give it up to return to writing with pen and paper. Use of word processing does not equate to finding the computer useful for writing; however, when responding to a question about how useful the computer is for writing, writers probably compare it to writing by hand and thus those who have shifted partially or completely to word processing would be unlikely to find the computer less useful than pen and paper.

This speculation about improving attitudes is based on the assumption that there is a choice about whether to use word processing. In a situation where there is no choice—e.g., in an office environment where word processing is required or in a school situation where papers must be word processed—there may be people who find the computer less useful, as they would prefer to write by hand, like one of the **skeptics** in the present study who very strongly preferred to write by hand due to high computer anxiety and lack of typing skills. Over time, this kind of individual may or may not try the word processor again.

Overall, then, the time span of the study was sufficient only to assess initial changes in attitudes towards the computer as a tool for writing, and to serve as a basis for speculations about how the students' patterns of change might evolve. On the other hand, the time was too limited for students to learn word processing skills well. A total of three hours was spent exclusively on teaching the basic skills of operating a computer and using the word processing program, including: turning on the computer, accessing the program, opening and closing files, typing with the computer keyboard, and moving the cursor. Although formatting and block moves and deletion were also explained to the class, most inexperienced students still had difficulty with these word processing functions. Indeed, many students needed help throughout the course to save their files and exit the program. If there had been sufficient time to give more training and more practice in word processor use, students may have learned word processing skills more quickly and/or thoroughly, and their attitudes might have been different or might have changed at a different rate.

Finally, the limited time of the lab sessions may have influenced writing patterns. Since only one to one-and-a-half hours a week were available for lab work, most students did part of their writing at home. While some of the students had computers available at home or at their office, others had no such easy access and thus had no option but to write by hand. If they had had greater access, they might have used the computer more.

7.3.4.2. Software and Hardware

The lack of time made it difficult to teach the majority of students anything more than the rudiments of the word processing system. In itself, *Microsoft Word for Windows* was satisfactory, as it was a user-friendly and fairly transparent system. Those subjects who had previous experience with other word processors found it simple to learn, with its easy-to-use icons and pull-down menus. However, those who had no previous experience with word processing found it difficult to understand certain basic concepts, such as word wrapping or file directories, and to learn how to manipulate the mouse.

Although the word processing system was, on the whole, satisfactory, there were technical problems with the computer lab. Because the computers were connected to the university network, students had to access the computer lab accounts through the network. This required them to press a certain sequence of keys and move through some introductory screens within a time limit; otherwise, they would connect to the wrong menu. This requirement probably baffled many students, most of whom did not know anything about networks, and may have contributed to anxiety about the technology being difficult and confusing. Furthermore, because of network problems, some computers would go off-line at times, and students would have to change to other workstations, sometimes requiring the whole peer group to move. Lastly, students could not directly print their documents but had to pass them on disk to be printed at the instructor's printer; this caused time delays and also did not give students the power to print at their own convenience.

7.3.4.3. Environment

Some of the above technical problems made the computer lab a less-than-ideal environment in which to work; at times there was an atmosphere of frustration with the computer. This frustration was exacerbated by the lack of a technical assistant during the writing sessions. Most students had questions or difficulties concerning the hardware and software, and the instructor had to spend much of the writing session answering software questions or solving computer problems. Furthermore, some students were reluctant to ask the instructor questions about the software because they would have had to ask them in English. Instead, they would either remain silent, or ask one of their peers for assistance in Cantonese. Although occasional questions to peers can help foster a sense of community and collaboration, there were times when an experienced student was spending 10 minutes of a 60-minute writing session helping peers. In this situation, although the instructor tried to redirect the questions to herself, students instead asked fewer questions. Had there been a Cantonese-speaking lab technician on hand, not only would these problems have been solved more easily, but the instructor would also have had more time to discuss the writing tasks with the students.

Despite the technical problems, most students liked the lab environment for writing, and rated it an average of 5 out of a maximum of 6 scale points, one of the highest ratings on the questionnaire. This positive response may have been an indirect effect of the structured use of the computer lab. In this investigation, students were not merely assigned to work at the lab for a certain number of hours, but instead went as a class and accomplished a clearly defined task each week. Furthermore, the peer feedback sessions were held in the lab, which on the one hand contributed to the structured atmosphere and encouraged consultation and feedback during writing sessions, and on the other hand offered flexibility, in that students could immediately start work when they finished their feedback discussion, without having to wait for the rest of the class to catch up.

The mean responses to the question about liking to write in the computer lab revealed the greatest difference between the two groups classified in terms of order of feedback from teacher or peers. Group A students may have liked writing more in the lab because they were the ones who received teacher feedback before peer feedback, but another possible reason is that they were a more sociable group. Even during the time spent in the classroom, Group A students collaborated more with each other and were livelier both among themselves and with the instructor. In contrast, Group B tended to be somewhat more serious,

210

and did not have extended group discussions either in the lab or in the classroom.[16]

7.3.4.4.   Instruction

The original design of the course included process writing elements, as students were required to write at least two drafts of each assignment and received peer feedback on their first draft. However, the course design planned for students to do most of their writing at home. In order to incorporate the computer component, three drafts instead of two were required for each assignment, and at least one hour a week was allocated for writing in the computer lab. In effect, this meant that students could not avoid writing three drafts, whereas in the previous semester some students, according to their instructors, were apt to skip over a non-final draft if not required to work on it in class. Furthermore, the modified course design increased class time spent writing. The increase in the number of drafts written and the greater amount of in-class writing may have influenced subjects' attitudes to their own writing. In other words, they may have believed that they improved their writing not only because they learned to use the word processor, but perhaps even more importantly because they were expected to spend more time writing. Also, because most of them did use the word processor to some extent, writing the three drafts was probably easier on the word processor than by hand and thus it was possible to demand more writing, as noted by Chadwick and Bruce (1989), without causing students to feel overburdened. Since they probably wrote more during the course of this study than they had in previous classes, the increase in writing activity may have contributed to positive attitudes and to improved writing quality.

One of the process writing aspects of the course was the feedback given by the teacher and by peers. The decreases found in the perceived usefulness of feedback might have been part of a novelty effect which made subjects feel that the feedback was initially more interesting than it was later. Or, there may have been something wrong with the way the feedback was carried out that caused the students to believe in it less

---

[16] Although the implication is that the differences in sociability were due to pre-existing characteristics (e.g., the 'personality' of individuals or of each group as a whole), these differences could also result from the order of feedback. From observations of eight Hong Kong secondary teachers' implementations of process writing with teacher and peer feedback (Pennington, 1995a,b), it can be concluded that Hong Kong students are generally more confident and positive about instruction when they receive teacher feedback initially on their writing; if this is delayed to a later stage in the writing process, they may incorporate feedback less and generally be less cooperative and interactive in the feedback process. (Editor's note)

over time. In the peer feedback sessions, however, only one of the small groups seemed to be what George (1984) defines as a 'dysfunctional' group comprised of individuals who engage in little discussion and quickly terminate the feedback activity; most peer groups were 'task-oriented' in that they were willing to talk and listen, as they engaged in an on-going, independent discussion. Observations of students, who spoke in Cantonese during the peer feedback sessions, recorded that they discussed their own reactions to content and organization, and solicited suggestions for improvement from one another. However, this observer's grasp of Cantonese may not have been sufficient to judge whether the comments were superficial or helpful. It would have been useful at the beginning of the study to model a feedback session to show students what kind of feedback they should give and how, though this sort of training was not included.

The fact that students continued to make changes after peer and teacher feedback had been given, even as their assessment of the usefulness of the feedback became less positive, might be an artifact of learning to use the computer and thus being able to make more changes. Or perhaps as students felt more confident about their own writing, they valued both peer and teacher feedback less, but continued to make changes based on their own increasing awareness of good writing standards. On the other hand, the lack of any general patterns may simply suggest that the usefulness and the effect of peer feedback depends on a writer's reaction to the individual class session and the specific assignment given.

Group A, who received teacher feedback first, believed on average that feedback was more useful and reported making more changes than Group B. Group A also responded more positively on most of the other questionnaire items. It is possible that this difference is related to the order of feedback, as incorporating teacher feedback before showing one's draft to peers might have made the peer feedback process less threatening and perhaps more useful as a result (*see also footnote 16—Ed.*).

7.3.4.5.   Age

The subjects were adults ranging in age from 36-57, two-thirds of whom had not had previous experience with word processing. Within this range, age did not seem to be a factor in previous exposure, as those with experience were found at various points within the age range, and both the oldest and youngest subject were familiar with word processing.

Since responses to writing on the computer were generally quite positive, it seems that age of these students did not make them resistant or fearful towards using the computer for word processing. In fact, they did not seem any more confused or anxious about working on the computer than novices among regular daytime students, who are in their late teens or early twenties. On the other hand, because they were older than the usual college student, these adults may have had higher motivation and self-confidence about improving their writing, which, in turn, may have made them more willing to learn new skills despite any anxieties they may have had. Kantrov (1991) suggests that older and more experienced writers may approach the word processor differently from younger student writers since they already have established writing processes. In this sense, age may have been a factor in the small amount of change in subjects' use of writing tools and their writing activity over the fourteen weeks of the study.

7.3.4.6.   Experience

Previous computer experience seems to be a strong factor influencing users' initial attitudes towards the computer as a writing tool; those with experience of computers were more positive at the beginning of the study than those without this experience. Those without computer experience tended to start with lower evaluations of their first encounter with the computer in the writing class, but then were likely to change their evaluation subsequently. Experience with word processing may have been an influence on the outcomes of this study in other, indirect ways. 37.5% of the students in Group A were experienced computer users, compared with 27% in Group B. Furthermore, based on personal observations, three out of the four students who seemed to use word processing with the greatest mastery were in Group A. In the Group A lab sessions, then, there were more experienced students who could not only answer peer questions on technical issues, but also serve as models for good use of word processors. The presence of these relatively skilled computer users in their group may have contributed to Group A's more positive attitudes towards working in the computer lab and to their more positive responses in general.

7.3.4.7.   Gender

As an influencing factor in the present investigation, gender *per se* seems to have been less important than experience. Proportionally more males than females (50% vs. 20%) had computer experience, which is consistent with the findings of previous studies (Badagliacco, 1990; Culley, 1988; Fetler, 1985) that males tend to be more encouraged by others to use computers, and to have earlier and greater exposure to them than females. If, however, experience is both a direct and an indirect influence on attitude, as discussed above, then the discrepancy between the sexes, though it originates outside the classroom, cannot be ignored.

7.3.4.8.   Second Language Status

In general, L2 writers have to contend with greater anxiety about writing (Phinney, 1991b), language difficulties (Pennington, 1993b; 1996b), and a greater cognitive burden when writing (Jones & Tetroe, 1987) than do those writing in their L1. Certainly, the writers in the present study, as returning adult students who had not used English on a regular basis since their college days, faced all of these difficulties. As suggested by previous studies, the attractiveness of computer-printed text (Huffman & Goldberg, 1987; Piper, 1987) and the ease of composing and revising (Hermann, 1986; Phinney & Mathis, 1990; Piper, 1987) may have contributed to their positive attitudes towards writing and the computer. Furthermore, the opportunity when word processing to "learn and use English in a novel way" (Lam & Pennington, 1995, p. 75) may have helped to counteract any anxiety they might have felt about the English language. Finally, as Pennington (1996b-d; this volume) proposes, these writers' cognitive burden may have been lessened by the more 'natural' computer writing process, in which writers generate and express ideas freely and then later evaluate and organize the generated text, rather than first formulating and organizing ideas and then later expressing them in linguistic form. These attributes may have made the computer a particularly valuable tool for the L2 writers in the present study and may have accounted in large part for the overwhelmingly positive responses of the students towards the computer.

7.3.5.   Implications for Teaching

Students clearly adapt in different ways to the introduction of the word processor to their writing milieu. Identifying their reactions to the computer as a writing tool can be useful for determining how to best help them adapt to a new computer writing environment. Writers who have a strong belief in the usefulness of the computer, or those referred to here as computer **devotees**, tend to have strongly positive attitudes about their own writing. In order to further the growth of these writers' skills, it may be useful to try to reinforce their positive attitudes about both writing and the computer. For example, writing teachers who are experienced computer users can encourage these learners to improve their writing by showing them how to use word processing tools to revise their work more effectively or to organize their ideas more logically. Teachers could also share their own 'tricks of the trade', in other words, discuss how they, as expert writers, take advantage of the functions of the word processor. Similar advice may be appropriate for the computer **enthusiasts**, who exhibit nearly as high levels of positive attitudes as the **devotees** towards the computer and towards writing. Furthermore, if writing teachers can find ways to motivate the **enthusiasts** outside the computer lab, it might be possible to bring them up to the same levels of motivation and interest as the **devotees**.

The computer **rededicateds**, over the course of the investigation, reported more positive attitudes than the **converts**; but by the time of the final assessment, the **converts** had caught up to or surpassed the **rededicateds'** levels of enthusiasm. Perhaps in order to avoid the **rededicateds'** temporary lull in enthusiasm, writing teachers can warn students that the computer is by no means a panacea for writing troubles. On the other hand, the novelty effect and its aftermath may be unavoidable for some writers with little or no experience of word processing. However, in the end it may not be anything more than a minor impediment, especially since the quality of the **rededicateds'** writing seemed to be unaffected, and since the later resurgence of their enthusiasm augurs continuing improvement.

For the computer **positives**, who are not strongly motivated about the computer or about writing and whose quality of written work seems rather low, it may be best to try to find another way to stimulate their interest. Since neither writing nor the computer appears to interest them greatly, appeals to other objectives such as improving language or developing communication skills may be more effective in motivating their learning.

The computer **converts** were novices to word processing and to computing, and thus were initially cautious about any benefit the computer could offer for their writing. However, in their final assessment, their positive attitudes towards the computer and towards writing reached, if not surpassed, the level of the **enthusiasts**. The majority of the converts also seem to have improved the quality of their writing over time. In line with their cautious approach, an unpressured, step-by-step exposure to word processing may be most appropriate for them. This would help relieve any initial anxieties they have, and encourage them to progress. Constant technical and emotional support may also be important to bolster their development of word processing and writing skills.

Finally, for the **skeptics**, it is clearly necessary to relieve their anxieties about writing and about computers; otherwise, their negative attitudes may continuously reinforce each other, raising anxiety even further and negatively influencing the quality of their writing. Reducing writing apprehension is a topic that has been discussed extensively by others who have explored the subject in detail. To relieve computer phobia, more experience with computers may work for a majority of people, but it cannot help everyone, as McInerney, McInerney, and Sinclair (1994) have shown. Some computer phobics may be better left alone, if such an option is available. However, if word processing is required by the circumstances, strong encouragement and reassurances, combined with extensive technical support, may go at least some way to helping the computer phobic **skeptic**.

Observation of the way writers use the computer and pen and paper may not always indicate how they adapt to computers, as in this study both tools were used in various combinations in all of the different categories of users. Therefore, some means of identifying how well writers are adapting, either through questionnaires and writing assessment instruments such as those used in this study or by some other means, may contribute to helping L2 writers increase their motivation and improve their writing when introduced to the computer as a writing tool.

7.3.6. Limitations

The nature of the research reported here is such that the adaptation patterns outlined are offered as only a preliminary classification scheme. The existence of these patterns needs to be verified, their definitions modified, and the categories developed further. In order to accomplish this task, a larger number of subjects is needed, as the twenty-seven adult Cantonese-speaking subjects in this study were insufficient to be able to generalize the findings. A larger subject pool is also necessary to test whether the relationships discovered here between positive orientation to the computer and writing motivation hold more generally. The nature of the connection—whether the relationship among the various aspects of writing attitudes, process, and product can be identified as causal or reciprocal, and to what extent—is an area of interest for further study. Larger subject pools and more rigorous assessments of writing quality are also necessary to clarify the relationship between attitude and product outcomes in a computer-mediated environment.

In addition to larger numbers of subjects to support more quantitative analyses, more detailed study of individual students' writing processes would be of value. In this study, self-reports of when and how the subjects used the two writing tools occasionally contradicted the observations of the researcher, and the data gathered were sometimes unclear. Reports from subjects should be augmented by videotaping or other forms of data recording and supported by interviews in order to investigate questions such as why students choose particular tools for particular stages of their writing.

Third, a longitudinal study over at least two semesters would be valuable, as this fourteen-week investigation has been sufficient only to reveal students' initial attitudes and the mere beginnings of changes in their writing process. Better conditions for an investigation in terms of technical support for students and improvement in the feedback process through modeling and training would also be helpful.

Finally, this study was conducted in a Hong Kong tertiary setting, with older working adults who presumably had well-established, though by no means necessarily effective, writing habits. To see whether the findings are generalizable to writers of other ages and from different linguistic, educational, and cultural backgrounds, it is clearly necessary to conduct other studies focusing on different populations.

7.4.   CONCLUSION

Despite the limitations and the necessarily tentative nature of the findings, it is hoped that this study has revealed some possible patterns of adaptations on the part of L2 writers when their writing environment is changed by the addition of the computer as a writing tool. Adaptation processes are important for human beings to understand because we are organisms that not only adapt to the environment, but also change that environment to suit our needs. In a sense, the present computer writing environment is the product of writers who demanded that technology serve their communication needs and who shaped the technology accordingly. If we as second language teachers and researchers can understand how writers adapt to writing on computers, if we can determine where and how the technology serves them best and where it does not meet their requirements, then we too can shape the writing technology of the future to best fit our students' (as well as our own) desires and aspirations as writers and as human beings who communicate.

APPENDIX 7.1.

Questionnaire on Computer Usage

PART 1 (all information in this section will be kept confidential and is for survey purposes only)

1. Name
2. Student number
3. Age
4. Sex
5. Department

PART 2

1. Do you own a computer at home?
2. Do you have access to a computer at your workplace?
3. Do you have access to a computer at any other place (friends' or relatives' homes, other organizations, etc.)? If so, where?

PART 3

1. Do you type your assignments and papers?
2. Do you word-process your assignments and papers in English?

If yes, what word-processing program do you use?

Microsoft Word for Windows	Word Perfect
PCWrite	MultiMate
Professional Write	Other: _____

I use word processing to:
(check as many as appropriate)

I use pen and paper to:
(check as many as appropriate)

_____	Jot down my ideas/brainstorm	_____
_____	Organize my ideas	_____
_____	Make an outline	_____
_____	Draft/compose	_____
_____	Revise for ideas and organization	_____
_____	Edit for language and mechanics	_____
_____	Type my final version	_____

_____   Check spelling   _____
_____   Proofread   _____

About how long have you been using word-processing?

_____ years   _____ months

3. Do you word-process in Chinese? What program do you use?

4. Do you use the computer for any other purpose?

__ Spreadsheet or other financial calculations   __ Statistics
__ Graphics or design   __ Programming
   Databases   Language
                                                        __ learning
__ Games   __ Other: _____

Please write the name of the program you use:

5. Do you use a computer mouse?

6. If you answered no to questions 2-5 above, have you ever touched a computer before, even if you do not use it on a regular basis? (Have you taken a computer course, tried it out, etc?) If so, please describe the situation.

APPENDIX 7.2.

Peer Response Guidelines (from Pennington, 1996b, p. 134)

PEER FEEDBACK

This is to help you give feedback to your classmates' writing in our peer feedback session. Give your response to each item below; the author will respond last. After each person has spoken, the group members discuss the responses to clarify and elaborate points, and to ask and answer questions. The discussion should continue until members reach a shared understanding and have no further points to discuss. Then, members should move on to the next item.

---

1. Summarize the content of the writing, as far as you are able.

2. State what you consider to be the main point.

3. Ask a question or questions about something you did not fully understand or about which you would like to know more.

4. Mention any possible confusions or errors in content or language.

5. State what you consider to be the most interesting or important aspect of the writing.

6. Give your own opinion about the topic.

7. Give suggestions for the continued development of the ideas expressed.

8. If there is time, bring up related topics for discussion.

APPENDIX 7.3.

Questionnaire on Assignment

ASSIGNMENT EVALUATION

Please take a moment to give your feedback on the assignment you have just completed. Your *honest* opinion is valuable since it can help to change and improve aspects of the next assignments, and of the course in general. Thanks.

Section 6 / 9 *(circle one)*   Assignment 1 / 2 / 3 / 4 *(circle one)*

Name: _____   Date: _____

Circle the number that best describes your experience and opinion according to the scale:

1) Developing the content of this assignment was:

       1   2   3   4   5   6
     very difficult   very easy

---

2) Organizing this assignment was:

       1   2   3   4   5   6
     very difficult   very easy

---

3) Expressing my ideas in this assignment was:

       1   2   3   4   5   6
     very difficult   very easy

---

4) The peer feedback on a non-final draft was:

       1   2   3   4   5   6
       not at all   very
       helpful   helpful

222

5) The teacher feedback on a non-final draft was:

1	2	3	4	5	6
not at all helpful					very helpful

6) The grammar feedback on the final draft was:

1	2	3	4	5	6
not at all helpful					very helpful

7) I made changes in my assignment after peer feedback

1	2	3	4	5	6
none at all					very many

What kind of changes? (*circle as many as appropriate*)

content / organization / expression / grammar

8) I made changes in my assignment after teacher feedback

1	2	3	4	5	6
none at all					very many

What kind of changes? (*circle as many as appropriate*)

content / organization / expression / grammar

9) I made changes in my assignment after grammar feedback

1	2	3	4	5	6
none at all					very many

What kind of changes? (*circle as many as appropriate*)

content / organization / expression / grammar

Below you will see different steps in the writing process. Please mark in the appropriate column whether you used the computer or pen & paper to complete any of these steps in your last assignment. __Do not__ use a tick (√) in the column; instead please write the version of the draft you were working on, as follows:

X = did not do this step
A = first draft   B = second draft   C = final draft

Each line may contain __more than one__ letter/answer.

	I used the computer	I used pen and paper
10) In this assignment, to:		
Jot down my ideas/brainstorm	_____	_____
Organize my ideas	_____	_____
Make an outline	_____	_____
Draft/compose	_____	_____
Revise the content of my paper (e.g., by adding new information)	_____	_____
Revise the organization of my paper (e.g., by moving sections)	_____	_____
Edit the language of my paper (e.g., by changing wording or grammar)	_____	_____
Type the final version of my paper	_____	_____
Check my spelling	_____	_____
Proofread the final draft	_____	_____
Other _____	_____	_____

Circle the number that best describes your experience and opinion according to the scale:

11) I find the computer useful for writing.

1	2	3	4	5	6
not at all					very much

12) I like writing in the computer lab.

1	2	3	4	5	6
not at all					very much

13) I like writing alone, at home.

1	2	3	4	5	6
not at all					very much

14) I feel my writing has improved.

1	2	3	4	5	6
not at all					very much

15) I write faster now than I used to.

1	2	3	4	5	6
not at all					very much

16) I write more than I used to.

1	2	3	4	5	6
not at all					very much

17) I find writing easier than I used to.

1	2	3	4	5	6
not at all					very much

18) I enjoyed this assignment.

1	2	3	4	5	6
not at all					very much

19) I feel nervous about writing:

    1   2   3   4   5   6
  not at all   very
                                     much

Complete the following sentences:

20) The easiest part of this assignment was _____

_____

21) The hardest part of this assignment was _____

_____

22) In contrast to past assignments, writing is becoming _____

_____

(DISTRIBUTED ONLY AFTER FINAL ASSIGNMENT)

LANG 1410 (CONVERSION)

Q1) Given a choice, **I myself** would have preferred to take: (circle one)

       computer section   non-computer section

Q2) I would recommend my **classmates** take: (circle one)

       computer section   non-computer section

APPENDIX 7.4.

Attitudinal and Affective Responses to Writing

	Mean Responses							
	Devotees	*Enthusiasts*	*Rededs.*	*Positives*	*Converts*	*Skeptics*	all groups	*sd*
Q12 all A's	5.50	5.35	5.03	5.00	4.43	4.13	5.00	0.90
Q12 final A	5.82	5.00	5.00	5.33	5.33	4.50		
Q13 all A's	2.40	3.60	3.70	3.70	4.20	2.40	3.50	1.40
Q13 final A	2.00	3.60	3.83	3.33	4.00	3.00		
Q14 all A's	4.85	4.10	4.09	4.17	4.04	3.38	4.20	0.90
Q14 final A	5.00	4.00	4.00	4.00	4.33	3.50		
Q15 all A's	4.85	4.25	3.99	4.08	4.00	3.38	4.10	0.90

8. Student E-mail Letters: Negotiating Meaning, Gathering Information, Building Relationships[1]

Leslie K. Nabors and Ethel C. Swartley

ABSTRACT

In this chapter, more than three hundred ESL student e-mail letters are analyzed to discover how students use language to negotiate form and meaning, gather information, and build relationships with others. Students' use of continuation and comprehension moves, and their negotiation of language, are described, and information request patterns are analyzed by type (direct/indirect), by culture of writer, and by topic. Twelve strategies employed by the students to build relationships are also discussed, along with pedagogical implications and suggestions for further research.

8.0. INTRODUCTION

The appearance of new technology always provides opportunities to apply established paradigms to the use of such technology. Electronic mail (e-mail), particularly, has changed the nature of communication in the present age and is challenging the distinction between spoken and written language. E-mail naturally has many of the elements of written language (Akinnaso, 1982; Biber, 1988; Halliday, 1989; Hoffman, 1996; Nabors, 1995), but includes many of the elements of face-to-face interaction cited by Goffman (1981) and Labov (1972) as well. Because of the speed with which information can be exchanged electronically, communicators can interact in a sort of 'slow motion' conversational style that incorporates the stages of (i) greeting, (ii) establishment of relationship and clarification of role, (iii) performance of task, (iv) re-establishment of relationship, and (v) parting—the five-episode social encounter structure noted by Clarke and Argyle (1982) in spoken language interactions. In

[1] The research and publication of this study was aided by a 1996-1997 PTE Project Award given by the Executive Board of PennTESOL-East, a TESOL affiliate drawing membership from eastern Pennsylvania, southern New Jersey, and Delaware (USA).

addition, the on-line conversations of e-mail interactions influence and are influenced by a social context (Fulk, Schmitz, & Schwarz, 1992).

In the study reported in this chapter, the researchers analyzed the language produced by ESL students in e-mail letters—specifically, exploring the students' use of language to perform three tasks traditionally studied in spoken language contexts: the negotiation of linguistic and structural meaning (Ellis, 1985; Gass & Varonis, 1985; Long, 1993; Pica & Doughty, 1988; Pica, Lincoln-Porter, Paninos, & Linnell, 1995; Varonis & Gass, 1985), the gathering and exchange of information (Gibbs, 1985; Thomas, 1985), and the construction of social relationships (Argyle, 1992; Brown & Levinson, 1987; Clarke & Argyle, 1982; Harre, 1985). Although e-mail is a written medium, each of these traditionally spoken communication tasks is present in the e-mail communications that we studied.

8.1. COMPONENTS OF INTERACTION

8.1.1. Negotiation

In the context of the present investigation, **negotiation** can be defined as a cooperative process in which "the speech addressed to learners is the result of an ongoing interaction between learner and native speaker" (Ellis, 1985, p. 70). It should be noted, however, that negotiation also occurs in L1 interactions and in communication between L2 learners. Negotiation serves two main functions. First, it helps manage discourse and prevent communication breakdown (Pica & Doughty, 1988). Second, it affords the learner access to comprehensible input and a measure of control over the language being learned. In this way, the negotiation process itself becomes an indispensable component of L2 learning.

Negotiation is often divided into specific categories or interactional features which describe language input and output. For example, Long (1983) described teachers' speech in terms of six interactional features of negotiated input: clarification checks, comprehension checks, clarification requests, self-repetitions, other-repetitions, and expansions. These same categories or features can be employed to describe learner output and, therefore, the interaction between an L1 speaker and a L2 learner. Further studies on the role of negotiation have explored such topics as the effect of language proficiency on the negotiation strategies used (Ellis, 1985) and the effectiveness of strategies used in learner-learner discourse (Gass & Varonis; Pica, Lincoln-Porter, Paninos, & Linnell, 1995; 1985; Varonis & Gass, 1985). Yet all these negotiation studies rest on one common assumption: that negotiation of meaning occurs in a spoken medium.[2]

However, negotiation may occur in written language as well: a dialogue journal is an example of written negotiation. Although e-mail messages have many characteristics of spoken language (Ferrara, Brunner, & Whittemore, 1991), in terms of the formal and functional characteristics of speech and writing, e-mail is closer to written text than to spoken discourse (Akinnaso, 1982; Biber, 1988; Halliday, 1989; Nabors, 1995; Hoffman, 1996).[3] Thus, it might be expected that the negotiation moves of e-mail communication would be different from those of spoken discourse as influenced by the electronic writing medium.

8.1.2. Information-Gathering

Argyle (1992) and Gibbs (1985) have both indicated that communication is facilitated when the communicators share some key information—information about what the speakers or communicators have in common and what each assumes about the other. According to Gibbs (1985):

> People need to know...information about the social setting, the particular roles that speakers and hearers play in conversations, the interaction of speakers' and hearers' beliefs, and their presuppositions about each other's plans and goals in different discourse situations. This pragmatic information constitutes the shared or mutual knowledge that allows speakers and hearers to achieve successful communication. (p. 97)

In addition, Brown and Levinson (1987) assert that a claim of 'common ground' or shared wants, goals, and values is one of the key elements of politeness and face-protection, which in turn facilitate relationship-building. In order to make claims of common ground, it is necessary for two communicators to know something about each other so that they are able to act on the information and wants that they both share. It can therefore be assumed that participants in the penpal project would need to gather some information about each other in order to be able to communicate satisfactorily.

---

[2] Linnell (1995) is an exception, as his study focused on negotiation occurring in simultaneous computer messages; however, this type of communication still differs greatly from asynchronous e-mail messages.

[3] For a discussion of the similarities and differences between e-mail and both spoken and written language, see Baron (1998). (Editor's note)

8.1.3. Relationship-Building

A number of studies have examined the relational use of language, though nearly all have had a focus on spoken language. Labov (1972), for example, demonstrated the need to distinguish between grammatical form and social function: a person may produce a grammatical statement, question, or imperative; but the action or intention behind these grammatical forms may be a refusal, an assertion, an information request, a command, a request for clarification, an answer, or any number of other actions. Goffman (1981) listed eleven such actions, or "interpersonal verbal rituals", which are part of conversational face-to-face interactions. Goffman (1981) claims that these interpersonal rituals:

> often serve a bracketing function, celebratively marking a per-
> ceived change in the physical and social accessibility of two
> individuals to each other, as well as beginnings and endings—
> of...a social occasion,...an encounter, an interchange. (pp. 20-
> 21)

Just as in other forms of interactive communication, some of these types of social 'bracketing' strategies can be expected to occur in e-mail communication.

In another relational language study, Harre (1985) refers to the "situational rhetoric", which appears in both spoken and written language. Harre (1985) defines this rhetoric as "a form of speech or writing that serves to create in the listener or reader a certain impression of the character and the moral qualities of the speaker or writer in a given situation" (p. 175). It can be assumed according to this notion of situational rhetoric that e-mail writers will choose certain words and language forms to project a desired personality or character that will, in turn, affect the reader's desire to interact with or build a relationship with the writer. Fulk, Schmitz, and Schwarz (1992) make a similar point in noting that the actions of the individual communicators within a computer-mediated communication context (in this case, an e-mail relationship) help to define that context and influence the communicators' future behavior in it.

Argyle (1992) examines how people relate to one another and the role that language plays in the formation of human relationships. For making friendships, Argyle lists nine verbal strategies:

1. paying compliments
2. pleasure talk about cheerful topics
3. agreeing
4. using names, especially first names and first person plural pronouns
5. being helpful - offering help, sympathy or information

6. humor
7. reaching for similarity and things in common
8. asking questions of personal interest that are not at the same time overly intimate
9. a degree of self-disclosure which matches or goes slightly beyond that of the other person

This list provides an excellent starting-point for the classification of relationship-building strategies in the context of e-mail letters.

Argyle (1992) asserts that relationships have six main features: goals, rules, activities, forms of attachment, concepts and beliefs, and skills. If these features are assumed to be present in all relationships, then in order to build e-mail relationships with penpals they have never met, the students of our study would have to develop these features through their use of written language. An additional challenge in forming these relationships by written rather than spoken means involves a negative association noted by Argyle, who found that strangers were rated least friendly based on an initial written exchange as compared to a first-time meeting conducted face-to-face, by video, or over the telephone.[4]

---

[4] It is worth investigating whether and to what extent people are specifically aware of the need to overcome the limitations of the non-verbal medium in initial—and indeed, continuing—contacts made by e-mail. Based on my own experience with e-mail and informal observations of other e-mail users, I would speculate that such awareness is not necessarily present at first and that it grows with time. My impression is that novice e-mail users may not specifically perceive any such limitations and may at first simply transfer the communication strategies or modes of another context such as letter-writing to that of e-mail. However, they soon learn (based on the structure and content of others' e-mail messages, and the feedback they receive as responses to their own e-mail messages, including respondents' misreading of their original pragmatic intent) that the constraints of the new context are different. They will then start responding to these new constraints, shifting over time to a more 'verbal'—or mixed—construction of communication, and eventually developing the new context independently.

I believe it is a general principle of adaptation to a new medium, mode, or context of behavior that people will first transfer the skills, behaviors, and values of what they perceive to be the closest 'old' (i.e., familiar) medium/mode/context to the new medium/mode/context and only gradually differentiate the old and the new (see Pennington, 1993d; 1996b, ch. 5, for a discussion of 'early-stage' and 'late-stage' forms of adaptation to a computer writing environment). Along the way, they may evolve processes and products which blend the old and new forms, as Baron (1998) has speculated in comparing e-mail communication to a creole and as I have discussed in relation to code-mixing (Pennington, 1998) and 'approach-mixing' in the English teaching of L2 speakers (Pennington, 1995a).

Consistent with the discussion presented here and elsewhere (Pennington, 1993c-d; 1996b-d; this volume), a 'developmental path' involving the stages of (i) transfer, (ii) blending, and (iii) independence would seem to apply to the acquisition of computer-

8.2.   STRUCTURE OF THE INVESTIGATION

8.2.1.   The Drexel E-mail Penpal Project

The investigation grew out of an e-mail exchange project between first (L1) and second language (L2) English writers at the Drexel University English Language Center (ELC). The ELC is an intensive English language program providing instruction to learners of English as L2 from around the world who come to study in the United States at the ELC facility, located on the Drexel University campus. Despite being surrounded by an American college campus, the international students at the ELC complain that they find it difficult to meet American students and to build American friendships which would enhance their language learning experience.

In 1993, the ELC began an ongoing e-mail penpal project with two purposes in mind: (a) to provide an authentic audience for students in the ELC's ESL writing classes and (b) to help ELC students build relationships outside the language program with non-ESL students on the campus. Non-ELC students with e-mail accounts were recruited via flyers to write to ELC students by e-mail. The flyers indicated that volunteers would have opportunities to "explore the world" by exchanging e-mail letters with an on-campus international student once a week over the course of one 10-week university term. Flyers were placed on prominent bulletin boards in the campus computing center, dormitories, classroom and laboratory buildings, and the student center. To join the program, the volunteers were asked to send an e-mail message indicating their interest to the ELC teacher in charge of the project. This ELC teacher then followed up each inquiry with the following e-mail message:

> Thank you for writing to me about an international penpal. Here's how it works. If you decide to participate, I will give your name and user ID to one of the international students studying in the English Language Center and ask him or her to write you an introductory message. After that, you should hear from your penpal about once a week, and I would ask that you also respond once a week so that your

---

based writing skills—whether in the context of 'plain' word processing or in an 'enhanced' electronic environment. The same sequence of stages can also be applied to learning a second language (Pennington, forthcoming a). Given the intransigence of first language transfer, it can be suggested that learners will benefit by using a second language in the context of new media, as these new tools and environments are more likely to inspire novelty and experimentation than those associated with literacy in the mother tongue (Pennington, 1996a; forthcoming b). (Editor's note)

penpal won't be disappointed. Since your penpal will be studying English as his or her second language, you should expect some grammar mistakes, etc., in his or her writing, but if there is something you really can't understand, please ask your penpal to explain it. This will really help your penpal to improve his or her writing. The purpose of the project for the ELC is to give our students a chance to practice writing in English and to get to know other people at Drexel. For you, I hope it will just be fun.

The ELC student participants in the project were chosen based on the number of volunteer penpals available each term and on their teachers' decision as to whether or not to use e-mail as a class activity. The ELC participants were told that they were expected to write to their volunteer penpal at least once a week and were asked to send a copy of their e-mail message to their English instructor. In order to encourage free and candid participation in the program, non-ELC volunteers were not required to submit their messages to the ELC teachers. In recognition of their participation in this project, the penpals were invited to meet the students at an end-of-term party.

8.2.2. Students

This chapter reports on findings from the first two years of the e-mail penpal project. During those two years, the project had 218 participants. One hundred sixteen of these were volunteer penpals—both matriculated university students and non-Drexel participants from the local community. Of the volunteers, 59 participants were L1 English-speaking Americans and 57 were international students with English proficiency of a higher level than that of any ELC student.

The other 102 participants were ESL students enrolled in ELC classes. These students came from multiple sections of four different courses:

- 30 students from Level 1 Writing (beginning or low level English learners)
- 46 students from Level 3 Writing (intermediate level English learners)
- 13 students from Level 4 writing (high-intermediate level English learners)
- 13 students from ESL Business Writing (intermediate through advanced level English learners)

The students came from a variety of cultural backgrounds. There were 8 students from the nations of Francophone Africa; 24 Chinese (from Taiwan, Hong Kong, and the People's Republic of China); 5 Europeans (from Poland, Russia, Spain, Italy and Greece); 18 Japanese; 28 Koreans; 13 Latin Americans (from Brazil, Venezuela, Peru, and Ecuador); 3 Middle Easterners (from Iraq, Israel, and Kuwait); and 3 Thais.

8.2.3.   Writing Task

For the ESL students, participation in the penpal project was a class assignment. In the general writing classes (Levels 1, 3, and 4), the assignment was introduced in the following way. Students were told that they would need to write at least once a week to an e-mail 'penpal' who would be a non-ESL student—either an American or an international student in another university department. The students were allowed to write about any topic they wanted, and they were told that their messages would not be graded for content or grammar. At the same time, they would need to send a copy of each of their letters to their teacher as proof that the assignment had been completed each week.

In the business writing class, the assignment was slightly more specific. These students were told that their penpal would be someone in the business field—either a business department student or faculty member, or someone currently working in business. The business writing students were told that they would need to write to their penpals seven times during the 10-week term (as opposed to every week) and that they would have opportunities to ask their penpals about American business practices and business education. As in the case of the general writing students, the business students were asked to send copies of all their letters to their instructor to demonstrate that their assignment had been completed.

8.2.4.   Data Collection

As the students sent copies of their letters to their teacher, she kept this corpus of student letters in a computer file. The characteristics of this corpus are summarized in Table 8.1.

As can be seen in Table 8.1, the corpus comprised 337 messages from the 102 ESL students. The average length of message was 12.58 lines of text, excluding address and headers. The average number of messages produced per student was 3.47 over a period of one ten-week term. While this seems like a small number considering the original assignment of one message per week, it must be noted that the first class week was spent introducing or reacquainting students with the hardware, software, and computer lab procedures. Likewise, the penpal party occurred in the final week of class, so students may have been less moti-

236

vated to communicate with their partners at this time since they would soon be meeting them face-to-face. The range of letters sent by students during the term also varied greatly, from a few single unsuccessful attempts at communication to one Level 3 student who sent eleven e-mail letters in ten weeks.

Class	No. of Students	No. of Messages	Avg. No. of Messages per Student	Avg. No. of Lines per Message	Range of No. of Letters per Student
Level 1	30	92	3.37	8.56	1-7
Level 3	46	147	3.34	14.24	1-11
Level 4	13	43	3.30	12.88	1-10
Business (levels 3-6)	13	56	4.30	14.51	2-7
Total	102	337	3.47	12.58	1-11

Table 8.1. Data and Subject Characteristics

8.2.5.   Data Analysis

After they were sent to the teacher, the student e-mail letters were printed, and each researcher coded the hard copies of the letters separately over a two-month period. The researchers initially coded for **negotiation of meaning** and **negotiation of form** (see Ellis, 1994, for a review). When we discovered that the corpus contained relatively few negotiation moves—fewer than three moves per student per group—we explored the letters further in order to find other indications of language learning or content learning in them. The results indicated that although the students were not explicitly addressing linguistic issues, other types of learning were occurring. For the purposes of this study, these other types are labeled **information-gathering** and **relationship-building**. First, however, we determined how the learners manipulated their language in order to achieve mutual understanding in their messages. Coding for negotiation followed the taxonomies found in Pica, Holliday, Lewis, Berducci, and Newman (1991). Since information-gathering and relationship-building appeared to be less thoroughly addressed by the linguistics literature, our coding was data-driven in these areas, although we later found that the patterns we discovered paralleled Argyle's (1992) psychological studies of spoken language. Any discrepancies in the coding were resolved by discussion between the researchers.

8.2.6. Hypotheses

In this study, we analyzed samples of e-mail in order to determine if, and if so how, negotiation of meaning and negotiation of form occur in the written context of e-mail. Concerning negotiation, we hypothesized that:

H 1.   The majority of utterances would be for the purposes of information-gathering and/or relationship-building.

H2.   Structural negotiation (*negotiation of form*) would occur more frequently at higher than at lower levels of English language proficiency.

8.3.   FINDINGS

8.3.1. Negotiation of Meaning

The most striking feature of the negotiation analysis is that the vast majority of negotiation moves were **comprehension** or **continuation** moves: approximately 80% were of these types. Many of the comprehension moves were simply signals that the penpal had actually received the previous message. This in itself was not surprising since, especially for first-time users, e-mail technology can seem a bit undependable and unpredictable. We can therefore say that in these cases, the technology and the task definitely impacted the language used.

Class	Comprehension Moves	Continuation Moves	Indication of Inability to Respond	Structural Negotiation
Level 1	1.20	0.46	0.23	0.10
Level 3	1.71	0.82	0.39	0.86
Level 4	1.30	0.46	0.23	0.07
Business (levels 3-6)	1.61	0.53	0.15	0.46
Total Average	1.50	0.63	0.29	0.13

Table 8.2. Average Number of Most Common Negotiation Moves by Class

238

Some learners were more adept than others at using English to signal comprehension and to indicate continuation of the topic. Marcella, from Venezuela, was able to organize her e-mail letters so that her penpal, Jonathan, could clearly follow their communication:[5]

> DEAR JONATHAN,
> IS VERY NICE THAT YOU HAD A ROOMMATE
> FROM VENEZUELA.... [Four lines of text omitted]
> I CAN SEE THAT YOU HAVE A BIG FAMILY,
> IS VERY HARD WHEN THE FAMILY AREN'T
> TOGETHER.... [Four lines of text omitted]
> NOW, I'M GONNA TO ANSWER YOUR QUES-
> TIONS. I'M LIVING DOWNTOWN CLOSE TO
> THE ART MUSEUM.... [Four lines of text omitted]

Here, in one of her first e-mail letters, Marcella was able to signal to Jonathan that she received his last letter by paraphrasing parts of his previous message (*is very nice that you had a roommate from Venezuela*) and she indicates that she will continue his topic on her living arrangements (*now, I'm gonna to answer your questions...*). Not all students were this successful in their communication. In fact, the third most prevalent type of negotiation move found in these letters was an **indication of inability to respond**.

These 'inability moves' usually indicated that the computer had caused some problems in the penpal relationship, although sometimes the learners gave some other reason for not having written in a long time. The following message combines two types of reasons, as Sunghee, from Korea, explains why her message is coming late:

> Last Friday, when I was writing letter to you, my
> compyuter had dark suddenly. And I couldn't find
> my letters. I disappointed at my fault. I had no time
> in last Friday. So after finish class I am writing letter
> to you.

Even though it is clear how the new technology could have caused some confusion or mechanical difficulty leading to a need for this type of negotiation, it is important to keep in mind that notification of inability to respond accounted for a relatively small portion of total negotiation moves. Other minor types of negotiation found in the corpus included

---

[5] Except where specific permission was obtained, all names have been changed to protect the anonymity of the participants. Otherwise, the e-mail messages in this chapter have been reproduced exactly as they appeared in the original letters, maintaining student errors in punctuation, spelling, and grammar.

clarification requests, self-repetitions, other repetitions, and structural negotiations. Of these, only structural negotiation, i.e., negotiation involving language, was considered to be significant for the purposes of this study.

Structural negotiation composed the fourth largest category of negotiation moves. Most of these instances of negotiation consisted of vocabulary questions, as seen in the following message from Jenny, a student from Taiwan:

> Rockerfaler Center is my favorite place. The big Christmas tree is ready. I probably will go there on Christmas. Will there be a lot of people there on Christmas eve? I heard on New Year Even there will be a "big apple" in Time square. What does this "big apple" mean?

This letter is particularly interesting since Jenny is really referring to two "big apples". The first one is the lit-up neon, fruit-like ball that drops at the countdown to midnight on New Year's Eve in Times Square. The other is the nickname for the city of New York. What is also intriguing about Jenny's use of this term is that she uses it correctly as a term, within quotes, in a complex structure *(I heard on New Year Even there will be a "big apple" in Time square)* before indicating that she does not know what this term means. Throughout our corpus, we find many instances in which students were able to request information of this kind, since they held the individual attention of their penpal.

One humorous exchange occurred between David and his penpal, as he responded to a previous letter:

> Hi! Missy:
> It is so nice to hear you tell me that you earn money last weekend, I believe you were so happy to do that. But, I can not realize the word's mean "UGH". what is it? Would you please explain it for me?

This request shows the benefits that e-mail can have over everyday conversation, as David would have correctly interpreted Missy's exasperated sigh had she been speaking with him in person. In this message, however, we see that David has the chance to gain a vocabulary item which most learners are never explicitly taught.

While there were some direct benefits to the ESL students in terms of learning to negotiate form and meaning in e-mail letters, the majority of e-mail exchanges did not focus on language *per se*, but on the culture of the host country and on the everyday lives of the students. These findings are discussed in detail in the next sections.

8.3.2. Information-Gathering

In this study, the only initial information every ESL student was given about his/her penpal was the person's name. In some cases, the instructor knew the penpal's major subject, hobbies, and gender, and this was also given to the ESL student partners; but since the volunteer penpals were not required to disclose anything about themselves to the penpal coordinator, in most cases the ESL students initially had very little knowledge about their penpals. They were therefore required to use their language abilities in English to learn the other information from their penpal that would facilitate a communicative relationship. The ways in which the students attempted to do this are the focus of discussion in this section.

Gibbs (1985) identified 13 different sentence forms in which his subjects made requests, but we looked at information requests more generally. The first request form we studied was the direct question, as in *"Are you interested in Japan?"* Secondly, we looked at indirect requests for information, such as *"I'd like to know something about your family."* Based on this division into **direct** and **indirect** requests, we were able to characterize a number of patterns in the way the ESL participants gathered information.

We first compared the number and percentage of direct vs. indirect requests produced at the different English proficiency levels represented in our study (Table 8.3). Few request pattern differences emerged from this comparison across the different classes, although students in the higher level courses made somewhat more requests than the other student groups. Direct questions were found to be more frequent at every proficiency level than indirect requests.

Class (No. of Relationships)	No. of Relationships with No Requests	Total No. of Requests	%Direct Requests	%Indirect Requests	Avg. No. of Requests per Relationship
Level 1 (30)	12 (40%)	75	84%	16%	4.00
Level 3 (46)	16 (35%)	111	75%	25%	3.70
Level 4 (13)	3 (23%)	47	79%	21%	4.70
Business (13) (levels 3-6)	1 (8%)	57	82%	18%	4.75

Table 8.3. Request Patterns by Class

When request patterns were studied by culture, the patterns were more striking (Table 8.4).[6] The percentage of relationships in which no information requests were made was highest among the Africans and Europeans, perhaps indicating that in these cultures there may be social mores against asking too many questions or that requests for information are not a necessary or accepted feature of communication. As in the comparison of requests by class, in every cultural group the number of direct requests was always higher than the number of indirect requests. However, the ratio of direct to indirect requests was greatest among the Asian and African students and smallest among the Europeans, Latin Americans, and Middle Easterners. Among the Middle Eastern students, the numbers of direct and indirect requests were almost equal.

These cultural request patterns call into question many prevalent cultural stereotypes. Most obviously, Asians are often stereotyped as indirect and fearful of asking questions, whereas in this study they showed a greater directness than any other cultural group. Likewise, Latin Americans and Europeans are stereotypically viewed as assertive and direct, but in this study they exhibited these tendencies perhaps less than expected and in fact were less direct in their requests than the students from Asia and Africa who are often compared with them in terms of language proficiency and culturally appropriate behavior. These findings may be examples of the empowering and equalizing effects of communicating by computer means, or they may be cases in which the widely believed stereotypes are not accurate.[7]

---

[6] Given the small number of requests and subjects in some cultural groups, these patterns should be taken as only suggestive of group differences which may or may not be generalizable to other studies. (Editor's note)

[7] It may be that the electronic environment serves to 'equalize' students in terms of communicative constraints in the sense that they are all facing the same novel conditions for interaction or in the sense that the constraints are reduced when communicating outside the real-time comprehension and production demands of face-to-face conversation or the genre demands of other written modes. An alternative explanation for the findings is that directness in some cultures is considered more appropriate in written than spoken modes, or more appropriate in certain types of role-relationships than others (e.g., indirectness, as in indirect or 'polite' requests, may be considered a sign of distance of formality and therefore in appropriate for close relationships). Differences in the proportion of direct and indirect requests might also be related to differences in the topics of interaction or the conversation style of individuals, especially in the smaller groups. A final possibility is a confounding of cultural and proficiency groups—if the Asian and African groups had proportionately greater representation at the lower levels of proficiency and/or the Latin Americans, Europeans, and Middle Easterners at the higher levels of proficiency—as direct strategies are linguistically less complex than indirect ones. Students at higher proficiency levels can be expected to produce both more indirectness and more variety in their requests. (Editor's note)

Cultural Group (No. of Students)	%Relation-ships with NoRequests	Total No. of Requests	%Direct Requests	%Indirect Requests	Avg. No. of Requests per Relationship
Korean (28)	39%	56	77%	23%	2.00
Japanese (18)	33%	53	81%	19%	3.00
Chinese (24)	12%	78	94%	6%	3.25
Thai (3)	0%	23	87%	13%	7.60
Middle Eastern (3)	0%	9	56%	44%	3.00
West African (8)	75%	8	88%	12%	1.00
Lat. American (13)	23%	44	70%	30%	4.40
European (5)	40%	8	63%	37%	1.60

Table 8.4. Request Patterns by Culture

In a classic study of conversation, Speier (1972) indicated that 'topic' is the main way in which participants to a conversation turn a social activity into an occasion for talk. Participants raise a topic which they assume will be of interest to other participants or which is capable of being developed by the other interlocutors. It was important to examine the topics chosen by the students in this study because they indicated the students' assumptions about their penpals' interests and the development of a shared interest base for facilitation of communication (Gibbs, 1985). Table 8.5 lists the most common types of information that the ESL students requested from their penpals.

general personal information	exchanging letters
home and housing	jobs and work
media	food
family	studies and school life
cultural exchange	miscellaneous
pasttimes	holidays
travel	languages

Table 8.5. Information Request Topics

Topic	No. of Occurrences	Topic	No. of Occurrences
Age	30	Homesickness	10
Alcohol	7	Impressions of Philadelphia/U.S.	26
Animals/Pets**	11	Invitations	68
Appearance*	5	Jobs	55
Books**	10	Likes/Dislikes*	8
Cities	12	Love/Boyfriends/ Girlfriends	12
Classwork/Studying	60	Major Subject	79
Computers	48	Marital Status**	6
Cultural Comparisons	28	Meeting People	30
Current Events/ News of Home	11	Money	14
Dorm/Home Life**	14	Movies/Movie Stars	36
English Ability	71	Music	30
ELC Activities/Outings*	9	Names	87
Exams	58	Nationality	92
Family	42	Negative Experiences	6
Food/Cooking	37	Returning Home	18
Friends and Classmates	23	Shopping/Purchases	22
Future Goals/Dreams	37	Smoking*	2
Health	10	Sports	44
Hobbies/Pasttimes/ Free Time	34	Teachers*	5
Holidays	26	Television	11
Home Country	29	Time/Time Constraints	24
Home Location/ Description***	31	Travel	69

Topic	No. of Occurrences	Topic	No. of Occurrences
Vacation	10	Why Wrote/ Didn t Write***	30
Visits from Friends/ Family	1	Why in America	16
Weather	2	Writing Letters (general)	29
Weekend/Activities**	27	Languages (not English)	29

* Occurred only in Levels 1 and 3
**Never occurred in Business group
***Never occurred in Level 4

Table 8.6. General Topics Chosen for Discussion in Messages

As can be seen in Tables 8.5 and 8.6, many of the topics chosen by the ESL students in our study matched those which Argyle (1992) found to be common in conversations among friends:

1. Sociability—jokes and chat about recent activities
2. Gossip—news about friends
3. Discussion of common interests
4. Provision of information and problem-solving
5. Social support for those in distress

Interestingly, several of these topics (gossip, jokes, and common interests) are also cited by Brown and Levinson (1987) as means of preserving 'face' and showing politeness—crucial elements in the building of relationships.[8]

---

[8] These forms of talk in fact generally function in whole or in part to express role-relationships and to establish a communicative structure or frame for interaction, rather than for the simple or literal transfer of information. As such they come under the heading of *phatic communication* (or, given their often ritual nature, what can alternatively be labeled *phatic communion*). (Editor's note)

8.3.3.   Relationship-Building

8.3.3.1.   Twelve Acts of Relationship-Building

Many of the interpersonal verbal rituals identified by Goffman (1981) occur in our student e-mail letters, including: giving praise, blaming, thanking, supporting, showing affection, showing gratitude, disapproving, indicating dislike, showing sympathy, greeting, and saying farewell. Moreover, although Argyle's friendship-forming strategies are based on spoken language, all nine strategies were used by the students in our investigation to varying degrees. We also identified several additional strategies in our student e-mail letters. The strategies identified in our corpus have been categorized into twelve **acts of relationship-building**. These relationship-building strategies based on our e-mail data are listed in Table 8.7 in order from most commonly used to least commonly used strategies, with a breakdown of these in each class shown in Table 8.8.

```
 1.  Communicating about Relationship
 2.  Giving Personal Information
 3.  Expressing Feelings and Opinions
 4.  Complimenting and Encouraging
 5.  Inquiring (General)
 6.  Comparing Preferences, Interests, and Commonalities
 7.  Relating Experiences
 8.  Sharing Plans and Dreams
 9.  Exchanging Culture and/or Language
10.  Talking about Family and Home
11.  Describing Abilities (and Inabilities)
12.  Apologizing
```

(These acts are listed from most to least frequent.)

Table 8.7. Twelve Acts of Relationship-Building

Relational Act	Level 1	Level 3	Level 4	Business	Overall Average
Communicating about Relationship	4.2	4.9	5.7	9.0	5.9
Giving Personal Information	3.8	3.5	3.5	3.8	3.6
Sharing Feelings	1.7	2.1	2.4	2.2	2.1
Complimenting and Encouraging	1.1	1.6	1.8	3.2	1.9
Inquiring	1.1	0.9	1.4	2.1	1.4
Preferences, Interests, Commonalities	1.5	1.5	1.5	0.6	1.3
Relating Experiences	1.0	1.2	0.9	1.2	1.1
Plans and Dreams	1.3	1.3	0.8	0.9	1.1
Exchanging Culture and/or Language	0.4	0.7	1.5	1.0	0.9
Family and Home	0.7	0.8	0.4	0.7	0.6
Abilities (and Inabilities)	0.7	0.4	0.5	0.4	0.5
Apologizing	0.5	0.5	0.1	0.4	0.4

Table 8.8. Average Number of Relationship-Building Acts Per Relationship

1. Communicating about the Relationship. Communication about the students' relationships with their penpals was the most common act of relationship-building in the e-mail letters of our study.[9] This communication involved defining and describing the relationship, reporting on its status, and inviting continuation of the relationship.

The ESL students viewed their relationships with their penpals in one of three ways: as friend, teacher, or counselor/advisor. Phanh, a student from Thailand, viewed his penpal as a friend, as shown in these excerpts from two of his letters:

---

[9] Note that for the most advanced Writing and Business groups, this type of act was especially common. (Editor's note)

7/15 Finally, I hope I will be your friend and I look forward to your letter. Best friend, Phanh

7/16 Dear Joe, I received your letter, I'm so glad and interested because when I have been staying here, I have not had an American friend because in ELC, there are all international students.

In contrast, many other students viewed their penpals as English teachers to help them with their language learning, as in the case of a Taiwanese student, Ying:

I am vary happy to know you. I am study English. I am English very poor. It is difficult for me to learn English...I hope you can to give me a little suggestion in learn English. Thank very mush.I'll get in touch with you by electronic_mail.

A few students seemed to view their penpals less as friends or teachers and more as expert advisors and counselors. Arturo, one such business writing student from Brazil, wrote this message to his penpal, a graduate student in the Accounting Department:

I would like to ask you a question about accounting. Free consulting please. I received some money in my cheking account from my father in law (SP?). Do I have to pay taxes on this money? Because as an international student I have to fill in a federal and state declaration.

Another way in which the students communicated about their relationships was in asking and telling whether or not letters to or from the penpal had been received. Although this relational act often confirmed successful letter exchanges, this category also often overlapped with the 'indication of inability to respond' category of negotiation discussed earlier. Here are two such examples from Julie, a Taiwanese student, whose penpal was also named Julie:

11/11 Hi, Julie! I was wrote letter to you in Nov.2. I was wait you letter.I don't know what's matter? I ask my husband. He said: You are send wrong.Isaid Iunderstood> He help me check the e-mail and again send. So it's late. Now I am understand send.

11/15 Hi,julie I have receive your message. I don't
know whay send to you is a blank message. I am
sorry! I think it possible is send wrong. Now I can
understand how send.

A third way in which students communicated about their relationship
with their penpal was through invitations. These invitations took many
forms, either invitations to physical events or one of four types of invitations to continue the relationship:

- Assigning a topic for the penpal's next letter—e.g., *"Please
  tell me about..."* (60 occurrences);
- Indicating a topic and/or intention of writing again—e.g.,
  "Next time I will tell you about..." (30 occurrences);
- General expectation of relationship continuation—e.g., *"See
  you later"*, *"Talk to you next time"* (68 occurrences);
- Putting responsibility for relationship continuation on the
  penpal—e.g., *"I will wait for you..."* (56 occurrences).

Some students seemed eager to meet their penpals face-to-face and
invited their penpals to continue their relationships in person, as in the
case of Marcella from Venezuela:

AMIGO,I'D LIKE INVITE YOU TO MEET ME
FACE TO FACE.WE, THE LEVEL 3a, ARE GO-
ING TO HAVE A PARTY ON TUESDAY...
PLEASE TRY TO COME, BECAUSE I WANT TO
TALK TO   YOU WITHOUT COMPUTERS.

2. Giving Personal Information. The second most common act of
relationship-building found in our students' letters was the giving and
exchanging of general personal information. The most common information exchanged was usually very basic identification data such as the
penpals' names, countries of origin, and major school subjects. Sometimes the sharing of this basic information led to deeper discussion in
later letters, as in the case of Speciosa from Rwanda, who wrote:

In your last letter, you asked me to give you the
meaning of my first name. Well! Speciosa is a latin
name...Normally it is one of the virgin Mary's
qualities and it mean 'pretty woman'. I don't know
why my parents chose this for me but I imagine that
they wanted me to be like the virgin Mary in my life.
In Rwanda, the names have alwasy a message for
people who will call us. By our names, we are dif-

ferent from other persons and this is so important
that we don't have family name in Rwanda. Did you
know this before?

As mentioned earlier, Argyle (1992) indicates that such types of self-disclosure aid the maintenance and formation of friendships. Thomas (1985) found that between students who did not know each other, self-disclosure on the part of one person was reciprocated at least 23% of the time with disclosure of personal information by the other person as well.[10]

3. Expressing Feelings and Opinions. A third strategy which the ESL students used to develop their penpal relationships was the expression of emotions and opinions. As might be expected from students studying in a foreign country, homesickness was a common theme, as shown in this example from Mee-Young, a Korean student studying both English and art:

> I WAS ABSENT A LOT LAST WEEK BECAUSE I
> WAS SO SICK. AND ALSO, I THINK I HAVE
> HOMESICK LITTLE BIT...UNTIL NOW, DUR-
> ING MY AMERICALIFE,I HAD MANY DIFFER-
> ENT AND DIFFICULT SITUATION AND EXPE-
> RIENCE. OF COURSE, I AM VERY LIKE AMER-
> ICA LIFE AND I AM SATISFIED...NOW, I
> KNOW WHAT IS FIBER ART...BUT, MORE
> AND MORE IT IS DIFFICULT TO EXPRESS
> MYSELF...ANYWAY, IT IS NOT EASY TO EX-
> PLAIN MY MIND. ART IS MY WHOLE LIFE. I
> CAN GIVE UP THE OTHER THING IF I WILL
> CONTINUE ART.

Students also expressed their feelings and opinions about things that were happening in the news, especially news about their home country. An Israeli student, Rachel, wrote this to her penpal:

> Today it's a very sad day in Israel and for the Is-
> raelie's peoples evry place and for all the jewish
> world. You probebly had heard about the terrorism
> action of the HAMAs the arabik radical movment,
> that killed 19 people and wounded 60 . I feel very

---

[10] Such self-disclosure encourages the production of more language as well. (Editor's note)

dad to start our letters with such a sad subject but i cann't stop thinking about that all the time.

Students also chose to share happy emotions with their penpals, as in the case of a Japanese student, Takio, when he heard this news about his favorite American professional basketball player:

Today I'm Vrey Very Very Very HAPPY.Because my god is come back.My real god is come back.Name is 'MICHAEL JORDAN'. This morning my friend said 'This morning on the redio said Michael Jordan is come back.' First i couldn't believe this but he said on the redio.Now i can believe this. This news is very big and very important for 'NBA'. And for me.

4. Complimenting and Encouraging. A fourth way in which the ESL students tried to develop their penpal relationships was through the use of compliments and words of encouragement. Ellis and Beattie (1986) assert that complimenting is a subtle way of showing a positive attitude toward other people. A Taiwanese student named Albert used this subtle, or not-so-subtle, method when he wrote in his third letter to his penpal:

I think you are so intelligent to handle both job and study.

Miyoko, from Japan, felt a need to acknowledge the encouragement she received from her penpal's letters by writing:

You always send a letter to me soon, moreover; you always try to make me fun. Thank you so much.

While students received encouragement from their penpals' letters, they were also sometimes in the position of giving encouragement as well, as in this series of excerpts from the letters of Zoe, a mainland Chinese student:

3/14 It is very sad to hear the bad news from your father-in-law. I think you have a good familly, you must love him very much. If I were you, I must be very sad, too. So it doesn't matter that you return my message late somehow...I hope you recover your sorrow fully.

3/16 I am glad you feel better now, I wish you eat more and sleep more. Health is most important thing. After I came here, I got sick several times due to the weather. If I feel uncomfortable, I might be in a bad mood. So you should be take care yourself and your family, nothing is more important than health.

5. Inquiring. A fifth means that the ESL students in our investigation used to develop and continue their relationships with their penpals was in the way of what we are labeling 'general inquiries'.[11] The most common of these were:

a. *"How are you?"* (47 occurrences)
b. *"How are you doing?"* (24 occurrences)
c. *"How about you?"* (15 occurrences)

(This question was sometimes used as a general inquiry and sometimes as a solicitation of an opinion.)

d. *"How was your....?"* (12 occurrences)
e. *"How about your....?"* (5 occurrences)
f. *"How do you do?"* (5 occurrences)
g. *"Are you busy?"* (5 occurrences)

In addition to these forms of inquiry, the students attempted, with varying accuracy, to use a variety of idiomatic expressions of the 'general inquiry' type, such as *What's up?* (sometimes written by the students as *What is up?*) and *How's it going?*

6. Comparing Preferences, Interests, and Commonalities. As noted above, Argyle (1992) listed sharing similarities as a verbal strategy for making friendships, and we found this strategy in the e-mail messages of the students in our study as well. For example, Kyoko, a Japanese student, used what she knew about her penpal to clearly create a basis for relationship in her first letter:

Anyway, I got an information that your hobbies are Playing golf, mountain bike, reading and rollerblading. We have two quite same hobbies and two similar ones. I like playing golf but I just began last summer. In spite of a not good player I enjoy play-

---

[11] These 'general inquiry' questions all function as conversation-starters and may be intended on any occasion as partially or wholly phatic. (Editor's note)

ing. If you know good golf links and shops, please
tell me....

7. Relating Experiences. Some students chose to tell their penpals
stories about their lives, most often about living as students in America.
Sometimes the experiences they related were positive, happy stories as in
this example from a Korean student, Hye-Young:

> And another news...I earned 180dollars at atlantic
> city casino...by just one quater.I ate seafood and I
> cross the sea that named bridge and tunnel.I felt first
> time great america.I never felt before.

Yet, many of the experiences that most demanded to be told were negative stories of adapting to urban life in the United States. Wen-Wen, a
student from Taiwan, told her penpal about such as experience:

> I am very busy for my term papers. But yesterday
> afternoon, I was robbed by two guys. Fortunately, I
> ran away and they did't get the money from me. But
> terribly , they robbed the other girl who walked after
> me, just one mimute after they tried to robbed my
> bag. I know that girl. Both of us were scared. Last
> night I could'nt pay attention to my class because of
> the bad experience. I don't know why they don't
> work and make money by themselves. However,
> they choose to be a robber. It's bad. The two guys,
> One is a child,around 15 year olds.He is so young,
> but he is teached to be a robber I feel so sad. Any-
> way, I still have to prepare my peper in library. I will
> more carefully to pass gym,the road where I met the
> two guys.

A Thai student, Bat, had this "terrible, rotten, no good, very bad"
weekend and felt compelled to tell his penpal about it:

> I had a bad holiday. I forgot my all of my key inside
> my apartment since Wednesday and the rental office
> was closed. So..nobody can help me open the door.
> I have to wait for the spare key until Monday morn-
> ing. Bad thing happened again, they did not find my
> key in their lcabinet and I have to call the lock
> opener...During the time I was a homeless, I stayed
> with my friend...We had a trip to Shenandoah Na-
> tional Park...Again, it was very foggy, rainy windy

and very cold so we couldn't see many view from
the top.

Although many of the experiences students shared contained the elements
of opinions and emotions, this category differs from Act 3 'expressing
feelings and opinions' in that the students used story-telling as a means
of illustrating or justifying their feelings or opinions.

8. Sharing Plans and Dreams. As the relationships between students and penpals deepened, the students began sharing information
about their plans and dreams as part of their e-mail letters. Initially, the
ideas shared were short-term plans about what the students wanted to do
after class or on the weekend. Sometimes the students shared more about
their long-term career and education goals, and sometimes the plans and
dreams shared were a combination of both long-term and short-term
goals, as in this letter from a Level 1 student from Brazil, Adriana:

> Today I will go to the ZOO wich my brazilians
> friends.
> I like animals, plants, plantation.
> When I came back to Brazil,I have a examination for
> my university.
> The test is very diffcult.
> I will be ZOO TECNIA. (I don't know in inglish).

9. Exchanging Culture and/or Language. One relationship-
building strategy found in the student letters of this study which would
probably not be found in other studies of relational language use by L1
English speakers is the exchanging of cultural information and language
instruction between the ESL students and their penpals. Several of the
ESL students greeted their penpals in their own L1 from time to time, and
several who came from countries which do not use a Latin alphabet
transliterated sentences into Latin characters. Many students also tried to
teach their penpals about their home countries, and this appeared to be
something often requested by the penpals themselves. Mickey, a Level 4
student from Japan, expressed this desire to his penpal:

> If you could come to Japan...you sould take suburb
> train or subway 'in the morning', because it is very
> very crowded...and you could know how hard to
> work Japan and it is 'not' true that we are rich as ev-
> erybody in other countries says.Everything is very
> expensive...It takes so long time to go to office or
> school...We have to work from morning to till late at
> night, we don't have long vacation etc. I'd like you

American to know about Japan not only cars and a high Japanese yen late but also real living way of Japanese.

10. Talking about Family and Home. A specific type of personal information that some of the students shared with their penpals was information and descriptions of their family and their lifestyle, both in the U.S. and in their home country. Jenny, a business writing student from Taiwan, shared this about her relationship with her family:

> I didn't stay at home since I was very young . Because my father had his business and my mother had to help him, I lived my grandparents' home. And the other reasons that I lived in my grandparents' house is my grandparents' house is in downtown, it is easy for me to go to school...I went home once a week. I think because of this, I am more independent in some way, and my parents always don't worry about me. They trust what I did.

11. Describing Abilities (and Inabilities). One of the less frequent ways the students attempted to build relationships with their penpals was by sharing information about their abilities and inabilities. The most common ability discussed, predictably, was English language proficiency, and language learning struggles and triumphs. Sang-Young, a student from Korea, expressed his frustration by writing, "*I can't talk with you because I can't write well. But I exert myself because I want to exchange views with you early.*"

While many authors have found that computers make writing easier for L1 and L2 writers in the long rum (see Pennington, 1996b, this volume), a number of students in the present investigation wrote to their penpals about their inability to use computers and their uncertainty of being able to successfully send e-mail to their penpals. Kwang-Shik, a Korean engineering student, expressed it this way:

> Last friday I send my letter to you but maybe you did't get it. It's my mistake because I am not accustomed to computer.Whenever I sit down in front of computer, I fill sick.In spite of my major is engineering,Idon 't like computer. It's my handcap.After fishing undergraduate school,I will change my major.

Less unique to the medium of e-mail and the cross-cultural relationships of this study were the discussions about abilities in sports and hobbies. In a particularly creative role-playing piece, a level 1 student from Japan shared his athletic strengths through the eyes of 'a friend':

> Hi!How's it going?Today one of my friends is going to tell you about me. That's as follows:....As you know, he's a ELC student from Japan.His block hair has a slignt wave.He's a medinm bulit and he's tall enongn to play basketball. When he was a high school student,he joined the basketball team.He was good at shooting .He really likes basket-ball...Anyway,he's such a nice guy.He can talk with anybody and make pepole laugh and even happy.I suggest you to meet him and talk with him in pe-son.....
> Did you get it? That's me.

12. Apologizing. The last and least common act of relationship-building found in these letters might actually be viewed as a means of re-building or maintaining a relationship rather than beginning a friendship. Several students apologized to their penpals, most often for not writing letters or for writing letters late, as illustrated by the second example given for negotiation (sec. 8.3.1). Since these actions (or lack of actions) could be considered face-threatening to the penpal and so damaging to the common relationship, the students used apologies to show that they did not wish the relationship to be interrupted (Brown & Levinson, 1987).

8.3.3.2. A Case Study in Relationship-Building

Appendix 8.1 shows the progression of one particular relationship be-tween a Brazilian student, Marcos, and his penpal, Anita, who was late in returning his first message. The case uses a number of the acts of re-lationship-building that we have just described (as listed in Tables 8.7 and 8.8).

Marcos' first message, dated 4/22, begins with a greeting and general inquiry (Act 5), moves next to expressing interest in the new relationship (Act 1), shares some personal information (Act 2), and then finishes up with an invitation for his penpal Anita to continue the relationship by sending a letter in return (Act 1 again).

Marcos returns to the computer center one week later to find no letter from his penpal and tries again to start the relationship, this time by giv-ing a terse greeting, encouraging her in what he perceives to be her diffi-cult studies that could be keeping her from writing (Act 4), giving more information about himself (Act 2), and then finishing up by sharing his feelings about the relationship's slow start (a combination of Acts 1 and 3).

Two weeks after his first letter, Marcos still has no letter from Anita, so he writes a letter of frustration to the teacher giving up on the relationship, only to discover a letter from his penpal in his mailbox the next day. He then writes back to try to repair the relationship's bad beginning. In this e-mail letter, he shares his feelings about the rocky start (Acts 1 and 3), tells more about the common interests he has with his penpal (Act 6), and invites Anita to write back more about these commonalities (Act 1).

By Marcos' fourth letter to Anita, the relationship seems to be on the mend. Marcos begins with a greeting and inquiry (Act 5), acknowledges Anita's second letter and the limitations on his own time for writing (Act 1), expresses his forgiveness of Anita's initial slow response (Act 3), compliments her on her studies (Act 4), mentions how one of their common interests has reminded him of their relationship (Acts 1 and 6), thanks Anita for her letter and invites her to write again (Act 1), and encourages her again in her studies (Act 4).

Marcos clearly shows the expectation in his first and second letter that if he discloses information about himself, Anita will do the same (as noted by Thomas, 1985); and in his third and fourth letters, he uses the verbal forms of agreeing and paying compliments to try to repair the relationship, or affirm a positive attitude toward it (Ellis & Beattie, 1986; Thomas, 1985). This case study demonstrates how the various acts of relationship-building that we have identified interact with one another to aid ESL students in getting to know strangers via e-mail. It also shows how students made use of individual acts multiple times, both in single letters and over the course of their relationships.

8.3.3.3. Relationship-Ending: Continuation and Decline

Argyle (1992) notes that friendship formation follows a pattern of six stages:

1. Proximity (making frequency of contact easier)
2. Similarity (though not necessarily of personality)
3. Rewardingness (meeting of each other's needs)
4. Development of regular meetings
5. Self-disclosure
6. Decline (moving away from each other)

The student-penpal relationships built through the Drexel E-mail Penpal Project were officially limited to the course of a 10-week academic term, and few relationships continued beyond the official time commitment.

Both students and penpals seemed to expect and accept the time limitations imposed by the university schedule, although participants in a few relationships desired continuation. Magdalene from Rwanda and her penpal were one such case. Magdalene wrote:

> 12/2 I'm going to tell you how we can meet : I have my classes at Drexel Matheson house from Monday to Thursday and Friday at Korman :from 9-10:30,and next class at Matheson. I also give you my adress at home:....
> I think we will have a party at Drexel on Tuesday, December 13...buy I don't know if I will be there. I have to begin my vacations because I will make my retreat...Please, could you say me how to meet before you will be flying to Mexico ? I will be very happy ! I'm already waiting !
>
> 12/9 About our meeting, I think it is impossible this time becaus e today is my last class for this term. I have to go to Massachusetts next Monday...I retourn for Winter therefore January...I hope to meet you that time. I have with me your adress and you have mine to. We can write.

Although most of the relationships built were limited in the way described above, the letter excerpts we have shared show that many of the relationships did fit Argyle's (1992) definition of friends:

> people who are liked, whose company is enjoyed, who share common interests and activities, who are helpful and understanding, who can be trusted, with whom one feels comfortable, and who will be emotionally supportive. (p. 49)

Many of the teachers whose ESL classes participated in the penpal project organized end-of-term parties for their classes and encouraged the ESL students to invite their penpals to these parties or to otherwise meet face-to-face. The results of these attempts to bridge the gap between the virtual world and the physical one were mixed. Turnout rate of volunteer penpals for the end-of-term parties averaged 25-30% of those invited, and few students ever met their penpals face-to-face. There seemed to be a variety of reasons for this. One was the difficulty of scheduling an actual meeting, as in Mindy and Chris's case:

> First, I need to apaligize to you . Because I don't
> konw you had an appoin ent with me ,I had not
> check my e-mail last week .So ,may be you mail me
> some massage but I really don,t know about that .
> Tonight,there is a party...I will to meet you first.Can
> you go with me?because I am not familiar with the
> road in philadelphhia...See you tonight!

We heard later from Mindy that Chris did not get her message in time to
make it to the party and she was left waiting at the appointed place, just
as he had been the week before.[12]

A second difficulty in moving from the written to the face-to-face relationship was in the ESL students' fear about transferring from a written
language to a spoken language situation. This insecurity was felt by students at both beginning and higher levels. Level 1 student Nayumi expressed it this way:

> I'm glad that you will come to our party.Thank you
> very much...At first I have to tell you that I can't
> speak English very well. And please speak slowly.
> Of corse I study English as hard as I can but....

Min, a Taiwanese student in Level 3, shared a similar concern:

> I am excited to know that you want to meet me face
> on face. But I worry about my spoken English. I can
> read, I can write, but I really can't speak well. I hope
> we can still communicate when we see each other.
> Anyway, I live in the [dormitory] and my room
> number is 406. If you have time, welcome to my
> room.

In addition to the difficulty of trying to arrange meetings, it seemed
that in many cases, both the volunteer penpals and the ESL students preferred to remain anonymous, perhaps because of the increased freedom
to take risks in the private computer environment (Pennington,

---

[12] In addition to the usual problems of transmission and reception of information in
spoken interactions, in e-mail communication, the physical and temporal gap in
transmission and reception creates a temporal gap in feedback that may produce anxiety and other sorts of problems. On the other hand, this gap may encourage the generation of lengthier and more thoughtful and involved responses. (Editor's note)

1996a,b).[13] Vivienne, a student from Hong Kong, expressed it to her penpal this way:

> Why everytime you want to meet me. I think if I meet you, may be I can't tell a lot of things to you. Now, I feel comfortable. Also, I feel some interesting about your face.

While many of the e-mail relationships formed did not end in a face-to-face meeting, they did not all decline and end without closure. Many of the students clearly acknowledged the end of their relationship with the penpal, often because they themselves were returning to their home countries and would not have access to e-mail there. Marcos Z was one of those who ended the relationship in an explicit way:

> Hello again..., sorry for didn't have time to go to your restaurant, but it's my last E-MAIL I'll send to you, I'm very pleasured to talk to you and you have untill saturday 19 to write to me...So I hope you enjoyed my E-mail letters...
> GOOD-BYE, YOUR BRAZILIAN FRIEND,
> Marcos Z!!!!!!

8.3.4. Limitations of the Investigation

This study, while one of the largest conducted to date on the e-mail letters of English L2 learners, is limited by several factors, most obvious of which is the limited perspective of the data itself. Since we analyzed only the ESL students' letters and not those of their English-speaking penpals,

---

[13] Indeed, one of the main attractions of computer communication is its simultaneously intimate and anonymous nature (Pennington, 1996a; this volume; forthcoming b). E-mail, as a medium for forming virtual connections or partnerships at a distance, would seem to be a less face-threatening context than various modes of real-time spoken interaction, including face-to-face as well as telephone communication. Moreover, in e-mail participants can choose the extent to which they construct the interaction as real or virtual. Participants can thus decide whether and the extent to which they use the e-mail exchanges to create a real relationship or to only roleplay a relationship in what remains only a nominal partnership—a chance or *ad hoc* pairing. Thus, e-mail provides an environment not only for engaging in (a type of real) communication but also for *simulating* communication. In fact, e-mail communication would seem to vary along a continuum from actual communication, involving real communicative purposes and relationship-building, to simulated communication involving roleplay, language play, or language practice (Pennington, forthcoming b). In any of these constructions, e-mail would seem to have particular value for L2 learners. (Editor's note)

we were able to study only one side of what were mainly two-way exchanges. Because of this, we may not have been able to see the extent to which the meaning of information was really negotiated, whether the information requested by one partner was supplied by the other, and whether or not the relationships built were equal in their level of self-disclosure and intimacy. In addition, the results of our data have been slightly skewed by our decision to include those 'relationships' in which only one letter was written by the ESL student to the penpal. These 'relationships' may in fact not have been relationships at all, failing due to inability of the penpal to respond, lack of interest in the relationship on the part of either writing partner, or failure of the ESL student to find and follow-up on the penpal's response letters.

Another limitation of our study is the effect of the computer and e-mail technology on many of the students and their relationships. Although the computer can reduce the negative affect associated with writing (Pennington, 1996b, this volume), we found that in many cases lack of familiarity with computers created a 'block' for some students trying to write to their penpals via e-mail, even though the students were generally well-motivated to 'meet' their penpals and to learn about computer communications. For these students, the quantity and, in some cases, the quality of what they were able to write and share with their penpals was limited by their speed and comfort level with the computer and the e-mail software employed, thereby limiting their ability and the time available for negotiating meaning, gathering information, and responding fully to the task of relationship-building.

Similarly, the ESL students in this study were limited in their access to the computer hardware for sending and receiving e-mail. Most did not have computers in their homes, and although they had independent access to the campus computer center during the week, most students used computers only on 'e-mail day' once a week when their class met in a computer laboratory expressly for the purpose of checking, sending, and receiving e-mail. If the students had had more open access to the technology over the course of the term, they may have exchanged more letters with their penpals than was dictated by the once-a-week requirement, relationships between penpals might have become more intimate, and a deeper exchange of information might have occurred.

The e-mail task itself affected the study in another way, as can be seen by comparing the assignment given to the students in the business writing course and that given to the students in the general ESL writing classes. Volunteer penpals with some background, experience, or education in business were specifically selected to write to students in the business writing course, thereby giving the students and their penpals an immediate sense of shared information and common experience. As Argyle (1992) points out, this shared or assumed information is a basic requirement of interaction. The students in the general writing courses were not guaranteed this interactional advantage, although when the interests of the penpals were known, they were matched as closely as possible with a student who had similar interests. This common interest, along with the fact that the business writing course met every day in a computer classroom rather than just once a week (as in the general courses), may account for the higher number of messages per student in the business writing course, as well as for some of the variation in the topic choices of the students in the different courses.

8.4.   IMPLICATIONS FOR LANGUAGE TEACHING

We are able to draw a number of conclusions about the use of e-mail for language teaching from the findings of the investigation. First of all, it seems clear that e-mail can be used effectively by language learners to facilitate contact with L1 speakers and with the target language culture. Our study shows that when presented as an opportunity to interact with L1 or advanced L2 speakers of the target language, the learners' e-mail writing produced a wealth of relational language. We also see that students were able to repair initially unsuccessful relationships through multiple attempts at communication in successive letters, a task which many language learners find extremely difficult in face-to-face interactions. This finding may relate to Pennington's (1996a,b) assertions about the freedom to take risks in a computer environment and with Spears and Lea's (1992) claims that computer-mediated communication may be an even more social medium "than the apparently 'richer' context of face-to-face interaction, and one that gives fuller rein to fundamentally *social* psychological factors" (p. 31). In addition, although students did not get much feedback on the grammar or surface structure of the language they used, they did receive reinforcement of their understandings of the meaning of words and ideas through the continuation of a topic in their penpals' letters. If the e-mail project undertaken for this study were adapted elsewhere, it seems that it might be especially useful for ESL and foreign language settings where authentic contact with L2 speakers is difficult.

At the same time, e-mail was not clearly of value in this setting for helping students develop greater control of vocabulary and structure. In the ESL student letters we studied, there were few instances of language negotiation or directly observable language improvement. Pennington (1996b) points out that the short timeframe of computer studies such as our one-term investigation may account for a lack of noticeable language improvement. Future longer-term studies that analyze the e-mail interactions of both ESL student and L1 English writers in relationship to one another may show more instances of negotiation and greater language development.

There would seem to be several conditions for deriving language development benefits from e-mail projects such as the one described here. One condition is that of 'goal-directed' communication (Hoppe-Graff, Hermann, Winterhoff-Spurk, & Mangold, 1985). The instructor's purposes for the e-mail assignment—both linguistic and relational—must be made clear, and the students' purposes for such activity should also be discussed. As Snyder (1993) found that word processing was most useful when combined with complementary writing instruction, the setting of goals for e-mail relationships should be accompanied by instruction in the language and processes necessary for achieving those goals.

In addition, as many researchers have pointed out, 'social setting' and 'conventional knowledge' are key components of communication. Since e-mail is a newly emerging field, it may be especially helpful in language teaching to accompany e-mail tasks with instruction about the unique environment of e-mail, background information about the correspondents, and the potential expectations of the participants for the e-mail relationships.[14]

8.5.   QUESTIONS FOR FURTHER STUDY

The study reported here raises a number of questions for further study of e-mail communication, especially as it relates to language teaching. In the area of negotiation, the most obvious question is: How can we increase the amount of linguistic negotiation between writers? Since e-mail is such a promising language learning tool and negotiation is such a basic part of learning, this seems to be a key question for ensuring the best use of e-mail in the language classroom. There are also many other areas to explore within the realm of e-mail communication. Migliacci (1996), for example, is currently analyzing other dimensions of the e-mail partner relationship, including the possible effects of gender on computer communication.

In the area of information-gathering, our study raises many questions about the cultural aspects of requesting as well as about how request patterns differ in written and spoken interactions. There is a need for further comparative studies across cultures, with an increased sample pool especially from Middle Eastern and European cultures. The request patterns of ESL learners in an e-mail context need to be compared with

---

[14]It might be of value to students to make explicit comparisons of e-mail communication with other types of communication, written as well as spoken. (Editor's note)

those of L1 English writers as well.[15] The type, the structuring, and the timing of requests within e-mail relationships should also be investigated.

A number of questions also arise from our survey of relationship-building. There seems to be a need for a separate in-depth study of each relationship-building act. What is the timing of the different kinds of information shared? At what point in an e-mail relationship is each act felt to be appropriate? What conditions must be met in the relationship before each partner feels comfortable disclosing certain types of information about him/herself? Are there cultural variations in the types of information that writers choose to share?

The reasons for deciding to meet or not to meet face-to-face when such a meeting is possible should also be explored. Are there cultural variations in the reasons behind these decisions, or is the decision based solely on individual factors? Are certain types of e-mail relationships more or less likely to lead to a face-to-face meeting?

We would also like to see this study replicated by others and to have the results of our study or others carried out with L2 learners examined in comparison to the relationship-building strategies used by L1 English speakers and writers. Additionally, it would be useful to compare our findings to similar studies conducted with learners of languages other than English to see what similarities and differences occur in the negotiation and relationship-building patterns of those languages.[16]

Finally, the acts of relationship-building found in the present study of e-mail letters need to be compared with the strategies used for building relationships in other situations. Are there significant differences in the strategies used in an e-mail context and the strategies used in spoken interactions, whether face-to-face, telephone, or video? Clarke and Argyle (1982) suggested that social encounters usually have a five-episode structure of greeting, relationship-establishment and role clarification, performance of a task, re-establishment of the relationship, and parting (p. 190). Do these five episodes occur in individual e-mail letters as well, and to what extent are they present in other types of social encounters that do not occur as face-to-face interactions? Only a deeper study of a more complete set of data can answer these many research questions.

---

[15] From the data of this study, it might be of interest to contrastively analyze the interactions of the 59 L1 English-speaking penpals vs. the 57 advanced L2 penpals. Procedures used in other e-mail investigations for capturing both sides of the e-mail communication would allow for additional analysis of the interactions. (Editor's note)

[16] This study can be compared in several respects with that of Slater and Carpenter (this volume), e.g., as done in the introductory chapter (Pennington, this volume). (Editor's note)

APPENDIX 8.1.

Relationship-building: The Case of Marcos

4/22 To Anita

Hello!
How are you doing? I hope you are very well.
I'm very glad to be your penpal. I believe that we can talk a lot by e-mail.
I'm from Brazil, I came here to study English....
Well I'm looking forward to receive your letter, as soon as you can response.
Ciao. MBA

4/29 To Anita

Hello one more time.
Well I think you're very busy, studying a lot. Very nice. Also I hope that you are enjoying your life here.
I can tell you that i'm having a lot of fun. I can play my favorites sports, play my guitar, do my work out, make new friends.
I was excited to be your penpal, but I'm so frustrated because I waited for one week your answer AND nothing happened. Well I wish on this time have more luck.
CIAO. MARCOS A_____

5/5 To teacher

Hello
Ok. Probably she does not received my letters. Well, I don't think so.
I believe that she just din't wanted to write back to me. So if you don't mind, I prefer to write to someone else.
Thank you for your time and I appreciated your attention.
Ciao.
Marcos

5/6 To Anita

Hi!
I have to tell you the truth, last friday I was so dessapointed with you
that I took you off from my computer. It is bad when you are expecting
some thing appear in your screem and nothing happen.
Well if you still have interest to be my penpal Ok. WELLCOME ONE
MORE TIME.
I think that I like every thing you like too...
I like your studies about wales and dolphins, I just love both of them.
When you have a chance, please tell me something more about that.
Well one more time, I'm really glad for you response my letter. Thank
you.

5/10 To Anita

Hei, how are you again?

I'm very glad for received one more letter from you. Today I don't have
enough time to write very well, But I can write somethings.
First of all I am not mad with you. Please, you don't need ask for for-
give you. I can understand you were very busy. In addition, congratula-
tions for you, I can see you are very smart. Only "A" in your degree...
Yesterday, I remind you. I was seeing TV, and suddenly appeared a
program about dolphins. It was very interesting.
One more time, thank you for write me again. I will wait for your next
letter.
Good luck in yours tests. Quimical and computer, isn't it? I hope you get
"AA"

Ciao.
Marcos A_____

9. Introducing E-mail into a Course in French as a Second Language

Paul Slater and Catrine Carpenter

ABSTRACT

This chapter evaluates a project which put students enrolled at a UK university in e-mail contact with university students in France as a way to further the goals of a second language curriculum in French. The e-mail contact, which was structured to aid in the completion of a course assignment, was not successful in achieving this goal due to problems of implementation and matching of student characteristics and interests. The problems are described and analyzed as a basis for making recommendations for future applications of e-mail under similar circumstances.

9.0. INTRODUCTION

The growth of the Internet presents those in education wishing to exploit it with a challenge to develop effective and pedagogically sound approaches to its use in different disciplines. Given that many language learners are studying with the explicit intention of improving their ability to communicate internationally, the communication potential of the Internet makes it a particularly valuable resource for this group. A group of educators at the Language Centre at the University of Brighton[1] undertook a literature review to determine how this new technology was being used to support the teaching and learning of languages. We identified work with e-mail as having the most potential for directly addressing our students' need for authentic communication in the target language, which was in this case French. We determined that by providing e-mail partners who were mother tongue (L1) speakers of French, our learners would have the opportunity to use their second language (L2) in genuinely communicative exchanges.

---

[1] Those involved in the project included: Elspeth Broady, Catrine Carpenter, Dominique Le Duc, and Paul Slater. A report on the project was presented at the Association of Learning Technology's Conference 'Virtual Campus, Real Learning', held in September 1997, Wolverhampton, UK.

To research this potential for genuinely communicative exchanges using the resources of the Internet, two of the members of the original group (the authors) decided to run a pilot project using e-mail with a group of our students in the UK and a paired group at a university in France. The discussion of this chapter presents the pedagogical benefits that we hoped to explore, the rationale behind the project framework, the practicalities involved, an assessment of the successes and failures of the project, and finally an account of what we learned and how we intend to improve future e-mail projects.

9.1.   THE PEDAGOGICAL BENEFITS OF E-MAIL

E-mail was selected as the focus of the project because it appeared to offer a range of attractive and worthwhile benefits. It was felt that by running our own project, we could see if the benefits to students described by other language educators could be replicated in the context of the learning of French in an English-speaking university. Since most studies of e-mail have been focused on the learning of English, an investigation in relation to the learning of another language seemed motivated. Moreover, while the practical benefits of e-mail use such as speed and flexibility of access are clear, the pedagogical benefits are less well documented and in our view require more investigation.

The literature on e-mail suggests that the pedagogical benefits associated with its use are not independent but rather from a series of interlinked effects. Fostering genuine communication in an L2 is an important factor in successful language learning but is difficult in a classroom. By arranging e-mail links between students, teachers provide a context in which authentic communication is relatively easy to generate. The provision of a context for authentic communication is the benefit most consistently associated with e-mail use (Brammerts, 1996a, 1996b; Calvert, 1996; Mason, 1993; Warschauer, 1995). The authenticity of the communication means that students' use of the L2 has a real purpose rather than being the type of abstracted or artificial language exercises that some class work can become. Higher motivation levels are generated by the real purpose underlying e-mail communication (Kornum, 1993), and increases in commitment can result in student texts of higher quality (Eck, Legenhausen, & Wolff, 1994). The production of such texts necessitates the type of deep level cognitive processing and intellectual involvement required for effective learning.

As possibly an "ideal tool for the autonomous learner" (Lewis, Woodin, & St. John, 1996, p. 117), we were interested to explore e-mail's potential in self-study. While different levels of student autonomy have been reported in the pedagogical literature on e-mail, those projects

268

which promoted an autonomous approach to e-mail use emphasized peer learning, with its associated pedagogical benefits such as high levels of student-to-student support (Brammerts, 1996b) and improved speech modeling (Kelm, 1996). Given the value of intercultural understanding to L2 development (Byram, & Morgan, 1994; Tomalin & Stempleski, 1993), we were also interested in the potential of e-mail links to foster improved intercultural understanding. If e-mail projects can raise cultural awareness in the way that some commentators suggest (Calvert, 1996; Kern, 1996; Korum, 1993), then this potential effect looked to be an interesting area to investigate.

9.2. PROJECT PREPARATION AND STARTUP

For the project to be successful, careful preparation and the establishment of details of structure, basic principles, and guidelines were essential. The key issues addressed by us in preparing for the project were: the nature of the e-mail groups and the links between them; the students' tasks to be performed using e-mail; deciding when the L1 and the L2 (both French and English) would be used in the exchanges; the level of student autonomy; the degree of integration of e-mail use with main course work; and methods of assessment of project effectiveness. Some of these decisions were determined by practicalities such as the student vacation dates but most were matters requiring a consideration of many factors and the weighing of alternatives.

9.2.1. Learner Autonomy or Program Control?

Looking at e-mail projects in the literature, we were struck by the contrasting levels of control teachers applied to students' work. Some emphasized teacher-led whole-class work, while others argued for student independence and autonomy. In different ways, both approaches attempt to confront the tendency in language teaching situations to encourage communication which becomes shallow, dull, and lifeless. If this is allowed to happen "students' messages can remain perennially brief and chatty, with little development and elaboration of language or thought" (Kern, 1996, p. 107). To avoid this tendency, some educators are moving away from individual 'penpal' exchanges to class exchanges with more focused, content-based curricular objectives (Kern, 1996; Riel, 1993). Other educators working with e-mail continue to advocate the autonomous approach, arguing that it is only when teachers relinquish control to students that the more educationally valuable authentic communication can take place (Hoffman, 1996).

269

These conflicting views on the appropriate level of student autonomy in e-mail projects put us in a dilemma. As members of a department fostering student autonomy, we favored the autonomous approach but were concerned that this might result in trivial exchanges. We decided to adopt a compromise. We provided students with a range of topics and allowed them each to select a topic for their individual projects. Communication over the Internet was not restricted to these topics, as students were allowed any informal contact they wanted with their e-mail partners, provided the thematic work that had been assigned as part of their French course was covered first. We hoped that this would provide an element of control and guidance while allowing enough freedom for authentic communication to take place.

9.2.2. Integration with the Curriculum

One of the key questions facing organizers of an e-mail project is the degree to which e-mail work is integrated into the curriculum. There are a variety of approaches. The e-mail work can be "a course in its own right, a compulsory or optional element of an existing course, or merely an optional extra available to those wishing to exploit it" (Calvert, 1996, p. 36). The idea of voluntary work, or e-mail work as an 'add-on' to the core curriculum, is viewed unfavorably by some who believe this usually results in projects ending in failure, as students seem unable to sustain effective levels of communication over the 'long haul' (Tillyer, 1996). Many American commentators on e-mail use now favor an approach in which e-mail work is more carefully planned and integrated within the larger course curriculum (Kern, 1996; Riel, 1993). However, the European commentators involved in the so-called 'tandem' e-mail work (e.g., Brammerts, 1996a,b; Calvert, 1996; Lewis, Woodin, & St. John, 1996) argue that a variety of approaches can be successful. Those committed to the tandem philosophy believe that effective e-mail work "is based on the principle of each partner following his/her own learning goals and methods" (Calvert, 1996, p. 36).

Whether e-mail work is integrated within the existing curriculum or applied as a supplementary activity, there must be parity in the degree of curriculum integration between paired institutions. Such parity helps to create an equal level commitment from participating students. Differing degrees of commitment between paired classes rapidly destroys the value of an exchange; one class will find the other overly demanding while the 'demanding' class views the other group of students as lazy or disinterested.

The degree of e-mail project integration with main course work also influences project work assessment. If the e-mail work is tightly integrated with a main course, then it will not need a separate assessment. If it is an 'add-on', students will want to know if work will be graded and, if it is, how that grade will influence a final overall course mark. If the work is not assessed, there is likely to be insufficient motivation for students to treat it seriously.

As our project was partly experimental, it would have been unfair to integrate the work too closely within the main course. The students would be the ones to suffer most if the project were unsuccessful. In consequence, we decided to run the project as a course add-on; but as the class instructors, we gave students support and guidance during class time. It was also decided that the project work would lead to an end-of-term student presentation based on the e-mail exchanges. We would assess this presentation, but the mark would not contribute towards the student's end-of-year mark.

9.2.3. Selecting Project Groups

In selecting students for the project, we identified those who were in our view likely to benefit most from an e-mail exchange and who would experience the least disruption to their existing course. We selected two first-year French groups studying linguistics and modern languages. One group had eleven students, and the other had twelve. Most were aged nineteen or twenty, from one of five nationalities: British, Greek, Moroccan, German, and French. These groups were chosen because we could incorporate the e-mail work into the 'integrated skills' section of their course, which is designed to develop students' communication skills. This intake of students was also the first to have had instruction in e-mail use built into their course. Finally, we knew that if the e-mail project was successful, then we would be able to build on that success and include further e-mail work into these students' second and third years of French study.

9.2.4. Pairing Languages

The pairing of students for an inter-institutional e-mail exchange can be done according to a shared L2, or it can involve two different target languages. There are negative and positive factors involved in pairing students whose target languages are different. One advantage of different language pairs is that in any exchange there can be one student who is an expert in the language of interaction. Such an 'expert' is unlikely to have an extensive knowledge of grammar. However, the expert, if an L1 speaker of the target language, will be able to produce authentic texts in that language and to competently assess a received text for meaning and grammatical acceptability. This possibility contrasts with e-mail exchanges where students are communicating in a common target language.

In such circumstances, without teacher intervention, there is a danger of incorrect, and uncorrected, language flowing between learners. The disadvantage for paired students studying each other's languages is that if the exchange is to be equitable, half of the communications will have to be in each language.

The decision was made to link our students to a group of L1 French-speaking students studying English in France, meaning that the e-mail exchanges would involve two target languages—French as L2 for our students and English as L2 for the French-speaking students. This type of exchange needs careful negotiations between teachers and students on both sides of the exchange to establish ground rules as to where and when the two languages are to be used. Texts composed by students in the language they are learning mean that their partners will read texts full of linguistic errors; on the other hand, the advantage of writing in their L2 is that students benefit from composing in that language and from partner feedback and correction. Alternatively, if messages are composed in the writer's L1, those receiving the message will be reading authentic texts with personalized communicative value in their L2.

To benefit from both approaches, it is necessary to vary the language used, so that the learners produce either alternate messages or parts of messages in the two languages. Initially, we decided that questions would be composed in the L2 of the sender and answers supplied by the addressee in the same language, i.e., our students would write questions in French and their e-mail 'keypals' would answer in French, and the French students would write questions to our students in English which they would answer in English. With this arrangement, students on both sides of the exchange would have opportunities both to write in their L2 and to read texts generated by L1 speakers. However, we accepted the need for flexibility and gave students the option to negotiate with their partners over language use.

9.2.5. Finding Partners

A variety of organizations are available to help link up language-learning students either on a class-to-class or student-to-student basis. Within the European context, the International Tandem E-mail Network has a system in which a student individually registers and is then allocated a partner.[2] On a whole-class basis, all the students will be individually allocated partners drawn from a variety of different institutions. Alternatively, the class teacher can try to find a partner class through personal

---

[2] Details of the procedure required for registering are available on the International Tandem E-Mail Network web site available at: http://tandem.uni-trier.de/Tandem/e-mail/infen.html

contacts and then establish the additional structure to make the project bilateral. We chose the latter option because it allowed us to plan, monitor, and evaluate the project more extensively and effectively in the hopes of gaining clearer and potentially more effective results.

Finding partner classes in the French higher education system was difficult. In our search for partner classes, we posted calls through the Intercultural E-mail Classroom Connections (IECC) service.[3] Our call went out to subscribers to the higher education list but produced no contacts. We eventually found a partner class through existing contacts we had with an Institut Universitaire de Technologie (IUT) in southern France. IUTs are further education colleges where students study vocationally orientated courses over a period of two years.

9.2.6. Finalizing the Project Arrangements

With our UK class selected, the partner class in France found, and project guidelines established, we completed our project plan and timeline, and agreed details with the partner teacher in France. The project was to run from early February to June, 1996. As the first step, the students would have the project explained to them and would receive additional instruction in e-mail use. Within each of the partner groups, students would be teamed with a co-class member. These same-group paired students would then be matched up with a pair in the partner class. By pairing students in each group, we hoped to avoid the problem of individual students being matched up with a student who, for whatever reason, failed to respond to the e-mail messages. It was hoped that with pair-to-pair mail, someone in each pair would maintain the contact through whatever difficulties arose during the course of the project. After pairings had been established, each pair would be given the e-mail addresses of their partners and would mail them an introductory e-mail message.

9.2.7. Presenting the Project to the Students

After establishing contact, students would agree on a subject for discussion with their keypals from the range of topics we offered them, including 'university life', 'life in the university town', and 'job prospects in their home country'. For this initial project, the students were restricted to the subjects we had selected. Students were told they should exchange mail at least once a week, and ideally more often. Over a period of five weeks, they would gather information from their keypals for a presentation at the end of the spring term on the selected topic. At this time, they would also give written feedback on the project in questionnaire form, in

---

[3] This service can be accessed at: http://www.stolaf.edu/network/iecc/intro.html

addition to oral feedback in whole-class mode. On their return after the Easter vacation, the students would select a new topic and work to assemble information for a second presentation at the end of the summer term, when it was planned to evaluate the project a second time.

To prepare our students for the project and to get their reactions to the work, they were shown the project schedule, given the reasoning behind the project and its goals, and told how work would be assessed. They immediately raised a number of concerns. Although the bulk of the work was intended to take place outside of class, some students were worried about losing class time. They felt that this time could be better spent on other activities with which they were more familiar and secure. One student felt that they were being treated "like guinea pigs"; some were intimidated about having to use French, their L2, with L1 speakers of that language; others were anxious about using computers and e-mail. Because of these concerns, students were given the option to withdraw from the project, although none opted to do so. Although this was not an auspicious start, listening to the students gave us their perspective on the project plan and allowed us to provide them some reassurance.

9.2.8. Administering the Project

During an initial two-hour session, students reviewed the basics of e-mail use, including how to access their accounts and to send, receive, forward, and save mail messages. Once students were confident in using the e-mail system, the first exchange of mail took place. During these early exchanges, there were a variety of problems such as forgotten passwords and mail bouncing back. Most of these 'teething troubles' were resolved in the first two weeks.

Having trained the students to use the system and having helped them to establish contact with their partners, we then left them to communicate with their partners outside of class time. Subject areas were negotiated with partners, and an exchange of questions and answers began. During the project, twenty to thirty minutes of class time per week were devoted to monitoring student work and giving advice and support. Students also provided printouts of their exchanges, so that the course instructors could monitor the type of exchanges students were involved in and the level of language being used.

9.3. PROJECT OUTCOMES

At the end of the spring term, we assessed student reaction to the project using a questionnaire and a whole-class feedback session. Although many positive results were attested by individual students, the outcomes of the project did not in general meet our expectations. After reviewing positive and less positive outcomes below, we discuss project shortcomings and reasons for these, as a basis in the next section for making recommendations for future projects.

9.3.1. Positive Results

Our project work produced many of the benefits we were expecting. The students provided us with sufficient positive feedback for us to believe that e-mail work can be developed into a useful tool to support students' learning of an L2.

This positive feedback had a number of foci. The students valued the opportunity to use e-mail and to develop computer skills, and there were positive comments relating to the value of e-mail for language development. In terms of language benefits, students were enthusiastic about the extra practice in reading and writing French that the e-mail contact provided them. They valued the contact with L1 French speakers and the feedback on their French from someone other than their teacher. Some, though not all, appreciated the exposure to a more colloquial form of French than they were experiencing through their outside reading or during class time. Aspects of the intercultural contact were also positive; some students found the contact with young French people rewarding, commenting, for example, on how interesting it was to find out about aspects of French culture such as the education system.

9.3.2. Negative Results

From the beginning of the project, we were aware that it was not working as effectively as we had hoped. The students were satisfied with the technical training and support they received on the project, but problems stemmed from inadequacies in the quality and quantity of the mail received from their French partners. As the project centered around exchanges of information, this was a crucial factor for its success. Unfortunately, our students were unhappy with the responses they received to calls for information from their keypals. Most either received very little information from their partners, had to wait a long time for a response, or received information that was irrelevant to the questions asked. This generally low level of interest or cooperation from the French side of the e-mail exchanges was also reflected in the limited requests our students received from their overseas partners for reciprocal information. As a result, some students found themselves participating in the kinds of banal and non-informative exchanges that quickly lead to boredom. The imbalance in enthusiasm for the work was reflected in the number of messages sent from each side. In almost all cases, our students sent significantly more messages and messages of greater length than their keypals. The limited responses from their keypals left many of our students demoralized.

9.4.   DISCUSSION

9.4.1. Lack of Reciprocity

The different levels of project enthusiasm were caused in part by the different degree to which the e-mail work was integrated into the course of study. For a successful project, both sets of students must have similar tasks and overall aims for their project work so that they share similar levels of motivation and attitudes to the work. Although we had allocated class time to preparation and feedback on the project and had integrated the e-mail activity with the curriculum at our institution, the students in the exchange class seemed to view their e-mail work as very much an add-on to their core work. This was commented on by our students, one of whom wrote: "They (the partner class students) didn't seem to realise that getting information was important, even though we had explained. It was more of a leisure activity for our keypals than education." As Tillyer (1996) stresses, if e-mail work is based around having 'fun', when one group of students have had their fun, the impetus for the project runs out. If one group of students but not the other continues to need to make contact in order to complete assignments, they are likely to receive inadequate assistance from their partnered students.

This problem of inadequate response from the French partners stemmed from a failure to effectively incorporate into the work what Brammerts (1996a) considers central to the understanding of tandem language learning, i.e., the Principle of Reciprocity. He stresses that:

> Successful learning in tandem is based on the reciprocal dependence and mutual support of partners; both partners should contribute equally to their work together and benefit to the same extent. Learners should be prepared and able to do as much for their partner as they expect from their partner. (Brammerts, 1996a, p. 11)

Despite the high levels of good will between the two groups and the regular contact between teachers, this 'Principle of Reciprocity' did not sufficiently underlie the project and was reflected in the relatively poor response rates. Since the partner class teacher was not involved in the project from the onset, this finding suggests how difficult it maybe to achieve a full commitment from students when their teacher is not part of the process through which the original ideas and enthusiasm for a curricular innovation are generated.

9.4.2. Intercultural Problems

While much is made of the intercultural learning that can take place between the different language communities and cultures through e-mail communication, we saw in our students some intercultural friction. This aspect of e-mail exchanges has received little attention in the literature. One of the few to discuss it is Teichmann (1994), in reporting on an e-mail project she carried out:

> It sometimes seemed...as if teachers were fighting an uphill battle on the intercultural front. Not even the immediacy of modern telecommunications could completely compensate for this tendency to reject the foreign and different. (p. 68)

She gives examples of keypal behavior which demonstrate that "an impartial recognition of differences and non-judgmental discussion of them were often beyond the immediate horizon of the pupils involved" (Teichmann, 1994, p. 66). We observed this same type of shortcoming in our own students to a degree.

Interestingly, the cultural differences limiting the project's effectiveness were more complex than simply a matter of nationality. Our students were arts students studying French and linguistics. They were paired, however, with information technology students. We knew that this pairing might generate difficulties related to different interests and goals; and we suspect, as Calvert (1996) suggests, that there is an advantage in matching partners according to academic discipline. Unfortunately, we were not able to find such matched partners for our students. Our groups were also predominantly female, while the French group was almost entirely male. As a result of these factors, the two groups had few common interests. Regrettably, our students found it difficult to relate to the interests of the French group (e.g., comics, computers, snowboarding). It is likely that even if these two student groups were of the same nationality, they would also have had little to say to each other. Thus, students' background characteristics, interests, and fields of study comprise a factor which needs attention if useful language exchanges are to take place.

Where it is not possible to perfectly match groups, the solution to these breakdowns in communication may lie in a more structured project, built on a variety of task-based activities predetermined by the teachers.

Completing these sorts of activities would provide students with the incentive to exploit the opportunity to communicate.[4]

9.4.3. Problems of Structure

We believed that the work structure we established and the consistency with which we imposed it would be key to the project's success. Our semi-autonomous approach proved moderately successful but did not satisfy all the students, who provided us with conflicting feedback on the project's structure. When asked how the project work could be improved, a small proportion of the students said they would have wanted a more explicit structure, while another group argued that less structure would have allowed for more authentic communication with their keypals. A possible solution to these conflicting demands is simply to allocate time for both structured and unstructured communication, accommodating both types of student preferences.[5]

9.4.4. Summary

Our students were initially well-motivated, they participated in some authentic L2 (French) exchanges, and they achieved a degree of student autonomy based on peer learning. However, the success of the project was limited due to in large measure to insufficient quality and quantity of communication between partners. Although the positive outcomes did not occur on the scale we had hoped for, the work was experimental and offered many lessons for future work with e-mail. Based on our analysis of the effects and constraints of this project, we can say with confidence that we know what worked, what did not, and why. We are confident that improvements can be made in future projects and that the benefit to students from e-mail exchanges can be increased.

---

[4] A different type of solution might be to have students focus on relationship-building with their e-mail partner, thus gearing the exchange towards a conversational model (e.g., as in the e-mail project described by Nabors & Swartley, this volume). (Editor's note)

[5] It would be of value to carry out an investigation to compare these two types of e-mail activity in an explicit way, e.g., through a quasi-experimental controlled research design, on perhaps three groups—one of which receives a structured treatment, one unstructured, and one a combination of treatments. (Editor's note)

9.5.   IMPROVING FUTURE E-MAIL PROJECTS

In attempting to improve use of e-mail with L2 students, we have re-examined our own work and researched the work of others reported since we undertook this first project. In future work with e-mail some changes that we plan to make are minor, while others are more fundamental.

9.5.1.   Integration of E-mail into Coursework

The degree to which e-mail is integrated with main course work is critical for the success of a student partners project; our compromise did not work satisfactorily. The project was run in essence as an add-on to an already established main course. If this type of e-mail contact is to be successful, students must be highly motivated; the e-mail contact alone will not be sufficient to sustain student interest. We gave the students a task, but it was relatively unguided and its successful completion was totally dependent on information coming out of the e-mail contact. The e-mail response was at the center of the work assigned on the project, rather than being a supporting peripheral project task. As a result, the project succeeded or failed based on the degree of reciprocity between keypals. This factor of student response is not one over which a single teacher can have control. If the students in the two paired classes view the e-mail work in a significantly different way, this mismatch can have major effects on the outcome of the e-mail exchange.

Having reanalyzed successful projects reported in the literature, we believe that part of the solution to these problems is to make e-mail less central in project work and also to give it a supporting role for other class activities. In the Radio Gemini project, carried out jointly by Totton College and the Lycée Grignard (Barner, 1993), the students' main work was the production of radio broadcasts for transmission on local radio stations. The e-mail link provided the means of liaison for the production work.[6] It would be unrealistic to expect every class to be involved in such high profile work but the principle is important: e-mail, like other instructional tools or media, should not be placed center stage, but should be utilized as a means to an end.

9.5.2.   Enriching the Contact

A great deal of information can be conveyed by e-mail, but there is much that cannot. Thus, e-mail should not be the only medium of communica-

---

[6] Compare the tie-in of project work to a student on-line newspaper in Marcoul's (this volume) study. (Editor's note)

tion used by students. The exchange of texts between students is an excellent vehicle for language learning, but these textual exchanges can be enriched and enhanced with other instructional aids or media. A simple exchange of photos between paired classes can facilitate communication between partners by making the partner seem more real or interesting. This 'reality effect' can be further enhanced by an exchange of videos showing aspects of students' lives or, if possible, by face-to-face meetings between student groups (if they agree to this).[7] As students develop a greater awareness of their partners through various forms of contact, they are more likely to respect the 'Principle of Reciprocity' that is so central to effective e-mail projects for language learning.

9.5.3. Enriching The Task

Unlike traditional instructional tasks, in which learning takes place primarily in the classroom with the teacher as the main provider and peers as recipients, e-mail work involves two partners communicating with each other via the Internet. This means that the function of the teacher, the peers, and the classroom will necessarily evolve with the increasing use of e-mail. Teachers are increasingly becoming advisors and facilitators of learning, providing guidance and feedback, and seeking to monitor learning without controlling it. Students can benefit from individual support for their e-mail communication when and where it is required. Teachers will continue to provide language work in preparation for students' e-mail work. For example, students recounting their holiday experiences to their e-mail partners can benefit from work on past tenses.

The classroom can become a forum for discussion before and after e-mail communications, with peers acting as collaborators and resources. It then becomes desirable to divide the class into smaller groups to facilitate collaborative tasks and strategy building, such as discussing one's ideas, asking others about their opinions, and carrying out peer correction. Both the teachers and the students should collaborate in designing instructional tasks. The teacher can set the overall format of the task, while the students can be involved in selecting the task content. For example, in a writing context, the teacher could focus on the use of genres as the overall task framework, while the students are responsible for selecting their own topics. If the selected genre is narrative, students could produce a story on any topic, while for a contrastive essay, students could select an issue of their choice to develop in this genre. To ensure that students will take responsibility for their own learning, as part of an e-mail project they might be required to write a learning contract and to

---

[7] As noted by Nabors and Swartley (this volume), students may not always want such contact. (Editor's note)

keep a diary on their learning experience. Whereas students need to be given as much freedom as possible, care must be taken to establish a structure for pedagogical tasks with clear objectives and criteria.

9.5.4. Internet Resources

E-mail work can also be supported, supplemented, and enriched by other media forms of communication available via the Internet. Students can exchange photos, audio recordings, and even videos electronically. The World Wide Web can be used to publish materials for joint discussion (see Hoffman, 1996, for some discussion of resources). Students could also use some of the synchronous net-based means of communication now available to help develop relationships that might lead to and support further interaction. Brammerts (1996a) has suggested the use of the synchronous text-based communication medium of MOOs (Multi-User Domain Object Orientated) as a pedagogical resource "Occasional meetings between partners in a MOO are obviously helpful; there they can quickly answer questions, sort out problems and build on the relationships they have made" (p. 15).

Developments in the electronic medium are currently so rapid that a variety of synchronous means of audio communication are already available, such as Microsoft's *Netmeeting* and Netscape's *CoolTalk*. These tools offer the user the ability to conference in real time using text supplemented by a shared whiteboard and full audio communication via the Internet.

9.5.5. Adding Value To E-mail Exchanges

Pedagogical value can be added to exchanges in the form of research-based learning using e-mail communications as the raw data for linguistic analysis. E-mail exchanges are encoded as digital data which can be electronically saved and submitted to a variety of analyses. Eck, Legenhausen, and Wolff (1994) stress the value of students comparing their own work with an L1 speaker text of the same type, a process which can be assisted by the use of electronic dictionaries and concordancing packages. Eck, Legenhausen, & Wolff (1994) comment that among their German students in an e-mail project "the motivation to work with their own texts and compare them with native speakers' texts was extremely high" (p. 56). While our students did some linguistic work using the data from the exchanges, we are considering developing this aspect of e-mail work further and perhaps instituting it earlier in future projects.

9.5.6. Fine-Tuning

In future projects, we will improve on the design of the present project in a number of other ways. Closer contact with partner teachers will be established before the project starts and then maintained for the duration of the project. More closely matched assignments or tasks will be agreed between teachers on both sides of the exchange before the project gets underway. Students will moreover be given a more explicit and extensive presentation about the rationale and objectives of the project. In our presentation of the e-mail project to the first cohort, we failed to stress sufficiently the benefits they might gain from communication with L1 speakers. Some of the students participating in the project said they would have appreciated clearer guidelines for aspects of the exchanges. To that end, students will be given advice at the beginning of the project about when to use which language in their communications. We will also suggest how and when to provide correction or feedback to partner students. Overall, we want to encourage students to develop additional strategies enabling them to make better use of the exchange and so enhance their learning experience. Despite our desire to establish a clearer structure in future exchanges, we shall continue to observe one of Tillyer's guidelines for successful e-mail projects: "Be flexible and prepare to make adjustments as necessary" (Tillyer, 1996, p. 5).

Each group of students has a different dynamic and adjustments made to an institutional program which might have made it more productive for that group might make it less profitable for another group. We recognize that the imposition of tighter structuring and control might provide one group of students the framework which they need to work productively, but which for another group could be stifling and counterproductive. Sensitive monitoring of student exchanges should allow teachers to adjust approaches for use of e-mail to fit the characteristics of different students groups and educational settings.

9.5.7. Measures of Effects

Our project was assessed on qualitative feedback from students via questionnaires and whole-class feedback. Students are an important source of data, but the information they provided us may reflect group dynamics, other elements of their course, their attitude towards and experience in the larger university, or aspects of their social life, rather than only the e-mail exchange. The students are also not necessarily able to accurately assess pedagogical aspects of the work they are either currently pursuing or have recently completed. In future projects, we would like to apply research methodologies which provide some objective measures of any language learning benefits achieved through e-mail.

9.6.   CONCLUSION

The critical question on the use of e-mail for L2 learning is whether or not it brings sufficient language learning gains to justify the effort involved in establishing and managing it as part of an educational curriculum. Our initial trials produced mixed results, including some which provide useful directions for the future. We are confident that any negative aspects of e-mail use can be minimized through careful planning and guided execution of task-based work. In particular, this project demonstrates the importance of building up shared interests and goals, and a strong sense of commitment on both sides of an e-mail partnership, in order to provide the motivation needed to ensure productive communication and to sustain that communication over an extended period of time.

10. Composing with Computer Technology: A Case Study of a Group of Students in Computer Studies Learning French as a Second Language

Isabelle Marcoul and Martha C. Pennington[1]

ABSTRACT

This chapter reports on an investigation of writing in French as a second language which aimed to discover the best practice for developing composition skills among a group of English-speaking students that would make use of their degree specialization and technical skills in computer studies. During seven weeks, the writers had to produce written compositions at first with pen and paper, then a word processor, and finally as a hypertext file to be set up on the World Wide Web. Part of this exercise was for the purpose of developing articles for an electronic newspaper created by the students. The use of three different media to produce writing makes it possible to compare outcomes of each in the training of the students' skills and in their written products. The study emphasizes the role of multimedia presentation on writing and draws conclusions in the way of guidelines for students' writing and composition assessment in computer contexts.

10.0.   INTRODUCTION

A central problem in teaching French to a group of computer studies students who take a class in French for Computing as part of their degree course at City University of London has been the training of their written skills. Writing is often perceived as a difficult skill area by the students in this course, who tend to achieve poor results in composition. Because writing is part of full competence in a second language (L2) and is one of the skills tested in the course, it is considered important to increase the chances of the students concerned to achieve better results in this area of language skill. Since the students are enrolled in a 'specific purposes' course, the acquisition and improvement of their French language is to be

---

[1] The first author is largely responsible for this research. The second author advised on the design of the study and assisted in writing up the findings in the present report.

carried out in relation to the students' main subject area, which in this case is computer studies. In this context, using a word processor or other computer tools is not only for the purpose of learning or practicing a language. Rather, the main objective of these specific purpose language courses is to master a language to be used in the context of the workplace and its technology.

In the project that is the focus of the present chapter, the first author, who is the tutor on the French for Computing course, sought to combine students' knowledge and skills in information technology [IT] with training in writing to produce tangible work in the way of web pages. It was decided to investigate the compositions produced by the students using three different media—pen-and-paper, word processing, and hypertext—as a way to draw preliminary conclusions about how technology influences the students' composition and to find ways of using the different media to enhance their chances of success. The intention was to assess students' work with the three media and to produce guidelines for composition—in particular, regarding a standard for a good web page.

This research is relevant to today's educational context, as teaching and learning are being influenced by technology with the great increase in the presence of computers in society. Document and report writing by computer means, in addition to data presentation and access, have become important elements of office work; and there is a need for ongoing training in the use of technology as part of most workers' continuing education. This influence of technology on work is described in the context of the Multilingual Information Society program adopted by the European Commission (Rédacteurs Software Documentation Limited, 1996) as follows: "For more and more people language technology, though they may not label it as such, provides the tools with which they work, learn and relax; it is an unobtrusive part of their daily life" (p. 22). There is no possibility of going back to a world where handwriting is used to produce office documents. In today's international workplace, IT skills have become a prerequisite, and an additional language can also be a great asset. It is therefore relevant that students preparing for work as computer specialists should receive adequate training in writing combined with their IT skills. It is also essential in today's society that language teachers adapt their teaching to the demands of the workplace.

10.1.   RESEARCH FRAMEWORK

10.1.1. Project Focus

Writing is a difficult task because of its degree of complexity. In the words of Hayes (1996):

> Writing depends on an appropriate combination of cognitive,
> affective, social, and physical conditions if it is to happen at
> all. Writing is a communicative act that requires a social con-
> text and a medium. It is a generative activity requiring motiva-
> tion, and it is an intellectual activity requiring cognitive pro-
> cesses and memory. (p. 5)

Since the early 1970's, much research has been conducted in the attempt
to establish the nature of writing competence. As stated by Hillocks
(1987):

> Research on the composing process indicates that writing is an
> enormously complex task, demanding the use of at least four
> types of knowledge: knowledge of the content to be written
> about; procedural knowledge that enables the manipulation of
> content; knowledge of discourse structures, including the
> schemata underlying various types of writing (e.g., story, ar-
> gument), syntactic forms, and the conventions of punctuation
> and usage; and the procedural knowledge that enables the pro-
> duction of a piece of writing of a particular type. (p. 73)

The use of computer media in the last thirty years or so has brought a
different perspective to ways of generating and presenting text. Computer representation has moreover extended itself beyond the written
word: with the use of multimedia, the communicator is dealing with
sounds, images, animations, and other tools which convey meaning different from written text and which could alter the process of writing.
Bates (1995) argues that "[t]hese representational possibilities of media
are particularly important for non-academic learners, who often require
concrete examples or demonstrations rather than abstract theory" (p. 8).

Computer technology offers interactivity, flexibility, autonomy, and
power to its users. According to Reinking (1986), the use of e-mail or
the exploration of virtual environments on the Internet provides the opportunity to expand the context of interaction amongst users and the
freedom to move at one's very own pace in a controllable environment.
There is in this type of technology an element of discovery, which provides an opportunity to explore. As Boyles (1995) suggests, computers
may have changed the way in which learners interact with information
and with each other.

Although writing is largely a cognitive activity, it cannot be performed without physical tools and resources. In order for multimedia to
be worthwhile to writers, it must offer resources for creating representations and document structures. As has been speculated for word processing (Pennington, 1993c; 1996b,d), perhaps this technology can help
writers overcome cognitive limitations such as short-term memory.

However, writers still need to learn to use the medium as effective support for writing activity and goals.

The focus of the present project is on the effective use and interactive development of computer students' IT skills and their L2 (in this case, French). The researchers opted to focus on the influence of the use of three different writing means—pen-and-paper, word processor, and hypertext programming—on the production of students' writing and on the assessment of the different written products created. The analysis of the students' production and its assessment should highlight both the strengths and the weaknesses of the technology. The analysis should also aid the selection of an approach to instructing students' writing skills and offer some direction for students to improve their writing in the context of their work environment.

10.1.2. Instructional Orientation

From a psychological perspective, Krashen's model (e.g., Krashen, 1981, 1982) provides some basic assumptions regarding optimal input for language acquisition that are relevant to the teaching of writing. These involve four characteristics that must obtain for learners to receive optimal input, which can be applied to the present context of research as follows:

> **Comprehensibility.** In the present context, this implies that the students would develop their L2 writing skills using a technology that they understood and could apply according to their own level of knowledge and skill. They could also receive advice from a writing tutor who would strive to present clear instruction and who could also serve as a facilitator to clarify any points while students were writing.

> **Focus on Meaning.** According to Krashen (1982), writers "should simply write..., using what they intuitively feel they need to... make [their work] comprehensible" (p.186). Following Krashen's advice, the students would be left free to follow their instincts when writing, and to make use of any technical or human resources they wished in the creation and expression of meaning.

> **Exposure to Sufficient Quantity of Authentic Material.** Electronic sources of information involving foreign language materials have become a reality on the Internet. Students would therefore be encouraged to find material for composing in French by browsing the World Wide Web.

High Interest or Relevance of What is Taught. Consistent with Krashen's views, Freeman and Sanders (1987) observed: "If students could feel that their writing serves a function relevant to their lives and interests perhaps they would be more willing to work on their writing tasks until the writing is truly completed and not merely handed over to the authorities" (p. 644). It was thus felt important to let the students write about topics they knew and enjoyed.

Although writing practice does not necessarily improve the quality of writing, the tutor felt that it was important to encourage the students to write. It was felt that students' reluctance to write or negative attitudes toward writing could be reduced by offering non-judgmental or positive feedback from the tutor and other students. Consistent with the selected approach inspired by Krashen, the students were instructed not to worry about grammar or surface errors when writing in French. In addition, as a way to make writing a more enjoyable task and a more appropriate learning experience, the students were free to choose any subjects they wanted to write about (other than subjects promoting violence, racism, or sexism).

10.1.3. Analytical Orientation

Written composition can be analyzed at three levels which may be affected one way or another by this technology. As described by Braddock, Lloyd-Jones, and Shoer (1963), these are: surface, meaning, and environmental levels.

The **surface level** deals with the language of the composition, i.e., its grammar, vocabulary, and the types of errors made in sentence structure. The analysis at this level allows the tutor to discover the students' proficiency in French as L2.

The **meaning level** involves the content of the composition, i.e., the kinds of ideas that are being explored. In this connection, it is important to find out whether the students use written French based on memorized sentences or are able to produce their own original text of coherent ideas. Organization into paragraphs is included in this level of analysis, as each paragraph is considered to represent a developed idea.

The **environmental level** deals with the type of presentation produced by the three different computer means. This level of analysis is especially important in the present research project because the use of multimedia tools allows a great variety of presentation styles. The environmental level also emphasizes the importance of each means in the production of written texts, as each can influence writing in a positive or restrictive manner.

10.1.4. Aims and Expectations

At the end of the research project the tutor aimed to:

- Decide on the best method of training the students to compose in French with the aid of computer media;

- Assess the work produced in an original manner, especially for web pages: there is a need to research assessment standards, as material on L2 acquisition and web authoring is sparse;

- Offer guidelines to the students for creating good quality composition for web pages;

- Publish students' work on the World Wide Web.

The objectives were not to see whether any linguistic improvement could be recorded during the limited time of research. Rather, the tutor wanted to observe how computer studies students would react to the different means of composing texts, recording the differences that occurred when the three media were being used, as a way to help develop effective use of media to enhance the French writing of this specific group of students.

It was expected that it would be possible to observe differences at the three levels of analysis as defined above in how the students produce and react to their written work, based on the characteristics of the different media. These expectations, as laid out below, can be taken as a set of informal hypotheses against which the research results will be interpreted.

a. *In their approach to correction and revision.* Because of its editing tools, word processing should make a consistent difference in error correction. Students will revise their text significantly better at the surface level and will make more corrections at all levels when using word processing than in the other writing modes.

b. *In their language.* Because of its additional resources, hypertext will allow a more unconventional use of language than the other two means of writing. At the surface level, structural errors will be less frequent with hypertext and word processing than in pen-and-paper mode, where these are more difficult to correct.

c. *In the way meaning is conveyed.* Students will develop their ideas more fully and with more originality when using the extra resources of hypertext than when using the other computer media.

d. *In their approach to presentation.* Hypertext presentation will be influenced by the cyberspace culture, giving freedom of expression to the students to create less conventional or formal types of text than in the other modes.

10.2. PRELIMINARY PHASE

10.2.1. Students

Before beginning any writing, the students were required to fill out a questionnaire about themselves focusing on their linguistic background and writing skills. Key results are shown in Table 10.1.

Language Spoken	French	English	3rd lang.	4th lang.
	100%	100%	29%	19%
Years Spent Learning French	2	3	4	7	8
	25%	25%	14%	30%	5%
Hypertext Skills	Skilled	Basic or No Knowledge		Professional Level
	90%	10%		30%

Table 10.1. Students' Skills and Language Background

Twenty-one students participated in the research. The age range varied from 19 to 28 years old, with 10 female students and 11 male students. Two subjects were English, 10 were from the United Kingdom but belong to a second-generation group whose parents immigrated to England. This means that they had learned languages other than English as children. Nine were L2 English speakers who came from Europe,

China, Arabian countries, or Africa. All of them had spent two to eight years learning French and, 19 had learned another language besides English or French. Six had learned a fourth language other than English or French, mastering the four languages to different standards. The majority of the students had passed a general level (GCSE) French examination, and six of them had passed an advanced level ('A-level') examination in French. Four students had spent some time in France (less than a year) and kept regular contact with French mother tongue (L1) speakers and used French with them. Three students had not taken any kind of examination in French, though they had been taught French at secondary school for two or three years and had taken some private tuition in French before the course had started. All of the subjects, without exception, found writing the most difficult skill to master in French, followed by speaking.

The majority said they had been taught French in a communicative approach, with the exception of three students who appeared to have been taught mainly in a more conventional way with an emphasis on grammar. Fifteen out of 21 claimed to have a general knowledge of French grammar and grammatical terminology, while the remaining six found grammar difficult. However, the tutor had difficulty in describing to the class the types of errors they were making in writing and speaking using conventional grammatical terminology. Thus, it appears that all students had only a limited knowledge of grammatical terms. None of them had been taught specific study skills. Those who were in their final year of study and who had to complete a final written project with references had been given a list of books dealing with academic skills and writing style. In general, they knew little about these areas.

Subjects were either second- or third-year students in computer fields. Most of them had spent a year in industry gathering experience in the field of computing as part of their degree curriculum. Three specializations were represented in the group. The first was Computer Science, which is the most general subject in the area of computing. The second was Business Computing, which centers on computer systems in the field of business. The third is Software Engineering, which is concerned with programming software.

Seventeen of the students had direct experience with hypertext and had learned the design of web pages at a professional level. Six of them had worked in companies specializing in that type of programming using complex tools such as JAVA, a sophisticated programming language. Only four out of 21 had very little or no experience of web page composition. All had extensive experience in word processing and knew how to use *Microsoft Word*. The majority of subjects regularly spent time on the World Wide Web, browsing sites on a weekly basis for an average of four hours. Six of them regularly browsed sites where the language used was not English. Ten of the students had created their own web sites.

These ten students belonged to what can be referred to as the popular dance music scene: they were involved with music recording software and were part of the 'rave music' movement and its associated culture.

To give a general description of the participants' identity, one can say that they were all undergraduates, young, and with IT experience, some knowledge of French, and a rich linguistic background. They had little conscious knowledge about academic skills and writing style. It was therefore decided to prepare them in composition basics before beginning the investigation of information technology on their written work.

10.2.2. Baseline Writing Assessment

Before the students were asked to produce compositions using the three different media, they had to write an essay on any topic they chose using pen and paper within a period of two hours. They were allowed to use their dictionary, coursebooks, and the tutor's and other students' help as desired. This was not a marked test but rather a baseline writing sample for assessment of students' writing skills. The analysis of their compositions showed that the class could be divided into two levels in French writing: lower intermediate, the equivalent of 200 hours of teaching, and upper intermediate, the equivalent of 300-400 hours of teaching. None of the students were entirely fluent or had an advanced understanding and control of the written language. Their presentation of ideas suffered from problems of unclear meaning, lack of organization, and errors in surface form. Thus, it seemed necessary to spend some time on teaching the ways ideas can be presented in writing essays.

10.2.3. Writing Instruction and Generation of Starting Guidelines

In the first part of the project, the tutor offered instruction in French composition. Advice on essay writing was derived from *Study Skills in English* (Wallace, 1980) and *A Study Skills Handbook* (Smith & Smith, 1990). The main topics discussed revolved around the tasks of generating text in planning, gathering information, note-taking, considering the audience, and organizing ideas. The students were asked to pay attention to examples of the types of compositions they were interested in writing. They were also asked to analyze samples of written work in French, working in groups of three to find the main ideas of the texts and how they were presented. This allowed the students to be exposed to a certain quantity of text. In an attempt to arouse the students' interest, model compositions were drawn from articles about computers or youth culture, as well as from texts downloaded from French sites on the Internet.

Students were also asked to analyze a French web site that they had to find by browsing the Internet.

A general discussion followed this preliminary work. The students had to discuss what, according to them, made a text clear and a web page interesting, even if they did not always understand the written words. As an outcome of this discussion the students developed a set of starting guidelines for the production of written text and web pages, as follows:

- Before starting to write, decide on only one topic, with the possibility of later adding subtopics.

- Plan the way ideas were to be presented by jotting down a list of main items of content and putting them into a logical order.

- Formulate each main idea as a sentence and revise them during the writing process.

- The dictionary is not always the most helpful way of checking on vocabulary; the tutor or other students might be of more use.

- Web pages need to be clearly designed, not overloaded with pictures and animations. A high percentage of the information on the World Wide Web is visual, with a small amount of sound.

- Web sites need to give a sense of unity of style in the way of: color, font, and use of graphics, pictures, sounds, etc.

At the end of this preliminary phase, in which the students' academic and linguistic background had been assessed, their writing skills analyzed, and their views on writing ascertained, they were informed about the research project and its procedures for generating and evaluating compositions in the three media, as described in the next section.

10.3.   TREATMENT PHASE

10.3.1. Procedure

The students had only 30 hours of French lessons before taking their final test. For the research project, only three sessions of two hours each could be dedicated to this writing exercise. It was therefore decided to follow a modified time-series design, assessing the written work of the group in three stages, starting with writing in the classroom using pen and paper, next using *Microsoft Word* as a word processor in the computer laboratory, and then using hypertext in the computer lab to create a web page for a student on-line newspaper. The hypertext exercise was linked to a graded, out-of-class assignment to create a web page in French and English. Each class time exercise could not last any more than two hours, which is generally the time allocated to the students to write an essay in French during their final test. The students were informed that in each session they would write a short essay (150 words or more) in French about any topic which would be suitable for SENAC, the students' electronic newspaper.

10.3.2. SENAC (Student Electronic Newspaper At City)

The SENAC on-line newspaper at City University of London is the result of a project set by the first author, who, as the tutor in the French for Computing course, took the opportunity to create an electronic newspaper where the students' work could be shown on the World Wide Web. A WWW student newspaper was made possible by the fact that the students involved in SENAC were computer-literate and experienced in hypertext composition. There was no need to train them in IT skills before starting this project. The four students from the treatment group who hardly had any web experience decided that they would still create a web page as part of their assignment, learning the necessary procedures on their own.

SENAC has different links containing articles produced by students. The articles are on a wide range of topics which are of interest to the students at the university, such as:

- News at City University

- Life in London: entertainment, sport, leisure, travel, going out, accommodation, transport, and personal experiences as a student

- A section called 'Blah Blah' for articles which do not fit into any other specific section but which address subjects of interest to the students

Each article is in the form of a hypertext document. From the beginning, SENAC has contained files with multimedia elements, mainly picture such as scanned photographs. Later some of the students' work added more complex features, such as by the use of JAVA, which enables the creation of hypertext documents with multimedia elements like video, animation, and sound effects. At the present time, the written text in SENAC is in French and English, but it is hoped that students in other language classes will produce work in German and Spanish in the very near future.

As part of the method used to investigate the students' writing, the tutor asked the students to design a web page to add to SENAC as a piece of coursework whose mark would count towards their final degree. As mentioned earlier, the creation of a web page can involve the use of elements other than written words, for example, video clips or sounds. These can be easily accessed from the Internet, though the downloading of data can take some time. As a two-hour session can prove disappointing in terms of the amount of hypertext material produced, students were given two weeks to complete their web page, which had to be written in French and English and would be graded as their final piece of coursework. This made it possible to research the style and the design of web pages with more material than those produced during the two-hour session. Thus, the students' work for pen-and-paper, word processing, and hypertext were assessed from two-hour sessions, whereas the graded web page was necessarily created over a longer, more open-ended period.

10.3.3. Data Collection

The students were required to keep records of all the changes they made during the time spent writing in French. They were given a diary to keep track of all these changes and an explanation of what to record. This part of the project was explained at great length and supported by written instructions and examples to make sure that there was no misunderstanding and that the students clearly understood the process of collecting data.

In their diary of the writing sessions, students had to produce the following sorts of information:

> *Records of the changes made in language* (**surface level**). Such changes include those in grammar, vocabulary, sentence structure, and spelling. This allowed the tutor to check the frequency and type of changes made by the students in language.

> *Records of the changes made in content and organization* (**meaning level**). The data recorded give information about what kinds of topics the writers selected and how many times they changed their topics, ideas, or paragraphs.

> *Records of changes made in presentation* (**environmental level**). This category includes changes in text style or layout as

well as means of representation other than the written word. In the hypertext condition, it includes the use of multimedia elements such as picture files (mainly known as *gif* or *jpg* files).

The students were to record changes they made of any of these types along with any other relevant observations about their work in each session. The tutor later classified the students' records at each session into the three categories of changes. During the writing sessions, the tutor sat next to two students at a time and observed what they were writing in their diaries. This procedure encouraged completeness and accuracy in what was being recorded, while also helping to discover any problems or misunderstandings and providing extra help as needed. In addition to seeing the students' work in progress, the tutor was able to view the final products of the two-hour sessions and the two-week course assignment. Changes in the students' work were tallied by a consideration of their self-report records in relation to the work produced and checked by the tutor four times to ensure accuracy. These tallies were supplemented by qualitative analysis of patterns in the students' work and records of this work.

10.4.   FINDINGS

Out of 21 participants, an average of 17 students attended the three sessions and produced compositions in each mode. Four students (as mentioned earlier), because of their lack of hypertext expertise, did not compose a web page during the session in the computer laboratory but did produce one as part of their coursework. Since the goal of the study was essentially a qualitative and practical one, that is, to describe the work produced under the different media as a basis for making recommendations for instruction, the data are analyzed in a primarily qualitative and interpretive manner. When the analysis of the three compositions allows for numerical comparison, the results are given as frequency data (Table 10.2.), and later in graphic form with the frequencies converted to percentages of the total per row. The computer program used to enter the quantitative data and produce graphs was *Microsoft Excel*, which was also used to calculate 1x3 chi-square distributions and probabilities for these, as shown in Table 10.2.

The chi-square values, which are large and highly significant, support the view, as presented below, of a different pattern of accent errors and revision changes—in terms of surface-level (grammar and mechanics), meaning-level, and environment-level (presentation) revision changes—in pen-and-paper, word processing, and hypertext modes. These figures are, however, only suggestive, as the differences in frequency of errors and of the different types of revision changes may be due in part to the different number of words produced in each writing mode.

WRITING MODE	Pen & Paper	Word Processing	Hypertext	Total	Row Chi-Square
Accent Errors	358	406	179	943	91.02***
REVISION CHANGES					
Grammar & Mechanics	256	388	88	732	185.31***
Meaning	51	88	114	253	23.76***
Presentation	9	87	360	456	446.96***

*** $p < 0.0001$

Table 10.2. Frequency of Accent Errors and Revision Changes (Grammar and Mechanics, Meaning, and Presentation, with Row Chi-Square Values (df = 2)

10.4.1. Surface Level: Language

10.4.1.1. Errors

It was observed from the information found in the diaries and the analysis of the written compositions that most students had problems with gender of nouns, case of pronouns, verb forms, prepositions, and idiomatic expressions. There were not many errors in sentence structure, but in general the structures students produced were simple ones. In this group, most of the errors in language produced during the three sessions were of the same type and order of magnitude, regardless of the means used to write, with one exception: accent marks. As shown in Table 10.2 (above) and Figure 10.1 (below), students made more accent errors in the word processing than in the pen-and-paper condition, and fewest of all in the hypertext (HTML) condition.

When the students had to write text for a web page in the laboratory, the tutor left an OHP slide on for the whole session showing the different tags used for accentuation in French on the World Wide Web. Hypertext does not always read accents unless the page is programmed to do so by the use of these tags. As an example, although the word *été* ('summer') can be written with ASCII codes like those used with *Word*, one can also use tags to write: 'été'; this is *été* for the WWW. It seems that fewer mistakes in accents were made when the students' attention was focused on avoiding this one type of error in relation to a particular medium. The fact that fewer errors were made in the pen-and-paper condition than in the word processing condition perhaps relates to the relative unfamiliarity for most writers of typing accented letters on a keyboard.

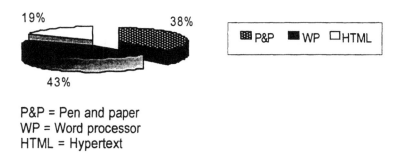

P&P = Pen and paper
WP = Word processor
HTML = Hypertext

Figure 10.1. Accent Errors

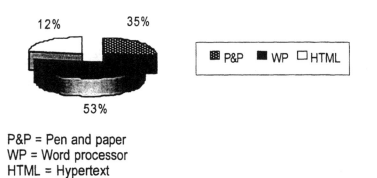

P&P = Pen and paper
WP = Word processor
HTML = Hypertext

Figure 10.2. Changes to Grammar and Mechanics

10.4.1.2. Changes in Grammar and Mechanics

Surface-level revisions, i.e., changes in grammar and mechanics, were most frequent when the word processor was used, as shown in Table 10.2. and Figure 10.2. Under this medium, the students concentrated on surface editing rather than major changes. The student writers in general spent more time revising their written text with *Word*, even though they could not use any spell-checking facility or other computer tool such as a grammar checker to comment on their production in French. They could, however, receive help from the tutor, their fellow students, and reference books such as a dictionary.

Attention was given to sentence structure although often the changes did not produce correct sentences. In the following example of a student's work on the word processor, the text has been changed as follows:

Version 1
Je suis parti a la vacance au moi d'Aout pour 2 semains, je suis visité les monuments de region et interét nationale.

Version 2
J'ai part en la vacance au Aout pour e deux semains, je suis visite les monuments regional et nationals. Il est très interessant.

Version 3
Je suis parti en la vacande au Aout pour 2 semains et j'ai suis les monuments regionalles et interessantes.

The student has written three versions, with changes resulting in problems of similar type and magnitude each time, such as mechanical errors in spelling and accent marks, and grammatical errors in tenses and sentence structure.

10.4.1.3. Type of Language

In the pen-and-paper and word processor modes, most of the text generated was based on a 'GCSE' level or secondary-school type of French. This type of writing has features reminiscent of the sentence structures and lexis of textbook French, which the students would have learned during their years at school when they were studying for the GCSE examination. The students' sentence structures and use of language in pen-and-paper and word-processed compositions were reminiscent of this early training and did not reflect their creativity or personal style.

The students' language was different in the hypertext condition. When working in hypertext, most of the students used language reflecting Internet jargon and their specific background and areas of interest. When students started creating their French web pages, they often used a translation of earlier web pages created in English that they had prepared for their personal pleasure or to communicate their personal interests on the Internet. Thus, at the surface level, the language and vocabulary they produced was often translated from their own English web pages. Some of the students managed to create lengthy documents with multimedia presentations from their original English web sites.

10.4.2. Meaning Level: Content and Organization

10.4.2.1. Topics

In general, students' approach to writing in an L2 reflects their early training and lacks incentives towards a more personal and reflective approach. When writing with pen and paper or word processor, the students in the present investigation wrote texts treating subjects dealt with during their previous learning experiences. Their written production lacked original content and style, and was more mechanical than creative, even when given the opportunity to produce free writing. When asked to comment about the source of inspiration for the topics they chose to write about, a large number of students said they wrote on topics which they had studied at school, such as family, travel, or studies, with descriptions written from a teenager's or secondary student's point of view. Table 10.3 lists the main topics selected by the students and the number of writers who chose them.

	P&P	WP	HTML
Holidays	6	9	7
University	2	5	3
Self	19	20	21
Cyberspace Culture	0	0	10
Pets	0	0	4
Family	19	11	10
Travel	10	7	6
Others	1	2	5

Table 10.3. Topics Selected by Students

301

Topics were more personalized in hypertext mode. For their web pages, most students decided to introduce topics related to their personal lives, showing pictures of themselves or loved ones, describing their dreams, experiences, personal characteristics, or job. Their topics also included cyberspace culture and were more varied in the hypertext mode, as shown by the addition of a category of 'pets' and more entries in the category of 'others'. Several chose to prepare web pages about traveling and holidays, but in this case they expressed a point of view more relevant to their age group instead of using pre-learned sentences reflecting a secondary student's concerns. Most kept in mind that they were writing for SENAC and were inspired by the list of articles and topics presented in this electronic newspaper.

10.4.2.2. Content and Originality

Students spent more time thinking about their subject matter and how to express it when creating web pages than in the other modes. Thus, a striking difference when hypertext was used was the greater attention the students put on content. In their work in the other two modes, less thought appeared to have been put into the ideas expressed. The production of written composition linked to multimedia tools seemed to push the students to think more about their ideas and to generate more original content. The length of the paragraphs was shorter in the hypertext mode than in the other writing modes, as the texts were often arranged around the multimedia tools used. Nevertheless, the texts generated in the hypertext mode contained more different ideas and more developed content than in the other modes, as paragraphs had been reworked more to produce clearer and more concise text.

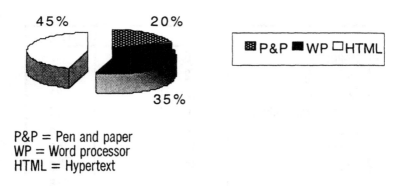

P&P = Pen and paper
WP = Word processor
HTML = Hypertext

Figure 10.3. Meaning Changes

302

10.4.2.3. Changes in Meaning

At the meaning level, there were more revisions made to ideas in hypertext mode than in word-processing mode and more changes in meaning in both of these modes than in pen-and-paper mode, as shown in Table 10.2 and Figure 10.3.

10.4.3. Environmental Level: Presentation

10.4.3.1. Handwriting

As compared to the hypertext and the word processor texts, the pen-and-paper mode produced some compositions that were at times unreadable. Some students who used a different alphabet in their L1 had not mastered the formation of the letters of the Roman alphabet to a consistently readable standard. Under the pressure to complete an essay within two hours, they produced texts with many scribbles and badly shaped letters that were difficult to read.

10.4.3.2. Presentation Changes

The students made far more presentation changes—e.g., in layout, format, or appearance of their documents—in hypertext than in the other two modes, as shown in Table 10.2. and Figure 10.4.

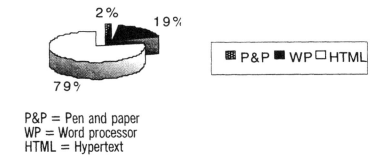

P&P = Pen and paper
WP = Word processor
HTML = Hypertext

Figure 10.4. Presentation Changes

303

10.4.3.3. Multimedia Style

In using hypertext, many design decisions had to be taken by the student authors regarding the use of non-textual elements and the creation of available routes (hypertext links) for readers. The most notable element in the hypertext mode was the major use of illustrations, which in the multimedia context often becomes as important as the written text. Many presentations used animations, pictures, and some JAVA programming that allowed the creation of sophisticated web pages. Some had an over-abundance of pictures and special effects such as flashing words, animated characters, and moving sentences, making it at times difficult to concentrate on the message or the text (see Appendix 10.2).

The students with more experience in web site design had developed their own, often highly original, presentation style, with emphasis on the use of color, drawings, or pictorial representation of letters and words. Some students also presented themselves as imaginary characters, often portraying themselves as comic strip characters or heroes. Those with less experience created web pages with only text and no pictures, with a format that looked very much like a normal typed page. Their composition structure borrowed considerably from conventional written style, with longer paragraphs than the work of the experienced HTML-using students.

Some of the students also added links to their web creations allowing potential readers to contact them by e-mail. Readers wrote comments, filling the pages with their feedback on the written text. This created an interaction between writers and readers that could help the writers improve or develop their web pages, while at the same time giving readers the opportunity to become involved in the development of those pages. However, most of the links were connected not to e-mail but to the students' own English web pages or to other web sites they liked and often visited. The readers were invited to click on links, for example, which showed e-mail conversations or descriptions of the popular music scene that included text, pictures, and sounds. These links brought the reader into the hypertext world of the designer, and into contact with links and jargon used in the cyberspace culture.

In some of the cases of the assignment, therefore, hypertext was used to design pages which opened into a new entire dimension that invited the reader to connect to less known cultures, providing information on cyberspace, its humor, and way of life. The most dedicated to this culture gave advice to the potential reader on the jargon and the culture itself.

10.4.4. Guidelines

At the end of the project, the group gathered for a last time to discuss what they thought made a clear web page. The ideas that came out of this discussion were compared with the first meeting when this same issue was discussed. The result was a final guideline sheet produced in order to help the students for future compositions in French in a hypertext format. These guidelines, included as Appendix 10.1, can be seen as a summary of experience on this project.

10.5.   DISCUSSION

As Hayes (1996) observed, writing can only exist in a social context and requires a medium. Under the influence of computer technology, the medium of writing is changing and so is the social context. From the results of this project, it can be concluded that each medium has influenced the students' writing and context of writing in different ways. There appeared to be little in the way of cumulative effects from one medium to the next in the series. Rather, in many ways, the hypertext condition showed striking discontinuities with the other writing conditions, even with its 'sister' electronic medium of word processing. Because of the uniqueness of the hypertext effects and because use of hypertext for web pages is the focus of investigation, the bulk of the discussion will be in that area.

10.5.1. Revision

Writing with a computer using a word processor facilitates production and revision of text to a greater extent than in pen-and-paper mode (Breese, 1993; Gallagher, 1988; Pennington, 1993b-c; 1996b-d; this volume; Williamson & Pence, 1989). It was therefore expected that students would revise their text significantly better at the surface level and would make more corrections and revisions when using word processing than in the other writing modes. It was further expected that structural errors would be less frequent with hypertext and word processing than in pen-and-paper mode, where these are more difficult to correct.

Consistent with expectation, students participating in the project made more corrections of what they considered mechanical and language errors in texts created on the word processor than in those created with pen and paper. This greater orientation to surface editing seems to stem from the fact that corrections are easily implemented with a word processor as compared to the pen-and-paper medium (Turkle, 1984). In pen-and-paper mode, the students produced what Bridwell (1980) called 'stuttering in writing', which could be directly observed on paper as text with scribbled words and drawn through sentences. According to Ihde (1979), writing with pen and paper is a slow process when, on the contrary, the use of a keyboard allows the display of ideas on the monitor as soon as they are conceived.

Word processing mode produced far more surface corrections than hypertext mode, which produced many changes not on the surface level but on the meaning level. The students changed their topics more and did more rewriting of paragraphs when writing in hypertext than in the other modes. Although students made more surface changes in word processing mode, these revisions did not always produce better texts. In contrast, the meaning changes made in hypertext mode resulted in texts of higher quality.

10.5.2. Presentation

At the presentation level, many changes affecting the style of a text can be very attractive to students, who in today's world of computer technology must be not only writers but also designers who have to plan, organize, and set goals for the layout and appearance of their documents. When working with hypertext, students in the present study often took a long time designing or redesigning their text presentation. In hypertext mode, they devoted more time and attention to the presentation of the text than to the correctness of their French language. The focus on presentation appeared to distract them from changes relevant to the surface level of their texts, but at the same time redesigning their presentation structures seemed to have been an incentive to think about the messages they were trying to convey under the hypertext mode. Perhaps the students spent more time considering the ideas they wanted to express because of a felt need to structure the text presentation to fit the hypertext medium. At the same time, it seems that having been inspired by their English web pages, they often concentrated on reducing their text to the closest translation they could possibly produce.

As anticipated, the students' hypertext presentation was influenced by the cyberspace culture. Many were inspired by the technological culture they are part of, which encourages freedom of expression and the creation of less conventional or formal types of text. Creating hyperlinks in a non-linear context gives students a new kind of freedom for presenting their ideas, by their associations in this specific environment. They also make it possible for the writer to associate thoughts to external representations (Sharples & Pemberton, 1992).

Those who were comfortable using their skills to create web pages often mentioned the fact that they liked this type of exercise because it gave them the freedom to show their own world. These students, when confident and skilled in the use of hypertext, were able to incorporate the reality of their own culture into their writing. Pictures, sounds, animations, and video helped them to give this reality a representation. The students with the least competence in French overused images, one of the easier options to incorporate into a web page, as it only takes a few minutes to scan a picture and put it into a picture format readable on the World Wide Web.

10.5.3. Use of Language

The use of pictures and sounds for a web page provides an excuse to minimize the number of words on the page. Yet the students used, on average, the same number of words in the three media. However, their sentence and paragraph structures were different in the web page environment as compared to the pen-and-paper and word processing environments.

An example is the web page created by a student called Simon. One of the links he created leads to a web page called *My Life/Ma vie* (see Appendix 10.2). The page shows a sort of frame divided into five rows, with a short sentence in French next to a small picture. When one clicks on each picture, it takes the reader to a bigger version of the picture. The picture has a subtitle in French as well. The vocabulary used is witty and informal. One caption reads: *This is me (after drinking) / Ça c'est moi (après avoir beaucoup bu)*. The picture shows the student and some lights on the street slightly out of focus. Another caption reads: *My beautiful holidays / Mes jolies vacances* and shows a picture of the Titanic. Humor is used thoroughly in this student's work. The student has achieved his aim in describing 'his life' as a witty and personal kind of curriculum vitae, talking about himself, his son, and his mother. Although he has not used many words in his web page, by careful selection and crafting of expression, he has still managed to tell the reader a great deal about himself in a memorable way.

As another example, Matthew, a student at the upper intermediate level with a good command of written French, created a web page which made references to goats. At first, this seemed very odd as a topic. Later in the written text, Matthew explained that it was his way to communicate with some of his friends:

> *I like cheese, in case you didn't know, because it's a fun fun dairy product. As dairy products go, cheese is a clear winner, although it would be unfair to say that dairy products are bad, since almost all are not only tasty, but nutritious, and therefore good for you too. Hurrah for cows, and all their milk. Also, on*

the subject of milk, goats are very cool too. I like them, and their predisposition for headbutting things.

If you've heard of Adam Sandler[2], then you might also have heard of the talking goat. A friend and I heard this once, and laughed. A lot. So we started calling each other "talking goat". From there, "goat" slipped into our everyday conversation pretty rapidly, and is now one of my favourite expletives, and/or insults. As in

1-"Bottom of the Goat, I got shot again in Doom"
2-"You mean old goat."

Here is Matthew's French version:

J'aime le fromage, si vous ne le savez pas, car c'est un produit laitier amusant. Dans le monde des produits laitiers, le fromage est un pur gagnant, mais il est injuste de dire que les produits laitiers soient ennuyeux, surtout que presque tous les produits sont délicieux et aussi nutritifs et donc bons pour vous aussi. Longue vie aux vaches et à tout leur lait.

En outre, au sujet de lait, les chèvres sont très à la mode aussi. Je les aime ainsi que leur prédisposition à tout frapper avec leur tête.

Vous avez entendu parler d'Adam Sandler et aussi de la chèvre qui parle? Un ami et moi l'avons écouté une fois et nous avons ri. Beaucoup!!!! Alors, nous avons commencé à nous appeler "la chèvre qui parle". De là le mot chèvre est apparu dans notre vocabulaire de tous les jours assez rapidement et le mot est maintenant l'une de mes expressions favorites et/ou insultes. Comme:
"Derrière la chèvre je suis encore mort"
"Tu es une vieille chèvre"

Je pense que cela perd un peu de son sens dans sa traduction...

---

[2] Adam Sandler, the comedian

> *De toute façon...Les expressions au-dessus je viens juste de trouver comment les produire, C'est très cool.*

Matthew's web page has a link to a web site whose main topic is goats and how to look after them. Matthew also created a web site in English to introduce himself and his interests. There the same use of witty and colloquial lexis can be observed.

It was anticipated that hypertext would allow a more unconventional use of language than the other two writing modes and this was found to be the case for the more experienced students. However, students who were less experienced in web pages and World Wide Web culture used less humor and more conventional vocabulary and forms of expression in their texts, which were often of a more serious and straightforward academic type.

10.5.4. Web Page Style

As expected, students developed their ideas more fully and with more originality when using the extra resources of hypertext than when using the other computer media. Students generally viewed web pages as informal environments where they could work with a sense of fun to develop personal topics. Like others who create web sites, the participants in this project were young people interested in topics related to youth culture.

For example, in one of Matthew's web sites, designed for his personal interest, he shows what is labeled as a picture of himself, but which is a cartoon character. Thus, on the web page he takes on a new identity, one which is very similar to that of characters in the "Dungeons and Dragons" type of game. This is an example of how virtual reality is adding its architecture to the world that Matthew has become part of. The use of open-ended stories and real-time games on the Internet such as simulations and role-playing MOOs (Multiple-user-domain Object Oriented) allow links to a world where the participants can pretend to be whoever or whatever they want to be, and where the form of language used does not have to meet external standards.

In a web page, writers can create their own expression and representation of knowledge working on "mosaics of information" (Marcus, 1993). In this way, the presentation in hypertext mode results in writers having more scope in the form and content of words and the text as a whole. The text becomes flexible in the sense that it is not the only modality in which information is presented. There is also an element of novelty in hypertext, which may encourage a more personal approach and less reference to the norms or standards of writing in other modes.

The style used on the Internet is influenced by the jargon of those computer users who are specialized in the creation of web pages. It is not a culture of very formal conventions for language or other aspects of presentation of information. Some informal conventions arose in the 1970's when hackers accessed telephone lines and created their own code names to avoid being identified. These code names developed into a mode of writing that makes use of letters combined with signs and numbers that is known as 'the alphabet of the hackers'. Using this alphabet, a name like *Walter*, for instance, can be written as *w@1+£r*. The conventions for expression in the impersonal world of cyberspace have thus become a means for people to personalize their messages and at the same time feel that they are participating in a special 'insider' culture, that of the Internet. Ironically, this culture is also one that is open to the world outside because of the access to the Internet by a large proportion of people around the globe.

In the world of hypertext, multimedia, and the World Wide Web, writers may develop their texts in relation to other modes of expression and in cooperation with readers who give input via electronic links to the web page. As Hunter (1998) has observed, there are similarities between the presentation characteristics of web pages and those of written texts in medieval times, when the written word was adorned with decorative elements and writers and readers could interact via annotation of texts. In the words of Hunter (1998):

> Medieval texts, famously, are often elaborately illustrated and displayed,...a function of the physical intimacy that people may have felt toward them. Certainly, when they were read, they were frequently written upon: with introductory material, with intertextual notes to sources or quotations, with intratextual notes to other places in the same manuscript that might be of interest to other readers, and with straightforward commentary (p. 3).

Hunter emphasizes the fact that the readers of Internet texts are part of a community "that legitimates physical interaction with the page in front of us. The knowledge on the page is never in isolation, and the text, although written, is flexible" (p. 3). She also sees in hypertext the conventions of oral transmission, though web creations are not, unlike their oral counterpart, ephemeral. They remain on the World Wide Web for as long as the writer wants them to be seen and commented upon.

Time is needed before it will be possible to assess the influence of these writers and these media on writing process and outcomes in the literate world. It is not yet obvious whether they will have a great influence on writing conventions as more and more web pages are being prepared for companies as part of their publicity strategy. With time, it can be expected that web page style—and computer writing more generally—will diverge more and more from traditional writing modes.

10.6.　CONCLUSION

Students now have the opportunity to compose a text with many tools which can aid the cognitive and physical activity involved in writing. The fact that all the students involved in the present study had access to and experience in the use of information technology expanded their learning opportunities and context. As seen in this project, the students used the word processor for editing and revising and the hypertext mode to express personal ideas that they took time to organize and plan. Considering the fact that the students' planning skills were limited, the use of hypertext technology seems to be a promising medium for increasing planning in students' writing. The creation of web pages also gave the students freedom and flexibility in writing, a skill that they at first perceived as difficult and not enjoyable. The production of web pages, above all, motivated the students to write and to express themselves in original ways.

The use of three media allowed students more choices with regard to their approach to written composition. Although handwriting is here to stay, the rapidly growing world of computers and the Internet has brought changes in the approach to writing in academic as well as non-academic contexts. Thus, students—and their teachers—need to adapt to computer technology. Through computer means they are able to interact, to participate in an 'on-line' culture, and to gather information, as they also develop and test their own ideas.

It is also important that student writers gain knowledge and insight into the conventions of written composition in order to produce a high standard of work in an L2. For this they will need to not only study those conventions but also creatively exercise their writing skills, using tools and resources which can enable them to design, compose, and analyze their own written work. Computer technology, although still in an early and immature state of development, can help the writer to present and manipulate ideas in a flexible way. Various computer media such as those used here allow for originality and expand the range of presentation styles, empowering the writer and helping to develop writing skills in conjunction with the technology. Hypertext, though sophisticated, has not yet reached its full potential but is nevertheless bringing users a different experience in writing, offering them the opportunity to write in a non-linear way and to gather additional resources from the World Wide Web.

The project led to recommended guidelines for quality standards of computer writing products. It is hoped that other teachers and students may find these of use, and that the students who participated in the present study will continue to develop and apply best practice combined with their IT skills. More time and research are nevertheless still needed to find out how the electronic medium can best be used in developing students' writing and in language instruction more generally. Equally important, more time and research is need to investigate the types of writing students are producing in electronic environments, and how their written texts are affected by, and in turn affect, other expressive modes.

APPENDIX 10.1.

Guidelines for Students

These guidelines were produced through discussion with the students at the end of the research period. The main issues involve organizing thoughts and designing good web pages.

Writing Compositions

- Write down your ideas and put them in a logical order.

- Select one topic.

- Divide the topic into subtopics and write one sentence to describe each.

- Try to write everything in French without translating from English.

- Use the dictionary: even if you cannot write a full sentence to describe your idea or subtopic and use a few words as a description.

- Write in the language that you feel most comfortable with to develop the flow of your thoughts on the topic you have selected.

- Take notes and collect information on the topic. Keep notes separate from the main page where you are writing, regardless of the medium used and look at them as you are revising your text and presentation. Question whether you have addressed all the elements you first decided to write about.

- Remember who your audience is.

- Revise your text and format.

Designing Web Pages

Using hypertext to create written compositions requires an understanding of visual style. A high percentage of web pages are visual, so use color appropriately. Remember that your web pages can be seen all over the world where color codes have different meanings to people of different cultures.

Recommendations:

- **Presentation style**: consider font, format of the pictures, and special effects. If special effects are used, too many words flashing or, moving may tire the reader. Be aware of the type of information associated with the colors on your web pages. Optical problems can be solved if colors do not clash (for example, red against blue or - green). Color-coding can help a user navigate through the web site.

- **Image format**: GIF files and JPEG files are the most commonly used; reduce their size. The JPEG files have more color depth and the GIF files are good for graphics and icons. Use them sparingly as too many pictures can take too much time to download, irritating the reader. Opt for clear fonts and a format which provides clarity.

- Choose the color in order to grab attention and to create an image. A particular color or a choice of two or three colors could be used through the whole web site in order to create a sense of unity. A neutral background enhances colored elements.

- Remember the constraints imposed by the technology: downloading time, speed of the technology, screens and monitors which can vary in performance, many black and white prints, short life of pages which are often technology driven, and limited capacity of the driver.

- Use the contrasts in luminance as well as hue between the text and the images. Consider the opportunity to use a three dimensional representation.

- Do not use too many links. Make sure that any links are well programmed and working. Don't link your site to another one which may not be running in the near future.

- Create a connection to receive e-mail feedback. Answer your e-mail when you are approached or contacted by a reader.

- Keep everything simple and clear in terms of text and limit the number of colors. However, remember that in the future web sites will have high multimedia capability. Be aware of the possibilities offered by the technology.

APPENDIX 10.2.

Sample Student Web Page

My Life:

< < < < M a - V i e > > > >

Choississez une photo, s'il vous plaît !

Ça c'est moi (après avoir beaucoup bu!!) -	⊠
Moi à trois heures du matin ! -	⊠
Mon fils (une vieille photo) -	⊠
Ma mère durant son enfance -	⊠
Mes jolies vacances -	⊠

-page-d'accueil-

REFERENCES

Acker, S. R. (1992). The storyteller's toolkit: Designing hypermedia group use knowledge systems. In M. Lea (Ed.), *Contexts of computer-mediated communication* (pp. 209-231). Hempstead, UK: Harvester Wheatsheaf.

Akinnaso, F. (1982). On the differences between spoken and written language. *Language and Speech, 25*, 97-125.

Akyel, A. (1994). First language use in EFL writing: Planning in Turkish vs. planning in English. *International Journal of Applied Linguistics, 4*, 169-196.

Akyel, A., & Kamıslı, S. (1996). Composing in first and second languages: Possible effects of EFL writing. *Odense Working Papers on Language and Communication, 14*, 69-105.

Al-Semari, O. (1993). *Saudi students' revising strategies in Arabic and English essays.* Unpublished Doctoral dissertation, Michigan State University.

Andrews, D. C. (1985). Writer's slump and revision schemes: Effects of computers on the composing process. *Collegiate Microcomputer, 3*, 313-16.

Argyle, M. (1992). *The social psychology of everyday life.* New York: Routledge.

Arms, V. M. (1982). *The computer kids and composition.* Paper presented at the annual meeting of the Conference on College Composition and Communication, San Francisco, CA. ERIC Document No. ED 217489.

Arndt, V. (1987). Six writers in search of texts: A protocol based study of L1 and L2 writing. *ELT Journal, 41*, 257-267.

Ashworth, D. (1996). Hypermedia and CALL. In M. C. Pennington (Ed.), *The power of CALL* (pp. 79-95). Houston: Athelstan.

Badagliacco, J. M. (1990). Gender and race differences in computing attitudes and experience. *Social Science Computer Review, 8*(1), 42-63.

Bangert-Drowns, R. L. (1993). The word processor as an instructional tool: A meta-analysis of word processing in writing instruction. *Review of Educational Research, 63*, 69-93.

Barker, T. T., & Kemp, F. O. (1990). Network theory: A postmodern pedagogy for the writing classroom. In C. Handa (Ed.), *Computer and community: Teaching composition in the twenty-first century* (pp. 1-27). Portsmouth, NH: Boynton/ Cook.

Barner, C. (Director). (1993). *Project Gemini: Is there anybody there?* Video produced for British Telecom Plc by Science Pictures for the BBC.

Baron, N. S. (1998). Letters by phone or speech by other means: The linguistics of e-mail. *Language & Communication, 18*, 133-170.

Bates, T. (1995). *Technology: Open learning and distance education.* London: Routledge.

Beach, R., & Eaton, S. (1984). Factors influencing self-assessing and revising by college freshmen. In R. Beach & L. Bridwell. (Eds.), *New directions in composition research* (pp. 149-170). New York: The Guilford Press.

Bean, H. C. (1983). Computerized word-processing as an aid to revision. *College Composition and Communication, 34*, 146-148.

Beattie, G. W. (1980). Encoding units in spontaneous speech: Some implications for the dynamics of conversation. In H. W. Dechert & M. Raupach (Eds.), *Temporal variables in speech: Studies in honor of Frieda Goldman-Eisler* (pp.131-143). The Hague: Mouton.

Beattie, G. W. (1983). *Talk: An analysis of speech and nonverbal behaviour in conversation*. Milton Keynes: Open University.

Benesch, S. (1987). *Word processing in English as a second language: A case study of three non-native college students.* Paper presented at the conference on College Composition and Communication, Atlanta, GA. ERIC Document No. ED 281383.

Bereiter, C., & Scardamalia, M. (1987). *The psychology of written composition*. Hillsdale, NJ: Lawrence Erlbaum.

Berens, G. L. (1986). Using word processors in the ESL composition class II. *TESOL Newsletter, 20*(6), 13.

Bernhardt, S. A. (1993). The shape of text to come: The texture of print on screens. *College Composition and Communication, 44*, 151-175.

Bernhardt, S. A., Edwards, P. G., & Wojahn, P. R. (1989). Teaching college composition with computers: A program evaluation study. *Written Communication, 6*, 108-133.

Biber, D. (1988). *Variations across speech and writing*. New York: Cambridge University Press.

Bisaillon, J. (1991). *Enseigner une stratégie de révision de textes à des étudiants en langue seconde, faibles à l'écrit: un moyen d'améliorer les productions écrites*. Publication B-182. Sainte-Foy: CIRAL, Université Laval.

Bisaillon, J. (1995a). Le comportement scriptural de quatre scripteurs en L2 ayant le traitement de texte comme support à l'écrit. In H. Knoerr (Ed.), *The use of new technologies in teaching and learning languages / Utilisation des nouvelles technologies en enseignement et apprentissage des langues* (pp. 6-18). CREAL, University of Ottawa.

Bisaillon, J. (1995b). Les nouvelles technologies dans l'enseignement, dites-vous? Vous m'en reparlerez! *Québec français, 98*, 102-104.

Bisaillon, J. (1997). Interrelations entre la mise en texte, la révision et le traitement de texte chez quatre scripteurs en langue seconde. *The Canadian Modern Language Review / La Revue canadienne des langues vivantes, 53*, 530-565.

Boomer, D. S. (1965). Hesitation and grammatical encoding. *Language and Speech, 8*, 148-158.

Borg, W. R. & Gall, M .D. (1989). *Educational research: An introduction*. White Plains, NY: Longman.

Boyles, R. (1995). A computer-based system of reading instruction for adult nonreaders. *AEDS Journal, 12,* 157-162.

Braddock, R., Lloyd-Jones, R., & Shoer, L. (1963). *Research in written composition*. Urbana, IL: National Council of Teachers of English.

Bradin, C., & Davis, T. N. (1995). Computers in Applied Linguistics Conference: Research Reports. *CAELL Journal, 5*(2), 30-35.

Brady, L. (1990). Overcoming resistance: Computers in the writing classroom. *Computers and Composition, 7*(2), 21-33.

Brammerts, H. (1996a). Tandem language learning via the Internet and the International E-mail Tandem Network. In D. Little. & H. Brammerts (Eds.), *A guide to language learning in tandem via the Internet* (pp. 9-22). Occasional Paper No. 46, Centre for Language and Communications Studies. Dublin: Trinity College.

Brammerts, H. (1996b). Language learning in tandem using the Internet. In M. Warschauer (Ed.), *Telecollaboration in foreign language learning* (pp. 121-130). Second Language Teaching & Curriculum Center. Honolulu: University of Hawai'i.

Breese, C. (1993). Computers and the writing process: A memo to the head. In M. Monteith (Ed.), *Computers and language* (pp. 57-73). Oxford: Intellect Books.

Bridwell, L. (1980). Revising strategies in twelfth grade students' transactional writing. *Research in the Teaching of English, 14,* 197-222.

Broady, B., & Kenning, M. M. (Eds.). (1996). *Promoting learner autonomy in university language teaching*. London: Association of French Language Studies/Centre for Information on Language Teaching and Research.

Brock, M. N. (1990a). Can the computer tutor? An analysis of a disk-based text analyzer. *System, 18,* 351-359.

Brock, M. N. (1990b). Customizing a computerized text analyzer for ESL writers: Cost versus gain. *CALICO Journal, 8*(2), 51-60.

Brock, M. N. (1991). Should we do what we can or can we do what we should? Three disk-based text analyzers and the ESL writer. In J. C. Milton & K. S. T. Tong (Eds.), *Text analysis in computer-assisted language learning* (pp. 109-128). Working papers from a seminar. Hong Kong: Hong Kong University of Science and Technology and City Polytechnic of Hong Kong.

Brock, M. N. (1993). Three disk-based text analyzers and the ESL writer. *Journal of Second Language Writing, 2,* 19-40.

Brock, M. N. (1995). Computerized text analysis: Roots and research. *Computer Assisted Language Learning, 8,* 227-258.

Brown, H. D. (1987). *Principles of language learning and teaching*. Englewood Cliffs, NJ: Prentice-Hall.

Brown, P. & Levinson, S. (1987). *Politeness: Some universals in language usage*. New York: Cambridge University Press.

Bruce, B. C., & Peyton, J. K. (1990). A new writing environment and an old culture: A situated evaluation of computer networking to teach writing. *Interactive Learning Environments, 1*(3), 171-191.

Bruce, B. C., Peyton, J. K., & Batson, T. (1993). *Networked-based classrooms: Promises and realities.* New York: Cambridge University Press.

Bruce, B. C., & Rubin, A. (1993). *Electronic quills: A situated evaluation of using computers for writing in classrooms.* Hillsdale, NJ: Lawrence Erlbaum.

Burton, P. (1994). Electronic mail as an academic discussion forum. *Journal of Documentation, 50,* 99-110.

Butler-Nalin, K. (1984). Revising patterns in students' writing. In A. N. Applebee (Ed.), *Contexts for learning to write: Studies of secondary school instruction* (pp. 121-133). Norwood, NJ: Ablex.

Butterworth, B. (1975). Hesitation and semantic planning in speech. *Journal of Psycholinguistic Research, 4,* 75-87.

Butterworth, B. (1980). Evidence from pauses in speech. In B. Butterworth, (Ed.), *Language production.* Vol. 1, *Speech and talk* (pp. 155-176). London: Academic Press.

Byram, M., & Morgan, C. (1994). *Teaching-and-learning language-and-culture.* Clevedon, UK: Multilingual Matters.

Calvert, M. (1996). The integration of e-mail tandem learning into language courses. In D. Little & H. Brammerts (Eds.), *A guide to language learning in tandem via the Internet* (pp. 35-42). Occasional Paper No. 46, Centre for Language and Communications Studies. Dublin: Trinity College.

Campbell, D. T., & Stanley, J. C. (1963). *Experimental and quasi-experimental design for research.* Chicago: Rand McNally.

Carrell, P. L. (1987). Text as interaction: Some implications of text analysis and reading research for ESL composition. In U. Connor & R. B. Kaplan (Eds.), *Writing across languages: Analysis of L2 text* (pp. 447-55). Reading, MA: Addison-Wesley.

Chadwick, S., & Bruce, N. (1989). The revision process in academic writing: From pen & paper to word processor. *Hongkong Papers in Linguistics and Language Teaching, 12,* April, 1-27.

Chanquoy, L., Foulin, J. N., & Fayol, M. (1996). Writing in adults: A real-time approach. In G. Rijlaarsdam, H. van den Berg, & M. Couzijn (Eds.), *Current research in writing: Theories, models and methodology* (pp. 36-43). Amsterdam: Amsterdam University Press.

Charolles, M. (1978).Introduction aux problèmes de cohérence de texte, *Langue française, 38,* 7-41. Paris: Larousse.

Chaudron, C. (1983). Evaluating writing: Effects of feedback on revision. Revised version of a paper presented at the 17th Annual TESOL Convention. Toronto. March 1983. ERIC Document No. ED 227706.

Clarke, D. & Argyle, M. (1982). Conversation sequences. In C. Fraser & K. Scherer (Eds.), *Advances in the social psychology of language* (pp. 159-200). New York: Cambridge University Press.

Cochran-Smith, M. (1991). Word processing and writing in elementary classrooms: A critical review of related literature. *Review of Educational Research, 61,* 107-155.

Cochran-Smith, M., Paris, C. L., & Kahn, J. L. (1991). *Learning to write differently: Beginning writers and word processing.* Norwood, NJ: Ablex.

Colley, A. M., Gale, M. T., & Harris, T. A. (1994). Effects of gender role identity and experience on computer attitude components. *Journal of Educational Computing Research, 10*(2), 129-137.

Collier, R. M. (1983). The word processor and the revision strategies. *College Composition and Communication, 34,* 149-155.

Collins, L. (1991). Wordpower: An examination of the role of computer as a facilitator for creativity in the writing of adolescent reluctant learners. Unpublished Masters thesis, University of Sheffield.

Crookall, D., Coleman, D. W., & Oxford, R. L. (1992). Computer-mediated language learning environments: Prolegomenon to a research framework. *Computer-Assisted Language Learning, 5*(1-2), 93-120.

Cross, G. (1990). Left to their own devices: Three basic writers using word processing. *Computers and Composition, 7*(2), 47-58.

Culley, L. (1988). Option choice and careers guidance: Gender and computing in secondary schools. *British Journal of Guidance and Counselling, 16*(1), 73-81.

Curtis, M., & Klem, E. (1992). The virtual context: Ethnography in the computer-equipped writing classroom. In G. Hawisher & P. LeBlanc (Eds.), *Reimagining computers and composition: Teaching and research in the virtual age.* Portsmouth, NH: Boynton/Cook.

Daiute, C. (1983). The computer as stylus and audience. *College Composition and Communication, 34,* 134-145.

Daiute, C. (1985). *Writing and computers.* Reading, MA: Addison-Wesley.

Daiute, C. (1986). Physical and cognitive factors in revision: Insights from studies with computers. *Research in the Teaching of English, 20,* 141-159.

Dam, L., Legenhausen, L., & Wolff, D. (1990). Text production in the foreign language classroom and the word processor. *System, 18,* 325-334.

Davidson, C., & Tomic, A. (1994). Removing computer phobia from the writing classroom. *ELT Journal, 48,* 205-213.

de Beaugrande, R. (1984). *Text production: Towards a science of composition.* Advances in Discourse Processes. Norwood, NJ: Ablex.

Dechert, H. W., & Raupach, M. (Eds.). (1980). *Temporal variables in speech: Studies in honour of Frieda Goldman-Eisler.* The Hague: Mouton.

Dechert, H. W., Möhle, D., & Raupach, M. (Eds.). (1984). *Second language productions.* Tübingen: Gunther Narr.

Dennett, J. (1990). ESL technical writing: Process and rhetorical differences. ERIC Document No. ED 322713.

Dimento, I. B. (1988). *The effect of peer response and self-evaluation on the quality of compositions written by twelfth-grade college preparatory students.* Unpublished Doctoral dissertation, Syracuse University.

DiPardo, A., & Freedman, S. (1988). Peer response groups in the writing classroom: Theoretic foundations and new directions. *Review of Educational Research, 58,* 119-149.

Dowling, C. (1994). Word processing and the ongoing difficulty of writing, *Computers and Composition, 11,* 227-235.

Dunn, B., & Reay, D. (1989). Word processing and the keyboard: Comparative effects of transcription on achievement. *Journal of Educational Research, 82,* 237-245.

Eastment, D. (1996). *The Internet and ELT: The impact of the Internet on English language teaching.* English 2000. Manchester: The British Council.

Eck, A., Legenhausen, L., & Wolff, D. (1994). Assessing telecommunications projects: Project types and their educational potential. In H. Jung & R. Vanderplank (Eds.), *Barriers and bridges: Media technology in language learning* (pp. 45-62). Frankfurt: Peter Lang.

Edelsky, C. (1982). Writing in a bilingual program: The relation of L1 and L2 texts. *TESOL Quarterly, 16, 211-228.*

Ellis, A., & Beattie, G. (1986). *The psychology of language and communication.* London: Weidenfeld and Nicholson.

Ellis, R. (1994). *The study of second language acquisition.* Oxford: Oxford University Press.

Ellis, R. (1985). Teacher-pupil interaction in second language development. In S. Gass & C. Madden (Eds.), *Input in second language acquisition* (pp. 69-85). Rowley, MA: Newbury House.

Emig, J. (1971). *The composing process of twelfth graders.* Research Report No. 13. Urbana, IL: National Council of Teachers of English.

Ericsson, K., & Simon, H. A. (1993). *Protocol analysis: Verbal reports as data.* Revised Edition. Cambridge: MIT Press.

Etchison, C. (1989). Word processing: A helpful tool for basic writers. *Computers and Composition, 6(2),* 33-43.

Faigley, L., & Witte, S. (1981). Analyzing revision. *College Composition and Communication, 32,* 400-414.

Faigley, L., & Witte, S. (1984). Measuring the effects of revisions on text structure. In R. Beach & L. Bridwell (Eds.), *New directions in composition research* (pp. 95-108). New York: The Guilford Press.

Ferrara, K., Brunner, H., & Whittemore, G. (1991). Interactive written discourse as an emergent register. *Written Communication, 8,* 8-34.

Fetler, M. (1985). Sex differences on the California statewide assessment of computer literacy. *Sex Roles, 13,* 181-191.

Flinn, J. Z. (1987a). Case studies of revision aided by keystroke recording and replaying software. *Computers and Composition, 5,* 31-43.

Flinn, J. Z. (1987b). Programming software to trace the composing process. *Computers and Composition, 5,* 45-49.

Flower, L. S. (1979). Writer-based prose: A cognitive basis for problems in writing. *College English, 41,* 19-37.

Flower, L., & Hayes, J. (1981). A cognitive process theory of writing. *College Composition and Communication, 32,*365-387.

Flower, L., Stein, J., Ackerman, J., Kantz, M., McCormick, K., & Peck, W. (1990). *Reading-to-write: Exploring a cognitive and social process.* Oxford: Oxford University Press.

Forgas, J. (Ed.). (1985). *Language and social situations.* New York: Springer-Verlag.

Frase, L. T. (1983). The UNIX Writer's Workbench software: Philosophy. *The Bell System Technical Journal, 62*(2), 1883-1890.

Freedman, S. W. (1987). *Research in writing: Past, present and future.* Technical Report No. 1, Center for the Study of Writing. Berkeley, CA: University of California at Berkeley.

Freedman, S. W. (1992). Outside-in and outside-out: Peer response groups in two ninth-grade classes. *Research in the Teaching of English, 26,* 71-107.

Freeman, E., & Sanders, T. (1987). The social meaning of literacy: Writing instruction and community. *Language Arts, 64,* 641-645.

Friedlander, A. (1990). Composing in English: First language effects. In B. Kroll (Ed.), *Second language writing* (pp. 109-125). Cambridge: Cambridge University Press.

Friedlander, A., & Markel, M. (1990). Some effects of the Macintosh on technical writing assignments. *Computers and Composition, 8*(1), 69-79.

Fulk, J., Schmitz, J., & Schwarz, D. (1992). The dynamics of context-behavior interactions in computer-mediated communication. In M. Lea (Ed.), *Contexts of computer-mediated communication* (pp. 7-29). New York: Harvester Wheatsheaf.

Gallagher, B. (1988). Microcomputer word processing and language teaching: issues, approaches and practical considerations. In Jung, U. O. H. (Ed.), *Computers in Applied Linguistics and Language Teaching* (pp. 79-88). Frankfurt: Peter Lang.

Garrett, M. F. (1982). Production of speech: Observations from normal and pathological language use. In A. W. Ellis (Ed.), *Normality and pathology in cognitive functions* (pp. 19-76). London: Academic Press.

Gass, S., & Varonis, E. (1985). Task variation and non-native/non-native negotiation of meaning. In S. Gass & C. Madden (Eds.),

Input and second language acquisition (pp.149-161). Rowley, MA: Newbury House.

Gaskill, W. (1986). *Revising in Spanish and English as a second language: A process oriented study of composition.* Unpublished Doctoral dissertation, University of California at Los Angeles.

Gee, J., & Grosjean, F. (1983). Performance structures: A psycholinguistic and linguistic appraisal. *Cognitive Psychology, 15,* 411-458.

Geertz, R. (1973). *The interpretation of cultures: Selected essays.* New York: Basic Books.

George, D. (1984). Working with peer groups in the composition classroom. *College Composition and Communication, 35,* 320-326.

Gerrard, L. (1989). Computers and basic writers: A critical view. In G. E. Hawisher & C. L. Selfe (Eds.), *Critical perspectives on computers and composition instruction* (pp. 94-108). New York, NY: Teachers College Press.

Gibbs, R. (1985). Situational conversations and requests. In J. Forgas (Ed.), *Language and social situations* (pp. 97-110). New York: Springer-Verlag.

Gibson, W. (1966). *Tough, sweet and stuffy.* Bloomington: Indiana University Press.

Goffman, E. (1981). *Forms of talk.* Philadelphia: University of Pennsylvania Press.

Goldman-Eisler, F. (1968). *Psycholinguistics: Experiments in spontaneous speech.* London: Academic Press.

Goldman-Eisler, F. (1972). Pauses, clauses, sentences. *Language and Speech, 15,* 103-113.

Goutsos, D. (1997). *Modeling discourse topic: Sequential relations and strategies in expository text.* Norwood, NJ: Ablex.

Grabe, W., & Kaplan, R. B. (1996). *Theory and practice of writing.* London: Longman.

Green, L. C. (1991). *The effects of word processing and a process approach to writing on the reading and writing achievement, revision and editing strategies and attitudes towards writing of third-grade Mexican-American students.* Unpublished Doctoral dissertation, University of Texas, Austin.

Greene, S., & Higgins, L. (1994). "Once upon a time': The use of retrospective accounts in building theory in composition. In P. Smagorinsky (Ed.), *Speaking about writing* (pp. 115-140). London: Sage.

Greenleaf, C. (1994). Technological indeterminacy: The role of classroom writing practices and pedagogy in shaping student use of the computer. *Written Communication, 11,* 85-130.

Gregg & E. R. Steinberg (Eds.), *Cognitive processes in writing* (pp. 3-30). Hillsdale, NJ: Lawrence Erlbaum.

Griffiths, R. (1991). Pausological research in an L2 context: A rationale, and review of selected studies. *Applied Linguistics, 12,* 345-364.

Grosjean, F, Grosjean, L., & Lane, H. (1979). The patterns of silence: Performance structures in sentence production. *Cognitive Psychology, 11*, 58-81.

Haas, C. (1989). How the writing medium shapes the writing process: Effects of word processing on planning. *Research in the Teaching of English, 23*, 181-207.

Hadenius, P. (1991). Pausmonster. En kvantitativ analys av pauser I skrivprocessen. IPLab Report No. 53, Department of Numerical Analysis and Computing Science. Stockholm: Royal Institute of Technology.

Halimah, A. (1991). *EST writing: Rhetorically processed and produced: A case study of Kuwaiti learners.* Unpublished Doctoral dissertation, University of Essex.

Halliday, M. A. K. (1985). *An introduction to functional grammar.* London: Arnold.

Halliday, M. A. K. (1989). *Spoken and written language.* New York: Oxford University Press.

Hanson-Smith, E. (1990). Word-processed composition. *TESOL Newsletter, 24*(3), 23; 24(4), 23.

Harre, R. (1985). Situational rhetoric and self-presentation. In J. Forgas (Ed.), *Language and social situations* (pp. 175-86). New York: Springer-Verlag.

Hartman, K., Neuwirth, C. M., Kiesler, S., Sproul, L., Cochran, C., Palmquist, M., & Zubrow, D. (1991). Patterns of social interaction and learning to write. *Written Communication, 8*, 79-113.

Hawisher, G. (1987). The effects of word-processing on the revision strategies of college freshmen. *Research in the Teaching of English, 21*, 145-159.

Hawisher, G. E. (1989). Research and recommendations for computers and composition. In G. E. Hawisher & C. L. Selfe (Eds.), *Critical perspectives on computers and composition instruction* (pp. 44-69). New York: Teachers College Press.

Hawisher, G., & Moran, C. (1993). Electronic mail and the writing instructor. *College English, 55*, 627-43.

Hayes, J. R. (1995). Un nouveau modèle du processus d'écriture (Trans. G. Fortier). In J.-Y. Boyer, J.-P. Dionne, & P. Raymond (Eds.), *La production de textes. Vers un modèle d'enseignement de l'écriture* (pp. 49-72). Montreal: Les Éditions Logiques.

Hayes, J., R. (1996). A new framework for understanding cognition and affect in writing. In C. Michael Levy & S. Ransdell (Eds.), *The science of writing: Theories, methods, individual differences, and applications* (pp. 1-27). Mahwah, NJ: Lawrence Erlbaum Associates.

Hayes, J. R., & Flower, L. S. (1980). Identifying the organization of writing processes. In L.

Hayes, J., & Flower, L. (1983). Uncovering cognitive processes in writing: An introduction to protocol analysis. In P. Mosenthal, L.

Tamor, & S. Walmsley (Eds.), *Research on writing: Principles and methods* (pp. 207-219). New York: Longman.

Hayes, J. R., Flower, L. S., Schriver, K. S., Stratman, J., & Carey, L. (1985). Cognitive processes in revision. ERIC Document No. ED 267 396.

Hayes, J. R., & Nash, J. G. (1996). On the nature of planning in writing. In C. M. Levy & S. Ransdell (Eds.), *The science of writing* (pp. 29-55). Mahwah, NJ: Lawrence Erlbaum.

Henderson, A., Goldman-Eisler, F., & Skarbek, A. (1966). Sequential temporal patterns in spontaneous speech. *Language and Speech, 9,* 207-216.

Herrmann, A. (1986). Teaching ESL students writing using word processing. *TESOL Newsletter, 20*(1), Supplement No. 3, 5-6.

Hillocks, G. (1987). Synthesis of research on teaching writing. *Educational Leadership, 44,* 73-82.

Hoffman, R. (1994). The warm network, electronic mail, ESL learners, and the personal touch. *On-CALL: The Australian Journal of Computers and Education, 8*(2), 10-13.

Hoffman, R. (1996). Computer networks: Webs of communication for language teaching. In M. C. Pennington (Ed.), *The power of CALL* (pp. 55-78). Houston: Athelstan.

Hoffman, R. (1996). Computer networks: Webs of communication for language teaching. In M. C. Pennington (Ed.), *The power of CALL* (pp. 55-77). Houston: Athelstan.

Hoppe-Graff, S., Hermann, T., Winterhoff-Spurk, P., & Mangold, R. (1985). Speech and situation: A general model for the process of speech production. In J. Forgas (Ed.), *Language and social situations* (pp. 81-95). New York: Springer-Verlag.

Huffman, D. T. & Goldberg, J. R. (1987). Using wordprocessing to teach EFL composition. *System, 15,* 169-175.

Hughes, A. (1988). Introducing a needs based test of English language proficiency into an English-medium university in Turkey. In A. Hughes (Ed.), *Testing English for university students* (pp. 134-153). Hong Kong: Modern English Publications and the British Council.

Hunter, L. (1998). Electronic etiquette in the global community. Lecture presented at Gresham College, London. April 1998.

Hyland, K. (1993). ESL computers: What can we do to help? *System, 21*(1), 21-30.

Ihde, D. (1979). *Technics and praxis.* Dordrecht: Reidel.

Jacobs, H. L., Zinkgraf, S., Wormuth, D., Hartfield, V. F., & Hughey, J. (1981). *Testing ESL composition: A practical approach.* Rowley, MA: Newbury House.

Janssen, D., van Waes, L., & van den Bergh, H. (1996). Effects of thinking aloud on writing processes. In C. M. Levy & S. Ransdell (Eds.), *The science of writing* (pp. 233-250). Mahwah, NJ: Lawrence Erlbaum.

Johnson, M. A. (1986). *Effects of using the computer as a tool for writing on the vocabulary, reading and writing of first and second grade Spanish-speaking students.* Unpublished Doctoral dissertation, Texas Women's University.

Jones, C., & Fortescue, S. (1987). *Using computers in the language classroom.* London: Longman.

Jones, S., & Tetroe, J. (1987). Composing in a second language. In A. Matsuhashi, (Ed.), *Writing in real time: Modelling production processes* (pp. 34-57). Norwood, NJ: Ablex.

Joram, E., Woodruff, E., Bryson, M., & Lindsay, P. (1992). The effects of revising with a word processor on written composition. *Research in the Teaching of English, 26,* 167-193.

Kamıslı, S. (1992). *Word processing and the writing process: A case study of five Turkish English as a second language (ESL) students.* Unpublished Doctoral dissertation, Columbia University.

Kantrov, I. (1991). Keeping promises and avoiding pitfalls: Where teaching needs to augment word processing. *Computers and Composition, 8,* 63-77.

Kelm, O. R. (1996). The application of computer networking in foreign language education: Focusing on principles of second language acquisition. In M. Warschauer (Ed.), *Telecollaboration in foreign language learning* (pp. 19-28). Second Language Teaching & Curriculum Center. Honolulu: University of Hawai'i.

Kern, R. (1996). Computer-mediated communication: Using e-mail exchanges to explore personal histories in two cultures. In M. Warschauer (Ed.), *Telecollaboration in foreign language learning* (pp. 105-119). Second Language Teaching & Curriculum Center. Honolulu: University of Hawai'i.

Kiefer, K. (1987). Revising on a word processor: What's happened, what's ahead. *ADE Bulletin, 87,* 24-27.

Kitchin, D. A. (1991). *Case study of ESL community college students using computer-based writing tools in a composition course.* Unpublished Doctoral dissertation, University of San Francisco.

Kornum, L. (1993). From foreign languages methodology point of view. In *LINGUA DELTA: Foreign Language Learning and the Use of New Technologies Conference Proceedings* (pp. 32-39). London: Commission of the European Communities.

Kowal, S., & O'Connell, D.C. (1987). Writing as language behavior: Myths, models and methods. In A. Matsuhashi (Ed.), *Writing in real time: Modelling production processes* (pp. 108-132). Norwood, NJ: Ablex.

Kozma, R. B. (1991). Computer-based writing tools and the cognitive needs of novice writers. *Computers and Composition, 8(2),* 31-45.

Krapels, A. R. (1990). An overview of second language writing process research. In B. Kroll (Ed.), *Second language writing: Research insights for the classroom* (pp. 37-56). Cambridge: Cambridge University Press.

Krashen, S. D. (1981). *Second language acquisition and second language learning*. Oxford: Pergamon Press.

Krashen, S. D. (1982). *Principles and practice in second language acquisition*. Oxford: Pergamon Press.

Krashen, S. (1985). *The input hypothesis: Issues and implications*. London: Longman.

Kroll, B. (Ed.). (1990). *Second language writing: Research insights for the classroom*. Cambridge: Cambridge University Press.

Kroonenberg, N. (1995). Developing communicative and thinking skills via electronic mail. *TESOL Journal, 4*(2), 24-27.

Kurth, R. (1986). Using word processing to enhance revision strategies during student writing activities. *Educational Technology, 27*, 13-19.

Labov, W. (1972). Rules for ritual insults. In D. Sudnow (Ed.), *Studies in social interaction* (pp. 120-169). New York: Free Press.

Lam, C. Y. P. (1991). *Revision process of college ESL students: How teacher comments, discourse types and writing tools shape revision*. Unpublished Doctoral dissertation, University of Georgia. *Dissertation Abstracts International, 52*, 4248A.

Lam, F. S., & Pennington, M. C. (1995). The computer vs. the pen: A comparative study of word processing in a Hong Kong secondary classroom. *Computer-Assisted Language Learning, 7*, 75-92.

Lansman, M., Smith, J. B., & Weber, I. (1993). Using the Writing Environment to study writers' strategies. *Computers and Composition, 10*, 71-92.

Lay, N. (1982). Composing processes of adult ESL learners. *TESOL Quarterly, 16*(3), 406.

Lea, M. (Ed.). (1992). *Contexts of computer-mediated communication*. New York: Harvester Wheatsheaf.

Levelt, W. J. M. (1989). *Speaking: From intention to articulation*. Cambridge: MIT Press.

Levy, C. M., Marek, P., & Lea, J. (1996). Concurrent and retrospective protocols in writing research. In G. Rijlaarsdam, H. van den Berg, & M. Couzijn (Eds.), *Current research in writing: Theories, models and methodology* (pp. 542-556). Amsterdam: Amsterdam University Press.

Levy, C. M., & Ransdell, S. (1996). *The science of writing*. Mahwah, NJ: Lawrence Erlbaum.

Levy, C .M., & Ransdell, S. (1996). Writing signatures. In C. M. Levy & S. Ransdell (Eds.), *The science of writing* (pp. 149-161). Mahwah, NJ: Lawrence Erlbaum.

Lewis, B., & Lewis, R. (1987). Do style checkers work? *PC World*, June, 246-252.

Lewis, T., Woodin, J. & St. John, E. (1996). Tandem learning: Independence through partnership. In E. Broady and M. M. Kenning (Eds.), *Promoting learner autonomy in university language teaching* (pp. 105-120). London: Association of French

Language Studies/Centre for Information on Language Teaching and Research.

Li, J., & Cumming, A. (1996). Word processing and ESL writing: A longitudinal case study. Unpublished ms. Modern Language Centre. Ontario Institute for Studies in Education.

Li, N. M. (1990). Writing with pen or computer? A study on ESL secondary school learners. Paper presented at the Annual World Conference on Computers in Education, Sydney, Australia. July. ERIC Document No. ED 322720.

Linnell, J. (1995). Can negotiation provide a context for learning syntax in a second language? *Working Papers in Educational Linguistics, 11*(2), 83-103.

Logan, S. (1988). A study of four undergraduate computer writers. *Collegiate Microcomputer, 6*(3), 135-146.

Long, M. (1980). *Input, interaction, and second language acquisition.* Unpublished doctoral dissertation. University of California at Los Angeles.

Long, M. (1981). Input, interaction, and second language acquisition. In H. Winitz (Ed.), *Annals of the New York Academy of Sciences: Native language and foreign language acquisition, 379,* 259-278.

Long, M. (1983). Linguistic and conversational adjustments to non-native speakers. *Studies in Second Language Acquisition, 5,* 177-193.

Long, M. (1985). Input and second language acquisition theory. In S. Gass & C. Madden (Eds.), *Input in second language acquisition* (pp. 377-393). Rowley, MA: Newbury House.

Loyd, B. H., Loyd, D. E., & Gressard, C. P. (1987). Gender and computer experience as factors in the computer attitudes of middle school students. *Journal of Early Adolescence, 7*(1), 13-19.

Mabrito, M. (1991). Electronic mail as a vehicle for peer response. *Written communication, 8,* 509-532.

Mann, W. C., & Thompson, S. A. (1988). Rhetorical structure theory: Towards a functional theory of text organization. *Text, 8,* 243-281.

Marcus, S. (1993). Multimedia, hypermedia and the teaching of English. In M. Monteith (Ed.), *Computers and language* (pp. 21-43). Oxford: Intellect Books.

Mason, R. (1993). Computer conferencing and the new Europe. In L. M. Harasim (Ed.), *Global networks: Computers and international communication* (pp. 199-220). Cambridge, MA: MIT Press.

Matsuhashi, A. (1981). Pausing and planning: The tempo of written discourse production. *Research in the Teaching of English, 15,* 113-134.

Matsuhashi, A. (1982). Explorations in the real-time production of written discourse. In M. Nystrand (Ed.), *What writers know: the language, process, and structure of written discourse* (pp. 269-290). New York: Academic Press.

Matsuhashi, A. (1987).*Writing in real time: Modeling production processes*. Norwood, NJ: Ablex.

McInerney, V., McInerney, D. M., & Sinclair, K. E. (1994). Student teachers, computer anxiety and computer experience. *Journal of Educational Computing Research, 11*(1), 27-50.

Migliacci, N. (1996). E-mail and ESL students: Student and teacher interactions in cyberspace. Paper delivered at the PennTESOL East Conference, Newark, DE. November 1996.

Miura, I. T. (1987). Gender and socioeconomic status differences in middle-school computer interest and use. *Journal of Early Adolescence, 7*, 243-254.

Murray, D. M. (1980). Writing as process: How writing finds its own meaning. In T. R. Donovan & B. W. McClelland (Eds.), *Eight approaches to teaching composition* (pp. 3-20). Urbana, IL: National Council of Teachers of English.

Nabors, L. (1995). Written text or spoken discourse? Using e-mail in the ESL classroom. Paper delivered at the PennTESOL East Conference. Philadelphia, PA. April 1995.

Neu, J., & Scarcella, R. (1991). Word processing in the ESL writing classroom: A survey of student attitudes. In P. Dunkel (Ed.), *Computer-assisted language learning and testing: Research issues and practice* (pp. 169-187). New York: Newbury House/HarperCollins.

Neufeld, J., Gaudiot, T., Wiley, M., & Rigley, H. (1986). *Its academic: A multi-skill approach to college writing*. New York: Holt, Rinehart and Winston.

Nichols, R. G. (1986). Word processing and basic writers. *Journal of Basic Writing, 5*, 81-97.

Nystrand, M. (1986). Learning to write by talking about writing: A summary of research on intensive peer review in expository writing instruction at the University of Wisconsin-Madison. In M. Nystrand (Ed.), *The structure of written communication* (pp. 179-211). Orlando: Academic Press.

Ogletree, S. M., & Williams, S. W. (1990). Sex and sex-typing effects on computer attitudes and aptitude. *Sex Roles, 23*, 703-712.

Okebukola, P. A. (1993). The gender factor in computer anxiety and interest among some Australian high school students. *Educational Research, 35*, 181-189.

Oliver, R., & Kerr, T. (1993). The impact of word processing on the preparation and submission of written essays in a tertiary course of study. *Higher Education, 26*, 217-226.

Olson, V. (1990). The revising processes of sixth-grade writers with and without peer feedback. *The Journal of Educational Research, 84*, 22-29.

Owston, R. D., Murphy, S., & Wideman, H. H. (1992). The effects of word processing on students' writing quality and revision strategies. *Research in the Teaching of English, 26*, 249-276.

Oxford, R. L. (1990). Research on second language learning strategies: What every teacher should know. *Annual Review of Applied Linguistics, 13,* 175-187.

Palmquist, M. E. (1993). Network-supported interaction in two writing classrooms. *Computers and Composition, 10,* 25-57.

Pennington, M. C. (1991). Positive and negative potentials of word processing for ESL writers. *System, 19,* 267-275.

Pennington, M. C. (1992). Beyond off-the-shelf computer remedies for student writers: Alternatives to canned feedback. *System, 20,* 423-437.

Pennington, M. C. (1993a). Computer-assisted writing on a principled basis: The case against computer-assisted text analysis for non-proficient writers. *Language and Education, 7,* 43-59.

Pennington, M. C. (1993b). A critical examination of word processing effects in relation to L2 writers. *Journal of Second Language Writing, 2,* 227-255.

Pennington, M. C. (1993c). Exploring the potential of word processing for non-native writers. *Computers and the Humanities, 27,* 149-163.

Pennington, M. C. (1993d). Modeling the student writer's acquisition of word processing skills: The interaction of computer, writing, and language media. *Computers and Composition, 10,* 59-79.

Pennington, M. C. (1995a). *Modeling teacher change: Relating input to output.* Research Monograph Series 5. City University of Hong Kong.

Pennington, M. C. (1995b). The teacher change cycle. *TESOL Quarterly, 29,* 705-731.

Pennington, M. C. (1996a). The power of the computer in language education. In M. C. Pennington (Ed.), *The power of CALL* (pp. 1-14). Houston: Athelstan.

Pennington, M. C. (1996b). *The computer and the non-native writer: A natural partnership.* Cresskill, NJ: Hampton Press.

Pennington, M. C. (1996c). The way of the computer: Developing writing skills in an electronic environment. In S. Fotos (Ed.), *Multimedia language teaching* (pp. 93-113). Tokyo: Logos International.

Pennington, M. C. (1996d). Writing the natural way: On computer. *Computer Assisted Language Learning, 9,* 125-142.

Pennington, M. C. (1998). Perspectives on language in Hong Kong at century's end. In M. C. Pennington (Ed.), *Language in Hong Kong at century's end* (pp. 3-40). Hong Kong: Hong Kong University Press.

Pennington, M. C. (1999). The missing link in computer-assisted writing. In K. Cameron (Ed.), *CALL: Media, design & applications* (pp. 271-292). Lisse: Swets & Zeitlinger.

Pennington, M. C. (forthcoming a). *Language learning: An introduction.* London: Arnold.

Pennington, M. C. (forthcoming b). Writing minds and thinking fingers. Plenary address. IATEFL Conference on CALL for the 21st Century. Barcelona. July 2000.

Pennington, M. C., & Brock, M. N. (1992). Process and product approaches to computer-assisted composition. In M. C. Pennington & V. Stevens (Eds.), *Computers in applied linguistics: An international perspective* (pp. 79-109). Clevedon, UK: Multilingual Matters.

Pennington, M. C., & Doi, T. (1993). Discourse management devices in the interlanguages of Japanese learners of English: An exploratory study. *Journal of Asian Pacific Communication, 4*, 67-90.

Pennington, M. & Esling, J. (1996). Computer-assisted development of language skills. In M. C. Pennington (Ed.), *The power of CALL* (pp. 153-189). Houston: Athelstan.

Pennington, M. C., & So, S. (1993). Comparing writing processes and products across two languages: A study of six Singaporean university student writers. *Journal of Second Language Writing, 2*, 41-63.

Perkins, D. (1985). The fingertip effect: How information-processing technology shapes thinking. *Educational Researcher, 14*(7), 11-17.

Perl, S. (1979). The composing process of unskilled college writers. *Research in the Teaching of English, 13*, 317-336.

Phillips, M. (1986). CALL in its educational context. In G. Leech, & C. Candlin (Eds.), *Computers in English language teaching and research* (pp. 2-10). London: Longman.

Phinney, M. (1989). Computers, composition, and second language teaching. In M. C. Pennington (Ed.), *Teaching languages with computers: The state of the art* (pp. 81-96). La Jolla, CA: Athelstan.

Phinney, M. (1991a). Computer-assisted writing and writing apprehension in ESL students. In P. Dunkel (Ed.), *Computer-assisted language learning and testing: Research issues and practice* (pp. 189-204). New York: Newbury House/HarperCollins.

Phinney, M. (1991b). Word processing and writing apprehension in first and second language writers. *Computers and Composition, 9*, 65-82.

Phinney, M. (1996). Exploring the virtual world: Computers in the second language writing classroom. In M. C. Pennington (Ed.), *The power of CALL* (pp. 137-152). Houston: Athelstan.

Phinney, M., & Khouri, S. (1993). Computers, revision, and ESL writers: The role of experience. *Journal of Second Language Writing, 2*, 257-277.

Phinney, M., & Mathis, C. (1990). ESL student responses to writing with computers. *TESOL Newsletter, 24*(2), 30-31.

Pica, T. (1987). Interlanguage adjustments as an outcome of NS-NNS negotiated interaction. *Language Learning, 38*, 45-73.

Pica, T. & Doughty, C. (1988). Variations in classroom interaction as a function of participation pattern and task. In J. Fine (Ed.), *Second language discourse: A textbook of current research.* Norwood, NJ: Ablex.

Pica, T., Holliday, L., Lewis, N., Berducci, D., & Newman, J. (1991). Language learning through interaction: What role does gender play? *Studies in Second Language Acquisition, 13,* 343-376.

Pica, T., Lincoln-Porter, F., Paninos, D., & Linnell, J. (1995). What can second language learners learn from each other? Only their researcher knows for sure. *Working Papers in Educational Linguistics, 11*(1), 1-36.

Pica, T., Young, R., & Doughty, C. (1987). The impact of interaction on comprehension. *TESOL Quarterly, 21,* 737-58.

Piolat, A. (1991). Effects of word processing on text revision. *Language and Education, 5,* 255-272.

Piper, A. (1987). Helping learners to write: A role for the word processor. *ELT Journal, 41,* 122-124.

Piper, A. (1996). Second language academic writers revising. Poster presented at the Conference on Second Language Acquisition and Writing: A Multi-disciplinary Approach. University of Southampton. July 1996.

Poulsen, E. (1991). Writing processes with word processing in teaching English as a foreign language. *Computers & Education, 16,* 77-81.

Rabinovitz, R. (1991). 15 writer's tools. *PC Magazine, 10*(16), 321-369.

Raimes, A. (1985). What unskilled ESL students do as they write: A classroom study of composing. *TESOL Quarterly, 19,* 229-258.

Raimes, A. (1986). *Exploring through writing.* New York: St. Martins Press.

Raimes, A. (1987). Language proficiency, writing ability and composing strategies: A study of ESL college student writers. *Language Learning, 37*(3), 439-467.

Rédacteurs Software Documentation Limited. (1996). Language and technology. *Multilingual Information Society.* Luxembourg: European Commission.

Reichardt, C. S., & Cook, T. D. (1979). Beyond qualitative versus quantitative methods. In T. D. Cook & C. S. Reichardt (Eds.), *Qualitative and quantitative methods in evaluation research.* Beverly Hills, CA: Sage.

Reid, J. (1986). Using the Writer's Workbench in composition teaching and testing. In C. W. Stansfield (Ed.), *Technology and language testing* (pp. 167-186). Washington, DC: TESOL.

Reid, J., Lindstrom, P., McCaffrey, M., & Larson, D. (1983). Computer-assisted text-analysis for ESL students. *CALICO Journal, 1*(3), 40-46.

Reinking, D. (1986). Six advantages of computer-mediated text for reading and writing instruction. *Reading Instruction Journal, 29,* 8-16.

Riel, M. (1993). Global learning through learning circles. In L. M. Harasim (Ed.), *Global Networks: Computers and international communication* (pp. 221-236). Cambridge, MA: MIT Press.

Robinson-Staveley, K., & Cooper, J. (1990). The use of computers for writing: Effects on an English composition class. *Journal of Educational Computing Research, 6,* 41-48.

Roblyer, M. D., Castine, W. H., & King, F. J. (1988). *Assessing the impact of computer-based instruction: A review of recent research.* New York: Haworth.

Rochester, S. (1973). The significance of pauses in spontaneous speech. *Journal of Psycholinguistic Research, 2,* 51-81.

Russo, J. E., Johnson, E. J., & Stephens, D. L. (1989). The validity of verbal protocols. *Memory and Cognition, 17,* 759-769.

Ruth, L., & Murphy, S. (1988). *Designing writing tasks for the assessment of writing.* Norwood, NJ: Ablex.

Sanders, T., Janssen, D., van der Pool, E., Schilperoord, J., & van Wijk, C. (1996). Hierarchical text structure in writing products and writing processes. In G. Rijlaarsdam, H. van den Berg, & M. Couzijn (Eds.), *Current research in writing: Theories, models and methodology* (pp. 473-492). Amsterdam: Amsterdam University Press.

Sayers, D. (1989). Bilingual sister classes in computer writing networks. In D. M. Johnson & D. H. Roen (Eds.), *Richness in writing: Empowering ESL students* (pp. 120-133). New York: Longman.

Schcolnik, M. (1990). Effect of task type on student performance. *CAELL, 1*(4), 18-20.

Schilperoord, J. (1996). The distribution of pause time in written text production. In G. Rijlaarsdam, H. van den Berg, & M. Couzijn (Eds.), *Current research in writing: Theories, models and methodology* (pp. 21-35). Amsterdam: Amsterdam University Press.

Seliger, H. W., & Shohamy, E. (1990). *Second language research methods.* Oxford: Oxford University Press.

SENAC: *http://www.city.ac.uk/linguanews* (As an ongoing project some links in SENAC are still under construction and some articles are being constantly adapted for this electronic newspaper before being transferred to the WWW. Articles in German and Spanish are soon to be added).

Severinson Eklundh, K., & Kollberg, P. (1992). *Translating keystroke records into a general notation for the writing process.* IPLab Report No. 59. Stockholm: Royal Institute of Technology.

Severinson Eklundh, K., & Kollberg, P. (1996a). A computer tool and framework for analyzing online revisions. In C. M. Levy & S. Ransdell (Eds.), *The science of writing* (pp. 163-188). Mahwah, NJ: Lawrence Erlbaum.

Severinson Eklundh, K., & Kollberg, P. (1996b). Computer tools for tracing the writing process: From keystroke records to S-notation. In G. Rijlaarsdam, H. van den Berg, & M. Couzijn (Eds.), *Current research in writing: Theories, models and methodology* (pp. 526-541). Amsterdam: Amsterdam University Press.

Sharples, M., & Pemberton, L. (1992). Representing writing: External representations and the writing process. In P. O. Holt & N. Williams (Eds.), *Computers and writing: State of the art* (pp. 319-336). Oxford: Intellect Books.

Sharwood Smith, M. (1993). Input enhancement in instructed SLA. *Studies in Second Language Acquisition, 15,* 165-79.

Siegman, A. W., & Feldstein, S. (Eds.). (1979). *Of speech and time: Temporal patterns in interpersonal contexts.* Hillsdale, NJ: Lawrence Erlbaum.

Silva, T. (1993). Toward an understanding of the distinct nature of L2 writing: The ESL research and its implications. *TESOL Quarterly, 27,* 657-677.

Silver, N. W. (1990). *The effect of word processing on self esteem and quality of writing among beginning English as second language (ESL) students.* Unpublished Doctoral dissertation, New York University.

Silver, N. W., & Repa, J. T. (1993). The effect of word processing on the quality of writing and self-esteem of secondary school English-as-second-language students: Writing without censure. *Journal of Educational Computing Research, 9 ,* 265-283.

Sirc, G. (1989). Response in the electronic medium. In C. M. Anson (Ed.), *Writing and response: Theory, practice, and research* (pp. 187-205). Urbana, IL: National Council of Teachers of English.

Smagorinsky, P. (1994), *Speaking about writing.* London: Sage.

Smith, C. (1989). Text analysis: The state of the art. *The Computer-Assisted Composition Journal, 3*(2), 68-77.

Smith, F. (1982). *Writing and the writer.* New York: Holt, Rinehart and Winston.

Smith, M., & Smith, G. (1990). *A study skills handbook.* Oxford: Oxford University Press.

Snyder, I. (1993). Writing with word processors: A research overview. *Educational Research, 35,* 49-68.

Snyder, I. (1998). *Page to screen: Taking literacy into the electronic era.* London and New York: Routledge.

Sommers, N. (1980). Revision strategies of student writers and experienced adult writers. *College Composition and Communication, 31,* 378-388.

Spears, R. & Lea, M. (1992). Social influence and the influence of the "social" in computer-mediated communication. In Spears & Lea (Eds.), *Contexts of computer-mediated communication* (pp. 30-65). New York: Harvester Wheatsheaf.

Speier, M. (1972). Some conversational problems for interactional analysis. In D. Sudnow (Ed.), *Studies in social interaction* (pp. 397-427). New York: Free Press.

Stallard, C. K. (1974). An analysis of the writing behavior of good student writers. *Research in the Teaching of English, 8,* 206-218.

Steelman, J. D. (1994). Revision strategies employed by middle level students using computers. *Journal of Educational Computing Research, 11,* 141-152.

Stoddart, B., & MacArthur, C. (1993). A peer editor strategy: Guiding learning-disabled students in response and revision. *Research in the Teaching of English, 27,* 76-103.

Stratman, J., & Hamp-Lyons, L. (1994). Reactivity in concurrent think-aloud protocols: Issues for research. In P. Smagorinsky (Ed.), *Speaking about writing* (pp. 89-112). London: Sage.

Stromqvist, S., & Ahlsen, E. (1998). *The process of writing – A progress report.* Department of Linguistics and SSKKII Center for Cognitive Science, University of Goteborg.

Sullivan, K., Kollberg, P., & Palsson, E. (1997). L2 writing: A pilot investigation using key-stroke logging. In L. Diaz & C. Perez (Eds.), *Views on the acquisition and use of a second language* (pp. 553-566). Barcelona: Universitat Pompeu Fabra.

Tardif, J. (1992). *Pour un enseignement stratégique. L'apport de la psychologie cognitive.* Montreal: Éditions Logiques.

Taylor, B. P. (1981). Content and written form: A two-way street. *TESOL Quarterly, 15,* 5-13.

Teichman, M., & Poris, M. (1989). Initial effects of word processing on writing quality and writing anxiety of freshman writers. *Computers and the Humanities, 23,* 93-103.

Teichmann, V. (1994). An Interdisciplinary project orientation using telecommunications media in foreign language teaching. In H. Jung & R. Vanderplank (Eds.), *Barriers and bridges: Media technology in language learning* (pp. 63-68). Frankfurt: Peter Lang.

Tella, S. (1992). *Talking shop via e-mail: A thematic and linguistic analysis of electronic mail communication.* Research Report No. 99, Department of Communication. Helsinki: University of Helsinki.

Thiesmeyer, J. (1989). Should we do what we can? In G. E. Hawisher & C. L. Selfe (Eds.), *Critical perspectives on computers and composition instruction* (pp. 75-93). New York: Teachers College Press.

Thomas, A. (1985). Conversational routines: A Markov chain analysis. *Language and Communication, 5,* 287-96.

Tillyer, D. (1996). Tending your Internet exchange: Pen pal projects need attention to thrive. *CALL Review* (September), 4-6.

Todman, J., & Portia, F. (1990). A scale for children's attitudes to computers. *School Psychology International, 11,* 71-75.

Tomalin, B., & Templeski, S. (1993). *Cultural awareness.* Oxford: Oxford University Press.

Tuman, M. C. (1992). *Word perfect: Literacy in the computer age*. London: Falmer Press; Pittsburgh: University of Pittsburgh Press.

Turkle, S. (1984). *The second self: Computers and the human spirit*. New York: Simon and Schuster.

Underwood, J. (1984). *Linguistics, computers, and the language teacher: A communicative approach*. New York: Newbury House.

Upitis, R. (1990). Real and contrived uses of electronic mail in elementary schools. *Computers and Education, 15*, 233-243.

Van der Pool, E. (1996). A text-analytical study of conceptual writing processes and their development. In G. Rijlaarsdam, H. van den Berg, & M. Couzijn (Eds.), *Current research in writing: Theories, models and methodology* (pp. 456-472). Amsterdam: Amsterdam University Press.

van Waes, L. (1991). *De computer en het schrijfproces: De invloed van de tekstverwerker op het pauze- en revisiegedrag van schrijvers*. Unpublished Doctoral dissertation, University of Antwerp.

van Waes, L. (1994). Computers and writing: Implications for the teaching of writing. In K. H. Pogner (Ed.), *Odense Working Papers in Language and Communication: More about Writing, 6*, 41-61.

Varonis, E. & S. Gass. (1985). Non-native/non-native conversations: A model for the negotiation of meaning. *Applied Linguistics, 6*, 71-90.

Vigner, G. (1982). *Écrire: Éléments pour une pédagogie de la production écrite*. Coll. Didactique des langues étrangères. Paris: CLE international.

Wallace, M. J. (1980). *Study skills in English*. Cambridge: Cambridge University Press.

Warren, E. (1997). The significance of pauses in written discourse: A comparison of native speaker and learner writing. In A. Archibald & G. Jeffery (Eds.), *Second language acquisition and writing: A multidisciplinary approach* (pp. 152-177). South-ampton: University of Southampton.

Warschauer, M. (1995). *E-mail for English language teaching*. Alexandria, VA: TESOL.

Watson-Gegeo, K. A. (1988). Ethnography in ESL: defining the essentials. *TESOL Quarterly, 22*, 575-592.

Wenrich, J. K. (1991). *The computer word-processing abilities of high reading / high language and low reading / low language sixth-grade students*. Unpublished Doctoral dissertation, Lehigh University. Dissertation Abstracts International, *52*, 1721A.

Wesche, M. (1994). Input and interaction in second language acquisition. In C. Gallaway & B. Richards (Eds.), *Input and interaction in language acquisition* (pp. 219-249). Cambridge: Cambridge University Press.

Whalen, K. L. (1992). *Approche cognitive et expérimentale de la production écrite: Comparaison des processus d'écriture entre l'anglais langue maternelle et le français langue seconde.* Unpublished Doctoral dissertation, University of Montreal.

White, L. (1987). Against comprehensible input: the input hypothesis and the development of second language competence. *Applied Linguistics, 8,* 95-110.

White, R., & Arndt, V. (1991). *Process writing.* Harlow: Longman.

Wilder, G., Mackie, D., & Cooper, J. (1985). Gender and computers: Two surveys of computer-related attitudes. *Sex Roles, 13,* 215-228.

Wilkins, H. (1991). Computer talk: Long-distance conversations by computer. *Written Communication, 8,* 56-78.

Williams, N. (1992). New technology. New writing. New problems? In P. O. Holt & N. Williams (Eds.), *Computers and writing: State of the art* (pp. 1-19). Oxford: Intellect Books.

Williamson, M. M., & Pence, P. (1989). Word processing and student writers. In B. Britton & S. M. Glynn (Eds.), *Computer writing environments: Theory, research, and design* (pp. 93-127). Hillsdale, NJ: Lawrence Erlbaum.

Womble, G. G. (1984). Process and processor: Is there room for a machine in the English classroom? *English Journal, 73,* 34-37.

Woodin, J. (1997). E-mail tandem learning and the communicative curriculum. *ReCALL, 9*(1), 22-33.

Wresch, W. (1984). Questions, answers, and automated writing. In W. Wresch (Ed.), *The computer in composition instruction* (pp. 143-153). Urbana, IL: National Council of Teachers of English.

Wresch, W. (1989). A history of computer analysis of student writing. ERIC Document No. ED 303 813.

Zamel, V. (1982). Writing: The process of discovering meaning. *TESOL Quarterly, 16,* 195-209.

Zamel, V. (1983). The composing process of advanced ESL students: Six case studies. *TESOL Quarterly, 17,* 165-187.

Zamel, V. (1985). Responding to student writing. *TESOL Quarterly, 19,* 79-101.